NIETZSCHE ON CONFLICT, STRUGGLE AND WAR

Nietzsche controversially valorizes struggle and war as necessary ingredients of human flourishing. In this book, James S. Pearson reconstructs Nietzsche's rationale for placing such high value on relations of conflict. In doing so, Pearson reveals how Nietzsche's celebration of social discord is interwoven with his understanding of nature as universal struggle. This study thus draws together Nietzsche's writings on politics, culture, metaphysics, biology and human psychology. It also overcomes an entrenched dispute in the critical literature. Until now, commentators have tended to interpret Nietzsche either as an advocate of radical aristocratic violence or, by contrast, a defender of moderate democratic contest. This book navigates a path between these two opposed readings and shows how Nietzsche is able to endorse both violent strife and restrained competition without contradicting himself.

JAMES S. PEARSON is Research Fellow in Philosophy at the University of Tartu. He is the author of numerous articles on modern German philosophy in journals including *Inquiry, Social Theory and Practice* and *The Canadian Journal of Philosophy.*

T0372702

MODERN EUROPEAN PHILOSOPHY

Titles published in the series

NIETZSCHE ON CONFLICT, STRUGGLE AND WAR

JAMES S. PEARSON

University of Tartu

CAMBRIDGE
UNIVERSITY PRESS

CAMBRIDGE
UNIVERSITY PRESS

Shaftesbury Road, Cambridge CB2 8EA, United Kingdom

One Liberty Plaza, 20th Floor, New York, NY 10006, USA

477 Williamstown Road, Port Melbourne, VIC 3207, Australia

314–321, 3rd Floor, Plot 3, Splendor Forum, Jasola District Centre, New Delhi – 110025, India

103 Penang Road, #05–06/07, Visioncrest Commercial, Singapore 238467

Cambridge University Press is part of Cambridge University Press & Assessment,
a department of the University of Cambridge.

We share the University's mission to contribute to society through the pursuit of
education, learning and research at the highest international levels of excellence.

www.cambridge.org
Information on this title: www.cambridge.org/9781009015776

DOI: 10.1017/9781009030519

First published 2022
First paperback edition 2024

A catalogue record for this publication is available from the British Library

Library of Congress Cataloging-in-Publication data
NAMES: Pearson, James Stephen, author.
TITLE: Nietzsche on conflict, struggle and war / James S. Pearson.
DESCRIPTION: Cambridge, United Kingdom ; New York, NY, USA : Cambridge University
Press, 2021. | Series: Modern European philosophy | Includes bibliographical references and index.
IDENTIFIERS: LCCN 2021023815 (print) | LCCN 2021023816 (ebook) | ISBN 9781316516546
(hardback) | ISBN 9781009030519 (ebook other)
SUBJECTS: LCSH: Nietzsche, Friedrich Wilhelm, 1844–1900. | Conflict (Psychology) | War
(Philosophy) | BISAC: PHILOSOPHY / History & Surveys / Modern | PHILOSOPHY /
History & Surveys / Modern
CLASSIFICATION: LCC B3317 .P38 2021 (print) | LCC B3317 (ebook) | DDC 193–dc23
LC record available at https://lccn.loc.gov/2021023815
LC ebook record available at https://lccn.loc.gov/2021023816

ISBN   978-1-316-51654-6   Hardback
ISBN   978-1-009-01577-6   Paperback

Contents

Abbreviations

Nietzsche's Writings

Cited numbers principally refer to section numbers. Thus, GS 21 = GS, Section 21. Where the sections of text are too long for the section number to be sufficiently informative, I provide a reference to the relevant volume and page in the KSA. Thus, GM I 13, KSA 5.279 = GM, Essay 1, Section 13 (KSA, Volume 5, page 279). Likewise, when citing Nietzsche's unpublished notebooks (his *Nachlaß*), I provide the KSA reference, giving the volume, notebook, fragment and page number. Thus, KSA 10:15[36], 488 = KSA, Volume 10, Notebook 15, Fragment 36, page 488. For texts that are not contained in the KSA (e.g., Nietzsche's lecture notes), I cite the KGW, giving the volume, part and page number. Thus, KGW II/5, 519 = KGW, Volume 2, Part 5, page 519. When citing Nietzsche's letters, I refer to the KGB, giving the volume, part and page number. Thus, KGB III/1, 182–183 = KGB, Volume 3, Part 1, pages 182–183.

KGW	*Werke: Kritische Gesamtausgabe.* Edited by Giorgio Colli and Mazzino Montinari. Berlin: de Gruyter, 1967–
KSA	*Sämtliche Werke: Kritische Studienausgabe in 15 Bänden.* Edited by Giorgio Colli and Mazzino Montinari. Berlin: de Gruyter, 1980
KGB	*Briefwechsel: Kritische Gesamtausgabe.* Edited by Giorgio Colli and Mazzino Montinari. Berlin: de Gruyter, 1977

Nietzsche's Published Works

AOM	*Vermischte Meinungen und Sprüche* (in *Menschliches Allzumenschliches II*) (*Assorted Opinions and Maxims*)
BGE	*Jenseits von Gut und Böse* (*Beyond Good and Evil*)
BT	*Die Geburt der Tragödie* (*The Birth of Tragedy*)
CW	*Der Fall Wagner* (*The Case of Wagner*)

D   *Morgenröthe* (*Daybreak* or *Dawn*)
DS   *David Strauss der Bekenner und der Schriftsteller* (*Unzeitgemäße*
             Betrachtungen I) (*David Strauss the Confessor and the Writer*)
GM   *Zur Genealogie der Moral* (*On the Genealogy of Morals*)
GS   *Die fröhliche Wissenschaft* (*The Gay Science*)
HH   *Menschliches, Allzumenschliches* (*Human, All Too Human*)
HL   *Vom Nutzen und Nachteil der Historie für das Leben*
             (*Unzeitgemäße Betrachtungen* II) (*On the Uses and*
             Disadvantages of History for Life)
SE   *Schopenhauer als Erzieher* (*Unzeitgemäße Betrachtungen* III)
             (*Schopenhauer as Educator*)
TI   *Götzen-Dämmerung* (*Twilight of the Idols*; references to this
             work include an abbreviated section title)
UM   *Unzeitgemäße Betrachtungen* (*Untimely Meditations*)
WB   *Richard Wagner in Bayreuth* (*Unzeitgemäße Betrachtungen* IV)
WS   *Der Wanderer und sein Schatten* (in *Menschliches,*
             Allzumenschliches II) (*The Wanderer and His Shadow*)
Z   *Also sprach Zarathustra* (*Thus Spoke Zarathustra*; references to
             this work include an abbreviated section title)

Nietzsche's Unpublished Writings

A   *Der Antichrist* (*The Antichrist*)
DW   "Die dionysische Weltanschauung" ("The Dionysian
             Worldview")
EH   *Ecce Homo* (references to this work include an abbreviated
             section title)
FEI   "Über die Zukunft unserer Bildungsanstalten" ("On the
             Future of our Educational Institutions")
GSt   "Der griechische Staat" ("The Greek State")
HC   "Homer's Wettkampf" ("Homer's Contest")
HGL   "Geschichte der griechischen Literatur" ("[The] History of
             Greek Literature")
PPP   "Die vorplatonischen Philosophen" ("The Pre-Platonic
             Philosophers")
PTAG   *Die Philosophie im tragischen Zeitalter der Griechen* (*Philosophy*
             in the Tragic Age of the Greeks)
RSG   "Der Gottesdienst der Griechen" ("The Religious Worship of
             the Greeks")

SGT   "Sokrates und die griechische Tragödie" ("Socrates and Greek Tragedy")

TL   "Über Wahrheit und Lüge im aussermoralischen Sinne" ("On Truth and Lies in an Extra-Moral Sense")

Burckhardt's Writings

All references to Burckhardt's writings give the GW volume and page number.

GK   *Griechische Kulturgeschichte: Vierte Band*
GW   *Gesammelte Werke.* 10 vols. Basel: Schwabe Verlag, 1978
KRI   *Die Kultur der Renaissance in Italien*
WBe   *Weltgeschichtliche Betrachtungen*

Kant's Writings

All references to Kant's writings give the AA volume and page number.

AA   *Gesammelte Schriften.* Akademie Ausgabe. Edited by Wilhelm Dilthey et al. Berlin: de Gruyter, 1902–
CJ   *Kritik der Urteilskraft* (*Critique of Judgment*)
CPR   *Kritik der reinen Vernunft* (*Critique of Pure Reason*)
IUH   "Idee zu einer allgemeinen Geschichte in weltbürgerlicher Absicht" ("Idea for a Universal History with a Cosmopolitan Purpose")
PP   "Zum ewigen Frieden. Ein philosophischer Entwurf" ("Perpetual Peace: A Philosophical Sketch")

Schopenhauer's Writings

All references to Schopenhauer's works give the SW volume and page number.

SW   *Sämtliche Werke.* 7 vols. Edited by Arthur Hübscher. Mannheim: F. A. Brockhaus, 1988
WWR 1 *Die Welt als Wille und Vorstellung, Band 1*
          (*The World as Will and Representation, Volume 1*)
WWR 2 *Die Welt als Wille und Vorstellung, Band 2*
          (*The World as Will and Representation, Volume 2*)

Works by Other Authors

BP   William Rolph. *Biologische Probleme zugleich als Versuch zur Entwicklung einer rationellen Ethik.* Leipzig: Verlag von Wilhelm Engelmann, 1884

DWB   Jacob Grimm and Wilhelm Grimm. *Deutsches Wörterbuch.* 25 vols. Munich: DTV, 1854–

EAG   Leopold Schmidt. *Die Ethik der alten Griechen.* 2 vols. Berlin: Wilhelm Herz Verlag, 1882

KJV   *The Holy Bible: King James Version.* London: Collins, 2011

KTO   Wilhelm Roux. *Der Kampf der Theile im Organismus: Ein Beitrag zur Vervollständigung der mechanischen Zweckmässigkeitslehre.* Leipzig: Wilhelm Engelmann Verlag, 1881

NPB   Giuliano Campioni, P. d'Iorio, M. C. Fornari, F. Fronterotta and A. Orsucci, eds. *Nietzsches Persönliche Bibliothek.* Berlin: de Gruyter, 2003

NWB   Paul van Tongeren, G. Schank and H. W. Siemens, eds. *Nietzsche-Wörterbuch. Band I.* Berlin: de Gruyter, 2004

OED   *Oxford English Dictionary.* 2nd ed. 20 vols. Oxford: Oxford University Press, 1989

Translations

Most of the translations from German contained in this book are my own; however, I have drawn on various existing translations, which are listed below.

Nietzsche's Writings

The Anti-Christ, Ecce Homo, Twilight of the Idols and Other Writings, translated by Judith Norman. Cambridge: Cambridge University Press, 2005

Beyond Good and Evil, translated by Judith Norman. Cambridge: Cambridge University Press, 2002

The Birth of Tragedy, translated by Ronald Speirs. Cambridge: Cambridge University Press, 1999

Daybreak, translated by R. J. Hollingdale. Cambridge: Cambridge University Press, 1997

The Gay Science, translated by Josefine Nauckhoff. Cambridge: Cambridge University Press, 2001

On the Genealogy of Morality, translated by Carol Diethe. Cambridge: Cambridge University Press, 2006

Human, All Too Human, translated by R. J. Hollingdale. Cambridge: Cambridge University Press, 1996

Untimely Meditations, translated by R. J. Hollingdale. Cambridge: Cambridge University Press, 1997

Thus Spoke Zarathustra, translated by Adrian Del Caro. Cambridge: Cambridge University Press, 2006

"On Truth and Lies in an Extra-Moral Sense," in *The Nietzsche Reader*, translated by Daniel Breazeale. Oxford: Blackwell, 2006

The Will to Power, translated by Walter Kaufmann and R. J. Hollingdale. New York: Vintage, 1968

Schopenhauer's Writings

The World as Will and Representation, Volume 1, translated by Judith Norman, Alistair Welchman, Christopher Janaway. Cambridge: Cambridge University Press, 2010

Kant's Writings

Kant: Political Writings, translated by H. B. Nisbet. Cambridge: Cambridge University Press, 2003

Acknowledgments

This book is a distant descendant of my doctoral thesis, and so first and foremost, I would like to record my gratitude to Herman Siemens, who supervised the original thesis at Leiden University. My debt to Herman cannot be overstated. He provided a deep well of expertise and critical feedback, without which this book would have been substantially worse off. I also received a wealth of insightful comments from Paul van Tongeren, Beatrix Himmelmann, Sebastian Gardner, Marco Brusotti and the anonymous referees who promptly reviewed the typescript for Cambridge University Press. A number of other colleagues and past supervisors have encouraged me over the years, and their generous support has indirectly been of integral value to this book project. These are Keith Ansell-Pearson, Timothy Morris, Johanna Oksala, Thomas Fossen and Eileen John.

I would like to give special thanks to Hilary Gaskin at Cambridge University Press. Hilary's judicious advice, diligent editorial work and not least of all, patience have been instrumental in bringing this monograph to fruition. I am also grateful to Frances Tye, who was of indispensable help in polishing the final text of this book.

On the financial front, I would like to acknowledge the Dutch Research Council (NWO), which funded my research at Leiden University; and the European Regional Development Fund, which financed my research at the University of Tartu.

The contribution of my brother, Harry Pearson, was also fundamental. Aside from being a steadfast presence throughout the writing process, his comments on an early draft of this book helped me keep obscure technical jargon to a bare minimum. My parents, Howard and Davy, then provided me with the firm base of unconditional support that one requires in order to carry projects of this magnitude through to completion. Among my friends, I am particularly grateful to Razvan Ioan, Matthew Dennis, Viktorija Kostadinova and Álvaro Cortina Urdampilleta. While I was writing this book, the many stimulating conversations that I enjoyed with these four friends had a formative influence on my philosophical outlook. I would also like to thank Jorrit Smit, Katia Hay and Céline Henne, who were all of significant help at various stages of the creative process.

This book contains material from a number of articles that I published either during or after my doctorate: Chapter 1 reworks material from "On Catharsis, Conflict and the Coherence of Nietzsche's Agonism," *Nietzsche-Studien* 45(1): 3–32; Chapter 2 contains material from "Nietzsche on the Sources of Agonal Moderation," *Journal of Nietzsche Studies* 49(1): 102–129; Chapter 3 is based on "United We Stand, Divided We Fall: The Early Nietzsche on the Struggle for Organisation," *Canadian Journal of Philosophy* 49(4): 508–533; and Chapter 4 is in part based on "Nietzsche on the Necessity of Repression," *Inquiry*, DOI: 10.1080/0020174X .2018.1529618. I am grateful to the publishers of the above journals for granting me permission to reuse this material.

Introduction

Ai! let strife and rancor
perish from the lives of gods and men [. . .]   (Homer, *Iliad*)[1]

One must realize that war is shared and Conflict is Justice,
and that all things come to pass [. . .]
in accordance with conflict.   (Heraclitus, Fragment 82)[2]

The above disagreement between Homer and Heraclitus hinges on
a thorny philosophical problem – namely, how should we value conflict? Should we follow Homer's Achilles and curse it as a burdensome
feature of human existence? Or should we side with Heraclitus and
praise it as something beneficial, as beneficial as justice even? No doubt
most of us are intuitively inclined to agree with Achilles. After all, do
we not tend to denigrate violence and strive to resolve the personal
conflicts that vex our day-to-day lives? And do we not do so in the
reasonable belief that peace and harmony are the fertile ground in
which well-being thrives?

But on the other hand, who would deny that competition is often
exhilarating; or that it can provoke us to pursue excellence and thereby
improve ourselves? Certainly, it seems that many of our most valuable
achievements – be it as individuals or collectives – are the hard-won fruit of
contest. And so to what extent should we consider conflict as something
desirable, as something for which we ought to actively strive?

Though numerous philosophers have grappled with this last question,
consensus has not been forthcoming. On the contrary, we find a marked
polarity in how different thinkers are inclined to value the phenomenon of
conflict; in other words, they tend to give conflict *either* a negative *or*
a positive coloration. As such, taken as a whole, they *reproduce*, as opposed
to resolve, the confrontation staged in our epigraph.

---

[1] Homer (2008, Book 18, l.107).   [2] Kahn (1979, 67).

I

When Empedocles distinguished between the cosmic forces of love and hatred, he thereby established himself as one of the first philosophers to cast conflict in a critical light: "things never cease their continual exchange, now through Love all coming together into one, now again each carried apart by the hatred of Strife" (quoted in Kirk et al. 1983, 287). In contrast to the unificatory force of love, he associates conflict with hatred, disintegration and death. Later, following the lead of Empedocles, Plato then states in no uncertain terms that "wickedness is discord and virtue harmony" (2005, 93e). And in the *Republic*, he frames social contention as an impediment to the healthy functioning of the body politic, and even as a precursor to violent sedition. In a similar fashion, he submits that disharmony between the appetitive and rational parts of the soul renders us incapable of executing our rationally chosen plans. With an eye to preventing such discord, in the *Republic* he provides his readers with a blueprint for establishing individual and collective harmony. Even if, like many members of the anti-conflict school, Plato often accepts dissensus and war as indelible facts of human reality, we find that he nonetheless yearns for an undiluted condition of harmony.

This Platonic campaign against discord is then vigorously continued by the Stoics and, later, in the medieval period, by Christian thinkers such as Augustine and Aquinas. In the *City of God*, for instance, Augustine laments the inescapable nature of social and psychological antagonism (i.e., for those who remain on this side of the afterlife); and he concludes that over and against the burdens of strife, "peace [*pacis*] is so great a good that [. . .] no word ever falls more gratefully upon the ear, nothing is desired with greater longing, in fact, nothing better can be found" (2003, 866). Likewise, in the modern period, Spinoza, Hobbes, Rousseau and Kant all comparably idealize peace and denigrate strife. And this venerable legacy is still very much alive today, perhaps most saliently in contemporary political philosophy. Thus, deliberative democrats, such as Habermas and the followers of Rawls, largely devote themselves to the task of promoting peaceful liberal social organization.[3]

Like Plato, many of these thinkers incite their readers to a struggle against discord; in this sense, they can be said to endorse conflict, though only as a means to its own overcoming – that is, *as a means to peace*. The later Kant, for example, sanctions both revolution and war on account of the fact that they tend to conclude in political treaties, which then have the

---

[3] This interpretation of Habermas and Rawls is prominent among agonistic democrats such as Mouffe (2000) and Honig (1993).

beneficial effect of fostering global peace. As such, in Kant's view, nature produces "concord among men [. . .] by means of their very discord" (PP, 8.360).[4] The idea that harmonious relations are born of antagonism is one that we subsequently encounter among various thinkers who follow in Kant's wake, though perhaps most notably in Hegel and Marx. For Hegel, the struggle of master and slave impels them toward conciliation – which is to say, into a state of harmonious mutual recognition. Likewise, Marx maintains that class struggle promotes the liberation of the proletariat, and with this, the establishment of lasting international peace.

By contrast, others take a more pessimistic view, theorizing that humans are condemned to suffer arduous psychological and interpersonal strife. In the words of Aquinas (1956, 164), for instance, the inescapability of psychological suffering entails that "no person is happy [*felix*] in this life." And in Augustine's view (2003, 859), thanks to the sinful, treacherous nature of man, even if "cities are at times exempt from [the bloodshed of sedition and civil war,] they are never free from the danger of them."[5] For these Christian thinkers, enduring peace is therefore ultimately confined to the heavenly realm of the afterlife.

But what about those who frame conflict in more favorable terms? Members of this camp – led by Heraclitus, who celebrates war as "father and king of all" (Kahn 1979, 67) – conceive struggle as a generative, dynamic, selective and strengthening process. They then contend that given these advantageous qualities, we ought to venerate certain forms of conflict. Mill, for example, argues that we depend upon others to challenge our beliefs in order for these beliefs to retain their vitality. A strong opinion, says Mill, "however true it may be, if it is not fully, frequently, and fearlessly discussed, [. . .] will be held as a dead dogma, not a living truth." He also defends moral disagreement on the grounds that ethical truths are often medial in nature, being generated in the very act of disputation; thus, "conflicting doctrines, instead of being one true and the other false, *share the truth between them*" (Mill 2015, 35, 45; emphasis mine). Subsequent to Mill, the social Darwinists give the pro-conflict approach a more sinister iteration. Herbert Spencer (1886, 48), for instance, famously argues that selective struggle promotes the "survival of the fittest." And on the basis of this idea, he further maintains that socioeconomic struggle, and the kinds of social hierarchy that are engendered by such struggle, are healthy natural phenomena, which therefore ought to be left unimpeded either by taxation of the rich or welfare aimed

---

[4] See also IUH, 8.25.   [5] See Aquinas (1956, Book 3, chap. 48) and Augustine (2003, Book 19).

at supporting the poor.[6] We find similar apologies for economic competition in the work of libertarians, who, like the early Spencer, extol the virtues of free market capitalism, and correspondingly agitate against the welfare state.[7]

Others, such as Weber and Durkheim, underscore the constitutive role that conflict plays in social life. In tacit opposition to the Empedoclean belief that discord has an essentially centrifugal effect, they maintain that society is irreducibly structured by the contention of its members. On their analyses, the competitive interaction of individuals and social groups, when effectively managed by state institutions, functions as a motor of social, political, economic and moral change.[8] In a similar vein, Carl Schmitt likewise theorizes that conflict plays a constitutive role within the body politic, though it is principally aggressive international conflict that Schmitt has in mind. His core claim in this respect is that the identity of a political community is grounded in its hostile opposition to an existential threat, or *enemy*.[9] Within the field of contemporary political theory, the foremost advocates of conflict are without doubt the agonistic democrats, some of whom have been directly influenced by Schmitt (e.g., Chantal Mouffe). Along with certain poststructuralist thinkers, such as Foucault and Lyotard, the agonistic democrats argue that difference and lively disagreement are profoundly advantageous when kept within moderate bounds; moreover, they submit that suppressing disagreement in the name of liberal consensus is likely to tyrannize minorities in a manner that directly contradicts the pluralistic essence of democratic politics.[10]

This schema is by no means exhaustive. And what is more, it is undeniably procrustean – there is a case to be made for reclassifying almost all of the abovementioned thinkers in the opposite group. Nonetheless, this dualistic schema sheds useful light on the battle line that cuts through existing philosophical accounts of the value of conflict. It also serves to illuminate the fact that the concept of conflict subsumes a rich variety of distinct phenomena. The semantic breadth of the term "conflict" is neatly captured by the OED. Here we are told that the term is Latinate in origin, "the participial stem of *confligĕre* to strike together, clash, conflict, contend, fight [. . .], < *con-* together + *flĭgĕre* to strike." Under this broad notion of

---

[6] This idea is particularly salient in the early Spencer (e.g., 1994).
[7] Within the domain of political philosophy, the *locus classicus* for this position is Nozick (1974).
[8] For an interpretation of Weber that highlights his affirmation of conflict, see Beetham (1985, 41ff.).
[9] See e.g., Schmitt (2002).
[10] See e.g., Connolly (1988; 1991); Honig (1993); Mouffe (2000); Tully (2008). Isaiah Berlin is another noteworthy proponent of agonistic politics.

"striking together," we also have the general definition of conflict as a "prolonged struggle"; then a more specific, physical definition of the term as "fighting, contending with arms, martial strife"; a psychological definition that describes it as a "mental or spiritual struggle within a man"; an epistemological or ideological definition of conflict as the "clashing or variance of opposed principles, statements, arguments, etc."; and finally, we have a definition of conflict that refers to a particular species of interaction between inanimate physical entities – namely, the "[d]ashing together, collision, or violent mutual impact of physical bodies," and "the strife of natural forces."[11] It thus becomes readily apparent that the quarrel between Homer and Heraclitus rests on a false dichotomy – conflict is neither "good" nor "bad" per se. It is rather a complex concept used to index a wide range of diverse relations, each of which may be said to have good or bad effects depending on (a) the circumstances in which they occur and (b) the standpoint of the individual making the relevant value judgment.[12] So before we can effectively analyze the *value* of conflict, and consequently establish ways in which we might go about cultivating its advantageous forms, we need to designate as clearly as possible what we *mean* by conflict. Insofar as this demands that we draw a clear conceptual map of the notion at issue, and critically assess the justifications for why we might value particular forms of conflict over others, our endeavor is unambiguously philosophical in kind.

Throughout the course of this book, I will be arguing that Nietzsche makes a seminal contribution with respect to this demanding cluster of tasks. As we will see, his writings disclose a balanced and coherent theory of conflict – one that sheds important light on both the positive and negative consequences associated with its various subspecies. This said, fully appreciating Nietzsche's contribution requires extensive interpretive work, and in order to faithfully reconstruct his position, it is vital that we examine it in its proper historical and intellectual context. Nietzsche formulates his own mature theory of conflict in dialogue with a very particular set of philosophical views. Sometimes this dialogue is deflationary in kind, as Nietzsche strives to demolish certain key positions that run counter to his own. But just as often it takes a more constructive form, and thus we frequently find him avowing and adapting the views of his contemporaries and predecessors. If we are to understand Nietzsche's unique philosophy of

---

[11] OED, "conflict, n." and "conflict, v."

[12] And indeed, closer examination of the disagreement between Heraclitus and Homer's Achilles reveals that they are largely talking about different forms of conflict.

conflict, we therefore need a general impression of the intellectual back-drop against which his views came into being. This will grant us an insight into the specific nexus of influences and concerns that inform his distinct-ive outlook. With this in mind, we ought to begin by setting the scene and making a prefatory survey of Nietzsche's interpretation of the history of the philosophy of conflict.

A Brief History of the Philosophy of Conflict

The Presocratics

During the early 1870s, while employed as a professor of philology at the University of Basel, Nietzsche worked extensively on Presocratic philosophy. The principal results of this research are to be found in a series of lecture notes (PPP) and an unfinished book manuscript (PTAG). The opposition of Anaximander and Heraclitus that we encounter in these two texts is of particular relevance to our broader study of Nietzsche's philosophy of conflict.[13] According to Anaximander, humans, like all other transient phenomena, are caught in a painful maelstrom of generation, struggle and death – the relentless stream of what Nietzsche calls *becoming* (*das Werden*). Beneath this stream, however, Anaximander conjectures that there must exist some unchanging, fundamental substratum from which transient beings emerge, and to which they eventually return upon their death or destruction. From these premises, he pessimistically infers that temporal existence consti-tutes an illicit escape "from eternal being, a wrong which is expiated with our demise [*Untergang*]" (PTAG 4, KSA 1.819) – transient life is marred by death and decay because it is in reality a form of metaphysical penance. In Nietzsche's view, in favoring the static, abstract realm of being, "Anaximander flees [from the world of injustice, of insulting deterioration] into a metaphysical fortress" (PTAG 4, KSA 1.820). Indeed, according to Nietzsche, there is something cowardly concealed in Anaximander's inability to recognize the protean world of birth, death and destruction as the *only* world.

PTAG frames Heraclitus as the antithesis of Anaximander. In the first place, Nietzsche's Heraclitus denies the existence of what Anaximander calls *being*, dismissing this idea as little more than a specious abstraction. By the same token, he repudiates Anaximander's dualism (i.e., of being *versus* becoming), opting instead for a *monistic* metaphysics according to which he conceives reality as an immanent condition of pure becoming (PTAG 5,

---

[13] For a more detailed analysis of Nietzsche's relation to Heraclitus, see Pearson (2020).

KSA 1.183). In disavowing the world of being, Heraclitus rejects the ground of Anaximander's claim that becoming is the result of a transgressive act of escape. The upshot of this is that Heraclitus correspondingly refuses to characterize becoming as a form of penance. Instead, he remarks the inherent order that governs the ubiquitous struggle of reality qua becoming, and on the basis of this observation he then affirms becoming as the manifestation of a divine law or *logos* (which Nietzsche sometimes construes as natural, scientific law).[14] How could this orderly world, flawlessly administered by the goddess of justice (*Dikē*) in accordance with divine law, "be the sphere of guilt, penance, condemnation and a place of execution [. . .]?" (PTAG 5, KSA 1.822). Convinced that struggle and flux are inherently governed by law, Nietzsche's Heraclitus thus proclaims that "war [*Krieg*] is common to all and *Dikē* is strife [*Streit*]" (PPP, KGW II/4, 272).

At this stage, Nietzsche takes Heraclitus' affirmation of war to be largely figurative in kind; that is, he takes Heraclitus to be metaphorically referring to a deeper, metaphysical "war [*Krieg*] of opposites" rather than specifically human, martial combat (PTAG 5, KSA 1.825). On Nietzsche's reading of Heraclitus, individual phenomena are the site of a dynamic struggle between opposed properties, each of which vies for concrete expression in reality. Honey, for example, is in part constituted through the relentless struggle of sweetness to suppress its opposite, the quality of bitterness. But sweetness can only hold out for so long (PTAG 5, KSA 1.825). With time the honey will decay, and bitterness will inevitably prevail. Likewise, the human body supervenes on a constant tug of war between health and sickness, and life and death. Needless to say, sickness and death inexorably win out in the long run. But as death and decay prevail in one location (in one body), elsewhere new humans come into existence, or grow healthier, and so from a cosmic standpoint, the turbulent poise of opposed properties is stably maintained. Crucially, within any pair of antagonistic qualities, there is never a *conclusive* victor. Dominance is only ever local and temporary. Through time and across the cosmos, these contraries are kept in a state of dynamic equilibrium: "the struggle [*Ringen*] continues for all eternity" (PTAG 5, KSA 1.825).

Since "all becoming emerges from the war of opposites," the cosmic antagonism described by Heraclitus functions as a vital source of generation (PTAG 5, KSA 1.825). Indeed, Nietzsche's reading gives a very concrete sense to the Heraclitean dictum that "war [*polemos*] is father of all" (Kahn 1979, 67).[15]

---

[14] See PPP, KGW II/4, 267, where Nietzsche interprets Heraclitus' vision as an intuition of scientific truth.
[15] N.B. Nietzsche refers to this fragment in GS 92 and BT 4, KSA 1.39.

What is also pertinent to our inquiry is that for Nietzsche this metaphysical worldview transfigures the ancient Greek penchant for agon – which was exemplified in the Olympic or Pythian games – into a cosmic "world principle" (*Weltprincip*) (PTAG 6, KSA 1.825). The contest of opposed properties theorized by Heraclitus is in Nietzsche's view akin to an agon between two equally matched wrestlers who, by virtue of their approximately equal ability, prevent one another from securing a quick or conclusive victory.

Although Heraclitus slips into the background for almost a decade, he noticeably reappears in Nietzsche's later writings – for example, in EH, where Nietzsche expresses an enduring sense of intellectual fraternity with his ancient forerunner:

> I generally feel warmer and in better spirits in [Heraclitus'] company than anywhere else. The affirmation of passing away *and destruction* [*Vergehens und Vernichtungs*] that is crucial for a Dionysian philosophy, saying yes to opposition and war [*Krieg*], *becoming* along with a radical rejection of the very concept of "being" – all these are more closely related to me than anything else people have thought so far. (EH BT 4)

This passage plainly demonstrates that the Heraclitean view of struggle as omnipresent and fecund remains front and center in the later Nietzsche's understanding of the history of the philosophy of conflict. But what this text also bears out is that his interpretation of Heraclitus has undergone a significant transformation. Whereas the early Nietzsche approximates the Heraclitean worldview to the nondestructive ancient Greek agon, with its measured quality of mutual restraint, the later Nietzsche accents the belligerent, annihilatory overtones of that very same worldview. This said, it would be rash to read this as an endorsement of militarism. As in Nietzsche's earlier reading of Heraclitus, the above passage invokes bellicose language in a *figurative* manner, that is, as a means of elucidating the intangible world of *ontological* opposition. This indicates that in reconstructing Nietzsche's philosophy of conflict, we need to be mindful of his predilection for deploying the vocabulary of war in a symbolic fashion.

Autocratic Opposition: Socrates and Plato

Compared with his eulogizing treatment of Heraclitus, Nietzsche's attitude toward Plato and Socrates is markedly more ambivalent.[16] To anyone familiar with Nietzsche's searching critique of Platonic idealism,

---

[16] On Nietzsche's conflicted attitude toward Plato and Socrates, see Lampert (2004); Acampora (2013), chap. 3). N.B. Nietzsche is on occasion critical of Heraclitus (see e.g., TI Reason 2).

the Platonic currents running through his early writings can come as something of a surprise. In "The Greek State" for example, which contains Nietzsche's first extended discussion of literal war, he espouses a quasi-Platonic utopia. In the *Republic*, Plato constructs an account of political and psychological harmony that he believes is capable of minimizing strife on both of these ontological planes.[17] He claims that such harmony is achieved by ordering each of these systems into a strict form of rationally governed hierarchy. In the individual soul, the faculty of rationality should thus rule over an individual's will and appetites; and, analogously, within the ideal polis, the irrational "appetites of the masses – the inferior people – are mastered [...] by the wisdom and appetites of the few" – an elite of rationally minded philosopher-kings, or *guardians* (*phylakes*) (Plato 2005, 431d). In GSt Nietzsche commends Plato's pyramidic conception of the "perfect state," judging it to be "certainly something still greater than is believed by even his warm-blooded admirers" (GSt, KSA 1.776). With an eye to improving on Plato's account, Nietzsche then outlines his own stratified vision of utopia. Echoing the *Republic*, in GSt Nietzsche's ideal political arrangement couples an aggressive foreign policy bent on war with an equally fierce domestic policy geared toward stamping out insurrection and thereby ensuring harmonious civil order.[18] Yet, unlike Plato, who proposes to ban the arts from his well-ordered republic, Nietzsche envisions political order as a *means to* cultural flourishing, which in his view stands as the final cause of human existence (GSt, KSA 1.772). It is therefore not the philosopher but the artistic genius whom Nietzsche places at the apex of his pyramidic utopia.

This early enthusiasm for Plato cools rather rapidly as we move into the middle and later phases of Nietzsche's philosophy. For instance, he persistently indicts Plato for promoting political harmony at the expense of sociocultural flourishing. According to Nietzsche, Plato harmfully campaigns to suppress the passions that underpin interpersonal competition – passions such as jealousy, vanity, egoism, ambition and the desire for glory.[19] For reasons that we will be exploring in Part I, Nietzsche conceives competition as a condition of collective and individual enhancement. On

[17] Though he does, in places, acknowledge the need for social strife (particularly athletic contest and war). See e.g., Plato (2005, 412b, 470b, 555a).
[18] This maps onto the distinction that Plato (2005, 470b) draws between foreign and civil war (i.e., *polemos* and *stasis*).
[19] See KSA 9:11[303], 557; WS 285; BGE 14; KSA 13:14[94], 272.

this view, Plato's hostility toward the affects that drive competition has the knock-on effect of discouraging human enhancement.

Plato is also integral to Nietzsche's understanding of *psychological* strife. Given that soul and state are structurally isomorphic for Plato (2005, 368c–369a), the same abstract principles of organization (i.e., Plato's theory of justice) apply to both. In a similar manner, Nietzsche often figures the human psyche as a mirror image of the body politic.[20] It should come as little surprise, then, that Nietzsche ultimately rejects the Platonic conception of psychic health for the very same reasons (*mutatis mutandis*) that he disavows Plato's political utopia – that is, because he believes it fosters an unduly pacific form of harmony, one that negates the vibrant tension that conditions human flourishing. Now, though, the contention that Nietzsche seeks to ensure is *infra*-personal, and refers to the relations that inhere between a person's various psychological drives. He objects that both Plato and Socrates wish to install reason as a cognitive tyrant charged with the task of subduing the agent's riotous instincts with draconian force. To be sure, Nietzsche thinks that this may well have been an advisable therapeutic *for Plato*, due to the fact that Plato's sensual impulses were "overpowerful," and thus warranted radical countermeasures (GS 372); under normal circumstances, however, such a "fanatical" course of treatment is, by Nietzsche's lights, "itself just a sickness" (TI Socrates 10).

Nietzsche is likewise critical of the way in which Socrates establishes rationality as the ultimate yardstick of argumentative strength, thereby discounting instinct, intuition, authority and rhetorical flourish as valid means of persuasion (SGT 1, KSA 1.541). In a word, according to Nietzsche, Socrates employs reason *despotically*: "As a dialectician, you have a merciless tool in your hands; dialectics lets you act like a tyrant" (TI Socrates 7). In a contest of speeches, the Socratic dialectician compels agreement through force of the better argument, where *better* now means *logically sounder*. Nietzsche flags two adverse side effects of this development. First, the spread of rationalism corrupts ancient Greek dramatic tragedy, which it renders excessively logocentric. This shift banishes the musical dimension of tragic theater, which Nietzsche takes to be an essential component of thriving culture (particularly in his early writings) (BT 14–15). Second, the shift toward rationalism alienates people from their instinctive, "unconscious wisdom," which Nietzsche takes to have been the fundamental source of ancient Greek creativity (SGT 1, KSA 1.541ff.). For these reasons, then, he believes that the immoderate use of

---

[20] See Parkes (1991) for a comparison of Nietzsche's and Plato's philosophical psychologies.

reason leads to cultural decay. But we should take care not to read these grievances as an outright rejection of the ancient rise of dialectics. For instance, Nietzsche praises Plato for his "development and internalization of the ancient agonistic gymnastics" (TI Skirmishes 23). And he applauds both Socrates and Plato for transfiguring physical wrestling into dialogical struggle – a type of struggle that proceeds not just *between* individuals, but also *within* them, that is, between their will, reason and passions.[21]

Finally, though arguably most importantly, we come to Nietzsche's rejection of Platonic idealism. Plato asserts that the changeable world that we perceive via our sense organs is in fact an illusion. True reality is in his view confined to the static realm of the ideal forms, which we can only access by means of rational reflection. Reprising his critique of Anaximander, Nietzsche thus brands Plato a "coward in the face of reality," and charges him with fleeing into the imaginary sphere of being and ideality (TI Ancients 2).[22] But what exactly does Nietzsche think that Plato is fleeing *from*? Shortly put, the world of "appearance, change, contradiction, [and] struggle [*Kampf*]." According to Nietzsche, Plato both denies and devalues the real, conflictual world in which we actually live. One of the principal ways in which he does so is by conceiving intimate rational knowledge of the eternal forms (particularly the form of the Good) as a prerequisite of living a virtuous life. Nietzsche takes this fixation on the eternal forms to be motivated by an unhealthy "desire for a world in which [appearance, change, contradiction, and struggle] are missing" (KSA 12:9[160], 430).[23] Hence, Nietzsche declares himself a "total skeptic when it comes to Plato" (TI Ancients 2).

But Nietzsche's chief complaint against Plato is that he helped lay the fundaments of Judeo-Christian morality, which in turn caused an epoch of cultural decline. Thus, Nietzsche proclaims that Christianity is in essence "Platonism for the 'people'" (BGE Preface). In order to fathom the full depth of this criticism, we should now turn to Nietzsche's philosophical engagement with Christian doctrine.

Conflict and the Christian Tradition

In Nietzsche's judgment, Christian thinkers are culpable of "cowardice and flight from reality" – that is, of fleeing into the artificial realm of "the 'ideal'" (much like Plato and Anaximander) (EH BT 2). To substantiate

---

[21] See TI Skirmishes 23, Socrates 8.   [22] See also D 448.
[23] And to be sure, in the *Cratylus* Plato explicitly rejects the Heraclitean worldview.

this charge, Nietzsche adduces Christianity's veneration of the afterlife (*Jenseits*) (A 62). He further points to the fact that Christian doctrine cherishes equality, chastity and absolute moral values, each of which betrays a fainthearted (and ultimately self-detrimental) reluctance to acknowledge the fluctuating nature of reality and the conditions of burgeoning life.[24]

These life-denying Christian proclivities are not, Nietzsche tells us, confined to the revealed doctrines of the Church; rather, in his view, they also permeate a substantial part of modern philosophy. Thus, he inveighs against Judeo-Christian thinkers such as Descartes and Spinoza for their "contempt [...] towards everything changing," a contempt that he believes deeply motivates their substance metaphysics. Philosophers of a Judeo-Christian cast, Nietzsche contends, yearn for an eternal realm of unchanging essences and a priori truths, one that exists beneath and behind the conflictual manifold of appearance. On a similar note, he reprimands Kant for contriving the noumenal realm as an epistemically secure space for Christian dogmas (such as moral freedom and the existence of God) (KSA 12:9[160], 430). And to the extent that Leibniz argues for "eternal concepts, eternal values, eternal forms, eternal souls," Nietzsche likewise accuses him of shoring up the unwholesome Platonic–Christian worldview (KSA 11:38[14], 613–615). In another, earlier note, Nietzsche further takes issue with Spinoza's wish for a rationally grounded condition of "concord [*Eintracht*] and absence of struggle [*Kampfes*]." For Nietzsche, this desideratum is premised on a fundamental error (*Grundirrthum*), and he compares the attainment of this end to a state of death (KSA 9:11[132], 490).

Reprising another of his cavils against Plato, Nietzsche then rebukes Christian theologians for propagating an insipidly pacifistic notion of individual happiness. Thus, quoting from Augustine's *Confessions*, he disparages what he sees as the Christian lust for "rest, lack of disturbance, repletion, unity at last and the 'Sabbath of Sabbaths'" (BGE 200). In contrast to this ataraxic conception of happiness, Nietzsche endeavors to illuminate the multiple ways in which psychological tension conditions individual well-being.[25]

Christian sociopolitical theory, Nietzsche claims, is likewise fueled by a small-minded hankering for unblemished peace. He pejoratively labels Christianity a "herd morality" on account of the fact that it belongs to a set of moral systems that promote ever-smoother socialization, and which

[24] See Chapter 4.   [25] As we will see in Part II of this book.

surreptitiously corral humans into a single, homogeneous flock (at the expense of their individual freedom). In lionizing neighborly love, turning the other cheek, pity and universal equality before God, Christianity represents the herd morality par excellence.[26] He then takes democrats, socialists, utilitarians, social Darwinists and Kantian moral philosophers to be the modern torchbearers of this Christian breed of herd morality – even if these movements may on the surface appear to be secular in nature (EH Destiny 4; BGE 201).[27] In spite of their differences, these schools of moral theory share a common desire to render man peaceful, altruistic and gregarious (this latter term being understood in its etymological sense of belonging to a flock or, in Latin, *grex*). This is why Nietzsche emphatically declares that "[m]orality in Europe these days is the morality of herd animals" (BGE 202).

Lastly, Nietzsche objects to the way in which Christianity and its pseudo-secular heirs critically engage with competing value systems. Christianity is, he insists, a slave morality, which is to say a morality formulated by those who are "violated, oppressed, suffering, unfree, exhausted, and unsure of themselves" (BGE 260). The sentiment that drives this morality is, he maintains, one of *ressentiment* (GM I 10). But this in itself is not what makes Christianity anathema to Nietzsche. What riles him is the Christian habit of directing this vengeful animus toward those of noble standing: since the adherents of slave morality are too weak to vent their hostility in open confrontation with their noble superiors, they instead pursue revenge by underhanded means. By branding noble upstanding virtues "evil" (*böse*), they insidiously rack the nobles with guilt, robbing them of their exuberant, self-assured health and thereby drawing them into the pathological dynamic of *ressentiment* (GM III 14–15).[28] Moreover, in positing its values in an absolute and universalizing manner, Christianity shows unrestrained intolerance for alternative moralities: "The church has always wanted to destroy its enemies" (TI Morality 3). In the Bible, this impetus is clearly discernible in God's jealous command-ment against the worship of false idols (KJV Exodus 20: 3–5), but it can also be seen in the Church's numerous historical campaigns against heresy (e.g., the Inquisition). Nietzsche takes this desire to eradicate one's opponents to

---

[26] See BGE 62; GS 377. I am bracketing out the distinction that Nietzsche draws between the Christianity of Christ and Pauline Christianity. Nietzsche takes the latter to be far more political in nature, and, unlike the former, to be quite open to (violent) struggle (see KSA 13:11[282], 108).

[27] Nietzsche refers to his campaign against these acolytes as his "struggle against *latent Christianity*" (KSA 12: 10[2], 453).

[28] For more on this dynamic, see Chapter 4.

be deeply injurious, since, recalling Mill, he believes that one's strength depends on the continued vigor of one's adversaries – opponents offer us the resistance we need in order to manifest, and further cultivate, our individual powers (EH Wise 7). He further underlines how Christianity's aggressive intolerance of its "evil" adversaries flies in the face of its professed love of peace and harmony: "[O]ne takes *war* [*Krieg*] to be *evil* – and yet wages war [i.e., against evil and sin]!" (KSA 13:11[297], 124). The key issue that this raises, and which we will be addressing over the course of this book, concerns whether Nietzsche's own radical critique of Christian doctrine – a critique which is itself often fueled by destructive intent – is able to escape the charge of hypocrisy.

The Christian drive to eradicate opposition flouts what Nietzsche considers to be the conflictual Heraclitean basis of thriving life. This explains why he portrays Christianity as "anti-nature" (*Widernatur*).[29] Indeed, most of the critical remarks that we have so far delineated boil down to a naturalistically grounded allegation of life-denial. Anaximander, Plato, Socrates and representatives of the Christian tradition all stand accused of turning away from nature, and likewise, of disregarding the principles of flourishing human life – an issue that Nietzsche variously thematizes under the headings of *décadence*, life-denial and later, nihilism.[30] But if Nietzsche's argument is to have any real force, we need to obtain a clearer view of the grounds on which he holds flourishing nature (which includes *human* nature) to be irreducibly structured by conflict. While Nietzsche certainly takes the germ of this idea from Heraclitus, it can also be traced back to his reception of thinkers such as Schopenhauer, Burckhardt and Darwin. It is therefore to these figures that we should now turn our inquiry.

Schopenhauer and the Struggle for Life

Of the various figures who shaped Nietzsche's conflict-oriented vision of nature, Schopenhauer is of paramount significance. Yet this line of influence takes a radically dichotomous form, with the early Nietzsche being just as ardent a *disciple* of Schopenhauer, as the later Nietzsche is a *detractor*. But nonetheless, as acolyte or adversary, throughout his working life Nietzsche remains in constant dialogue with the Schopenhauerian worldview. What is more, Schopenhauer's influence on Nietzsche is also exerted by proxy, that is, through the impact of Wagner and Burckhardt,

---

[29] See e.g., TI Morality 1; EH Destiny 7.   [30] See e.g., KSA 12:7[54], 313.

who, in their own distinct ways, were both self-professed Schopenhauerians.

For Schopenhauer, as for Heraclitus, conflict is universal: "Everywhere in nature we see conflict [*Streit*], struggle [*Kampf*], and the interchange of victory" (WWR 1, 2.174). He depicts the world of representation (i.e., the empirical world of phenomena) as a welter of individual entities, each of which is impelled by a forceful will to live. This impetus condemns them to a condition of fierce and often destructive strife. Organisms, for example, are driven to consume one another for the sake of nutrition, and are therefore locked in a brutal contest for energetic resources. For Schopenhauer, even the *inorganic* world is at variance with itself, as natural forces wrangle over matter (WWR 1, 2.364). He believes this notion of universal strife to be confirmed by, but not grounded in, empirical observation. The *necessity* of conflict is in his view entailed by the fact that every individual object at the empirical level of representation is the expression of a single unified *will*: a "blind urge" (*blinder Drang*) to overpower and consume that underlies all existence (WWR 1, 2.213). It is this noumenal will that constitutes the unitary metaphysical ground of phenomenal reality. Given that there is only one will, and it needs something to will *against*, something to *consume*, it must necessarily will against and consume itself; and thus the individual phenomena through which it expresses itself are correspondingly destined to devour one another.[31]

In PTAG (1873), written while Nietzsche still publicly subscribed to Schopenhauer's *Weltanschauung*, he compares this description of the world in terms of struggle to that of Heraclitus (PTAG 5, KSA 1.826). Yet Nietzsche highlights a substantial *evaluative* discrepancy between Schopenhauer's and Heraclitus' accounts. Whereas Heraclitus *esteems* the conflictual nature of existence, Schopenhauer deems it cause for pessimism. In Nietzsche's words, for Schopenhauer, the conflictual structure of reality proves existence to be driven by "a self-consuming, menacing and gloomy drive, a thoroughly frightful and by no means blessed phenomenon" (PTAG 5, KSA 1.826) – a far cry from the affirmation of *Dikē* that we find in Heraclitus.[32] This gloomy drive is the metaphysical will that Schopenhauer sees compelling the activity of every empirical object in existence. Indeed, the activity of willing is common to *all* phenomena at *all* times. But working on the assumption that all willing presupposes the absence of that which is willed, Schopenhauer characterizes willing as

---

[31] Schopenhauer's metaphysics will be further clarified in Chapters 1 and 3.
[32] For more on Nietzsche's interpretations of Heraclitus and Schopenhauer, see Pearson (2020).

a process marked by "need, lack, and thus pain" (WWR 1, 2.367). At a specifically human level, the suffering inherent to life is then compounded by the fact that even the sustained satisfaction of our will quickly elicits boredom, which we experience as even more painful than the regular hunger of willing (WWR 1, 2.369–370) – hence Schopenhauer's bleak conclusion that "it would be better for us not to exist" (WWR 2, 3.695). At bottom, then, his evaluative view of existence has far more in common with Anaximander than it does with Heraclitus.

With respect to the world as representation, Schopenhauer is then what we might call a hard determinist, and as part of this theoretical view, he claims that an individual's character is immutable and fixed for life. This flows into Schopenhauer's hard-line skepticism regarding prescriptive ethics (since he takes it to be futile to expect people to truly change their ways). Philosophy, he maintains, is a strictly *descriptive* discipline; it "can never do more than interpret and explain" reality (WWR 1, 2.320). And yet he nevertheless holds that certain fortunate individuals do in fact obtain release from the will to live, from its dolorous cycles of desire, satisfaction and boredom. For example, in beholding ideal art, Schopenhauer thinks that we can transcend, and obtain brief respite from, the sufferings inherent to temporal existence (WWR 1, 2.217ff.). Some are even fortunate enough to glimpse the illusory nature of individuality – they "see through the *principium individuationis*, the veil of *māyā*" (WWR 1, 2.438). Understanding the deeper unity of all things and the futility of willing cues these individuals to resist the egoistic dictates of their will to live. In other words, they *negate the will* and thereby achieve a temporary form of bliss (WWR 1, 2.456). This idyllic vision of life-denial is exemplified by the altruistic and ascetic figure of the saint. But even the saint's bliss is episodic and short-lived, being interrupted by the constant "spiritual struggle" he has to wage against the importunate demands of his egoistic body. Redounding of Aquinas and Augustine, Schopenhauer thus concludes that "on earth no one can have lasting peace" (WWR 1, 2.446ff.).

Already in the late 1860s, Nietzsche was beginning to harbor private misgivings regarding the coherence of Schopenhauer's metaphysics.[33] Nonetheless, his public allegiance persisted into the early 1870s, perhaps reaching its climax in his panegyric *Schopenhauer as Educator* (1874). But throughout this period his reservations continue to grow steadily, until finally, in 1876, with the publication of HH, he publicly disavows

---

[33] See esp. KGW I/4, 417–426.

Schopenhauer's philosophy. Throughout his later writings, he then develops a searching critique of Schopenhauer, taking particular issue with his pessimistic celebration of life-denial, which Nietzsche frames as an act of "*slander*" (*Verleumdung*) committed against reality (GS 370; TI Errors 6). He censures Schopenhauer for advocating not just idealism (EH BT 2), but also altruism, which Nietzsche takes to be in most cases harmful to all involved parties (D 113); thus, he vilifies Schopenhauer for being "hostile to life" (*Lebensfeindlich*) (A 7), and reiterates his disdain for those who, like Anaximander, flee from lived existence. Struggle and desire can, he reminds us, be just as *pleasurable* as they are painful. And openly scorning Schopenhauer's pessimistic conception of the will, he even contends that "willing liberates" (Z II Redemption, KSA 4.179).[34] Recalling his critique of Plato's idealism, however, Nietzsche conjectures that Schopenhauer's tranquilizing, quietist practical philosophy may have actually been a fitting ethos for Schopenhauer himself – "someone who suffers deeply, who struggles, is tortured"; but for those who possess a more vigorous constitution, he takes it to be a singularly detrimental therapeutic, one that ought to be avoided at all costs (GS 370).[35]

Burckhardt, Bismarck and the Rise of Realism

Another figure of seminal importance for Nietzsche's mature philosophy of conflict is the historian Jakob Burckhardt, a friend and colleague of Nietzsche at the University of Basel. Burckhardt's foremost intellectual contribution was his revisionist account of ancient Greek culture. During the eighteenth and nineteenth centuries, German academe (and culture in general) was in the grip of an idealizing obsession with the ancient Greeks, what is often referred to as "Grecophilia," or *classicism*. The movement encompassed figures such as Winckelmann, Goethe, Schiller, Herder, Hegel and Wagner. What unites this diverse group of thinkers is their shared tendency to paint a remarkably rosy portrait of the ancient Greeks, whom they depict as, among other things, healthy peace-loving paragons of beauty, or as culturally and politically cohesive proto-socialists.[36] The Grecophiles tacitly assent to Rousseau's conviction that decadent social institutions have corrupted

---

[34] Nietzsche's grounds for this view will be explored in Chapter 4.

[35] Hence, Nietzsche thought that Schopenhauer did, *malgré lui*, propound a prescriptive ethics – principally through his valorization of life-denial.

[36] For an apt example of German classicism, see Winkelmann's *Gedancken über die Nachahmung der griechischen Wercke in der Mahlerei und Bildhauer-Kunst* (1755).

man's primordial innocence. But somewhat diverging from Rousseau,
they maintain that this purity was best embodied by the Hellenes, whom
they hold up as an archetype of perfection – one for which modern
German culture accordingly ought to strive.[37]

Burckhardt considers this approach to antiquity to be unacceptably
distortive, and he therefore seeks to replace it with a more faithful image
of the ancient Greeks – what we might characterize as his turn toward
historical *realism*. The core idea that informs his philological writings is
that the excellence of the ancient Greeks was a function of their brutality,
belligerence and aggressively competitive spirit. For example, in WBe he
asserts that the Persian Wars "developed the powers of the Hellenes
gloriously in all ways" (WBe, 4.119). Martial conflict, he argues, stimulates
the organization of society into a functionally well-organized whole, and
further serves to propagate manly warrior virtues.[38] But in 1871, only a few
years after making these remarks, he presents a series of lectures in which he
conspicuously modifies his position. In these lectures (which were edited
into the text of GK), he ascribes the cultural success of the ancient Greeks
to their ability to *channel* their belligerent impulses into specifically agonal
forms of contest, which, as we will see in Chapter 2, he considers to be
categorically *non*-martial.[39]

Our survey of Nietzsche's reception of Heraclitus, Plato and Socrates
has already gestured toward the centrality of the ancient Greek agon for his
own unique philosophy of conflict; hence it is important that we note the
significant impact that Burckhardt had on Nietzsche's understanding of
the practice. Scholars have long since disputed the extent to which
Nietzsche's thoughts on this topic were shaped by Burckhardt; and to be
sure, Nietzsche's fascination with the agon predates his acquaintance with
Burckhardt. Nonetheless, there is persuasive evidence that Nietzsche
both knew of, and engaged with, Burckhardt's conception of agonal

---

[37] Note that notwithstanding the common features shared by German classicists, it was a highly diverse
movement; and certainly, many classicists acknowledged the extreme belligerence of the ancient
Greeks (e.g., Goethe), or were themselves ambivalent regarding the social value of war (e.g.,
Humboldt).

[38] See Chapter 1.

[39] At this juncture we should note a conspicuous lacuna in Nietzsche's writings on the history of the
philosophy of conflict. This concerns his neglect of the just war theory tradition, which tries to
determine the objective moral framework that applies to situations of martial conflict. The accounts
advanced by Aquinas, Augustine, Grotius and Suarez, for example, are left unmentioned by
Nietzsche, though he certainly seems to have been aware of this school of moral philosophy; indeed,
he parodies the orthodox view of *jus ad bellum*, stating that "it is the good war that hallows [*heiligt*]
any cause" (Z I Warriors, KSA 4.59) – of course, for just war theorists it is the just *cause* that
legitimates a given war.

conflict.[40] What is more, there can be no doubt that Nietzsche was sharply aware of Burckhardt's dispute with the Grecophiles, though his own position in this debate is somewhat changeable. In certain passages he appears to endorse moderate classicism, speaking of the legitimate, periodic need that cultures have for using history as a means of constructing exemplars – what he terms "monumental history" – even if this often comes at the expense of historical accuracy (HL 2, KSA 1.258–265).[41] Yet he more often than not firmly sides with Burckhardt. In TI, for instance, he censures the Grecophiles for their willful misrepresentation of historical fact, and more particularly, for their tendency to overlook the aggressive, orgiastic, or in other words "Dionysian," energies that turned the wheels of ancient Greek culture.[42]

Aside from Burckhardt, Nietzsche's realism has further key sources, most notably in Thucydides and Bismarck.[43] Thucydides, an ancient Greek general and historian, is best known as the author of *The History of the Peloponnesian War*, a sober account of ancient Greek pugnacity and politicking. The text had a decisive impact on Nietzsche's realist vision of ancient Greece, and he even goes so far as to label Thucydides an "antidote" to the fantasy of Platonic idealism (TI Ancients 2). As for Bismarck, the *Real-* and *Machtpolitik* that he espoused, and which dominated Prussian foreign policy throughout the latter half of the nineteenth century, left a deep impression on the early Nietzsche's worldview. In 1862 Bismarck (1928, 140) infamously asserted that "state health" could only be secured by means of "blood and

---

[40] For an overview of the debate concerning Burckhardt's impact on Nietzsche's agonism, see Acampora (1998, 559). As Acampora observes, while Nietzsche may not have attended all of Burckhardt's lectures on ancient Greece, he had two students make transcripts of the lectures, which he carefully studied, and some of which he copied into his notebooks. Note, however, that Acampora (2013, 211 [n.7]) ultimately downplays the influence of Burckhardt. See also Chapter 2, fn.3 below.

[41] See also BT 20.   [42] See e.g., TI BT 4; GSt.

[43] In dealing with the realist dimension of Nietzsche's thought, we should flag a further gap in his view of the history of the philosophy of conflict, namely, Hobbes. Nietzsche's familiarity with Hobbes is superficial at best, though the latter's account of the causes of war (Hobbes 1996: 86–90) has been highly influential in conflict theory. This said, Nietzsche does indirectly engage with many of Hobbes' ideas, and even borrows Hobbes' phraseology in describing the state of nature as a *bellum omnium contra omnes* (see e.g., GSt, KSA 1.772; TL 1, KSA 1.877; DS 7, KSA 1.194); however, his choice of words in this respect is likely down to the influence of Schopenhauer, who was himself fond of Hobbes' Latin turn of phrase (see e.g., WWR 1, 2.393). Indeed, the early Nietzsche's reasons for construing the state of nature in such belligerent terms are principally taken from Schopenhauer (and to some extent Darwin) as opposed to Hobbes. Schopenhauer's rationale for viewing nature in this way, which was outlined in the previous subsection, is quite distinct from that of Hobbes (which can be found in Hobbes 1996: 86–90). It is also worth noting that the realist Clausewitz, the author of an influential study of war, *Vom Kriege* (1832), is almost completely absent from Nietzsche's writings on military conflict.

iron." This saber-rattling rhetoric appealed to the young Nietzsche. As he writes in a letter of 1868, "Bismarck brings me immense pleasure. I read his speeches as if I was drinking a strong wine."[44] Although these speeches therefore left an impression on the early Nietzsche, it is Bismarck's political *deeds* that feature most prominently in his writings (e.g., in DS) – especially the Franco-Prussian war and the subsequent unification of Germany under Prussian rule in 1871. On the whole, though, Nietzsche's feelings toward Bismarck are deeply mixed, with his early affection turning to outright disapprobation in his later writings. His contempt culminates in 1888 with him dubbing Bismarck "the idiot par excellence." It is Bismarck's militaristic politics that especially vex the later Nietzsche, who describes them as nothing more than a waste of valuable manpower (KSA 13:25[13], 643). But aside from this, Nietzsche also derides the "cultural struggle" (*Culturkampf*) that Bismarck waged against the political influence of the Roman Catholic church.[45] Above all, Nietzsche is unable to abide the arrogant nationalism that fueled this *Culturkampf*. And so it is in direct opposition to Bismarck that Nietzsche declares his own "struggle for culture" (*Kampf für die Kultur*). In this countercampaign, Nietzsche exhorts his fellow Germans to rejuvenate their national culture principally by means of educational reform – and thus he seeks to offer his countrymen a softer alternative to the militaristic *Realpolitik* of Bismarck (SE 6, KSA 1.386).[46]

Darwinism and the Struggle for Survival

Though the later Nietzsche vociferously attacks Darwin, and in 1888 even proclaims himself to be "anti-Darwin" (TI Skirmishes 14), scholars generally agree that he did not actually read any of Darwin's major works.[47] His knowledge of Darwin was largely obtained secondhand, via Darwinists such as Lange, Spencer, Wilhelm Roux and William Rolph (among others), all of whom he studied with close attention.[48] The problem is that each of these thinkers misinterpret fundamental aspects of Darwin's theory. Rather unsurprisingly, as we will see in Chapter 4, Nietzsche himself then

[44] Letter to Carl von Gersdorff, February 16, 1868 (KGB I/2, 254).   [45] See e.g., SE 7, KSA 1.407.
[46] On the impact of Bismarck on Nietzsche, see Drochon (2016, chap. 6). For an overview of Nietzsche's intellectual debt to Thucydides, see Jenkins (2011).
[47] This claim is supported by the fact that NPB does not report any books by Darwin being in Nietzsche's library. See Richardson (2004, 16). Compare Johnson (2010, 3), who claims that "Nietzsche understood Darwin and the implications of his theories both early and well."
[48] Evidence of this can be found in NPB.

reproduces many of these exegetical errors. At first glance, Darwin formulates a conflict-infused account of nature that largely corresponds to Schopenhauer's outlook in WWR. Unlike Schopenhauer, though, Darwin is at pains to avoid metaphysical speculation, and, moreover, confines himself to the biological sphere. In a chapter of *On the Origin of Species* entitled "Struggle for Existence," Darwin (2009, 50) draws his reader's attention to the all-too-human mistake of conceiving nature as abundant and harmonious: "we forget that the birds which are idly singing round us mostly live on insects or seeds, and are thus constantly destroying life." It turns out that nature is pervaded by what Darwin denotes "the struggle for life." Organisms have to compete with one another for limited space, mates and natural resources, in addition to vying with the harsh "physical conditions of life." His argument for the necessity of natural conflict is broadly Malthusian in kind: since the growth in population of any organisms inhabiting the same environment will always exceed the available space and resources, organisms are inevitably driven into a destructive zero-sum contest for the space and resources that they require in order to survive (52).[49] Consequently, at any one time only a fraction of the total number of organisms striving to propagate themselves are able to actually do so. Darwin figures this struggle for existence as the driving force behind natural selection – only those organisms possessing advantageous variations are able to prevail in the struggle for life, forcing those that lack such traits out of existence.

In a note from 1872, Nietzsche explicitly states that he takes Darwinism "to be true" (KSA 7:19[132], 461). And not long after, in DS, he criticizes David Strauss for *claiming* to be Darwinian and yet shying away from (what Nietzsche considers to be) the brutal ethical ramifications of Darwin's vision of nature qua "bellum omnium contra omnes." In Nietzsche's view, any resolute Darwinist must acknowledge that man, like all other animals, has evolved by "gradually eliminating the other, weaker examples of his species." This fact, he tells us, should translate into a moral code that eschews equal rights and ensures the "privileges of the strong" (DS 7, KSA 1.194–195). It is furthermore worth noting that this concern with the unpalatable ethical consequences of Darwinism is one that Nietzsche shares with many of the social Darwinists (though particularly Spencer).[50]

Over the course of his middle period, Nietzsche begins to question the validity of Darwin's theory of evolution. At first he endeavors to elaborate and correct, as opposed to debunk, what he takes to be Darwin's theory of

---

[49] See Malthus (1798, chaps. 3 and 8).   [50] See fn.6.

evolution. For example, in HH 224 – the preparatory note for which is entitled "On *Darwinism*" (KSA 8:12[22], 257) – Nietzsche asks whether it is only through the "struggle for existence" (*Kampf um's Dasein*) that man evolves and grows stronger. After all, he contends, strength alone can be ossifying, and although sick and deviant individuals might *appear* maladaptive from a Darwinian point of view, they can, in point of fact, serve as agents of vibrant change. Nietzsche thus maintains that such individuals enable evolution and development. His argument, however, is founded upon a misreading. Darwinism does not posit that individuals and societies only develop by means of a brutal, warlike "struggle for existence," nor that the biologically "fittest" individuals or groups are the *physically* strongest. Indeed, for more discerning Darwinists, the struggle for existence usually takes the *indirect* form of a struggle to accrue resources and outbreed one's competitors (i.e., without direct physical combat); and moreover, "the fittest" simply designates those organisms most capable of survival and reproduction (which may very well include those that we consider to be in some way sick or deviant). Hence, while HH 224 illuminates some counterintuitive consequences of Darwin's evolutionary theory, it does not correct said theory (as Nietzsche implies).

Not long after, in 1881, Nietzsche begins reading Wilhelm Roux, an evolutionary biologist who, like the Nietzsche of HH, also seeks to supplement Darwin's theory of evolution. The core idea of Roux's magnum opus, KTO, is that natural selection and the "struggle for survival" proceed *within*, as well as *between*, organisms – that is, between their various component parts (e.g., their cells, tissues and organs). Nietzsche accepts a great deal of Roux's theory, though not without significant exceptions and qualifications (which we will examine in depth in Chapter 4). Most importantly, he charges Roux with having committed an anthropomorphic fallacy. When we refer to entities as "struggling," Nietzsche thinks that we thereby presuppose that such entities are motivated by human affects (e.g., those of striving, hoping, hating, etc.); hence, we cannot talk about the "struggle" of the component parts of an organism in a scientifically realist manner. To illustrate this point, we might imagine visiting a fairground and spectating an intricate clockwork boxing match "fought" between two automata. Since "conflict" implies at least one sentient thing consciously struggling for some represented end, or at least motivated by some conscious emotion, it would be incorrect to claim that any real conflict was taking place between the two fairground machines. And yet Nietzsche maintains that the vocabulary of struggle *can* usefully illuminate nonhuman relations – namely, insofar as it can provide us with a "manner of speaking" (*Sprechart*) or "image-language" (*Bilderrede*) that enables us to meaningfully discuss and analyze various obscure natural processes (KSA 9:11[128], 487).[51] Throughout this book, we are going to need to bear in mind that Nietzsche deepens this critique of scientific objectivity, especially in the later writings. In trying to supersede scientifically realist views of natural phenomena, Nietzsche does not simply offer us his own alternative realist theories. Rather, as will become clear in Chapter 4, he presents his own theories as competing *interpretations*, perspectives or hypotheses – as stronger, more effective *Bilderreden* that in no way pretend to explain the world objectively, *as it really is*.

From the mid-1880s onwards, Nietzsche adopts a predominantly hostile attitude toward Darwinism. His chief objection concerns the teleological presuppositions that he mistakenly imputes to Darwin's theory of evolution. Nietzsche thus rejects the idea that organisms struggle to survive, arguing that proper observation reveals that they only do so under conditions of dearth, which are in fact extremely rare. Nature, he argues, is not ordinarily "a state of need, a state of hunger, but rather abundance, opulence" (TI Skirmishes 14), and under such normal circumstances, "struggle revolves everywhere around preponderance, around growth and expansion" (GS 349).[52]

Nietzsche's second objection applies more specifically to *social* Darwinism. He argues that where there is widespread struggle for existence among humans – that is, acute selective pressure – this weakens and mediocritizes the embattled population: "the weak keep gaining dominance over the strong, – there are more of them, and besides, they are cleverer" (TI Skirmishes 14).[53] His point is that biological fitness is inimical to the noble kinds of health and strength that he believes we ought to esteem. This view stands in stark opposition to that of the social Darwinists, who tend to exalt the idea that natural selection favors more pacific, socialized human beings

---

[51] As Müller-Lauter (1978) remarks, Nietzsche's stance toward Roux undergoes some important permutations. These will be touched upon in Chapter 4.

[52] See also KSA 13:14[123], 305. Note that these objections miss their mark. First, Darwin does not claim that organisms caught in the struggle for existence need to be *consciously* struggling for their existence. He rather speaks of organisms as having incompatible "tendencies" (and not conscious ends), though he does sometimes slip and describe them as "striving" (see e.g., Darwin 2009, 54); moreover, what Darwin describes them as "tending" toward is "increase" (*not* survival) (ibid.). Finally, he accepts that nature *is* often abundant and that the struggle for survival is usually episodic or seasonal (51) (though in Nietzsche's defense, *on the whole* nature *is* nonetheless marked by scarcity for Darwin).

[53] See also KSA 13:14[123], 303–304; KSA 13:14[133], 315.

(because pacifism facilitates cooperation, which in turn increases evolutionary fitness).[54] In Nietzsche's opinion, though, this peaceable type of human
represents the quintessence of mediocrity.

But all this invective should not distract us from the substantial overlap
that exists between Nietzsche and the social Darwinists. Nietzsche was
intimately familiar with the writings of Spencer, Rolph, Bagehot, Haeckel
and Galton, and, like them, was taken with the idea of applying recent
advances in evolutionary biology to issues of a social and ethical nature.
Though this is not the place for an extended comparison, it is worth
highlighting a few pertinent points of convergence. First, as we will see
throughout our study, Nietzsche, like the social Darwinists, maintains that
social competition, when properly regulated, can strengthen humankind
(though Nietzsche's conception of "strengthen" is largely at odds with that
of the social Darwinists).[55] Second, Nietzsche often speaks of *racial* forms
of struggle, superiority and purity in ways that clearly recall Haeckel,
Galton and Bagehot (as well as Gobineau and Wagner, whose theories of
racial superiority predate Darwinism).[56] But as many commentators
emphasize, Nietzsche's notion of "race" (*Rasse*) should not be conflated
with that of his racist contemporaries.[57] Third, Nietzsche frequently
defends the idea that eugenics are a necessary condition of social health –
a core tenet of social Darwinism. While some texts show him to be in favor
of merely positive eugenics (i.e., regulating marriages and incentivizing
stronger individuals to procreate) (e.g., KSA 11:34[176], 480), others more
controversially sanction negative eugenics – for example, the sterilization,
or even extermination, of "decaying races" (e.g., KSA 11:25[211], 69).[58] At
first blow, these remarks may strike the reader as ample justification for
boycotting Nietzsche. However, as we will see in the final chapter and
conclusion of this book, these ideas are not as outlandishly racist or
malevolent as might at first appear to be the case, nor can they be discarded
offhand as irrational outbursts. The question is, then, what kind of
grounds could Nietzsche possibly give to support these immoderate prescriptions? And, moreover, how do these recommendations hang together
with his pointed criticism of destructive struggle?

This prefatory survey of the rich variety of influences that shaped
Nietzsche's thoughts on conflict prompts a number of caveats and

---

[54] This idea is particularly prominent in Spencer (1882), and Rolph's BP, both of which Nietzsche read
and annotated (see NPB). On Nietzsche's reception of Spencer and the social Darwinists, see
Richardson (2004, chap. 3.1).

[55] Compare e.g., Spencer (1994), and Nietzsche's HC.   [56] See e.g., D 272.   [57] See Chapter 4.

[58] On Nietzsche's endorsement of eugenics, see Richardson (2004, 142–143, 146).

questions for our broader inquiry. First, much like the social Darwinists, Nietzsche tries to ground his ethical philosophy in a particular vision of nature (even if, for Nietzsche, this vision is not scientifically realist in kind, as it is for the social Darwinists). In order to reconstruct the normative aspect of his philosophy of conflict, then, it is imperative that we first excavate its descriptive, theoretical foundations. The pressing question is therefore: How does the mature Nietzsche conceive nature as struggle? If he initially adheres to a blend of Schopenhauer and Darwin, only to categorically repudiate these influences in the later phases of his thought, what kind of theoretical framework does he construct as a replacement? Only by ascertaining why he abandons his earlier intellectual allegiances will we be able to grasp the complex rationale that underpins his own unique description of nature qua conflict.

Our overview has also shown how Nietzsche warns against philosophies that overvalue pacific harmony. To vie for a world in which peace reigns, to the complete exclusion of conflict, is to strain for a world that simply cannot exist – it is to simultaneously deny and flee from reality, to press for nonbeing. For Nietzsche, such philosophies fail to affirm life, and thereby furtively promote psychological ill-health, physical degeneration and cultural decay. And yet he nonetheless acknowledges the allure of such theories, and the fact that once adopted they are not easily relinquished. If we wish to resist the seductive force of these theories, it stands to reason that we need a comprehensive, deterrent vision of the harmful effects that Nietzsche ascribes to the fantasy of frictionless harmony. This goes hand in hand with the need to elucidate why he thinks we stand to profit from adhering to a more conflict-oriented conception of both the world and human flourishing – where "flourishing" is understood in terms of the extension and diversification of human possibilities. How must we amend our understanding of conflict if we wish to genuinely *affirm* the world in which we live, and with this, to meaningfully enhance human life? Given that life enhancement and life affirmation form the normative bedrock of Nietzsche's philosophical project, it seems only fitting that we make this question the cornerstone of our analysis.

From the above, we can already see that for Nietzsche human flourishing is conditioned by contention across a range of different ontological domains: biological, cultural, political, metaphysical, psychological and epistemic modes of conflict are all particularly significant in this regard. In what follows, however, our focus will be on the particular import of *social* struggle. It is not without reason that we should place the social dimension of Nietzsche's philosophy at the center of our inquiry. As we will presently see, this facet of his thoughts on conflict has not only attracted the greatest amount of critical attention, but has furthermore generated deep controversy and confusion. Yet what our introductory survey should have made abundantly clear is that one cannot consider Nietzsche's mature understanding of social struggle in isolation from his wider philosophy of conflict. As I just mentioned, we need to pin down his conflict-oriented description of nature, since it is this description that determines his vision of man's healthiest place in the natural order of things; but further, given that Nietzsche follows Socrates and Plato in drawing a relation of analogy between the structure of the state and that of the psyche, properly analyzing his social theory of conflict is necessarily going to involve examining his parallel account of psychological health.

Lastly, our precis demonstrates that Nietzsche in no way thinks that any and all struggle is benign or ought to be propagated – thus we saw him castigate both Bismarck's militarism and the destructive attitude that he believes Christianity adopts toward its adversaries. It is only *particular* species of struggle that, under certain conditions, facilitate health according to Nietzsche. However, before we can establish why and how he thinks these species ought to be separately fostered, they need to be conceptually isolated. As we shall now see, though, this task is complicated by the apparent wooliness of Nietzsche's vocabulary of conflict.

Nietzsche's Ambiguous Vocabulary of Conflict

One of the obstacles facing us as interpreters of Nietzsche's writings is that his encomiums to conflict seem to refer to a wide variety of qualitatively distinct modes of relation. For example, he affirms the fact that *life (Leben)*, understood in the most general sense, "must be struggle [*Kampf*]" – that is, a struggle for power, a struggle to incorporate, command and exploit, to become "master over what is [...] weaker" (Z II Self-Overcoming, KSA 4.148).[59] Then, on a more bellicose note, he writes that he esteems peace only "as a means to new wars [*Kriegen*]" (Z I Warriors, KSA 4.58).[60] He also entreats us to commence the "struggle" (*Kampf*) for cultural renewal "with the elimination [*Ausscheidung*]" of those parts of ourselves and society that he believes have become harmful to us (BT 23, KSA 1.149); elsewhere he advocates "waging war [*kriegführen*] with oneself" (BGE 200); and he furthermore claims that without *Kampf*, "everything becomes *weak*,

---

[59] See also BGE 259.
[60] See also Z IV Kings 2, KSA 4.307. Note that this inverts Kant's view (see p. 2).

man and society" (KSA 9:11[193], 517); finally, he praises the ancient Greek love of "contest" (*Wettkampf*) or "agon" (*Agon*) on account of its culturally stimulating effects – indeed, he goes so far as to declare that the ancient Greeks' "entire art cannot be thought apart from contest [*Wettkampf*]" (HH 170).

The underlying referent of Nietzsche's plurivocal affirmation of *Kampf* is thus prima facie unclear. Dictionaries of (the history of) German reveal that the noun *Kampf* rivals its English analogue "conflict" in terms of its ambiguity, signifying not only "a physical (armed) struggle [*Ringen*] for victory," but also "'contest' [*Wettkampf*], above all in sport"; moreover, it can further refer to "ideological or spiritual [*geistig*] struggle" (Paul 1992, 446–447). We might perhaps expect *Krieg*, commonly translated as "war," to have a more univocal signification – that is, for it to straightforwardly designate military combat. And certainly, Hermann Paul's dictionary recounts how *Krieg* came to replace the late-medieval German term *urliuge* (which signified any armed form of conflict); yet Paul also indicates that, historically speaking, *Krieg* had the far more general meaning of "every kind of hostility [*Feindseligkeit*]" or "strife [*Streit*] (also in words)" (490). These dictionaries therefore shed remarkably little light on *what* exactly Nietzsche is endorsing in his Heraclitean "affirmation of opposition and war [*Krieg*]" (EH BT 3).

This semantic ambiguity is without doubt most obtrusive in the social dimension of Nietzsche's philosophy. When he extolls war (*Krieg*), for example, is he affirming violent, martial struggle (as many, such as his fascistic readers for example, are wont to argue [see e.g., Bäumler 1931])?[61] Or should we take the view popularized by Walter Kaufmann (1974, 386) that in most of Nietzsche's "notorious remarks about 'war' [. . .] the word is used metaphorically," that is, as a vehicle for *spiritual* war. If we turn to his conception of contest (*Wettkampf*) or agon (*Agon*), we then find that certain commentators take this concept to subsume violent forms of conflict (e.g., Ruehl 2003), while others read it as a categorically *non*-violent mode of contention (e.g., Siemens 2001a).[62] And textual evidence for each of these apparently incompatible interpretations is readily forthcoming.[63] Likewise, there are texts in which Nietzsche conceives the exploitative struggle intrinsic to life as a naked, *amoral* and unmeasured form of conflict; yet there are numerous other texts in which he then characterizes this struggle as intrinsically restrained.[64] Finally, we have the struggle for elimination, which Nietzsche consistently valorizes as a vital life-process. At times he figures this as a nondestructive act of

---

[61] For more examples, see Chapter 1.　　[62] For more examples, see Chapter 2.　　[63] See Chapter 2.
[64] See Chapter 4.

"excretion" (*Ausscheidung*), as an act of "generosity" (*Freigiebigkeit*) even, one that bequeaths fertilizing dung to others (KSA 9:11[134], 492). Texts abound, however, in which he contrarily figures this eliminatory life-process in far more destructive terms, for example, as one of "excision" (*Ausschneidung*) or "destruction" (*Vernichtung*) (EH M 2; KSA 13:23[10], 611).

In the first place, then, our task is of a *descriptive* sort. We need to conceptually map the philosophical terrain upon which Nietzsche is maneuvering. This will involve demarcating the key species of conflict with which Nietzsche is concerned and then enumerating the qualities that he most consistently predicates to each of these. Throughout this study, I will be defending the idea that we can fruitfully divide the principal forms of human conflict advocated by Nietzsche into the following four categories (though it is important to note, however, that these are not all mutually exclusive):

1. Struggles of annihilation (*Vernichtungskämpfe*): violently unmeasured struggles-to-the-death, in which individuals or social groups strive for one another's physical destruction. War (*Krieg*), murder (*Mord*) and violent duels (*Duellen*), among other things, belong to this category.[65]
2. Agonal struggles (*Wettkämpfe*; *Agonen*; *Wettstreite*): measured, nonviolent, nonexploitative struggles fought between approximately equal individuals or social groups.
3. Incorporative struggles (*Kämpfe um Einverleibung*): measured struggles of individuals or social groups to *subjugate* (*beherrschen*; *einordnen*; *unterwerfen*; *anpassen*; *assimilieren*) and *exploit* (*ausbeuten*; *ausnützen*) their inferior counterparts by incorporating them into a functional hierarchy – that is, *without* destroying them.
4. Exclusionary struggles: unmeasured struggles of individuals or social groups to eliminate those entities that they believe themselves unable to fruitfully incorporate. This includes the repression (*Unterdrückung*), repulsion (*Zurückstoßen*), excretion (*Ausscheidung*), excision (*Ausschneidung*) or destruction (*Vernichtung, Zerstörung*) of entities that are either redundant or detrimental.

This fourfold schema does not of course represent an exhaustive typology of the forms of conflict dealt with by Nietzsche (e.g., we might also think of anarchic conflict as another significant subspecies). Indeed, as we

---

[65] Note that even if war falls under the general heading of "unmeasured conflict," this does not mean that Nietzsche considers all wars to be motivated by the goal of all-out extermination. On this point, see Chapter 1 (fn.1).

reconstruct his philosophy of conflict, we will be touching upon many subsidiary species of struggle that are absent from the above taxonomy. Nonetheless, over the forthcoming chapters we will see that through the prism of this schema we obtain a coherent and illuminating view of Nietzsche's mature philosophy of conflict.

Evaluative Ambiguity

In addition to the task of conceptually isolating these different (though often interrelated and overlapping) categories of conflict, we are faced with the further challenge of determining the normative stance that Nietzsche assumes toward each of these categories. Close inspection of the texts in which he is specific in his use of the concept of conflict reveals, somewhat confusingly, that he both valorizes *and* denigrates each of the four key species of conflict enumerated in our schema. In his notorious essay GSt, for example, which unambiguously focuses on *martial* conflict, Nietzsche confesses to singing a "paean to war [*Krieg*]" on account of its culturally beneficial effects (GSt, KSA 1.774). And yet, in HC he approves of the ancient Greeks' disdain for the evil Eris goddess (*die böse Eris*) – the deity symbolizing the impulse to engage in "hostile annihilatory struggle" (*feindseligen Vernichtungskampfe*) (HC, KSA 1.787). In the same essay, he then praises what he calls "contest" (*Wettkampf*) or, following the ancient Greeks, "agon" (*Agon*); but notwithstanding this approbation, elsewhere he warns *against* the competitive "agonal" spirit of the ancient Greeks, which he argues almost invariably led to destructive, socially injurious eruptions of civil war whenever it spilled over into the political sphere (WS 226).

We encounter a similar ambivalence in Nietzsche's views on exploitation. For instance, though he often affirms exploitation as a vital life-process (e.g., in BGE 259), he also speaks critically of the attempt made by the weak to parasitically attach themselves to the strong, exploiting them for purposes of shelter and protection (e.g., in KSA 11:36[21], 560). Finally, he equivocates regarding the normative status of the struggle to eliminate the recalcitrant or degenerate parts of one's society or self. On the one side, he censures Christians for trying to amputate their troublesome psychological impulses – a practice encapsulated in the Gospel maxim that "if thy right eye offend thee, pluck it out" (KJV Matthew 5:29) (TI Morality 1); likewise, he rebukes what he takes to be Christianity's quest to expunge its ideological enemies (TI Morality 3). On the other side, this disapproval notwithstanding, he implores us to "prune" (*beschneiden*) our intractable instincts (TI Skirmishes 41). Further, he infamously calls for "the merciless destruction [*Vernichtung*] of everything degenerate and parasitic" from society (EH BT 4), and other texts indicate that he envisions this as an act of eliminatory "excision" (*Ausschneidung*).[66]

This apparent vacillation presents a very real threat to the practical applicability of Nietzsche's thoughts on conflict. How can one coherently implement such apparently incompatible prescriptions? We might be tempted to account for this seeming inconsistency by ascribing it to Nietzsche's supposed disregard for the principle of noncontradiction, or to his philosophical method of seeking a richer view of phenomena by analyzing them from as many partial angles as possible – what is often referred to as his "perspectivism." Such a conclusion would be premature, however, and should only be conceded as a last resort, that is, after we have earnestly examined whether or not his myriad thoughts on conflict are in fact united by some underlying systematic principles.

In trying to present a coherent account of Nietzsche's normative stance toward conflict, we are not in virgin scholarly territory. On the contrary, the critical debate around this topic has a long and heated history. The problem is that instead of *reconciling* Nietzsche's apparently incompatible views on conflict, commentators tend to latch onto *either* his celebration of measured (i.e., restrained, moderate and nondestructive) forms of conflict *or* his praise of unmeasured conflict. Thus, there are those who brand Nietzsche as an advocate of belligerence, that is, as an author bent on inciting violently unmeasured struggle. These are the proponents of the so-called *hard* reading. Historically speaking, the foremost defender of this interpretation is his very own sister, Elisabeth Förster-Nietzsche, who conscripted his writings as intellectual support for German aggression in the Great War.[67] Subsequently, Alfred Bäumler, in his book *Nietzsche, der Philosoph und Politiker* (1931), portrayed Nietzsche as a fascistic thinker for whom the only alternative to European nihilism was a militaristic form of German imperialism. In many ways, Heidegger's Nietzsche of the 1930s and early 1940s likewise belongs in this same vein of interpretation.[68] In reaction to his appropriation by fascists, anti-fascist commentators then responded by denouncing Nietzsche as a diabolical warmonger.[69] Taken together, these bellicose interpretations form what I will be calling the *militaristic* reading.

---

[66] See e.g., KSA 13:23[1], 600.
[67] For an insightful overview of this influence, see Ascheim (1994, esp. 142) and Niemeyer (2009, 188–189).
[68] For more on this issue, see Young (1997, 140ff.).
[69] See e.g., Russell (2004, 693); Nolte (1963, esp. 533–534).

While there had often been voices calling for a softer reading of Nietzsche (particularly in francophone quarters), moderate interpretations were for a long time lacking in the anglophone world; that is, until the publication of Walter Kaufmann's seminal *Nietzsche: Philosopher, Psychologist and Antichrist* (1974). Kaufmann's book sanitized Nietzsche, rendering him admissible for those of liberal political persuasions. With respect to the subject of our inquiry, Kaufmann makes two significant interpretive moves. As previously mentioned, he proposes that Nietzsche's commendations of war ought to be read as metaphorically signifying the spiritual war that Nietzsche wanted us to wage against our passions. Continuing this line of interpretation, he then seeks to depoliticize Nietzsche altogether, arguing that Nietzsche is above all concerned with private *self*-cultivation, which is best achieved through the nondestructive sublimation of our impulses (418, 306). But despite this antipolitical reading, Kaufmann also brought Nietzsche's early unpublished essay HC, with its marked social concerns, to the attention of anglophone commentators. In HC, Nietzsche sanctions measured modes of social competition over and against murderous martial conflict. The rediscovery of this essay inaugurated a new wave of Nietzsche research, one that often construes HC as the hermeneutic master key to Nietzsche's wider philosophical project. However, against Kaufmann, these readers, who are generally of a liberal-democratic stripe, seek to *re*-politicize Nietzsche's thought; but in contrast to the earlier militaristic readings, they attempt to forge a more democratic image of Nietzsche. Thus, they contend that the notion of agon endorsed in HC is in fact exemplified in democratic contest. Indeed, they submit that Nietzsche prescribes the *transformation* of unmeasured, belligerent antagonism into measured, nonviolent contest, principally by means of democratic political institutions.[70] This is what I will be referring to as the *agonistic* reading of Nietzsche. Along with others who strive to read a more democratic impetus (though not necessarily an agonistic one) into Nietzsche's works (e.g., Cavell 1990; Conant 2001), these interpreters defend what is often called the *soft* reading.

In reaction to this wave of soft readings, an evolved version of the hard reading then came into being. Advocates of this revamped hard reading foreground the sheer weight of antidemocratic sentiment that permeates the corpus, and on this basis, argue that democratic readings are simply untenable. In addition to citing the wealth of texts in which Nietzsche

---

[70] See e.g., Acampora (2013); Connolly (1991); Hatab (1995); Owen (1995); Schrift (2000); Strong (1988).

extols the virtues of war, these readers further maintain that Nietzsche wishes to instigate an amoral, and often murderous, form of aristocratic struggle – one that demands the exploitation and exclusion of the weaker members of society.[71] Throughout the course of this book, I will be referring to this interpretation as the *radical aristocratic* reading.[72]

Though not all of the aforementioned commentators fit neatly into the camps to which I have assigned them, the above should suffice to illustrate that the anglophone critical literature tends to reinstate the discord that we originally discovered in Nietzsche's writings themselves. That is to say, they are at loggerheads insofar as they *either* characterize him as a hard thinker, who encourages unmeasured conflict, *or* as a soft thinker, who exclusively endorses some breed of measured contest. This is the hermeneutic aporia that this book will be concerned with addressing. Against these contradictory readings, my thesis is that *both the early and the later Nietzsche can be read as valorizing both measured and unmeasured social conflict.*

The keystone of my systematic reading is the fact that whenever Nietzsche endorses a particular type of conflict, he does so in a manner that is virtually always context dependent. Indeed, he assiduously refrains from positively valuing any mode of conflict in an unconditional fashion. Moreover, his prescriptions are *coherently* conditional, and hence their variegated nature will be seen to generate no serious contradiction.

Outline of This Book

In order to defend my thesis that Nietzsche should be read as promoting both measured *and* unmeasured conflict, I employ two argumentative strategies. In Part I, I focus on illuminating Nietzsche's persistent esteem for both annihilatory *and* agonal forms of struggle (i.e., *Vernichtungskampf* and *Wettkampf*), and I do so in the context of both his earlier and later writings. This demonstrates that neither the exclusively measured, agonistic reading, nor the exclusively unmeasured, militaristic reading constitute adequate interpretations of Nietzsche's philosophy. In Part II, I then contend that Nietzsche (both early and late) recommends a form of struggle that *combines* measured exploitative conflict (i.e., incorporation)

---

[71] See e.g., Appel (1999); Detwiler (1990); Dombowsky (2004); Warren (1991).

[72] I have taken the adjective "radical aristocratic" from George Brandes (1915), who designates Nietzsche's philosophy "aristocratic radicalism." In a letter to Brandes, Nietzsche himself affirms the epithet (i.e., of *aristokratischer Radikalismus*) as "very good." See letter to Georges Brandes, December 2, 1887 (KGB III/5, 206).

and unmeasured eliminatory conflict (i.e., exclusion). This dual struggle for exploitation and exclusion is what I will be referring to with the overarching term *organizational struggle*.

The first chapter examines Nietzsche's thoughts regarding physically destructive conflict (*Vernichtungskampf*; [1] in the above schema) and, more specifically, war. I debunk the exclusively agonistic reading by showing that throughout his writings Nietzsche gives a wide variety of reasons as to why we ought to value mortal forms of combat. I further contend that many of these arguments are underpinned by a quasi-Schopenhauerian ontology of physically destructive conflict. According to this ontology, the impetus to engage in violently destructive struggle is *untransformable*. Nietzsche conceives war as an ineluctable feature of life because he believes humans to be defined by an irresistible drive for physically annihilatory conflict. The periodic release of this ever-accumulating urge is, in Nietzsche's view, socially cathartic, and to this extent enables flourishing. This thesis is deeply problematic for his agonistic readers, however, all of whom take Nietzsche to be pursuing the *transformation* of destructive into constructive struggle. My solution to this apparent contradiction is to suggest that Nietzsche's problematic conception of destructive conflict is for the most part confined to his early writings. As he moves away from Schopenhauer, from whom he inherits this idea, he reconceives destructive conflict as the *contingent* expression of a general impulse to overpower others. Insofar as this impulse is not *necessarily* murderous, it can be granted an outlet in nonviolent modes of conflict.

In Chapter 2, we will then turn to the counter-concept of *Vernichtungskampf*, that is, agon, or *Wettkampf*. With an eye to deflating the exclusively militaristic reading, I defend the claim that in both his earlier and later writings, Nietzsche values a specifically agonal type of contest: a measured form of nonexploitative, nondestructive conflict that takes place between adversaries that are approximately equal in ability. In doing so, I also endeavor to address the striking lack of agreement between current interpretations of Nietzsche's agonism. In the first place, it is unclear what Nietzsche actually means by agon. While some claim the concept picks out a distinctly nonviolent form of conflict, others maintain that it can legitimately be used to refer to physically destructive conflict (and thus that we can talk about war as an instance of agon). Second, there is then disagreement regarding the social conditions under which Nietzsche believes that agonal relations can and should obtain. Some commentators submit that he at least implicitly defends the idea that such relations both can and should be democratically realized across the breadth of society; by contrast, others maintain that he only endorses agonal struggle, and indeed only holds it to be truly possible, among an elite minority of equals. Finally, interpreters are divided regarding the *means* by which Nietzsche thinks agonal conflict is most effectively realized. Some defend the idea that his agonism is secured by an internal, self-initiated shift of attitude on the part of each contestant vis-à-vis their adversaries; others, though, claim that agonal relations can only be imposed externally, by means of fashioning a balance of powers within which contending parties are unable to domineer over one another on account of their being too equally matched. The position that I develop over the course of this chapter is that for Nietzsche (a) agon is decidedly nonviolent; (b) all can participate in some form of agonal contest; and (c) the measure of the agon is founded upon a *combination* of endogenous and exogenous restraint.

In Part II (Chapters 3 and 4), I analyze a conceptually unique, third form of conflict that pervades Nietzsche's writings – what I call *organizational struggle*. We will see that this *sui generis* mode of opposition fails to fit the *Vernichtungskampf–Wettkampf* dichotomy analyzed in Part I. Moreover, we find that Nietzsche prescribes organizational struggle in a far more widespread manner than either *Vernichtungskampf* or *Wettkampf*. Indeed, he formulates and prescribes organizational struggle as a remedy to the pathology of disintegration that he sees plaguing modernity. In a manner analogous to the biological process of digestion, organizational conflict consists of both a measured struggle to incorporate that which is serviceable (*Einverleibung*), and an unmeasured struggle to exclude, excrete or eliminate that which is redundant or potentially harmful (*Ausscheidung*) ([3] and [4] in the above schema). Taken together, these two complementary processes comprise the struggle to order the discordant elements of any system into a functional hierarchy, and, further, the struggle to augment that hierarchy by incorporating new material. My chief objective in this part of the book will be to systematically explicate the dual logic (of incorporation and exclusion) that constitutes the unified dynamic of organizational struggle.

We begin in Chapter 3 by examining how the early Nietzsche conceptualizes this struggle for organization in his *Untimely Meditations*. I argue that during this phase of his philosophy he adheres to a quasi-Schopenhauerian account of how healthy organization arises. Crucially, we find that this theory presupposes the existence of metaphysical essences or Ideas that teleologically organize entities from within. Such essences establish holism by means of selectively overpowering and assimilating the opposed entities that they need in order to materially realize themselves. My claim is that this is a *measured* dynamic insofar as what is incorporated is preserved, albeit in a position of subservience to the superordinate Idea. In contrast to Schopenhauer, though, Nietzsche lays far greater emphasis on the way in which such assimilation is necessarily married to an *unmeasured* process of exclusion. I then unpack how Nietzsche applies this abstract model of organization to the concrete problems of individual and social disintegration. Chapter 3 concludes with an account of how Nietzsche's eventual rejection of metaphysics (in his middle and later writings) undermines the metaphysical presuppositions that condition the synthetic program that he constructs in UM.

In the final chapter of this book (Chapter 4), we then explore how the later Nietzsche reconceives the foundations of organizational struggle subsequent to his rejection of metaphysics. We reconstruct how he draws on the natural sciences – particularly the work of Darwinists such as Rolph and Roux – in order to formulate a novel model of healthy organization. This new model, which falls within his general theory of the will to power, is free of the metaphysical baggage that rendered his earlier account of organizational struggle inadmissible. But despite these foundational modifications, we nonetheless see that his later notion of organizational conflict still comprises a dual process of, on the one hand, a measured struggle to incorporate that which is serviceable into an existing hierarchy, and, on the other, an unmeasured struggle to eliminate that which cannot be usefully incorporated. Furthermore, we find that Nietzsche continues to view nature in terms of necessary, ubiquitous struggle. *Pace* his radical aristocratic readers, who construe Nietzschean exploitation as an unmeasured mode of activity, my contention is that he conceives healthy instrumental relations as inherently measured in kind. However, although incorporation should, on my interpretation, be conceived as measured, we nonetheless find it to be conditioned by the unmeasured struggle for elimination, which forms an integral part of organizational struggle. Thus, against Nietzsche's agonistic readers, who tend to interpret him as an opponent of exclusion, I underscore how this process is in fact essential to his notion of sociopolitical health. Finally, on the psychological plane, our analysis is found to contradict those who argue that for Nietzsche self-cultivation exclusively involves the measured sublimation of our troublesome impulses. Our study of Nietzsche's theory of organization reveals that far more radical, exclusionary spiritual exercises are in his view required to achieve psychological coordination.

The book concludes with a summary of how the greater part of
Nietzsche's mature thoughts on conflict form an internally consistent,
interlocking whole. In other words, we review how he can be said to
prescribe destructive, agonistic, exploitative and exclusionary forms of
conflict under distinct yet compatible sets of conditions. I then assay
some of the ethical implications of our inquiry, and gesture toward how,
in light of our findings, we might profitably reformulate our conception of
conflict. Though I advance a systematic reading of Nietzsche's writings,
I do not wish to give the impression that this reading is free of remainders;
I therefore close by trying to shine a light on some of the anomalies and
tensions that are generated by my exegesis.

PART I

Agon Versus War

Reasons for War

In today's predominantly liberal climate, it comes quite naturally to us to read Nietzsche as a thinker who was fundamentally opposed to murderous conflict; and certainly, throughout his *oeuvre*, he repeatedly articulates a preference for measured modes of struggle – such as *Wettkampf* or agon – over and against those of an unmeasured, destructive sort. The allure of reading Nietzsche in this way is then intensified by the prevalence of agonistic interpretations in the critical literature. These interpretations persistently foreground texts that appear to demonstrate his wholehearted opposition to destructive struggle. In this chapter I want to assess the extent to which Nietzsche's writings *resist* this interpretive approach. More specifically, I want to explore the affirmative stance that he adopts toward *physically* destructive, interpersonal conflict, or what he refers to as *Vernichtungskampf* (GSt, KSA 1.787; BT 15, KSA 1.100). This species of *Kampf* encompasses any struggle motivated by the belligerent desire to physically annihilate one's adversary – everything from individual acts of murder or attempted murder, up to and including large-scale military conflicts, or what we might term *war*.[1]

The tendency to read Nietzsche as an agonistic philosopher, hostile toward struggles of annihilation, can be traced back to Walter Kaufmann. According to Kaufmann (1974, 220), Nietzsche affirms the fact that "the barbarian's desire to torture his foe can be sublimated into the desire to defeat one's rival, say, in the Olympic contests [. . .] or into the efforts of a Plato to write more beautifully than the poets." And as we saw in our

---

[1] In war the aim of each of the opposed groups is seldom to destroy their adversaries *absolutely*. Rather, the goal is more often than not merely to force them into *submission*. Nonetheless, at the level of the individual combatants, war comprises a multitude of smaller-scale instances of mortal combat. Nietzsche himself repeatedly blurs the distinction between murder and war– for example, by placing them both under the heading of *Vernichtungskampf* (see e.g., HC, KSA 1.784–785; or KSA 10:1[34], 18: "War [*Der Krieg*] as the permitted form of neighbor-murder [*Nachbar-Mordes*]"). Hence, although wars invariably involve unmeasured conflict, they usually exhibit degrees of measure when viewed as wholes.

introduction, Kaufmann makes the further claim that Nietzsche only promotes martial conflict "metaphorical[ly]," that is, in order to foster *spiritual*
struggle (386). The key thesis running through Kaufmann's exegesis is that
Nietzsche seeks a *transfiguration* of destructive conflict into measured, intellectual opposition. This idea has been echoed by a number of other influential commentators. Christa Davis Acampora (2013, 4), for example,
comparably underscores the transformative impulse that informs
Nietzsche's attitude toward *Vernichtungskampf:* "From early in his career
Nietzsche was interested in how human capacities for and tendencies toward
aggression, struggle, and resistance could be channeled, sublimated, or
redirected." This transformative interpretation of Nietzsche's practical philosophy of conflict is, however, radically at odds with the ontology of
physically destructive struggle that he presents across a significant number of
texts. In short, in these texts we encounter an ontology of *Vernichtungskampf*
that, in certain cases, rules out the possibility of meaningful agonistic transformation. This is because he describes struggles of annihilation as a *necessary*
and therefore, to some extent at least, *immutable* feature of human existence.
But what further contradicts the agonistic reading is that far from ruing the
inevitability of violent strife, Nietzsche accents its potential value.

The *locus classicus* of agonistic interpretations of Nietzsche's thought is
without question HC; yet, in GSt – part of the very same collection of
unpublished essays as HC – he presents us with an apology for war that is
curiously incompatible with the tone of HC, and that would seem to lend
at least some credibility to the militaristic reading. With an eye to clarifying
this incompatibility, this chapter begins by reconstructing the peculiar
etiology of *Vernichtungskampf* that Nietzsche develops in GSt. We will
see how, and why, he figures struggles of annihilation as the cathartic
expression of an *essentially* destructive and unstoppably accreting drive. We
will further discover that he innovatively grounds this theory in a fusion of
Aristotle's philosophy of mind and Schopenhauer's metaphysics. But I also
want to draw attention to how, in HH, when he openly disavows
Schopenhauer's metaphysics, he continues to conceive war in terms of
cathartic release, and, moreover, to praise its socially beneficial effects. We
will then turn our critical gaze to Nietzsche's later period, focusing on his
notorious portrayal of the pillaging blond beasts in GM. Here, once again,
we will see that he appears to unscrupulously affirm violent conflict as an
act of healthy ventilation.

Although opponents of the agonistic reading cite these texts as
evidence of Nietzsche's esteem for war and violence, none track the
complex and protean theory of catharsis on which his acclamations are

grounded.[2] The agonistic readers, on the other hand, understandably overlook, if not consciously suppress, these problematic texts.[3] *A fortiori*, it remains to be seen whether Nietzsche develops a cathartic ontology of violence that coheres with the transformative dimension of his practical philosophy of conflict. In what follows, I will defend the claim that he does indeed achieve such coherence. Although we will find that his early, metaphysically grounded conception of violent struggle is incompatible with an exclusively agonistic reading, we will see that his later cathartic model of violence can, for the most part, be reconciled with his transformative project.

1.1 Murder and Metaphysics in the Early Nietzsche

1.1.1 *Catharsis*

Before we explore the way in which Nietzsche's treatment of *Vernichtungskampf* is informed by the notion of catharsis, we first need to pin down how he conceives this notion. The Greek noun *kátharsis*, from which the English "catharsis" derives, is standardly glossed as "purification" or "cleansing," or in German, as *Reinigung* (Liddell and Scott 1961, 851; Pape 1914, 1282). In addition to signifying the quotidian act of washing physical dirt off oneself, it can, by extension, be used metaphorically to refer to the process of religious purification, or *ablution* – that is to say, the spiritual act of cleansing oneself of sin. As Nietzsche points out in his early historical study of Greek religious ceremony, a murderer could be washed with holy water and thereby cleansed of contaminating miasma (RSG, KGW II/5, 504–511).

There is then the specifically medical definition of catharsis. According to Hippocratic medicine, the body is composed of four humors, or fluids, and the essence of health is said to lie in the harmonious balance of these fluids. Catharsis then refers to the act of purgation required to re-establish harmony should any one of these humors become excessive.[4] We might compare this usage to that of the English verb "to let" (in the sense of "bloodletting"). One could purge an excess of black bile, for example, either by ingesting a particular medicinal preparation or by performing certain religious rites (Abdulla 1985, 14).

Next, we have the aesthetic conception, which is most notably formulated by Aristotle in his *Poetics*. Aristotle (1991a, 49b27) theorizes that one

---

[2] See e.g., Appel (1999, 147); Dombowsky (2014, 75; 2004, 89–96).
[3] Acampora (2013), for example, does not once refer to GSt.   [4] See Liddell and Scott (1961, 851).

of the chief functions of tragedy is to bring about a catharsis of the fear and pity that has become pent up within members of the audience.[5] The vagueness of Aristotle's brief remarks, however, has fueled a lengthy and ongoing philological dispute. With respect to our current purposes, the most relevant fault line in this debate is that which runs between the contrary interpretations of Lessing and Bernays. The former, in his *Hamburger Dramaturgie*, argues that tragic catharsis is a process by which passions undergo moral "purification" (*Reinigung*) and are thereby transformed into practical virtues (Lessing 1890, 262).[6] He marshals André Dacier's hypothesis that going through the compassionate and fearful experience of beholding a tragic protagonist's downfall renders the possibility of *our* being struck by similar misfortunes less fearsome. In acquainting us with the possibility of such calamities, tragedies strip them of their terrifying element of surprise, giving us, in theory, the ability to face them with greater fortitude should they actually come to pass. In this way, the outburst of emotion evoked by tragic drama has the power to transfigure the paralyzing vice of fear into the virtue of courage (261).

Jacob Bernays, though, accuses Lessing of moving too far from the letter of Aristotle's text. Through a close and historically contextualized reading, Bernays argues that Aristotle's conception of "catharsis" can only be fully grasped in relation to the term's *medical* signification. Bernays maintains that, akin to the medical conception, Aristotle's psychological notion of catharsis implies the "discharge" (*Entladung*), but *not* "transformation" (*Verwandlung*) or further "suppression" (*Zurückdrängung*), of a pathological accretion; however, it is now accreted *affects*, as opposed to humors, that are being purged (Bernays 1857, 144). The defining features of Bernays's conception of catharsis, qua raw discharge, can be summarized as follows: first, we have a pathologically accreted affect; then, second, the further excitation of this affect (e.g., by spectating tragedy), which brings it to the point of rupture; subsequently, third, the unrefined, raw discharge of this affect; and finally, fourth, the restoration of healthy affective equilibrium. While Bernays's reading may not be entirely original, it has been unquestionably influential – indeed, it inaugurated the now commonplace translation of *kátharsis* as *Entladung* ("discharge") (Most 2009, 60).[7]

---

[5] See also Aristotle (1991b, 1341b20–1341b32).

[6] As Emden (2018, 6) remarks, the moral interpretation of catharsis was later reiterated by Leonhard Spengel.

[7] For more on the questionable originality of Bernays's exegesis, see Abdulla (1985, 17).

There is strong evidence that Nietzsche consciously adopted Bernays's conception of catharsis. We find this in HGL, where Nietzsche recounts how ancient Greek religious ceremonies could purge not just sin, but also overloaded affects. For example, through the performance of rhythmic music, the Greeks believed that they could placate their gods by inducing a release of divine ferocity (*ferocia*). Further, Nietzsche tells us, they were convinced that art could function as a means of cathartically regulating their own oversaturated affects. To this end, tragedies, symposia and orgiastic cults would employ combinations of dramatic action, rhythmic music and wine to induce a state of "frenzy" (*Taumel*) or "excess" (*Übermaaß*), which would trigger the "discharge" (*Entladung*) of any overloaded affects, thereby restoring inner harmony and "equilibrium" (*Gleichgewicht*) (HGL, KGW II/5, 285–286).[8] This discussion of catharsis in terms of raw or untransformed discharge (*Entladung*), without any mention of moral transformation, implies that even early on Nietzsche was operating with Bernays's conception of catharsis.

BT indicates that in addition to being sympathetic to Bernays's view, Nietzsche was well aware of his dispute with Lessing. For example, he directly refers to "[t]he pathological discharge [*Entladung*] which Aristotle calls catharsis, and which leaves the philologists uncertain whether to count it amongst the moral or medical phenomena" (BT 22, KSA 1.142). Yet, in contrast to his apparent agreement with Bernays in HGL, in BT Nietzsche rejects *both* theories as insufficient explanations of the effect of tragedy. His objection is that neither of these conflicting interpretations are aesthetically attuned. Looking back on BT in 1888, Nietzsche denies the idea that the true function of tragedy is to facilitate the "purification" of a "dangerous affect"; its final purpose is rather, he asserts, to grant audiences a pleasurable, Heraclitean insight into the joyfully destructive essence of reality – that is, reality understood as becoming (*Werden*) (EH BT 3; TI Ancients 5).

Notwithstanding these criticisms, the dynamic model of cathartic discharge (*Entladung*) recurs throughout BT (Most 2009, 60–62). Thus, Nietzsche claims that in spectating tragedy we can be said to satisfy our need to "discharge" (*entladen*) our "musical excitations" (BT 24, KSA 1.49–50). Moreover, the musical satyr chorus of early Greek tragedy – representative of the primordial oneness of reality (*das Ureine*) – is said to need to "discharge" (*entladen*) itself in Apollonian images; indeed, according to Nietzsche, it was this choral ventilation that gave rise to the dialogue and stage action of tragedy (BT 8, KSA 1.61–62).

---

[8] See also GS 84.

The concept of catharsis therefore plays a leading role in Nietzsche's early vision of ancient Greek tragedy and religious practice. What remains to be determined, though, is the way in which this model structures Nietzsche's early sociopolitical theory as much as it does his early reflections on aesthetics.

1.1.2 Violent Discharge in "The Greek State"

In seeking to establish the role of catharsis in Nietzsche's early political theory, our first port of call ought to be GSt, one of the most overtly political texts of his early period. The content of GSt was originally composed as part of an early draft of BT (KGW III/5, 142–155);[9] however, Nietzsche subsequently decided to cut this material and leave it unpublished.[10] And yet he later reworked the excised passages into a polished essay (i.e., GSt), which he gifted, along with HC and three further essays, to Cosima Wagner in the Christmas of 1872. On this account, it warrants far more attention than a mere discarded note.

The essay was an obviously backhanded gift since it contained a thinly veiled attack on Cosima's husband, Richard Wagner. While the latter was ostensibly Nietzsche's friend at the time, this was understandably not to be the case for much longer. GSt abjures Wagner's humanist conviction that higher culture demands the liberation of the ordinarily oppressed masses, which is in turn only secured through periodic social revolution (Wagner 1850b, 40–45). The essay also targets Wagner's later claim that patriotic militarism is socially destabilizing and therefore ought to be considered a blight on the polity (Wagner 1911, 12). Finally, GSt aggressively rejects the rosy Grecophilic picture of ancient Greece, a vision to which Wagner emphatically subscribed. Nietzsche thus takes up Burckhardt's realist project, dispassionately examining the extent to which violence, slavery and war might stand as conditions of higher culture.[11]

Throughout this period, Nietzsche persistently seeks to identify the bases of what he calls "true culture" (wahre Kultur), by which, broadly speaking, he means a noble, unified and artistically productive form of society. He takes ancient Greece to be prototypical in this respect; modern Germans, by contrast, embody the opposite of this ideal – that is,

[9] See also KSA 7:10[1], 333–349.
[10] Martin Ruehl (2004, 83) has speculated that the content of GSt was removed from the final draft of BT at the behest of Wagner.
[11] For an insightful account of how Nietzsche's defection from Wagner to Burckhardt informs the composition of GSt, see Ruehl (2004).

a decadent and disintegrated pseudo-culture (GSt, KSA 1.764). In his endeavor to unearth the roots of cultural health, Nietzsche rebels against the socialist and communist yearning for a society grounded in peaceful relations of substantive equality. For Nietzsche, such an end would entail forfeiting culture altogether. In his eyes, the state (*Staat*) is predicated on slavery. And since the edifice of higher culture is undergirded by the state, it too is conditioned by slave labor. Crucially, Nietzsche maintains that *war* is the principal means by which a state procures such slaves. Culture is in this way perpetually born of violence (GSt, KSA 1.767).[12] Indeed, Nietzsche rather gorily compares a "magnificent culture to a victor dripping with blood, who, in his triumphal procession, drags the vanquished along, chained to his carriage as slaves" (GSt, KSA 1.771).

But *how* does slavery enable higher culture for Nietzsche? Briefly put, the leisure time required by artistic geniuses to produce their *chefs-d'oeuvre* is a function of the surplus generated by an economic base of slave labor: "through [the slaves'] extra work, that privileged class is to be removed from the struggle for existence [*Existenzkampfe*], in order to produce and satisfy a new world of necessities" (GSt, KSA 1.767).[13] But this arrangement is not all bad for the toiling masses, Nietzsche reassures us. Now echoing Wagner, he maintains that the artist dignifies, and even endows with significance, the otherwise meaningless existence of the plebeian majority.[14] Once this pyramidal state, with its inegalitarian division of labor, has been forged by means of war, it serves to shield the genius from violent conflict for extended periods of time, thereby allowing his works to attain fruition – *constant* war would, by contrast, constitute an impediment to cultural success. So far, then, his apology for war is premised on the idea that it represents a necessary condition of cultural productivity, an objective that forms the normative ground of Nietzsche's broader ethical framework.

In probing the question as to how culture and violence might be complementary instead of antagonistic, Nietzsche continues the realist legacy of Jakob Burckhardt, and before him, Machiavelli.[15] In the first part of *The Culture of the Renaissance in Italy* (entitled "The State as Artwork"), Burckhardt traces the way in which Renaissance states were

---

[12] See also GM II 17, KSA 5.324.
[13] This idea is conspicuously Aristotelian. See Irwin (1988, 411ff.) on the relation of slavery and cultural praxis in Aristotle.
[14] GSt, KSA 1.776; compare Wagner 2011, 27–29.
[15] Machiavelli (1998, 59), for example, counsels his prince that he "should never lift his thoughts from the exercise of war, and in peace he should exercise it more than in war."

born out of an unpalatable admixture of violence and despotism. He draws, for example, a causal relation between struggles of annihilation and artistic excellence, and hypothesizes that the violence committed by the Baglione family in fifteenth-century Perugia, where the twelve-year-old Raphael was growing up, likely inspired the painter's masterful depictions of St. George and St. Michael (KRI, 3.20).[16] And in GK, he calls attention to just how integral both slavery and war were to the fabric of ancient Greek life. As he matter-of-factly puts it: "genocide [*Ausmorden*], sale into slavery [...], wastage [*Ödelegen*] and destruction [were] the order of the day" (GK, 8.259).

But as GSt continues, Nietzsche's defense of war begins to evince distinct parallels with Bernays's account of catharsis. Indeed, we see him graft the cathartic dynamic described by Bernays onto a Schopenhauerian metaphysical framework – invoking a combination of the two theories in order to substantiate his belief in the inevitability of war. To fully appreciate the role played by catharsis in GSt, we therefore first need to make an excursus into Schopenhauer's covert presence in the text. Crucially, as we already noted in our introduction, in GSt Nietzsche follows Schopenhauer in assuming the natural state of humans to be one of *bellum omnium contra omnes* (war of all against all). What we now need to establish, then, is precisely why Schopenhauer takes this to be the case.

In *The World as Will and Representation*, Schopenhauer conceives the world as having two aspects: that of "will" – the Kantian noumenal realm, or world in itself, as it exists independent of human perception; and that of "representation" (*Vorstellung*) – the phenomenal world of objects and appearance. Schopenhauer rejects Kant's claim that because the noumenon lies beyond the reach of sensible intuition, it can only be legitimately conceived in negative terms, that is, as "something in general outside our sensibility" (CPR, 3.209). He looks within himself and claims that he has nonintellectual intuition of one particular object: his own body. And what does he find? Namely, that it's characterized by a unitary *striving*, or "*will*" (WWR 1, 2.123). He then makes the abductive, analogical argument that the noumenal aspect of every other object is in all likelihood characterized by the same kind of abstract striving (WWR 1, 2.123–126). And we should recall that for Schopenhauer, willing is marked by lack and pain.[17] Moreover, the world as will subsists as an atemporal unity, being ontologically prior to the

---

[16] See also the section of KRI entitled "War as Artwork" (3.67–68). On a similar note, Burckhardt describes Delphi as "above all the great monumental museum of the hatred of Greek against Greek, of mutually inflicted suffering immortalized in the loftiest works of art" (GK, 5.285).

[17] See Introduction, above.

plurality constructed by the intellect. At the most abstract level of the world as representation, there exists an atemporal multiplicity of Platonic Ideas. These constitute the ideal form of every possible species of representable phenomenon (WWR 1, 2.154). But diverging from Plato, Schopenhauer speculates that these Ideas are caught in a bitter struggle for matter, which they need in order to make themselves manifest at the concrete, temporal level of representation. This contentious state of affairs is captured in the following passage, which Nietzsche directly quotes in PTAG:

> The underlying, persisting matter must constantly change form as mechanical, physical, chemical and organic appearances, following the guiding thread of causality, all crowd around, greedy to emerge and tear the matter away from the others so they can each reveal their own Idea. This conflict [*Streit*] can be traced through the whole of nature, indeed nature exists only through this [...]. (WWR 1, 2.175; PTAG 5, KSA 1.826)

In the case of living organisms, this antagonism is most salient in their struggle for resources, which are requisite for individual survival, maturation and reproduction. On this view, destructive conflict is a metaphysical necessity for a number of different reasons. First, the situation is one analogous to that described by Malthus and Darwin, though their naturalistic observations are now given a speculative *metaphysical* foundation: there is a superabundance of competitors in a zero-sum struggle over limited resources, which renders destructive conflict an ineluctable fact of existence; in Schopenhauer's own words: "each only has what it has torn away from another; thus, there is a constant mortal struggle [*Kampf um Leben und Tod*]" (WWR 1, 2.364). The second reason adduced by Schopenhauer is that members of the animal kingdom are forced to consume either one another, or members of the plant kingdom (a fact to which any food chain readily testifies) (WWR 1, 2.175).

There is then a third, more fundamental reason. Schopenhauer maintains that the conflict that we find at the level of representation "basically stems from the fact that the will needs to live off itself because there is nothing outside of it and it is a hungry will" (WWR 1, 2.183). In his view, the noumenal will is *unitary* (since plurality is a product of the human mind); but since the will must will *for* and *against* something, it must therefore be divided against itself, it must be "self-ruptured" (*selbstentzweit*) (WWR 1, 2.175), and condemned to "maul itself" (*sich selbst zerfleischen*) (WWR 1, 2.364). In this regard, the symbol of the ouroboros aptly captures the essence of Schopenhauer's self-consuming will. But what is of singular importance for our line of inquiry is that since every appearing phenomenon is an embodiment of this will, they are, according to Schopenhauer, each metaphysically bound to replicate its inner nature: "That is why everyone wants everything for themselves, wants to possess or at least control everything, and wants to destroy [*vernichten*] anything that opposes them" (WWR I, 2.391). We can syllogistically formulate this argument as follows:

The Metaphysical Instantiation Argument

1. The will is characterized by destructively conflictual activity;
2. Every extant individual is an instantiation of the will;
3. Therefore, every extant individual is necessarily characterized by destructively conflictual activity (behavior).

Despite the metaphysical necessity with which individuals express the characteristics of the will, Schopenhauer nonetheless claims that rule of law and state institutions can suppress such strife within the social sphere. This is achieved by threatening citizens with punishment, which deters them from engaging in violently destructive struggle with one another; however, says Schopenhauer,

> [. . .] if Eris [the ancient Greek goddess of strife and discord] has been driven happily from within, she will appear from without: when she has been banished in the form of a conflict [*Streit*] between individuals through the institution of the state, she will return externally as war [*Krieg*] between nations and demand on a large scale and in a single blow, as an accumulated debt, the bloody sacrifices that prudent measures had withheld from her on a smaller scale. (WWR I, 2:413–414)[18]

   In this depiction of the collectively swelling urge for conflict, we can readily discern the affinity between the dynamic described by Schopenhauer at a metaphysical-social level and that described by Bernays's Aristotle at the aesthetic-psychological level. Let us now return to GSt in order to analyze how Nietzsche brings about a more complete rapprochement of these two dynamic models of accumulation and discharge. One of the notable differences between (the early) Nietzsche's and Schopenhauer's will-based metaphysics is the recurrent reference to *discharge* (*Entladung*) that is so striking in the former, though largely absent from latter. This is particularly salient in GSt. For Nietzsche, as for Schopenhauer, the level of appearance is necessarily a "reflection" (*Spiegelung*) of the "contradiction [that is] the essence of the

---

[18] Compare Burckhardt's argument that war is practically "unavoidable" in WBe (4.118). For Burckhardt, the necessity of war is premised on empirical-psychological, rather than metaphysical, grounds: it is the drive to test one's strength against another that leads so ineluctably to war, which he thus conceives as a kind of gauge (*Maßstab*). This compulsion for comparison is posited by Burckhardt as an essential quality of man, and since the only way in which it is fully satisfied at an international scale is through war, he avers that large-scale military conflict is for all intents and purposes inevitable (even if it can be compressed into periodic outbursts).

primal one [*Ureine*]" – the "primal one" being Nietzsche's way of referring to
the Schopenhauerian world-will (KSA 7:7[157], 199–200); however, in GSt,
what the will ultimately strives to realize in appearance is genius, beauty, and
redemptive works of art. It is only by means of these that Nietzsche thinks that
the will is able to marvel at itself and attain temporary solace and redemption
from its otherwise unending torment (GSt, KSA 1.770–771). Yet Nietzsche,
reprising an argument that derives from Hartmann, holds that beauty and
cultural development are foreclosed by the natural struggle for existence (the
Kampf ums Dasein).[19] These two originary tendencies of the primordial will
are, in the state of nature, incompatible, and hence the drive for art ends up
being suppressed by its antagonist. In order to allow the will to express its
artistic impulse, which is the mainspring of cultural flourishing, the state
(*Staat*) must impede the struggle for existence. Recalling Schopenhauer,
though now invoking the Aristotelian vocabulary of "discharge," Nietzsche
further argues that the state is incapable of altogether inhibiting the destructive
dynamic that structures existence; rather,

> after states have been founded everywhere, that drive [*Trieb*] of *bellum omnium
> contra omnes* is concentrated, from time to time, into dreadful clouds of war
> between nations and, as it were, discharges itself [*entladet sich*] in less frequent
> but all the stronger bolts of thunder and flashes of lightning. But in the intervals,
> the concentrated effect of that *bellum*, turned inwards, gives society time to
> germinate and turn green everywhere, so that it can let the radiant blossoms of
> genius sprout forth as soon as warmer days come. (GSt, KSA 1.772)[20]

From this it is evident that, although the destructive drive for all-out war is
depicted as irreducible, the political apparatus of the state *is* able to
temporarily inhibit this proclivity, constraining it to short though severe
outbursts. This ensures periods of peace and stability, during which the
genius can work unhampered by the tumult of war. This cathartic dynamic
thereby enables the flourishing of culture.[21] So, while Nietzsche denigrates
generalized struggle for existence insofar as it frustrates genius and culture,
he endorses belligerent explosions of violently destructive conflict on
account of their beneficial effect on culture.[22]

[19] On the Hartmann connection, see Gerratana (1988, esp. 418–421). See also KSA 7:7[24], 143–144. On
the notion of the *Kunsttrieb* and its roots in Häckel and Schiller, see Moore (2002, 89–96). See also
WWR 2, 3.390ff.
[20] See also KSA 7:10[1], 344.
[21] See also KSA 7:7[121], 169–170; GSt, KSA 1.772–777. Compare Hobbes's (1996, 89) criticism that in
times of war there are "no Arts; no Letters; no Society."
[22] GSt, KSA 1.772: "For this Helen [i.e., Greek culture], [the state] waged those wars – what grey-
bearded judge would condemn this?"

In this depiction of energetic build-up followed by qualitatively untransformed discharge, we bear witness to Nietzsche invoking the Bernaysian
model of catharsis in order to explain sociological phenomena.[23] What is
more, elsewhere in GSt, Nietzsche expands upon his apology for war in
a way that brings the influence of Bernays into clear relief. He conjectures
that it was by means of their political drives (*Triebe*) that the ancient Greeks
managed to suppress the impulse for all-out war, but these drives eventually
became overdeveloped and "overloaded" (*überladen*). The consequent excess
of political activity had the adverse effect of hindering cultural development
and fomenting violent political rivalries, eventually culminating in revolution and war (GSt, KSA 1.771). Nietzsche therefore suggests that pathological
accretion occurs in the very drives contrived to *inhibit* the struggle for
annihilation. As a result, war ensues, and the destructive energies accreted
in the collective will are vented in a quantitatively more condensed, but
qualitatively *untransformed*, manner (in accordance with Bernays's, rather
than Lessing's, theory of catharsis). Nietzsche asserts that these violent
outbursts show that "from time to time the will needed [*gebraucht*] such
self-lacerations [*Selbstzerfleischungen*] as a valve, in accordance with its terrible nature" (KSA 7:7[121], 170).[24] He thereby grounds the necessity of
violent catharsis in the "metaphysical instantiation" argument.

According to this ontology, episodic struggles for annihilation are postulated as an obligatory lesser evil (the greater being a perpetual condition of
war resembling the Hobbesian state of nature). The newly regulated (*reg-
uliert*) – that is, moderated and rehabilitated – political drives can be directed
toward the generation of genius "with new and surprising force." Nietzsche
therefore concludes that "in this sense the dreadful spectacle of these self-
rending [*sich zerreißenden*] parties is something venerable" (KSA 7:7[121],
169–170). Note that while this compression of violent conflict may seem to
suggest that we ought to classify such wars as "measured" (in contrast to the
entirely unmeasured *bellum omnium contra omnes*), this measure takes the
form of mere temporal constraint, and the concrete mode of behavior in
question remains essentially murderous and hence *unmeasured*.[25]

In figuring this dynamic as one that generates an end-state of healthy
equilibrium (i.e., between the political, destructive and artistic drives) all
four of the aforementioned criteria required to label a given energetic
economy "cathartic" in Bernays's sense of the term have been fulfilled: (1)

---

[23] For more on the influence of Bernays on Nietzsche's conception of catharsis, see Emden (2018).
[24] See also KSA 7:7[169], 205; KSA 7:7[122],175; KSA 7:7[64], 153; BT 22, KSA 1.141; BT 4, KSA 1.39.
[25] On the possibility of measure in war, see fn.1.

there is an initial condition of pathological accretion, followed by (2) a process of active stimulation and (3) raw, untransformed discharge, which culminates in (4) the restoration of a healthy state of equilibrium. Yet two questions now present themselves: what happens to Nietzsche's position regarding *Vernichtungskampf* when he (a) definitively repudiates the quasi-Schopenhauerian metaphysical foundations upon which he constructs his earlier cathartic model of violence, and (b) embarks on a project calling for the ostensibly total transformation of destructive into productive conflict?

1.2 War in the Wake of Metaphysics

Six years after writing GSt, in HH (1878) Nietzsche comes to openly disavow his Schopenhauerian roots. Yet his notebooks reveal that he had been gestating this damning critique for at least ten years. The key fragment in this respect, entitled "On Schopenhauer" (1868) (KGW I/4, 417–426), rejects the notion of "will" as a "clumsily coined, and very encompassing word" (419). Schopenhauer's world-will supposedly subsists in total independence of the realm of objectivity, and so cannot, *ex hypothesi*, be conceived as an *object* of knowledge; but in Nietzsche's view, Schopenhauer disregards this constraint and consequently falls into incoherence. Otherwise put, in trying to describe the characteristics of the world as will, Schopenhauer inadvertently construes it as an object of knowledge. As Nietzsche sees it, "all the predicates of the [Schopenhauerian] will are borrowed from the world of appearance" (424). In the first part of HH, Nietzsche then deepens this line of criticism, commending the "more rigorous logicians, [who] having clearly identified the concept of the metaphysical as that of the unconditioned, consequently also unconditioning, have disputed any connection between the unconditioned (the metaphysical world) and the world we know" (HH 16).[26] Nietzsche therefore favors a return to the negative conception of the thing in itself as an "ungraspable X," à la Kant, if not the complete abandonment of philosophical inquiry into the existence of things in themselves (a position to which he would later commit with resolution [e.g., in TI Fiction]).

This argument rules out the possibility that properties such as "self-consuming" or "self-lacerating" could be predicated to the world in itself (i.e., to the will); further, it deflates the idea that *any* features of the world in itself could be expressed at the level of objectivity. With this, Nietzsche debunks the metaphysical instantiation argument; but this then leads to

---

[26] See also HH 9, 13, 15, 17, 21.

the collapse of the cathartic model invoked in GSt, which we found to be grounded in this argument. An unstoppably accumulating drive for *Vernichtungskampf* can no longer be posited as a metaphysical necessity. It is perhaps unsurprising, then, that alongside his renunciation of Schopenhauerian metaphysics we bear witness to Nietzsche canvassing alternative theories of belligerent struggle – theories to which we should now turn in our inquiry.

1.2.1   The Ontology of Agonal Transformation

One of the most notable ways in which Nietzsche departs from the ideas that he espouses in GSt is in his formulation of an *agonal* conception of *Vernichtungskampf*. Although we will be making a comprehensive analysis of Nietzsche's conception of the agon in Chapter 2, it would serve us well to foreground the principal ways in which his agonism is at odds with the cathartic model of GSt. It is intriguingly in HC that we find the clearest articulation of this novel conception of violently destructive struggle. This fact is arresting because, as mentioned above, HC was written in the same year (1872), and belongs to the same collection of essays, as GSt; hence, we might reasonably expect the two essays to be ontologically congruent with one another. But in HC, Nietzsche is pointedly critical of even short outbursts of belligerent conflict, appearing to concur with Hesiod's indictment of the "evil Eris" goddess, the deity responsible for *Vernichtungskampf* (HC, KSA 1.785). Nietzsche disparages struggles of annihilation on account of their being antithetical to the categorically *non*-murderous, culturally productive species of conflict personified by the "good Eris" goddess. This beneficent form of struggle is what Nietzsche refers to as agon (*Agon*) or contest (*Wettkampf*), and was exemplified in the contests fought between ancient Greek poets, politicians, musicians, athletes and dramatists. Indeed, Nietzsche tacitly calls for the *complete* transformation of struggles of annihilation into such measured modes of contention; this prescription is implied in HC by his unqualified affirmation of the way in which ancient Greek culture grew out of the condition of *Vernichtungskampf*, by which it was plagued prior to the arrival of Homer.[27]

---

[27] Note that in KSA 7:16[26] we discover a rare instance of Nietzsche trying to conceptualize agonal transformation within a Schopenhauerian metaphysical framework: "1. Problem: how does the will, that fearsome thing, become purified and refined [*geläutert*], i.e., converted and transformed into nobler drives? [. . .] Influence of art on the purification of the will. The contest [*Wettkampf*] emerges from war? As an artistic game and imitation?" (403).

HC characterizes the figure of the genius (*Genius*) as the key trigger of this historical shift. The decisive move made by this exalted figure, Nietzsche explains, is that he *acknowledges* the terrible impulse for war. Instead of falling into a state of pessimistic resignation when faced with the *bellum omnium contra omnes*, the genius asks: "what does a life of struggle [*Kampf*] and victory want?" (HC, KSA 1.785). The response given to this question, in HC and HH at any rate, is that the psychological drive (*Trieb*) that motivates *Vernichtungskampf* is directed toward the general goal of engaging in contest and achieving victory. Nietzsche no longer postulates an essentially destructive "drive of *bellum omnium contra omnes*." Within this alternative dynamic, the impulse that drives people into struggles for annihilation is of a markedly more *plastic* sort. In virtue of this plasticity, it can obtain release in *agonal* competition, which grants people an opportunity for contest and victory, though now through measured, non-murderous species of conflict. In spotlighting the possibility of such transformation, the (poetic) genius enables, and initiates, a move away from all-out *Vernichtungskampf* and toward agonal community: "The poet educates: he knows how to transfer [*übertragen*] the tiger-like mutilating drives [*Zerfleischungstriebe*] of the Greeks into the good Eris. Gymnastics [is] the idealized war [*Krieg*]" (KSA 7:16[15], 398). In WS 226, this transformative process is brought into even sharper relief:

> *Greek prudence.* – Since the desire for victory and pre-eminence [*das Siegen- und Hervorragenwollen*] is an inextinguishable trait of nature, older and more primitive than any respect for and joy in equality, the Greek state sanctioned gymnastic and artistic contest [*Wettkampf*] between equals, that is to say, marked off an arena where that drive [*Trieb*] could be discharged [*sich entladen*] without imperiling the political order. With the eventual decline of the gymnastic and artistic contest the Greek state disintegrated into inner turmoil. [...]

It is now the drive for "victory" (*Siegen*) and "pre-eminence" (*Hervorragen*), as opposed to murderous *bellum*, that Nietzsche posits as the operative immutable impetus, or "inextinguishable trait of nature." What remains unchanged from GSt, though, is his conception of conflictual activity in terms of cathartic *discharge*. To be sure, during this period, he still considers the cathartic dynamic of "[a]ccumulation and discharge [*Entladung*] in forceful, temporally discrete bursts" to be a "fundamental principle of the Greek character [*Wesens*]"; indeed, he explicitly describes such discharge as a "necessity" (KSA 8:5[147], 79). Given what Nietzsche writes in WS 226, however, we can surmise that in this note he is not referring to the discharge of a drive for specifically destructive struggle. The kind of drive that he more likely has in mind is one pressing for *ascendancy*, conceived in general terms. This said, it is crucial to bear in mind that this drive *can* still express itself destructively if it is not carefully channeled into suitable social practices, such as the agon for example. My interpretation of these texts is further confirmed by what Nietzsche writes in AOM 220. In this aphorism, he attributes the cultural success of the ancient Greeks to the fact that

> They do not repudiate the natural drive [*Naturtrieb*] that finds expression in the evil qualities but regulate it, and, as soon as they have discovered sufficient prescriptive measures to provide these wild waters with the least harmful means of channeling and outflow, confine them to definite cults and days. [...] One granted to the evil and suspicious, to the animal and backward, likewise to the barbarian, the pre-Greek and Asiatic, that still lived on in the foundations of the Hellenic nature, a measured discharge [*eine mässige Entladung*], and did not strive after their total annihilation [*Vernichtung*].[28]

In light of the picture that Nietzsche paints in WS 226, we can interpret the fundamental "natural drive" to which he refers here in AOM 220 as a malleable drive for struggle and ascendancy. What is more, the hydraulic metaphors that he deploys in this passage strongly imply that this drive *demands* expression, and thus that some form of cathartic model is still very much at play. But once again, this drive is no longer conceived as being *intrinsically* destructive, or even harmful ("evil"), in nature. With the aid of the state, the energy bound up with this plastic drive can be safely bent away from the kinds of lethal behavior through which it is otherwise prone to seek expression.

HC and the above-cited texts from the late 1870s imply that violently destructive struggle is, contra Schopenhauer and GSt, neither metaphysically nor psychologically necessitated; it is rather the expression of a polymorphous impetus for combat, victory and overcoming (in many ways prefiguring his mature theory of the will to power).[29] From the perspective of HC and HH, then, the dilemma posed by GSt between perpetual or episodic war appears to be false. As such, the Bernays-inspired model of social catharsis that Nietzsche constructs in GSt is incompatible with his *transformative* cathartic theory.

---

[28] See also KSA 8:5[146], 78–79.

[29] See also D 189, where he describes this drive as the "most violent water," which drives "individuals and peoples" forward, and often into wars (*Kriege*), and he locates its source in the human "need for the *feeling of power* [*Machtgefühls*]," a conceptual precursor of his later theory of the will to power.

Before moving on, we should consider a potential objection to my claim that these two ontologies of destructive struggle are mutually exclusive. Maybe, so the objection goes, instead of being immutable, our predilection for mortal combat can only be transformed *up to a point*, beyond which individuals are compelled to engage in war; perhaps Nietzsche thinks that we can modulate a *portion* of our belligerent energies, but are always left with an accumulating remainder that demands periodic release in mortal strife?[30]

The chief problem with this attempt to reconcile the two cathartic theories outlined above lies in its patent lack of textual basis.[31] The only support for such an interpretation of GSt is where Nietzsche states that "the concentrated effect of that *bellum*, turned inwards, gives society time to germinate and turn green everywhere" (GSt, KSA 1. 772). Creatively read, this might imply that although destructive energies can be channeled into agonal practices and thereby temporarily rendered productive, the force of this energetic inflow inevitably exceeds our best efforts to manage it. The result is a burst dam, and a torrent of violently uncontrolled behavior. However, carefully considered, this fairly abstruse statement does not posit the substantive transformation of accumulating destructive energies, and further, we should not overlook that Nietzsche makes no mention of agon in GSt. Indeed, the passage at hand is certainly not describing a process by which destructive energies are being canalized into an *outlet* – they are at best simply "turned inwards" and "concentrated." Hence, GSt still seems to suggest that *every* drop of violent energy must ultimately be granted ventilation in savage violence.

But even if we assent to this charitable interpretive strategy, this still does not do enough to salvage the agonistic reading. Nietzsche would still be positing an ever-mounting debt of violently destructive energy, one resilient to our best efforts at transformation; and he would still be sanctioning the raw discharge of this energy as a precondition of sociocultural health. The reading of Nietzsche as a general advocate of agonism would therefore nonetheless be vitiated.

1.2.2 *Nietzsche's Realism: War as a Cultural Stimulant*

We might easily come away from the above with the impression that in HH Nietzsche exclusively encourages the agonal transformation of our

---

[30] We might compare this idea to Freud's (1966, 150–151) account of the limits of sexual sublimation.
[31] That is, in his early- and middle-period writings. We do find some cursory support for such an idea in the later text TI Ancients 3.

murderous impulses. Such a view, however, is contradicted by the host of unequivocally pro-war aphorisms that we find throughout the very same book. From this alternative hermeneutic angle, HH might strike us as having less in common with HC, and far more with GSt. To the extent that these aphorisms cast further doubt on the agonistic reading, they merit our critical attention.

What is of particular interest about these texts is their *realist* bearing, and, following on from this, the fact that they make no recourse to the shaky metaphysical speculation that underpins GSt. Nietzsche's realist consider- ations further diverge from GSt on another significant point. Violently destructive struggle is no longer praised as an *outlet* enabling the *discharge* of energy (as in GSt); rather, in HH, war is affirmed as a *source* of sociocul- tural energy, an idea that is unmistakably indebted to Burckhardt. We should briefly sketch Burckhardt's position since this will grant us a richer insight into the substance of Nietzsche's own unique claims.

Quoting Peter Lasaulx, Burckhardt defines an aging culture as one that "no longer carries a certain mass of unused energy from which it can refresh and rejuvenate itself." In such cases, Burckhardt agrees with Lasaulx that regeneration is possible if the exhausted society is invaded by a younger, culturally flourishing people. By way of illustration, he points to the Teutonic invasions of the late Roman Empire. He submits that for any culture, suffering defeat in a war of colonization represents a "necessary moment of higher development" (WBe, 4.117, 4.161).[32] Against Lasaulx, however, Burckhardt stipulates that suffering colonization is by no means a *guarantee* of cultural rejuvenation; he contends, for example, that the Mongols tended to have a culturally devastating effect whenever they invaded a given civilization. Regeneration therefore depends on being annexed by the right *kind* of culture.

But Burckhardt reserves his most laudatory remarks for the *active* pursuit of warfare. In his view, a "genuine war, with existence at stake," constitutes a healthy crisis. It can have an enlivening, ordering and discip- lining effect, and can stamp out the cowardly foibles that individuals have the luxury of nurturing in times of peace: "Wars purified the atmosphere like thunderstorms, steeled the nerves, shook the passions [*Gemüter*], and generated the heroic virtues on which states were originally founded, in place of enervation, mendacity and cowardice" (WBe, 4.118). War has the further benefit of motivating societies to organize themselves in what Burckhardt considers to be a vastly more efficient manner. Given that

---

[32] See also Flaig (2003, 145–147).

a community can usually only overcome an existential military threat by fighting as a functionally organized whole, effective preparation for war requires unifying the body politic. In times of peace, Burckhardt claims, people grow dissatisfied with social inequalities. The consequent demand for egalitarian rights then drives social disorder, which in turn effects a general weakening of the social whole. By contrast, in times of war, all willingly submit to hierarchical organization because all know this to be the most effective strategy for success – it is in this way that Burckhardt thinks egoism is overcome by the brute desire to prevail in the face of possible extermination (ibid.).[33] Military conflict structures and mobilizes the political body, transforming it into a potent, well-oiled war-machine.

Yet for Burckhardt it is only *large-scale* struggles of annihilation that qualify as genuine instances of cultural crisis. And he does not think that modern wars deserve this appellation. They are, he argues, too small and temporary to touch upon the quotidian existence of European citizens. He thus presciently warns that modern wars merely postpone an inevitably approaching "major crisis" (*Hauptkrisis*). But this is not necessarily a welcome prospect, since for Burckhardt it is perfectly possible for cultures to be eradicated by such crises (WBe, 4.119–120). Once again, then, meaningful regeneration is in no measure guaranteed by military conflict.

In HH, Nietzsche concurs with Burckhardt's position in almost all of its essentials. In HH 444, for example, he writes that war "barbarizes and thereby makes more natural; it is the winter or hibernation time of culture, mankind emerges from it stronger for good and evil." Like Burckhardt then, Nietzsche believes that exhausted cultures even stand to gain from suffering defeat, namely, insofar as this frequently initiates a regenerative period of cultural hibernation. Taken on its own, this terse affirmation of war is not particularly cogent. But in light of our analysis of Burckhardt, we can infer some of the empirical–historical grounds that likely inform Nietzsche's provocative assertions.

In HH 477 (entitled "*War* [*Der Krieg*] *indispensable*"), Nietzsche expounds his own position with somewhat greater depth. In this aphorism, he also makes a dramatic shift vis-à-vis the necessity of struggles of annihilation. He no longer conceives such conflict as a metaphysically necessary *release* of accrued energy, but rather as a prudential necessity, since it *generates* and *augments* the energy that cultures require to thrive. We know of no other means, he asserts,

---

[33] Note that in GK Burckhardt is far more skeptical regarding the cultural benefits of war (see Chapter 2 of this book).

by which that rude energy that characterizes the camp, that profound impersonal hatred, that murderous cold-bloodedness with a good conscience, that common fire in the destruction of the enemy, that proud indifference to great losses, to one's own existence and that of one's friends, that inarticulate, earthquake-like shuddering of the soul, could be communicated more surely or strongly to exhausted peoples than every great war communicates them: the streams and currents that here break forth, though they carry with them rocks and rubbish of every kind and ruin the pastures of tenderer cultures, will later under favorable circumstances turn the wheels in the workshops of the spirit with newfound energy.

War goads individual self-cultivation – it steels us – and on this account Nietzsche esteems it as a wellspring of socially beneficial energy. Echoing Burckhardt, he claims that by actively participating in war, a people can foster the virile warrior virtues and brave sangfroid that foster cultural flourishing.[34] Similarly, in HH 235, he posits social violence as a prerequisite of genius. Violence is, he submits, the source of a genius's burning *passion* (*Leidenschaft*). Peace, by contrast, represents an agent of cultural decay and mediocrity. Hence, Nietzsche poses the following rhetorical question: "Ought one therefore not to desire that life should retain its violent character, and that savage forces and energies continue to be called up again and again?" Notice that the fundamental normative criterion in these aphorisms is that of cultural flourishing. Without war, cultures grow weary (*matt*), as in the case of modern Europe. Consequently, Nietzsche seconds Burckhardt's verdict, ominously prescribing Europe "the greatest and most fearful wars" (HH 477).[35]

Before moving on to Nietzsche's later writings, we ought to remark how these ideas align with current empirical research, which refutes hydraulic-drive theories of aggression. Hydraulic-drive theories – exemplified by the work of Freud (1955) and Lorenz (1998) – depict inherently violent, destructive energies not just as an intrinsic feature of human nature, but as psychologically accruing in the manner of steam pressure mounting in a sealed vessel. Actively engaging in or watching violent activity is then said to ventilate such pressure and return the individual to a healthy mean. Recent empirical studies, however, have demonstrated that such hydraulic theories of aggression do not, in point of fact, hold water. Neither spectating nor participating in violence has an observable cathartic effect. On the

---

[34] On this point, see also GS 283. The idea also resurfaces later, in 1887, in GS 362.

[35] Bataille (2015, 165) comments that for Nietzsche war energizes a culture by exploding suffocating social and moral orders: "Even these catastrophes seemed preferable to him [Nietzsche] to stagnation, to the lie of bourgeois life, to the vulgar happiness preached by moralists."

contrary, to borrow Plato's turn of phrase, there is ample evidence to suggest that such activity "feeds and waters the passions" (Plato 2005, 606 c–e). Engaging in or watching violent behavior *exacerbates* violent inclinations.[36] Furthermore, while humans seem to possess certain instincts that make them prone to aggression, the bulk of violence research suggests that homicidal behavior is *learned*, and therefore in no way compelled by a "natural," let alone unstoppably accreting, psychological drive.[37]

Yet Nietzsche's position in HH 477 goes beyond this empirical research in two important ways: first, for Nietzsche, engaging in violence stimulates not just specifically violent behavioral dispositions, but rather kindles the individual and society in a more widespread manner. Second, and directly following from this, Nietzsche *valorizes* the stimulation occasioned by violent behavior, whereas contemporary theorists are by default critical thereof. This said, in HH 477, Nietzsche takes care to qualify his affirmative remarks. The energetic torrent that bursts forth in warfare is, he warns, prone to inundate, as opposed to irrigate, tender fledgling cultures.[38]

As such, not only does Nietzsche repudiate the Schopenhauerian metaphysics of GSt, but his affirmative stance toward struggles of annihilation becomes markedly more nuanced. Murderous conflict is no longer posited as a metaphysical necessity, but as an instrumental condition of social vitality, *in some cases*. Yet, if a culture is to survive in the long run, periodic military conflict is nonetheless "indispensable" (*unentbehrlich*). There is no hope of Kantian "perpetual peace." The best-case scenario is that we forever oscillate between the contented stability of peace and the regenerative fervor of war – between rest and motion. What we now need to establish is whether Nietzsche cleaves to this position in his later writings.

1.3 Violent Naturalism in the Later Nietzsche

1.3.1 *Raw Catharsis in the* Genealogy of Morals

On the basis of GM I 11, Fredrick Appel (1999, 147) claims that the later Nietzsche sanctions the "instinctive need to purge creative tension"

---

[36] See e.g., Baumeister and Bushman (2003, 485–487).

[37] See e.g., Kivivuori et al. (2011, 105–109).

[38] Note that we also uncover staunchly negative appraisals of *Vernichtungskampf* (and especially war) before, during and after Nietzsche's middle period. See e.g., BT 15, KSA 1.100; DS, KSA 1.160; HH 481; AOM 320; WS 284; A 48; KSA 12:9[126], 410; KSA 13:14[182], 369; KSA 13:15[38],438. See also Niemeyer (2009).

through the raw discharge of violently destructive energy. And certainly, there is a case to be made that Nietzsche's Bernays-inspired ontology of murderous violence makes a comeback in his later writings.

In GM I 11, Nietzsche sketches an idealized picture of his infamous "blond beasts," a community of brutal aristocrats who live in a stringent form of society structured around the principle of mutual restraint. However, in contrast to the moderation that these nobles exercise toward one another, their struggle against outsiders is void of all restraint. Beyond the confines of their narrow circle – that is, "where the strange [and] the foreign begin" – Nietzsche's blond beasts enjoy

> freedom from every social constraint, [and] in the wilderness they compen-
> sate for the tension which is caused by being closed and fenced in by the
> peace of the community for so long, they *return* to the innocent conscience
> of the wild beast as exultant monsters, who perhaps go away having
> committed a hideous succession of murder, arson, rape and torture, in
> a mood of bravado and spiritual equilibrium [*Gleichgewicht*] [. . .]. At the
> center of all these noble races we cannot fail to see the beast of prey, the
> magnificent *blond beast* avidly prowling round for spoil and victory; *this
> hidden center needs release* [*Entladung*] *from time to time, the beast must out
> again, must return to the wild* [emphasis mine] [. . .]. (GM I 11, KSA 5.275)

It would thus appear that Nietzsche has reverted to the Bernays- and Schopenhauer-inspired cathartic argument for the necessity and desirability of unrestrained violent contention. We have a potentially pathological build-up of specifically violent energy, accompanied by the need for periodic release. Ventilation is then achieved through the unrefined dis-charge of such energies in murderously violent behavior.[39] What is further implied in this account is that such outbursts reinstate a healthy condition of inner equilibrium (*Gleichgewicht*).

The unmeasured eruptions depicted in GM I 11 are affirmed by Nietzsche as innocent, irrepressible expressions of strength. And only two sections later, he likens these violent explosions to the instinctive (and therefore innocent) necessity with which an eagle kills the lambs that it needs to survive, as well as to the natural necessity with which a lightning bolt flashes (GM I 13, KSA 5.278–279). Just as a bolt of lightning simply *is* its flash, the nobles simply *are* their callous forms of activity, and they possess no substantial self, let alone a libertarian free will,

---

[39] On the potentially pathological consequences of overaccumulation, see GM II 11, KSA 5.312, where, in the case of the ascetic, this destructive impetus ends up discharging *internally* due to a lack of external outlets. See also BGE 76.

to which moral responsibility could possibly be ascribed. The destructive urges of the nobles therefore cannot, and indeed *should* not, be kept in a state of perpetual restraint – "*the beast must out.*"

But on what grounds does Nietzsche assert this necessity? In a word, the essentially destructive metaphysical will, which compelled martial violence in GSt, has now been replaced by an immanent account of *life* as necessarily destructive in kind. Indeed, Nietzsche explicitly states that "life, in its basic functions [*Grundfunktionen*], is injurious, violent, exploitative and destructive [*vernichtend*], and it cannot be thought of without these characteristics" (GM II 11, KSA 5.312). This is one of Nietzsche's more ruthless figurations of what he calls the "will to power" – the fundamental dynamic that structures existence. In this guise, the will to power is an eruptive, brutal and destructive struggle for assimilation, growth and expansion. Nietzsche seeks to demonstrate that within any natural system, while exploitation and destructive conflict may be *locally* inhibited – for example, at a human level, through the imposition of law – this only ever occurs as a means to forming stronger unities of power (*Macht-Einheiten*) more capable of brutally struggling against *other*, external entities. In Nietzsche's own words,

> states of legality can never be anything but *exceptional states*, as partial restrictions of the true will to life, which seeks power and to whose overall purpose they subordinate themselves as individual measures, that is to say, as a means of creating *greater* units of power. (GM II 11, KSA 5.312)

As such, these fundamental biological processes (*Grundfunktionen*) can only ever be *displaced*, never extinguished. To pursue their universal suppression, as Nietzsche believes Christianity is guilty of doing, is to pursue an actively hostile relation to life itself.[40] Since humans cannot help *but* embody these vital *Grundfunktionen*, they are naturally (i.e., psychologically and physiologically) compelled to engage in struggles of annihilation.

The Bernays-inspired cathartic model of GSt was found to be conditioned by the existence of a distinctly destructive energy that unstoppably accretes. In GM, the will to power is at least in part conceived as just such a kind of energy. As we have seen, Nietzsche attributes an ineradicably destructive component to the will to power. At the level of human existence, this

---

[40] Although note that insofar as both Christianity and its secular analogues rapaciously pursue mastery over their opponents and even life itself, Nietzsche sees them as hypocritically embodying the very characteristics of life qua will to power against which they are ostensibly struggling (see e.g., GM III 11, KSA 5.362–363).

component demands periodic discharge in the act of *Vernichtungskampf.* But in distinction to GSt, Nietzsche now suggests that this ferocious energy originates *immanently*, that is, from the ontological structure of life itself, as opposed to *transcendently*, in the noumenal realm of the Schopenhauerian will. In this way, Nietzsche can be said to substitute the *Metaphysical* Instantiation Argument with a *Naturalistic* Instantiation Argument:

The Naturalistic Instantiation Argument

1. All living entities are necessarily characterized by will to power;
2. Will to power is necessarily characterized by violently destructive activity;
3. Humans are living entities;
4. Therefore, humans are necessarily characterized by violently destructive activity (behavior).

Despite this naturalistic modification, these texts nonetheless betray a blatant reversion to the cathartic model that Nietzsche espouses in GSt. But does this mean that the later Nietzsche makes a wholesale return to the position that he implicitly rejected in HH? And do these passages from GM not undermine his transformative project in just the same way as did GSt – that is, in proposing that we can only ever *displace*, and never transform, our violent behavioral inclinations? The ontological obstacle of immutability has once again reared its ugly head.

As we will presently see, the later Nietzsche remains committed to the project that he pioneers in HC and HH of agonally transforming violent conflict. And there are a number of strategies available to the interpreter wishing to reconcile this later transformative impetus with the raw cathartic model presented in GM. In their own way, each of these strategies supports the idea that the problematic texts in GM can be set apart as exceptions, anomalies even, diverging quite radically from the dominant drift of Nietzsche's mature thought.

The first reason we might justifiably fence off this cluster of texts is that in no other enumeration of the basic functions (*Grundfunktionen*) of life does Nietzsche mention destructiveness; rather, he consistently underscores the functions of overpowering, exploitation, instrumentalization and domination.[41] It is *these* activities that I would argue best capture what the later Nietzsche holds to be the fundamentally ineluctable characteristics of life, nature and the world as will to power. Pivotally, as we will

---

[41] See KSA 12:1[30], 17; KSA 11:40[7], 631; BGE 259.

see in the following section, these are remarkably plastic characteristics, ones that do not necessarily have to express themselves in violent struggle.

Taking a more focused look at GM's place in the later corpus, we begin to uncover further reasons for setting GM I II apart. As Marco Brusotti (2012, 106, 126) has observed, in GM Nietzsche is principally attacking Eugene Dühring's contention that the concept of justice stems from the desire for revenge, which is reactively evoked whenever we suffer an injury.[42] Nietzsche saw Dühring (among others) as representative of a wider tendency within the human sciences to give explanatory priority to the reactive sentiments (e.g., "hatred, envy, resentment, suspicion, *rancune* and revenge"). He objects that because thinkers of this ilk are caught in the rancorous spirit of Christian *ressentiment*, they cannot help but view the world through the distorting lens of reactivity.[43] As an alternative to this tendency, Nietzsche wishes to introduce a new "funda-mental concept" (*Grundbegriff*) to the sciences – namely, that of "actual activity" (*eigentliche Aktivität*) (GM II II, KSA 5.310 and GM II 12, KSA 5.315–316). He thus endeavors to foreground the motivational force of "actual active emotions such as lust for mastery, greed and the like," affects he takes to be of "higher biological worth" (GM II II, KSA 5.310). In line with this enterprise, he seeks to convince his readers that nobility and freedom are distinguished by just such activity. Unlike the weak and the slavish, his nobles act with spontaneity and aggression, which Nietzsche defines as the essential characteristics of flourishing life itself, which is to say, of healthy will to power. His nobles are simply not prone to the kind of brooding and protracted resentment that culminates in calculated ven-geance; they are instead conceived as an outpouring of aggressive, unre-strained and at times necessarily *destructive* force. If they do react, they do so *immediately*, without thereby being poisoned by toxic *ressentiment*.

So it is largely in opposition to Dühring that Nietzsche constructs the active–reactive dichotomy (out of which thinkers such as Deleuze have gotten so much philosophical mileage). Brusotti persuasively argues, how-ever, that, following GM, Nietzsche abandons this conceptual dyad. Upon reading the works of the psychiatrist Charles Féré in 1888, Nietzsche comes to realize that instantaneous reaction is symptomatic of mental infirmity and neuroticism (Brusotti 2012, 115–117; Féré 1888). From this point on, Nietzsche ceases to associate strength with the kind of unrestrained,

---

[42] See GM II II, KSA 5.310–313; GM III 14, KSA 5.370.
[43] The argumentation in which this accusation is grounded will be analyzed in Chapter 4.

automatic and spontaneous discharge that we saw the blond beasts destructively unleashing upon outsiders. Instead, he now identifies strength with
slow, considered and deliberate reaction (TI Germans 6; EH Wise 2; KSA
13:14[102], 279). In this way, we might take Nietzsche's violent characterization of will to power in GM as an (over-)reaction to Dühring, with
whom Nietzsche is far less concerned as of 1888. Consequently, there
appear to be legitimate grounds for discounting the raw cathartic model
that we find in GM as a developmental anomaly. The chief disadvantage of
this interpretive strategy, though, is that Nietzsche deploys precisely the
same cathartic model in 1888, in TI Ancients 3, where he speaks of the
ancient Greeks' "strongest instinct, the will to power," and the "uncon-
trollable force [*unbändigen Gewalt*] of this drive [*Trieb*]." This "explosive
material," he tells us,

> vented itself outwardly in terrible and ruthless hostility: the city-states tore
> each other apart so that the citizens in each one were able to find peace from
> themselves. [. . .] [T]he bold realism and immoralism characteristic of the
> Hellenes was a necessity [*Noth*] [. . .].

Evidently, then, even in late 1888, Nietzsche still adheres to the idea that
under conditions of health, the will to power necessarily expresses itself in
violent, combative outbursts.

   The final justification for hermeneutically segregating the figure of the
blond beast lies in the character's potentially rhetorical status. What is
more, this status may also be able to account for Nietzsche's remarks in TI
Ancients 3. Agonistic commentators tend to charitably construe the blond
beast either as a caricature of evil from the perspective of the slaves (Hatab
2008b, 48–49), or as a mere symbol of unrestrained passion that Nietzsche
himself "does not glorify" (Kaufmann 1974, 225). While the blond beast is
not so easily reduced to a mere chimera or symbol, there is some textual
basis for conceiving the figure as a rhetorical device engineered by
Nietzsche as part of his transformative project. On this reading, the
blond beast functions as a polemical character (or caricature), akin to
Rousseau's or Hobbes's men in the state of nature, and therefore *not* as
a normative ideal.

   In the relevant passages, one of Nietzsche's underlying complaints is that
Europeans have lost their fear of man. With this loss, he continues, we
simultaneously lost our admiring love of man (GM I 11, KSA 5.275–276).
Being surrounded by "failed, sickly, tired and exhausted people," such as
prevail today, erodes our sense of reverence for humankind. Nietzsche's
contempt for this mediocre human type in many ways recalls his fear of

a future dominated by the "last man." Though these "last men" are, as a kind of herd-animal, maximally socialized and highly adept at surviving, they are entirely incapable of developing themselves, and hence fail to elicit our esteem.[44] The rhetorical function of the blond beast, and arguably also of the ancient Greeks in TI Ancients 3, is thus to give Nietzsche's readers an inspiring "glimpse of something perfect, completely finished, happy, powerful, triumphant, that still leaves something to fear!" (GM I 12, KSA 5.278). Yet this does not mean that Nietzsche enjoins us to emulate the behavior of the blond beasts. Even in GM, he qualifies his eulogy, warning that we "may be quite justified in retaining our fear of the blond beast at the center of every noble race and remain on our guard" (GM I 11, KSA 5.277).

In light of this caveat, it is vital that we take care not to confound the blond beast with the figure of the overman (*Übermensch*), who *does* in fact represent a Nietzschean normative ideal.[45] It is tempting to equate the two figures because the overman–last-man dyad, so prominent in Z (e.g., in Z I Preface, KSA 4.20), appears to be mirrored in GM, where the blond beast is juxtaposed with the mediocre man of the present. But the mere fact that both overman and blond beast are comparably opposed to mediocrity does not entail that they are therefore interchangeable. Indeed, close reading turns up a significant degree of conceptual discrepancy between the two characters. First, the only mention of the overman in GM is in relation to Napoleon, whom Nietzsche considers a "synthesis of *brute* and *overman* [*von* Unmensch *und* Übermensch]," which strongly suggests that Napoleon's brutish and beastly (*unmenschliche*) traits are not part of his *Übermenschlichkeit* (overmanliness) (GM I 16, KSA 5.288). Moreover, Nietzsche's examples of blond beasts are for the most part historical – for instance, the ancient Greeks and the Vikings (GM I 11, KSA 5.275) – yet he explicitly states in Z that "[n]ever has there yet been an overman" (Z II Priests, KSA 4.119). Finally, when he *does* look to the past in search of exemplars, he certainly doesn't confine himself to blond beasts, often preferring to invoke artists such as Leonardo da Vinci, Homer and Goethe.[46] So, even though there may be some conceptual overlap between the two figures, the overman cannot be reduced to the brutal figure of the blond beast without doing significant interpretive violence to the letter of Nietzsche's later writings.

---

[44] See Z I Preface 5, KSA 4.19–20.
[45] For an interpretation that equates the two figures, see Brennecke (1976).
[46] See e.g., BGE 200; KSA 12:9[157], 428.

With the polemical figure of the blond beast, Nietzsche wishes to illuminate not just the feebleness of modern Europeans, but, moreover, the *contingency* of this feebleness, and in this way to open our eyes to the possibility of fashioning and achieving alternative ideals. As in the opening paragraphs of HC, in which he also accents the violent character of the pre-Homeric Greeks, he may well be calling forth these destructive energies in order for us to *harness and sublimate* them into culturally productive forms of behavior. Acknowledging and invoking the blond beast within ourselves would then stand as a condition of bridling this beast, which would in turn then stand as the keystone of *Übermenschlichkeit*. However, this last attempt to exegetically isolate the blond beast has an unfortunate drawback: it has to concede that Nietzsche's galvanizing genealogy is founded upon an ontology of violent energy that contradicts the very transformative project for which he is trying to galvanize us. And yet his wider transformative project is certainly not undone by such texts. As we will now see, during the 1880s, and alongside this problematic essentialist conception of violence, Nietzsche also draws on the natural sciences to further develop the transformative notion of catharsis that we found in embryo in HC and HH.

1.3.2   Grounding the Transformative Project

In order to grasp the later Nietzsche's transformative ontology of violence, we need to begin by analyzing the influence of the chemist and physicist Julius Robert Mayer on Nietzsche's writings in the 1880s. Mayer's formative impact in this regard can be traced back to Peter Gast, one of Nietzsche's closest friends, who in 1881 sent Nietzsche a copy of Mayer's *On Release* (*Über Auslösung*).[47] In this short tract, Mayer presents his natural-scientific notion of "release" (*Auslösung*), which Nietzsche subsequently assigns a leading role within his later philosophy.[48] Mayer posits two species of causal relation: the first circumscribes cases in which a given cause is equal to its effect (in obvious accordance with the principle of the conservation of energy, also developed by Mayer). The second (which he does not think can be reduced to the first), comprises causes that trigger a chain reaction, or the (often sudden) release of large quantities of stored energy, as in the case of an explosion for instance. Thus, the energetic input required to pull the trigger of a gun seems to be far outweighed by the

---

[47] See letter to Heinrich Köselitz, April 16, 1881 (KGB III/1, 84–85).
[48] Yet note that Nietzsche nonetheless rejects Mayer's atomism. See letter to Heinrich Köselitz, March 20, 1882 (KGB III/1, 182–183).

energy thereby released in the firing of the bullet. While this is merely characteristic of "very many" natural processes according to Mayer (1893, 443), he deems the living, organic world to be "tied to an uninterrupted process of release [*Auslösungsprozeß*]" (442).[49] In humans, for example, nerve impulses represent a weak motor activity capable of triggering disproportionately great muscular movements. When kept within moderate bounds (*gewisse Grenzen*), these internal releases elicit a pleasurable sensation, such as that which we experience when exercising our muscles in recreational sport. Mayer further adds that this pleasurable sensation is closely connected to the feeling of health, which indexes "an undisturbed release-apparatus [*Auslösungsapparat*]" (443).

Mayer also discusses another comparable sensation of pleasure bound up with the process of release. This concerns the enjoyment that humans take in triggering *external* releases – in firing guns for example. He also refers to external "releases of a criminal sort," speculating that

> were our planet so constituted for it to be possible for each and every person to detonate it with a keg of dynamite, one would at any given time certainly find enough people prepared to sacrifice their own life exploding our beautiful earth into outer-space [. . .]. (446)

The takeaway point in these remarks is that the human urge for destructive discharge is not due to a build-up of any *intrinsically* destructive drive or species of energy, nor is it motivated by any anticipated pleasure in the destructive aspect of the act per se. Mayer's project implies that we would have no interest in destroying the world if we had to do so with shovels over the course of millennia. The incentive here lies in the pleasure we hope to achieve in triggering *a disproportionate release of energy*, which is only contingently associated with such explosively destructive behavior.

Nietzsche places Mayer's conception of "release" at the heart of his later ontology. Indeed, he comes to frame *release* (*Auslösung*) as *the* fundamental vital process: "above all," he declares, "something living wants to release its force" (KSA 12:2[63], 89).[50] But since one cannot have release without some prior accumulation, he likewise frames the ability to *accrue* energy as an essential feature of thriving life. And according to Nietzsche, geniuses and stronger human types are distinguished from *hoi polloi* insofar as they inherit, or are capable of accumulating, exceptionally great quantities of force (TI Skirmishes 44; KSA 12:10[165], 553). As such, the will to power

---

[49] For a comprehensive review of Mayer's influence on Nietzsche, see Mittasch (1952, 114ff.).
[50] See also KSA 11:27[3], 275; BGE 13.

does not merely designate a process whereby living entities greedily accrue power *in potentia*, but equally the subsequent process of actually releasing or discharging such potential – that is, power *in actu*.[51]

To be sure, according to this formulation of the will to power, there remains a certain *demand* for release that harkens back to the Bernays-inspired model of catharsis. And yet, in contrast to that earlier model, engaging in violently destructive struggle is no longer conceived as either metaphysically or naturalistically necessary. Even in 1883, Nietzsche states that the force accrued by human agents can, as Mayer indicates, be ventilated via an array of different activities:

> [...] *one and the same feeling of force can release itself* [*sich entladen*] *in a thousand ways*: this is the "freedom of the will" – the feeling that with respect to the necessary explosion, hundreds of actions would serve equally well. The feeling of a certain *arbitrariness* of the action with respect to this relief of tension. (KSA 10:7[77], 268)[52]

For Nietzsche, as for Mayer, there exist myriad behaviors through which this abstract, polymorphous force can obtain release. Like the "desire for victory and pre-eminence" described in WS 226, it is remarkably plastic. Thus, in one note from 1887, when he has more fully formulated his notion of the world as will to power, Nietzsche refers to the many "modes of expression and metamorphoses of the one will, which is inherent in all events, the will to power," which he goes on to characterize as a "wanting-to-become-stronger" (KSA 13:11[96], 44). At the level of human behavior, the discharge of this will to power can assume an infinitude of different forms: for example, just as we have seen that it can discharge itself in physically destructive behavior, or as we will witness in later chapters, sociopolitical oppression, it can equally obtain release in acts of artistic creativity.[53] Within this account of release, we might say that physically destructive behavior would be reduced to the status of a merely *possible* (though nonetheless *probable*) corollary of the release of power. Just as was the case with the individuals that Mayer theorized would gladly detonate the earth, the urge is one toward release, not physically destructive conflict per se. This opens up an ontologically coherent space for exclusively agonistic readings – that is, to the extent that it *theoretically* allows

---

[51] See KSA 13:11[114], 54, where the inheritance and discharge of power are clearly key to Nietzsche's conception of strength. See also KSA 13:15[78], 455 and BGE 208 for examples of Nietzsche applying this discharge model to the sociopolitical realm.

[52] See also KSA 9:11[31], 453.

[53] See e.g., KSA 12:7[3], 256: "One must examine the artist himself, and his psychology (critique of the drive to play as a release of force [*Auslassen von Kraft*], a pleasure in change, in impressing one's soul on something foreign, the absolute egoism of the artist, etc.)."

for the unlimited channeling of energy away from *Vernichtungskampf.* But note that Nietzsche does not consider complete transformation to be a *concrete* possibility. He still argues that accrued energy is de facto often released through impulsive, violent acts. This idea is particularly conspicuous in an aphorism from 1881 (though observe that Nietzsche composed this text prior to fully articulating his theory of the will to power in the mid-1880s):

> The act of violence as a consequence of passion, of anger for example, is to be understood physiologically as an attempt to prevent a threatening attack of suffocation. Countless acts of arrogance vented on other people have been diversions of a sudden rush of blood through a vigorous action of the muscles: and perhaps the whole phenomenon of the "evil of the strong" belongs in this domain. (D 371)[54]

Nietzsche's depiction of violence as a means of obtaining cathartic release at once explains and de-moralizes this unpalatable feature of human life: the "evil" of the strong "harms others without giving thought to it – it *has* to discharge itself" (D 371).[55] Likewise, exultant feelings (*Gefühle*) pent up in the *demos* have a strong tendency to discharge themselves in war, and princes, knowing very well how to exploit this brimming "feeling of power" for their own belligerent designs, offer military action to their subjects as an opportune vent (D 189).[56] In a similar manner, Nietzsche seems to think that the de facto way in which nations tend to pursue power accumulation is through "war and conquest" (KSA 13:14[192], 378). The upshot of these later realist arguments is that Nietzsche can be said to naturalize, explain, de-moralize and even, to some extent, *encourage* struggles of annihilation in a way that still seriously jars with the agonistic reading of his later practical philosophy.

Although Nietzsche does not explicitly refer to release (*Auslösung*) in the context of his post-1880 writings on war, there is nonetheless telling evidence that the concept had a molding effect on his treatment of the topic. An apposite example can be found in GS 23, where Nietzsche contests the assumption that pacific cultures are guilty of being lax. Often, beneath their veneer of lassitude, he tells us, "the ancient civil energy and passion, which received a magnificent visibility through war and competitive games, has now transformed itself into countless private passions and has merely become less visible" (GS 23). This picture of once destructive, though now productively modulated, energies is again sharply incompatible with the ontologies of

---

[54] See also D 356.   [55] Compare GS 218.   [56] See also GS 38.

violent strife that he advances in GSt and GM. But perhaps more interestingly, this aphorism signals an important change of tack from the argument
that we uncovered in HH 477. In the first place, cultures that have lost their
taste for war are not necessarily weary, as Nietzsche suggests in HH 477.
Closer scrutiny may very well reveal such cultures to have fruitfully canalized
their combative energies into nonmartial pursuits – a process which he
unambiguously praises in GS 23 for kindling the "flame of knowledge."
Furthermore, the aphorism implies that a nation's martial and cultural
undertakings stand in a zero-sum relation to one another – that is, as opposed
to being, under the right conditions, mutually complementary, as is suggested
by HH 477.[57]

A similar zero-sum dynamic is also discernible in one of his final
notes, presciently entitled "*Last consideration.*" In this fragment from
the 1888–1889 *Nachlaß*, we can see that in the last days of his working
life Nietzsche maintains a view of war that gels with Mayer's notion of
release, and which is correspondingly at odds with the Bernays-
inspired cathartic model that we uncovered in GSt and GM:

> Were we able to dispense with wars, so much the better. I would know how
> to make more serviceable use of twelve million, which is the yearly cost of
> Europe's armed peace; there are other means of honoring physiology than
> through the military hospital . . . (KSA 13:25[19], 646)

Despite the subjunctive mood, this shows that altogether dispensing with
war remains a conceivable possibility for Nietzsche. Furthermore, eradicating war, and thereby freeing up millions of men usually engaged in
standing armies, would allow their energy to be put to more profitable
ends – for example, as he mentions in an earlier draft of this note, toward
"the grandiose and higher work of life" (KSA 13:25[14], 644). As such, the
later Nietzsche can be said to promote the collective transformation of
belligerent into cultural perfectionist agency in a manner consonant with
the energetic economy presaged in HC and HH. Physically destructive
behavior is therefore possible (and indeed probable), but not necessary. It
lies well within our power to affirm and embody the *Grundfunktionen* of
life without lapsing into violent conflict.

---

[57] This zero-sum relation is prefigured in DS 1 (KSA 1.160–161). Compare GS 283, however, where he
suggests that by cultivating a warlike age, endowed with manly warrior virtues, we enable
a subsequent age in which these virtues are channeled into the *cultural* struggle for knowledge. In
this picture, the trade-off between martial and cultural activity is thus strictly age specific, and
a wider historical view may reveal that an increase in militarism leads, in the long run, to
a corresponding increase in culture.

1.4 Conclusion

The presence of a sustained agonal impulse running through Nietzsche's writings should not distract us from the fact that we must reject the defining thesis of the agonistic reading – that is, the claim that his evaluative attitude toward *Vernichtungskampf* is best described as disparaging and that he is above all concerned with the transformation of violent antagonism into more benign modes of contest. The key obstacle for agonistic readings lies in the modal status that Nietzsche ascribes to murderous violence. In both his early and later writings he conceives such violence as a *necessary* aspect of human existence – *metaphysically* necessary in the case of GSt, and *naturally* necessary in that of GM. The problem is trenchant: Nietzsche postulates theories that entail the *impossibility* of the agonal project with respect to certain forms of destructive behavior. These theories affirmatively posit violent strife as an essential component of thriving human life. The normative cost of acquiescing to such essentialist ontologies of physical violence, however, is that we (potentially inadvertently) relinquish the ideal of transformation as a coherent or even conceivable possibility. On this account, we should exercise extreme circumspection when faced with such hypotheses.

Alongside Nietzsche's essentialist, metaphysical conception of violence, we also found that he develops an alternative, naturalist–realist conception. According to this rival conception, Nietzsche regards violent strife as the contingent expression of a polymorphous impetus toward power. And we established that Nietzsche's later ontology of destructive conflict is best conceived in terms of this transformative model. En route to this mature theoretical view, however, we tracked him moving through a number of competing models. For the sake of clarity, we ought to briefly summarize the key points on this developmental arc.

His initial essentialist ontology was found to be rooted in a commitment to Schopenhauer's metaphysics; we then saw that after disavowing this metaphysical framework, he gravitates toward Burckhardt's historical–realist view. In tandem with this realignment, he then begins to develop what I have been calling his "transformative" model. Over the course of the 1880s, under the influence of the natural sciences, he proceeds to bring this model to full development. Although his earlier raw-catharsis model arguably makes a reappearance in GM and TI (though now in naturalized form), my contention has been that these texts serve a rhetorical function and should therefore not be taken as representative of his later thought, which lays the accent on transformation. Crucially, this move opens up an

ontologically coherent space for agonal transformation. However, we
should not lose sight of the fact that even within this somewhat softer
view, Nietzsche maintains that struggles of annihilation remain a highly
probable feature of human life.

The second fundamental problem for the exclusively agonistic reading
concerns the normative value that Nietzsche ascribes to physically destructive strife. We have ascertained at length that he affirms struggles of
annihilation, and does so on the basis of an array of distinct reasons.
Where he adopts his essentialist ontology of violence, he tends to hold
that compressing the release of belligerent energy into short-term bursts
represents a precondition of higher culture, as well as a hale expression of
both power and freedom. On the other hand, based on his realist observations, he argues in HH that martial conflict, as opposed to being an
exhaust, may in fact constitute a *source* of energy, demolishing moribund
cultural practices and fostering noble warrior virtues.

It should be stated that the aim of this chapter has not been to give an
exhaustive account of Nietzsche's conception of *Vernichtungskampf*. To be
sure, throughout his *oeuvre*, he attributes this species of conflict to a motley
of different causes, many of which we have not had sufficient space to
examine. For example, in BT, he describes how murderous conflict can
issue from collectively unrestrained egoism (BT 15, KSA 1.100); and later,
in A, he facetiously claims that war is caused by God, who deploys it as
a means of keeping humankind divided against itself and distracted from
science (A 48).[58] Strangely enough, though, we do not find natural scarcity
listed among Nietzsche's catalogue of potential incentives for human
violence. This is conspicuous because it is scarcity of resources that not
just Malthus, but also many today, single out as one of the primary drivers
of physically destructive conflict.[59]

Rather than seeking to exhaustively expose Nietzsche's thoughts on
Vernichtungskampf, we have been pursuing the more modest goal of
bringing into clear relief why he posits war and violence as preconditions
of cultural flourishing. In the process of doing so, however, we have
observed that far from affirming *Vernichtungskampf* without qualification,
he indicts various species of violence for *hampering* cultural growth. Even
in GSt Nietzsche staunchly criticizes unrelenting, universal states of war;

---

[58] Note that we have also not yet thematized Nietzsche's later demand for the "destruction of millions
of failures" (KSA 11:25[335], 98), which has often been interpreted as a proto-Fascist campaign for
ethnic cleansing (Detwiler 1990, 113). This issue will be examined in Chapter 4.
[59] See e.g., LeBlanc (2003).

and in HH 477 he draws our attention to the detrimental effect that wars often have on fledgling cultures. The evaluative criterion that Nietzsche uses to distinguish between better and worse forms of *Vernichtungskampf* is therefore ultimately cultural health. His thoughts concerning struggles of annihilation should accordingly be read with the following question in mind: To what extent do the distinct forms of actively murderous struggle enable a culture to become a productive whole? To be sure, in our analysis of HC and HH, we found that Nietzsche invokes this very same cultural criterion in order to valorize the agonal transformation of unmeasured violence; but to claim, in the manner of his agonistic readers, that this captures Nietzsche's wider thoughts on conflict is to whitewash over the strong affirmative vein running through his views on violent struggle. We must therefore take care not to inversely distort the tenor of his philosophy in trying to correct tendentious militaristic readings.

CHAPTER 2

Bounding Nietzsche's Agon

In light of the various justifications for war that were enumerated in the previous chapter, it is perhaps understandable that many have read Nietzsche as an outright warmonger. Such readers tend to reduce his sociopolitical philosophy of conflict to an endorsement of violently unmeasured struggle. Nietzsche, they claim, vociferously incites war as a remedy to modern Europe's ills. And congruent with this interpretation, numerous commentators hold him at least partly responsible for Germany's aggressive role in the two world wars. As was mentioned in our introduction, this tendency to read Nietzsche in a belligerent light is just as pronounced among his adherents as it is among his detractors. For example, Nietzsche enthusiasts such as Bernhardi, Bäumler and Elisabeth Förster-Nietzsche all read his philosophy as a literal call to arms. Likewise, on the critical side, Bertrand Russell (2004, 693) avers that Nietzsche's works are informed by a generally militaristic impulse, it being "obvious" that "in his day-dreams he is a warrior, not a professor; all of the men he admires were military."[1] In a similar vein, Ernst Nolte (1963, 533–534) disparages Nietzsche as a philosopher of pitiless intolerance, one who wantonly incites his readers to physically and ideologically exterminate the decadent elements of modern culture – be these moral systems, political regimes, philosophical worldviews or even human beings.

En passant, we have already seen that Nietzsche advocates a measured (i.e., nondestructive) form of social conflict modeled on the ancient Greek practice of agon. Although this practice was typified in the athletic, equestrian and dramaturgical contests that took place at the official games in Olympia and Delphi, it was equally embodied in the ancient Greeks' more general obsession with competition. Indeed, in almost every sphere of civic life they strenuously vied to excel one another. It is crucial to

---

[1] For a detailed review of the various journalists and intellectuals who read Nietzsche as a warmonger, see Martin (2006, 147–166); Ascheim (1994, esp. chap. 5 and chap. 8).

remark, however, that the Greeks themselves had no explicit theory of agon. This is no doubt one reason why the modern conception of agon is so inconveniently nebulous.[2] And Nietzsche's account of agonal contention might strike us a particularly severe example of this conceptual wooliness. The critical literature certainly gives us this impression. Yet, in what follows we are going to find that we can dispel much of this apparent indeterminacy by means of a close and historically contextualized reading of his writings on the topic of agonal struggle. Whereas in the previous chapter we rebutted the exclusively measured, agonal reading of Nietzsche by highlighting his valorization of war, this chapter adopts the contrary argumentative strategy. Our critical target is now the exclusively *unmeasured* militaristic interpretation of his thought, which we will overturn by elucidating his sustained affirmation of agonal conflict.

But in order to defend the broader, overarching thesis of this book – that Nietzsche's philosophy of conflict is largely coherent and systematic – we must first overcome three points of scholarly contention concerning Nietzsche's agonism. The current chapter will be structured around each of these in turn. The first and most pressing issue is that while Nietzsche's agon is usually read as nonviolent in nature, a number of commentators take it to be inclusive of violent, unmeasured forms of strife (such as war). This is what I will be referring to as the *destructive* reading. Against this interpretation, in the first section of this chapter, I contend that agonal conflict is *intrinsically* nondestructive (i.e., measured) for both the early and the later Nietzsche. This leaves us with the task of ascertaining how he conceives the type of measure peculiar to the agon. And so we arrive at our second obstacle, which regards the social scope within which Nietzsche thinks agonal measure is (a) *possible* (a descriptive question) and (b) *desirable* (a normative question). On the one side we find interpreters who suppose that agonally measured conflict is only deemed possible or desirable by Nietzsche within the narrow confines of an aristocratic elite. On the other side then stand his democratically minded readers, who take him to be campaigning for the society-wide application of his agonal ideal. Caught between these two extremes, we are left with little clue as to the true scope of Nietzsche's agonal recommendations. In the second section of this chapter, though, we will break this stalemate by splitting his agon in two: Discerning analysis will reveal that although Nietzsche retains an elitist conception of the agon qua contest for glory, he nonetheless affirms that individuals of *every* capacity and social standing can conceivably engage in a more general agon to excel their peers.

---

[2] See Kalyvas (2009, 18).

Our third problem relates to Nietzsche's observation that agonal conflict "unfetters the individual" but also, simultaneously, "bounds" (*bändigt*) him (KSA 7:16[22], 402). But how does agonal conflict restrain in the very act of rousing? By what mechanisms does it prevent the contest from devolving into a violent free for all? In other words, what is the concrete *source* of the agon's measure? As it stands, there are two incompatible responses to this question. One set of interpreters maintains that such restraint is rooted in a subjective shift of attitude on the part of agonal adversaries; consequently, each adversary acknowledges their counterpart and treats them with due sporting respect. Yet in contrast to this reading, others maintain that the attitude of agonal contestants is no different from that which drives struggles of annihilation. Agonal measure, they contend, is grounded in a balance of powers; hence, in their view, agon can only be said to obtain between approximate equals. By virtue of this equality, contestants are able to keep one another's tyrannical aspirations in mutual check. Against these contrarily one-sided readings, we will see that for Nietzsche both self-restraint *and* approximate equality represent necessary conditions of agonal measure.

In order to resolve these three scholarly disputes, it is imperative that we reconstruct Nietzsche's position with reference to its proper historical context. This will provide us with the hermeneutic lens that we require to bring the coherence of Nietzsche's agonism into sharp focus. The most pertinent points of reference are to be found in Burckhardt's *Griechische Kulturgeschichte* (1898–1902 [1978]),[3] Ernst Curtius's "Der Wettkampf" (1864),[4] George Grote's *A History of Greece* (1851)[5] and Leopold Schmidt's *Die Ethik der alten Griechen* (1882).[6] In order to appreciate the specificity of Nietzsche's standpoint we must first obtain a clear grasp of how he appropriates and synthesizes the conceptions of agonal competition advanced by his

---

[3] We know that Nietzsche and Burckhardt had lengthy discussions regarding the content of the lectures on which GK is based (and which were delivered from 1872 to 1886). See for example, Nietzsche's letter to Erwin Rohde of December 21, 1871 (KGB II/1, 257) (sent shortly prior to Nietzsche's composition of HC, and while Burckhardt was composing GK), where Nietzsche writes of having spent "several beautiful days with Jakob Burckhardt, during which time [they] discussed much concerning the ancient Greeks." See also Ruehl (2004, 91, 96 [n.44]). This gainsays Acampora (2013, 211 [n.7]), who insists that the influence of Burckhardt on Nietzsche is negligible. See also above, Introduction (fn.40).

[4] James Porter (2009, 11) writes that both Nietzsche and Burckhardt "adored" Curtius's study. See Janz (1978–1979, 1:491). There is also evidence that Curtius influenced Burckhardt's agonal interpretation of the Greeks (Ottmann 1999, 49 [fn.22]).

[5] Grote's influence on Nietzsche is overt in KSA 7:16[39], 407.

[6] For evidence of Schmidt's influence on Nietzsche, see e.g., KSA 10:7[161], 295. For an overview of this connection, see Orsucci (1996, 248–275).

predecessors. Let us begin by examining how this holds with respect to the first of the three aforementioned debates, which concerns the disputed relation of agonal conflict to struggles of annihilation.

2.1 The Relation of Agon to Annihilation

The destructive interpretation of Nietzsche's agonism is particularly problematic with respect to the principal thesis of this chapter – namely, that Nietzsche's endorsement of agon proves that he advocates for a *measured* form of social conflict, and so cannot be construed as an uncompromising militarist. The issue at stake is that the destructive reading understands Nietzsche's conception of agon as coextensive with, or at least inclusive of, unmeasured physical conflict (i.e., struggles of annihilation; *Vernichtungskämpfe*). The Nazi ideologue Alfred Bäumler, for example, puts forward a distinctly militaristic interpretation of Nietzsche's agon. He interprets HC as an unqualified celebration of the "pleasure of victory" (*Lust des Sieges*), and reads Nietzsche's interpretation of Heraclitus as an endorsement of naked political power struggle (Bäumler 1931, 63–64).[7] On the basis of this exegesis, Bäumler then argues that Nietzsche prescribes "danger and war" as a remedy to modern European decline (172); indeed, he concludes that Nietzsche "belongs to the age of great wars" (183). In this way, he equates Nietzsche's affirmation of agonal contest and victory in HC with an affirmation of martial conquest. While it has now become orthodox to read Nietzsche's conception of agon as a nonviolent mode of opposition, a number of recent commentators go against the interpretive grain, asserting that the concept *does* in fact subsume physically unmeasured species of conflict.[8] One pivotal way that commentators tend to run these concepts together is by reading HC as continuous with the militaristic sentiments of GSt, which might seem legitimate given that

---

[7] For a summary of Nietzsche's understanding of Heraclitus, see the Introduction to this book.

[8] For examples of the orthodox, nonviolent reading of Nietzsche's agon, see Acampora (2013, 18–25); Siemens (2001a, 101); and Kaufmann (1974, 220). However, note that Acampora (2013, 189), who reads HC as an unequivocal endorsement of nondestructive conflict, nevertheless views Nietzsche's later "agonal practice" as inclusive of destructiveness. The foremost *destructive* reading is advanced by Martin Ruehl (2004, 91), who argues that in GSt, "Nietzsche describe[s], with obvious relish, the Greek *agon* as 'the bloody jealousy of one town for another, one party for another, this murderous greed of those petty wars.'" Similarly, Dombowsky (2004, 43–44) claims that in GSt, Nietzsche affirms, "without utilizing the term, the Greek *agon*." Finally, Müller (2005, 78) asserts that for the early Nietzsche "the agon chiefly denotes the heroic duel to the death."

the two pieces belong to the same collection of essays.[9] But does this expansive notion of agon bear scrutiny?

To be sure, subsuming physically destructive modes of conflict under the concept of agon is perfectly consistent with historical usage. In ancient Greek the term *agón* principally denoted any "gathering [or] assembly; [. . .] especially met to see public games," or a "contest for a prize at the games." But it could also refer to "contests in general," or "generally, struggle." Further, it was specifically used to signify "struggle[s] for life and death" or "battle[s]" (Liddell and Scott 1961, 18–19). In post-classical Latin, *agon* was then used to signify (among other things) martyrdom.[10] And surveying historical dictionaries of German, one can see that *Wettkampf* has also been used to refer to measured and unmeasured types of conflict alike.[11] Looking to Nietzsche's influences, specifically Curtius and Burckhardt, we again discover that *Wettkampf* ("contest"), *Krieg* ("war"), and mortal violence are by no means mutually exclusive notions. We ought to now take a closer look at the conceptual overlap suggested by Nietzsche's precursors, since this will enable us to establish precisely how Nietzsche deviates from convention when he recasts the *Wettkampf-Vernichtungskampf* dyad in his own writings on the ancient Greek agon.

2.1.1   An Evolving Conceptual Distinction

Ernst Curtius (1864, 3–4) pioneers the idea that what distinguishes the ancient Greeks from other cultures is their "competitive lust for action" (*wetteifende Thatenlust*). He writes of their joyful desire to engage in competition and thereby prove themselves superior to their adversaries. For the Greeks, he continues, the good life lay not in security or material comfort (as it does for modern individuals) but in "struggle and striving" (*Ringen und Streben*), and he further claims that their immense cultural achievements directly stemmed from their consuming desire for competitive victory. In this sense, Curtius uses the term *Wettkampf* to signify any struggle for ascendancy in which the value of contention is placed over and above that of Arcadian contentment.

Nothing in this general vision of *Wettkampf* is incompatible with military conflict; indeed, Curtius submits that the ancient Greek agon began as a martial contest of tribes vying for political dominance. What

[9] See for example, Dombowsky (2004, 94); Müller (2005, 83); Ruehl (2004, 91).
[10] See entry for "agon" in Wölffin (1900–).
[11] See entry for "Wettkampf, m.," in DWB. The first definition of *Wettkampf* is given as an "opposition [*Auseinandersetzung*] of two or more opponents," the examples for which include military struggles.

motivated this tribal rivalry, says Curtius, was the desire of each tribe to prove the excellence of their unique "particularity" (*Eigenthumlichkeit*), that is, their collective idiosyncrasy, as expressed in their "constitution, art, and customs." The chief means by which they sought to demonstrate their superiority was by *annihilating* their rivals (though as Curtius points out, this would negate the very grounds of the victorious tribe's particularity, since it was defined through its opposition to that of the eliminated tribe).[12] Never in history, asserts Curtius, has any "contest of forces [*Wetteifer der Kräfte*] unfolded so much energy" as in ancient Greece, in this all-out tribal contention (5–7).

Curtius goes on to recount how the later Hellenes subsequently used religion to engineer a stabler, institutionalized form of agon, or what he calls the "regulated contest" (*regelmäßige Wettkampf*). It is this regulated mode of contest that Curtius wishes to cultivate in German educational institutions. He argues that encouraging spiritual competition (*geistigen Wettkampf*) in this way would likely have a tonic effect on academic practice (19ff.). Although Curtius unequivocally favors this bounded species of *Wettkampf*, his wider use of the concept nevertheless encompasses *all* forms of struggle driven by the desire for contest and victory.

Jakob Burckhardt, by stark contrast, eschews Curtius's use of the term, opting instead to completely dissociate the notion of agon from martial conflict. In his view, the Greek agon only emerges with the passing of "the heroic age" of warfare. Only *then* is a new form of victory instituted – one sharply distinguished from the kind of victory realized in the destruction of one's adversary. He describes this novel, "agonal" species of victory as "the noble victory without enmity [. . .], the peaceful victory of an individuality" (GK, 8.89). His account in GK traces the birth of the agon back to a burgeoning of the aristocracy, which, thanks to its slaves, enjoyed the time and wealth needed to engage in this new form of contest. The "purpose of life and ideal" of these aristocrats was "struggle [*Kampf*], *but less war than contest among equals* [*weniger der Krieg als der Wettkampf unter Gleichen*]" (GK 8.118, emphasis mine).

Like Curtius, Burckhardt accents the way in which the cultural brilliance of the ancient Greeks was a function of their agonally competitive spirit. He conceives the agon as a "universal ferment" (*allgemeines Gärungselement*) – one that, under conditions of social freedom, acted on "every desire and ability" (GK 8.84). From this alone, we can see that

---

[12] N.B. Burckhardt puts forward a similar view, see Chapter 1 (fn.18), above.

Burckhardt takes "agon" to be conceptually distinct from "war" – in his view, the respective notions refer to mutually exclusive states of conflictual affairs (even if both are similarly motivated by a desire for victory).[13] To fully articulate this division, Burckhardt invokes Hesiod's characterization of the two Eris goddesses, or goddesses of strife:

> In Hesiod we find the lore of the agon as it manifests itself in civic and rural life, i.e., a kind of competition [*Konkurrenz*] that is only a parallel to the aristocratic and ideal agon. This is associated with his doctrine of the evil [*bösen*] and the good [*guten*] Eris, of which we read at the beginning of *Works and Days*. The latter was the first to be born (while the evil Eris would be only a degeneration [*Ausartung*] into war and strife [*Krieg und Streit*]), and Hesiod seems to find her not only in human life but also in elemental Nature, for Cronos had placed her among the very roots of the earth. It is the good Eris who awakens even the indolent and unskilled to industry; seeing others rich, they too bestir themselves to plough and plant and order their houses, so that neighbor vies [*eifert*] with neighbor in striving for wealth [*Reichtum*]. (GK 8.89)

Burckhardt appears to concur with Hesiod's separation of war and *Wettkampf*, and his corresponding association of each with a distinct Eris deity. The good Eris symbolizes competition (*Konkurrenz*, *Agon*), and manifests herself in *productive* activity (i.e., plowing, planting and ordering one's house); conversely, the evil Eris manifests herself in the *destructive* activity of war and violent strife.

In his analysis, however, Burckhardt does not draw an absolutely clear-cut line between *Wettkampf* and mortal combat. For instance, he acknowledges the often-fatal consequences of the official agon, particularly the pankration – a no-holds-barred contest that combined boxing and wrestling, and which was unchecked by rules except those prohibiting biting and eye-gouging. In such fights, people often lost teeth, fingers were broken, and "on account of choking, appalling blows to the abdomen, etc., fatalities were not uncommon" (GK 8.98–99).[14] Thus, although intentionally killing one's opponent was officially proscribed, fatalities were nonetheless tolerated as par for the course.

It should also be observed that in Burckhardt's citation of Hesiod, while the twin godheads are depicted as mutually exclusive in *conceptual* terms,

---

[13] Though Burckhardt only distinguishes "Wettkampf *unter Gleichen*" from "Krieg," we find that, unlike Curtius, he generally refrains from using the term *Wettkampf* (or *Agon*) to refer to martial conflict.

[14] Burckhardt also writes that artistic contests often descended into frenzied chaos, with spectators frequently murdering one or more of the contestants (GK 8.113). He also recounts how the crippling weight of envy, animosity and the shame of defeat drove some competitors to suicide (GK 8.103–104).

the two species of conflict that they respectively symbolize are nonetheless figured as standing in *genetic* relation to one another. Yet Burckhardt formulates this relation in a manner quite distinct to that of Curtius, who conceived war as originary, and the "regulated contest" as emerging only later, by dint of human artifice. For Burckhardt's Hesiod, though, this relation is inverted, and it is the *good* Eris who is the "first to be born"; the evil Eris (i.e., "war and strife"), by contrast, is the subsequent result of human degeneration (*Ausartung*). So, although Burckhardt takes the Greek agonal age to be *historically* posterior to the belligerent heroic age, his interpretation of Hesiod implies that the agonal impulse is ultimately *genetically* prior to the impulse for war. We should now determine where Nietzsche sits in this debate.

2.1.2   The Early Nietzsche (1869–1880)

To be sure, on occasion Nietzsche can be found to use the term *Wettkampf* to signify unmeasured physical conflict – specifically, the seething life-and-death struggle that pervades nature, as described by Schopenhauer, Hobbes and Darwin. For example, in an early *Nachlaß* note, he refers to the Schopenhauerian will as "death-dealing [*tödtend*] (in nature, in the contest [*Wettkampf*] of the weaker and the stronger)" (KSA 7:21[15], 527).[15] There are then further texts that appear to support the idea that Nietzsche's agonism is compatible with warmongery. For instance, in the opening paragraphs of HC, he marvels at how the Greeks – widely considered to be "the most humane humans of all time" – could have been so violent and cruel, and have taken such pleasure in the horrors depicted in the *Iliad*. Further, he denounces our "emasculated concept of modern humanity," and our corresponding inability to conceive these aspects of Greek culture as anything but an aberration. Indeed, in HC it is against the backdrop of this failing that Nietzsche endeavors to recuperate a vision of humanity compatible with such apparently savage tendencies (HC, KSA 1.783).

   This desire to acknowledge *Vernichtungskampf* as an intrinsic part of our humanity certainly recalls the affirmation of war and its artistic representation that we encountered in GSt. As we saw in the previous chapter, in GSt he applauds ancient Greek warmongery, as depicted in the *Iliad*, as the ultimate foundation of Greek society and culture (KSA 1.771). But does this warrant reading GSt and HC as conceptually continuous with one

---

[15]   In his lecture notes, Nietzsche, recalling Burckhardt, writes that contestants' lives were often at stake in ancient Greek contest (HGL III, KGW II/5, 290).

another? And can we define Nietzsche's agonism in such expansive terms? The previous chapter already gestured toward the fact that we must answer both of these questions in the negative; however, we now ought to seek a more comprehensive explanation as to why this must necessarily be the case.

Let us begin by scrutinizing Nietzsche's statements regarding violence in the opening paragraphs of HC. Casting his eye back to pre-Homeric Greece, he describes a savage world of unrelenting, violent strife – one in which "the cruelty of victory is the pinnacle of life's jubilation." Note that this roughly maps onto Burckhardt's description of the belligerent "heroic age." During this ferocious epoch, it was deemed just, "according to the *rights* of war [*Krieges*]," to enslave or put to death the inhabitants of a conquered city. This vicious, Calliclean world was one devoid of meas- ure, a world in which justice denoted nothing more than the will of the heroically mighty. And in his endeavor to expose the violent roots of Greek civilization, he reiterates the claim that we found in GSt that Greek culture was born of murderous strife: "just as, in truth, the concept of Greek law developed out of *murder* and atonement for murder, finer culture, too, takes its first victor's wreath from the altar of atonement for murder" (HC, KSA 1.785).

According to Nietzsche, the horror inherent in any violent epoch has certain ramifications for the spiritual *Weltanschauung* of those forced to endure such times. Individuals subjected to unremittingly baleful conditions of this sort often come to equate life with suffering and punishment. The ubiquitous violence of the pre-Homeric, heroic age thus tends to generate a pessimistic outlook, what Nietzsche refers to as a "disgust with existence" (HC, KSA 1.785). This form of pessimism is exemplified, he claims, in ancient Greek Orphism (though Nietzsche's turn of phrase strongly implies that he also has the post-Homeric philosophies of Anaximander and Schopenhauer at the forefront of his mind).[16]

But this is not the only possible spiritual response to such a world. The Greek genius, Nietzsche tells us, formulates a quite contrary answer to the question "What does a life of combat [*Kampfes*] and victory want?" Rather than deeming life-*denial* the appropriate response to the horrifying char- acter of existence, "the Greek genius acknowledged the once so terribly present drive, and regarded it as *justified*" (HC, KSA 1.785–786). Crucially, the drive (*Trieb*) that the genius acknowledges is the drive for "struggle and

---

[16] For an overview of Nietzsche's interpretation of Anaximander and Schopenhauer, see Introduction.

the pleasure of victory," what in WS 226 he refers to as "the desire for victory and pre-eminence." If we look to the *Iliad*, we find this impulse typified in Achilles' desire "[e]ver to excel, to do better than others" (Homer 2008, VI, l.208). What Nietzsche is suggesting is that in evaluating the heroic world, the genius places the accent on the supreme joy of victory. In so doing, the genius dispels the pessimist's dispiriting fixation on the prevalence of crushing defeat, subjugation, slavery, war and murder.

In speaking of the Greek "genius," Nietzsche is ostensibly referring to Homer, or at least some form of archetypal Greek spirit epitomized by Homer. Certainly, Nietzsche believed Homer to have ingeniously aestheticized brutal war in such a way as to render it at least tolerable, if not actually affirmable.[17] Homer's deceptive portrait of the heroic world makes it appear "lighter, gentler, warmer, its people, in this warm multicolored light, better and more likeable" (HC, KSA 1.784). Nietzsche also describes the figure of "the poet" (*der Dichter*) as he who overcomes the brutal "struggle for existence insofar as he idealizes it into a free contest [*freien Wettkampfe*]" (KSA 7:16[15], 398). Nietzsche is nevertheless remarkably reticent when it comes to expounding how Homer concretely contributed to the advent of the Greek agonal age. After all, as Nietzsche would have undoubtedly been aware, agonal games are depicted in both the *Iliad* and the *Odyssey*, which clearly indicates that the agon predated Homer.[18]

If we read HC in conjunction with BT, we can begin to see why Nietzsche might think that Homer enabled the proliferation of nondestructive modes of contest. In BT 15 he speaks of how a life of relentless violence engenders a socially widespread condition of suicidal melancholy, which he terms "practical pessimism." People simply cannot bear to go on living given the burdensome prevalence of war. However, he adds, this defeatist sentiment only arose "where art, in some form or another, did not appear as a remedy and defense against that blight" (BT 15, KSA 1.100). Homeric art offered people solace, and thereby protected them from the specter of despondency. In painting the atrocities of the heroic age in such a beautifying light, Homer enabled the Greeks to

---

[17] There are a number of potential reasons why Nietzsche refrains from explicitly designating Homer as his aestheticizing genius. First, he no doubt also wants to connote Heraclitus, who similarly fits the description of one who affirms the justice inherent to a life of conflict. Second, Nietzsche may be invoking a more embracing notion of *Genius* – namely, as the "spirit" of a group or community (a use that we find in GS 354 for example).

[18] See, for example, the funeral games held in memory of Patroclus in Book 23 of the *Iliad*, and the games played by the Phaeacians in Book 8 of the *Odyssey*. See Homer (1975).

affirm a life of action – indeed, we might go further, and infer that for Nietzsche, what Homer enabled was a life suffused with specifically *agonal* modes of action.[19]

What we can conclude from the above is that Nietzsche's praise of the *Iliad* in HC is not to be confounded with praise of its *content* (i.e., war and violence). He is rather admiring the beautiful *form* that Homer brings to this content – he thus applauds the *Iliad* as an "artistic play [*Spiel*] and imitation" of the heroic world of war. And he further intimates that this ingeniously transfigured reflection is "a precondition of the contest [*Wettkampfes*]" (KSA 7:16[26], 404); but note that it is at most merely a *precondition* (*Voraussetzung*) of *Wettkampf*, and not *Wettkampf* itself. Consequently, Nietzsche's celebration of the *Iliad* in HC should not be interpreted as an affirmation of violent struggle (as it is in GSt).

From this it should already be plain that the genius does not affirm and embrace conflict and the pleasure of victory *tout court*, as the destructive interpretation of the Nietzschean agon would have us believe. On the contrary, Nietzsche acclaims how, in recognizing the drive for conflict and victory, the genius enabled the Greeks to *transfigure* its destructive content, to fashion ways of satisfying this drive without engaging in war and murderous violence. As we discovered in Chapter 1, this process of channeling energy away from socially pernicious forms of antagonism represents the essence of the *Wettkampf*, which functions as a nondestructive means of achieving the underlying end previously sought in war (namely, triumph).

Following Burckhardt's lead, Nietzsche likewise invokes Hesiod's theogony of Eris in order to illustrate the way in which *Wettkampf* is *conceptually* distinct from struggles of annihilation but nonetheless *genetically* related thereto. Yet, as the following passage illustrates, his figuration of the good–evil Eris dyad departs from that of Burckhardt in some key respects.

> One should praise the one Eris as much as blame the other, if one has any sense; because the two goddesses have quite separate dispositions. One promotes wicked war and feuding [*Krieg und Hader*], the cruel thing! [. . .] Black Night gave birth to this one as the older of the two; but Zeus, who reigns on high, placed the other on the roots of the earth and amongst men as a much better one. She drives even the unskilled man to work; and if someone who lacks property sees someone else who is rich, he likewise hurries off to

---

[19] See also KSA 8:11[20], 205–206 and KSA 8:5[165], 86–87. Acampora (2013, 51) elaborates this line of interpretation.

sow and plant and set his house in order; neighbor competes [*wetteifert*] with neighbor for prosperity [*Wohlstande*]. This Eris is good for men. Even potters harbor grudges against potters, carpenters against carpenters, beggars envy beggars and minstrels envy minstrels. (HC, KSA 1.786)

Nietzsche thus follows Burckhardt in sharply discriminating between the species of conflict respectively symbolized by the good and evil Eris siblings. He associates the latter with "hostile struggle[s] of annihilation" (*feindseligen Vernichtungskampfe*) – that is, with the "murder," "war," "strife" and "wanton cruelty" that characterized pre-Homeric ancient Greece. By contrast, the good Eris, "as jealousy, grudge and envy, goads men to action, not, however, the action of the struggle of annihilation [*Vernichtungskampfe*] but the action of the *contest* [*Wettkampfe*]" (HC, KSA 1.787).[20] In this way, Nietzsche draws an exclusive conceptual line between *Vernichtungskampf* (falling under the banner of the evil Eris) and *Wettkampf* (falling under the banner of the good Eris).

But how does this terminological distinction cash out in practical terms? And *why* does Nietzsche endorse *Wettkampf* as "good"? In short, because the good Eris elicits egoistic emotions – such as envy and ambition – which propel individuals to engage in personally and socioculturally *constructive* modes of praxis (KSA 9:11[303], 557). These emotions spur people to pursue excellence in the hope of positively outdoing their adversaries. In Nietzsche's view, the synchronic, community-wide push for individual self-cultivation issues in widespread collective flourishing. Yet, as he further notes, "the kernel of the idea of the Hellenic contest" does not merely consist in the mutual stimulation that contestants elicit in one another – rather, this kernel additionally comprises the mutual *moderation* that emerges when these contestants "reciprocally hold one another within measured bounds [*der Grenze des Maaßes*]" (HC, KSA 1.789). As a result, the ambition of each agonal individual is kept within socially productive limits, and they are prevented from growing excessively dominant and thereby stifling the contest. The evil Eris is in contrast distinctly *unmeasured* (*grenzenlos*). She promotes socially detrimental modes of action, driving individuals to sabotage or eliminate their opponents in their pursuit of victory.[21]

---

[20] See also KSA 7:16[19], 400: "The Hesiodic Eris is commonly misunderstood: that which drives people to war and strife, the evil; that which drives them to the ambitious deed, the good." On the good–evil Eris distinction, see also KSA 7:16[19], 400; KSA 7:16[26], 404; SGT 1, KSA 1.545; D 38; HH 170; WS 29.

[21] See WS 29, where Nietzsche distinguishes good and evil Eris in terms of the way in which individuals attempt to equal their opponents – that is, whether they try to do so by pulling their opponent *down* to their level (bad) or by raising themselves *up* to the level of their opponents (good). While this aphorism sets the goal as *equality* and not victory (as in HC), it nonetheless sheds important light on

Insofar as the agon promotes self-cultivation, Nietzsche takes it to be one of the fundaments of ancient Greek education; thus, he recounts how "Greek education decreed that every aptitude must unfold itself in struggle" (HC, KSA 1.787).[22] Chiming with both Curtius and Burckhardt, he further theorizes that the ancient Greeks' ethos of contest was the driving force behind their impressive cultural flourishing. Artists, for instance, impelled by their envy and ambition, tirelessly strained to outdo one another: "their entire art cannot be thought of without contest: the Hesiodic good Eris, ambition, gave their genius wings" (HH 170; see HC, KSA 1.790). Note that in trying to justify nondestructive, agonal contention, Nietzsche is invoking the very same cultural criterion that he employed in GSt to justify martial struggle.

Wettkampf is therefore presented as deeply *productive* in nature. Individuals are driven by reciprocal stimulation to compete and prove themselves predominant *at a given practice*, as opposed to through a direct clash of mortal force. As we established in the previous chapter, Nietzsche also underscores how this allows for the "measured discharge" (*mäßige Entladung*) of a range of aggressive, though not necessarily destructive, human affects (such as envy, ambition, jealousy, hatred and rage). Absent the agon, these would have to be discharged in violent and potentially seditious activity (KSA 8:5[146], 79; KSA 7:16[18], 399). Nietzsche's agon is therefore not, like Burckhardt's, "without enmity." It is rather suffused with a controlled species of animosity. Nietzsche further distinguishes himself from Burckhardt by conspicuously suppressing the often-fatal practical reality of agonal contest. He thereby presents us with a highly stylized vision of the ancient Greek agon, one that artificially amplifies the disjunctive conceptual relation of *Wettkampf* and *Vernichtungskampf.*

If we simply focus on how Nietzsche discriminates between these two antithetical notions, however, we run the risk of glossing over what we identified above as the guiding purpose of HC – namely, to show how "[t]hose capacities of [man] which are terrible and are viewed as inhuman are perhaps, indeed, the fertile soil from which alone all humanity, in feelings, deeds and works, can grow forth" (HC, KSA 1.783). We might reformulate this by saying that Nietzsche, again following the example of Burckhardt, seeks to underscore the *genetic* relation of *Wettkampf* to *Vernichtungskampf*. Though he indexes the distinct parentage of the two Eris goddesses – with one being born of "the black night," and the other

the way in which Nietzsche conceives the opposed dynamics of *Wettkampf* and *Vernichtungskampf*. See also D 369.
[22] See also KSA 7:16[4], 394; KSA 7:16[14], 397.

being engendered by Zeus – he echoes Burckhardt in suggesting that the two forms of conflict that they respectively personify stand in genetic relation to one another. According to Burckhardt, as in the proem to Hesiod's *Works and Days*, we saw that it was the *good* Eris who was born first, with the *Vernichtungskampf* emerging from the degeneration of *Wettkampf*. Nietzsche, though, curiously inverts the order of derivation, designating the evil Eris "the older of the two." But this raises the question as to why he would make such a radical interpretive move.

In the first place, Nietzsche's motivation appears to be purely philological. Note that in the proem of *Works and Days* itself, the good Eris *is* said to be genetically prior, and Nietzsche's translation is, strictly speaking, simply incorrect.[23] But he may think such creative translation is warranted given that he considers the very idea of the good Eris to be the illegitimate interpolation "of a Hesiodic rhapsode." Indeed, the sole textual basis for the notion of a good Eris is the proem to *Works and Days*, a text that Nietzsche considers to be unambiguously apocryphal. In his view, the aforementioned rhapsode fabricated the good Eris in order to "justify" "competition [*Wettstreit*] among poets" (which Hesiod's text would otherwise not sanction). Nietzsche thinks that we need to go to *Theogony* if we want Hesiod's true position, which in Nietzsche's view is that "the evil Eris is [. . .] ancient [*uralt*]" (KGW II/2, 360–361).[24] In modifying the proem to *Works and Days*, it is therefore likely that Nietzsche thought of himself as making a philological amendment, thereby bringing the spurious text closer to what he considered to be Hesiod's true stance.

This said, Nietzsche's reasons for inverting the order of birth given in the proem to *Works and Days* are probably chiefly philosophical in kind. We should bear in mind his vested interest in locating the origin of man in a gruesome world devoid of measure. This would enable him to argue that brutal measurelessness constitutes an inextricable part of our ancestry and inheritance. Cruelty and excess are not foibles of a wicked minority whose originally "good" natures have been contingently corrupted by society (as Burckhardt's Hesiod, much like Rousseau, would have it). Violent dispositions lie at the very heart of all that we vaunt as human. What gave the

---

[23] See Hesiod (2006b, 87–88 [ll.11–26]): "For the one [Eris] fosters evil war and conflict – cruel one, / no mortal loves that one, but it is by necessity that they honor / the oppressive Strife, by the plans of the immortals. But / the other one gloomy Night bore first; and Cronus' high-throned / son, who dwells in the aether, set it in the roots of / the earth, and it is much better for men."

[24] However, what *Theogony* actually states is merely that "Deadly Night [. . .] bore hard-hearted Eris" (Hesiod 2006a, 20–21 [ll.23–25]; modified translation).

ancient Greeks their extraordinary cultural fertility was their ability to avail themselves of their natural impulses, putting them to socially beneficial ends, what Nietzsche calls "the application of that which is harmful to that which is useful" (KSA 7:16[18], 399).[25] But this transformative exploitation of our primitive nature presupposes that we recognize these dark impulses and acknowledge their intrinsic place within our conception of humanity. Little wonder, then, that Nietzsche considers modern man's attempt to hew his natural, animalistic urges from his notion of humanity to have had such a debilitating effect.

This account of the genetic relation of *Wettkampf* and *Vernichtungskampf* reveals that in Nietzsche's eyes the two concepts share certain qualities in common. Both forms of conflict are driven by the desire for victory, and are associated with a similar cluster of aggressive affects. And yet they remain conceptually distinct. Each picks out a discrete set of human behaviors – chiefly distinguished in terms of the absence or presence of measure (i.e., restraint). Let us now examine how Nietzsche maintains this view in the later phases of his philosophy.

2.1.3   The Later Nietzsche (1881–1889)

As we enter the 1880s, explicit discussion of agonal conflict (*Wettkampf*) conspicuously wanes, almost to the point of complete disappearance. Nonetheless, close inspection of the later Nietzsche's sparse account of agonal conflict reveals that he upholds the nondestructive definition that we identified in his earlier writings. For instance, in a note from 1881 he tells us that

> Greek lawgivers promoted the agon in order to divert the thought of contest [*den Wettkampfgedanken*] away from the *state* and achieve political calm. [...] Contemplation regarding the state was supposed to be diverted through agonal agitation – indeed, one was supposed to engage in gymnastics and poetry. This had the side-effect of making the citizens strong, beautiful and decent. (KSA 9:11[186], 514)[26]

Here the agon is associated with "political calm" and engaging in "gymnastics and poetry." Further, it is plainly distinguished from civil war, though Nietzsche once again postulates that it draws on the same well of energy as destructive conflict, channeling potentially detrimental impulses into socially beneficial praxis, making the citizens "strong, beautiful and decent."

---

[25] See also AOM 220; KSA 9:11[186], 514.   [26] See also WS 226.

The disjunctive conceptual relation between the later Nietzschean agon and mortal forms of combat is evinced by a number of further texts. For example, in 1883 he describes the agonal feeling (*das agonale Gefühl*) as that which "desires to triumph before an audience and must make itself intelligible to this audience" (KSA 10:8[15], 339). This implies that his understanding of agon is closely related to the markedly nonviolent poetic or dramaturgical Greek contest, for it is only in such contests that one needs to make oneself "intelligible" to one's audience.[27] And the following note shows that even while formulating his notion of the world as will to power, he continues to conceptualize *Wettkampf* as an essentially measured form of interaction:

> The *free, moderate* [*Mässigen*] invented the *contest* [*Wettkampf*] as the ever-increasing refinement of that need to express power: through the contest *hubris* was prevented: which emerged as a result of the long dissatisfaction of the desire for power. (KSA 10:7[161], 295)

The agon represents a *refinement* (*Verfeinerung*) of the way in which individuals express their power.[28] Moreover, as he indicates earlier in the same note, agonal conflict is defined by *Aidos* – "a kind of *disgust* at the *injury* of honorable individuals." Pivotally, in this account it is *measure* (*Maß*) that distinguishes agonal conflict. Struggles in which one seeks to harm one's opponent are, by contrast, marked by "*excess* [*Übermaß*], in the joyful instinct for hubris" (ibid.).

In 1888, after a lengthy absence from his published writings, the agon suddenly makes a reappearance. Thus, in TI he writes of how the form of philosophical debate pioneered by Socrates and Plato constituted "a new form of *agon*" (TI Socrates 8), that is, "a further development and internalization of the ancient agonal gymnastics" (TI Skirmishes 23). Although Nietzsche in many ways construes this type of spiritualized agon as a decadent aberration, it is even further removed from struggles of annihilation than its physical counterparts in wrestling and gymnastics.

In TI Ancients 3, which we already touched upon in the previous chapter, Nietzsche rebukes the disempowering and sanitizing effect that ancient Greek philosophers tended to have on their surrounding culture; but what should be remarked is that throughout this critique, he maintains a clear *conceptual* distinction between agonal practices and violent conflict,

---

[27] See also D 175 where he distinguishes between personal contest (*persönliche Wettkampf*), which in his view dominated ancient Greek society, and war (*Krieg*), which dominated that of the ancient Romans. See also KSA 10:8[15], 339.

[28] See also GS 13.

while nonetheless accenting their *genetic* relation. Marveling at the "unbounded force" (*unbändige Gewalt*) with which the ancient Greeks ventilated their will to power, he writes the following:

> I saw all their institutions grow out of the preventative measures they took to protect each other against their inner *explosives*. [. . .] People needed to be strong: danger was close [. . .]. And even in their festivals and arts they only wanted to feel that they were in a position of *superiority*, to *show* that they were in a position of strength: these are ways of glorifying oneself and, at times, making oneself into an object of fear [. . .]. Philosophers really are the decadents of the Greek world, the counter-movement to the ancient, noble taste (– to the polis, the agonal instinct, the value of breeding, the authority of descent).

Nietzsche implies that agonal institutions were constructed in order to bound (*bändigen*) the otherwise destructive force of the will to power. Thus, he once again drives a conceptual wedge between measured agonal conflict – which he equates with the "festivals and arts" enjoyed by citizens living under conditions of infra-polis peace – from the unrestrained modes of belligerent conflict that inhered at the level of inter-polis relations.

But despite the conceptual disjunction that Nietzsche cuts between *Wettkampf* and *Vernichtungskampf*, he nonetheless postulates a strong connection between these two species of conflict. They are *both* expressions of the *one* will to power, and measured, agonal conflict is developed as an alternative to the often-deleterious effects of this impulse when left unchecked. Again, as in GM, Nietzsche is trying to show how the cultural strength of the ancient Greeks – particularly their art and (agonal) institutions – grew out of a need to locally restrain and moderate the otherwise "unbounded force" of the will to power, to transform the raw "agonal instinct" for discharge and overcoming into agonal conflict proper. In Nietzsche's view, the potency of ancient Greek culture lay in its ability to harness the productive potential of this tremendous force.

The conditions under which this transformation takes place will be expounded later in this chapter. For now, our objective has been to show that Nietzsche, unlike Curtius, persistently conceptualizes agonal struggle in *opposition* to struggles of annihilation – in other words, for Nietzsche, the two types of conflict are mutually exclusive. And yet, both the early and later Nietzsche consistently posit a *genealogical* link between *Wettkampf* and *Vernichtungskampf*. In reading Nietzsche's praise of agon as an endorsement of physically destructive conflict, commentators therefore commit a genetic fallacy. That is to say, they confound the agon with its dark and violently unmeasured origins.

2.2   Democracy or Aristocracy? The Inclusivity of Nietzsche's Agon

Having determined that Nietzsche's endorsement of agon does indeed refer to a *measured* form of conflict – insofar as agonal contention is *categorically* nondestructive – we now need to establish the *scope* of this endorsement. The point in contention concerns the social inclusivity of his ideal agon. On the democratic side of the debate, Lawrence Hatab (1995, 120) argues that although the Nietzschean agon "eschews equal results and even equal capacity," it demands equality in the sense of equal *opportunity*. In political terms, this "agonistic openness" translates into the "open, fair opportunity for all citizens to participate in political contention."[29] For Hatab (2002, 140), the ideal Nietzschean agon is structurally democratic by virtue of such openness, and only aristocratic to the extent that it distinguishes between winners and losers, thereby "apportioning appropriate judgments of superiority and inferiority."[30] Elsewhere, Hatab construes this openness as the equal opportunity of citizens to compete for *political* power, where "losers must yield to, and live under, the policies of the winner" (1995, 63). The rationale informing this notion of "agonistic openness" is that excluding individuals from the contest betrays a cowardly and disempowering "flight from competition, a will to eliminate challenges" (122). On this reading, then, agonism requires that contestants are receptive to any would-be challenger, regardless of their social standing or capacity.

In the opposite camp are those who maintain that the Nietzschean agon is confined to a select "community of agonistic 'friends' founded by the *Übermensch*" (Conway 1997a, 29);[31] or an elite "aristocratic inner circle" (Appel 1999, 141). Fredrick Appel repudiates the democratic reading, which he dismisses as misleading and contrived. In its place he presents us with a picture of Nietzsche as a dyed-in-the-wool aristocrat. But what does "aristocracy" mean in this context? On the one hand, says Appel, it refers to a minority of individuals selected solely on the meritocratic basis of superior *capacity* – that is to say, not on account of birthright or wealth (140). On the other hand, Appel attributes a more conventional notion of aristocratism to Nietzsche, one that refers to the oppressive rule of a few higher

---

[29] See also Hatab (1995, 100, 220 and 121–122).
[30] See also Hatab (2002, 142). David Owen (1995, 144–146) comparably suggests that the Nietzschean democratic agon is aristocratic only insofar as it establishes a rank order of values (i.e., in designating what counts as excellence).
[31] See also Conway (1997a, 54).

individuals over an enslaved majority. Furthermore, he posits a line of
continuity running between HC and Nietzsche's later affirmation of
aristocratic power struggle. In his view, HC venerates the way in which
ancient Greek society forged "a constructive outlet for the potentially
destructive wills of competitors, thereby [. . .] fostering its high culture."
"Casting his eyes to the future," Appel continues, "Nietzsche wishes to
foster a space of contest and rivalry with a similar function. 'Who can
command, who can obey – *that is experimented here!*'" (140, quoting Z III
Tablets 25, KSA 4.265). Thus, much like Hatab, he understands the
Nietzschean agon as a mode of struggle in which the principal stake is
political power over one's adversaries. Yet, unlike Hatab, he proposes that,
beyond the confines of this aristocratic inner circle, Nietzsche maintains
that the majority of individuals ought to be reduced to a politically
excluded and murderously oppressed body of slaves (147).

   What then is the social scope of Nietzsche's agonism? This question can
be divided into two parts. First, does Nietzsche think that it is *possible* for
just anyone and everyone to participate in agonal conflict (or is such
conflict somehow elitist *by definition*)? Second, supposing the answer to
this question is affirmative, does he hold it to be *desirable* that every
member of society participate in open agonal conflict, or is Nietzsche's
endorsement limited to particular social subgroups? For reasons that will
become apparent, we should not take it for granted that Nietzsche's
descriptive and normative conceptions of agon have the same extension.

   In trying to glean an insight into the aristocratic dimension of Nietzsche's
agon, it behooves us to begin by dissecting Burckhardt's view in GK, which
relevantly draws a tight connection between the ancient Greek agon and the
noble social classes. Indeed, Martin Ruehl (2003, 78) has claimed that
Burckhardt is the primary source of Nietzsche's conception of agon "as an
essentially aristocratic notion that belonged to a pre-democratic age." But as
we will now discover, while Ruehl is correct to identify a line of influence here,
his aristocratic reading nevertheless unduly distorts Nietzsche's true position.

2.2.1   Burckhardt

According to Burckhardt, the driving force of the ancient Greek agon was
the aristocratic ideal of *kalokagathia*, "the unity of nobility [*Adel*], wealth
and excellence [*Trefflichkeit*]" (GK, 8.82). The agon, he tells us, initially
emerged as a cultural practice confined to the noble social classes. The
leisure time required for engaging in the ostensibly useless practice of
athletic and equestrian contest was largely a function of the surplus labor

generated by the *banausoi* (manual laborers) (ibid.). As such, the practice of agon emerged by virtue of the socioeconomic conditions of landed aristocracy. It should be emphasized, however, that Burckhardt does not think that agonal culture was possible within tyrannous societies (such as Sparta, for example). Tyrannies tended to be organized around purely utilitarian goals, and therefore proscribed the apparently extravagant practice of agonal contest, favoring work and military exercise instead (ibid.).

Notwithstanding these aristocratic fundaments, Burckhardt considers social inclusivity to have been a necessary precondition of the agon. Thus, he writes that "every native Greek could participate" in agonal contest, and points out that such inclusivity would have been impossible in caste-based societies – such as ancient Egypt for example. Higher-caste members of stratified societies were, generally speaking, averse to competing before those of lower social strata, and contests were usually fought before a king, whose political favor was offered as the victor's prize (GK, 8.85). Only in ancient Greece, which is to say, "only in free and small aristocracies could [the agonal] *will to distinction among one's equals*, before elected or otherwise objectively selected judges, come into bloom" (ibid.; emphasis mine). But the sort of aristocracy that Burckhardt has in mind is far from that of an *exclusively* hereditary nobility; indeed, he indexes the abundant social mobility that characterized this "agonal age" of ancient Greek history. For instance, lower-standing Hellenes could become aristocrats simply by migrating to one of ancient Greece's many burgeoning colonies (GK, 8.82).

Burckhardt goes on to recount how this agonal spirit spread beyond the boundaries of the aristocratic sphere, eventually becoming a ubiquitous feature of ancient Greek social life. "Whenever and wherever many Greeks gathered, agonal contests arose almost as a matter of course" (GK, 8.88): "We see it in the conversations and round-songs of the guests in the symposium, in philosophy and legal procedure, down to cock- and quail-fighting or gargantuan feats of eating" (GK, 8.86). Any free individual could, according to Burckhardt, participate in agonal contest. Even when it came to the official agonal games (such as were held at Delphi), anyone could, *de jure*, take part provided they had sufficient funds to cover their travel, bed and board and the required religious offerings (GK, 8.95). Naturally, due to these costs, the *de facto* rule was that institutional agonal games remained the privilege of wealthy aristocratic families. It is also worth noting that women, slaves and metics were in most cases officially debarred.[32]

---

[32] Burckhardt does, however, note that women were, in some instances, allowed to compete in the official agon (GK, 8.141–142).

In trying to determine the inclusivity of Burckhardt's conception of agonal conflict, it is important to remark that he took the widespread agon "in civic and rural life" to be "a kind of competition [*Konkurrenz*] that [was] *only a parallel to the aristocratic and ideal agon*" (GK, 8.89; emphasis mine). And yet, though it is the noble agon that he holds in the highest regard, this does not prevent him from endorsing the pervasive culture of agonal contest. Indeed, he emphatically praises the latter on account of the culturally leavening effect that it had on ancient Greek society (GK, 8.84).

But what did Burckhardt think was the end sought by those who engaged in agonal contest? In short, above all else, the goal of manifesting *excellence*, a value that shaped every facet of ancient Greek spiritual and physical life, as every member of society relentlessly endeavored to excel their peers (GK, 8.89). Whereas in WBe, Burckhardt contends that it was by means of military struggle that poleis measured themselves against one another, in GK he avers that it was agonal contest that fulfilled this vital function.[33] He further claims that the fundamental goal of the ancient Greek *Wettkampf* was "victory in itself," irrespective of any instrumental ends that might be served by such victory (GK, 8.100). This supposition is buttressed by the fact that prizes in the official agonal games were in themselves worthless. As Curtius (1864, 14) observes, the most common prizes – "the crown of leaves, the branch" – had "no value other than as symbols of victory." Expanding on this point, Burckhardt maintains that immortal glory was the ultimate goal sought in contest; hence, victory at Olympia "counted as the highest on earth, insofar as it guaranteed the victor that which was the ultimate aim of every Greek: to be admired in life, and glorified in death" (GK, 8.100). Though Burckhardt acknowledges that contestants often conceived victory as an indirect means of acquiring public influence, he in no measure conceives political power as the chief incentive for contest; nor does he imply that the aristocratic agon sorted victors and vanquished into political relations of command and obedience.[34]

Andreas Kalyvas (2009, 24) argues that what differentiates the classical age from the earlier, archaic age of ancient Greece is its *democratization* of the agon – in other words, in the classical age we bear witness to an

---

[33] On his position in WBe, see Chapter 1, fn.18 of this book.

[34] On political influence as an agonal incentive, see GK, 8.203. Here Burckhardt laments the fact that with the onset of the democratic age, "[v]ictories at Olympia and elsewhere no longer guaranteed the slightest influence in the polis, which was the general object." He thereby implies that political influence was indeed the desideratum sought in true agonal contest.

"encounter of the democratic logic of equality with the aristocratic spirit of excellence." Burckhardt would at least partially assent to Kalyvas's claim that within the classical polis, "the aristocratic spirit became increasingly detached from its social and material bases, as additional social groups were gradually forming and participating in their own multiple agonistic spheres." In this way, we might label the agon aristocratic, less by virtue of the social standing of its participants than on account of the ethos or set of values to which its participants subscribed – an ethos that was ultimately rooted in the aristocratic classes. But what is unique to Burckhardt's view is the contention that the ancient Greek agon depended on the *conservation* of these aristocratic roots.

Burckhardt theorizes that the emergence of the *artistic* contest initiated the deracination of the agon from its aristocratic native soil; indeed, this relatively novel type of contest heralded the demise of Burckhardt's ideal agon. Since the aesthetic agon did not require expensive equipment, nor even participation in the official games, anyone could participate given the requisite talent. As such, once the agon proliferated beyond athletics and horseracing, it became an entirely public affair. Even shepherds could now compete in their own unofficial singing competitions (GK, 8.114).[35] In particular, Burckhardt shines a light on the way that artistic contest enflamed a cult of *celebrity* (*Zelebrität*). This process, he claims, drew attention away from the victors of the primarily aristocratic, physical agon (GK, 8.150). Unlike Curtius (or Nietzsche, for that matter), Burckhardt grants the artistic agon scant attention, and the little he does have to say on the topic is for the most part disparaging, his unmistakable preference being for the physical, sporting agon.

Following the advent of the musical agon, both philosophical dialogues and judicial trials began to assume a discernibly contestatory character (GK, 8.114–115). For Burckhardt, this development triggered the disintegration of the genuine ancient Greek agon: As the practice of oral contest became more widespread, the now vocal and quarrelsome demos began to demand that its leaders pander to its every whim. This process of decline and debasement was then accelerated by Socrates, whom Burckhardt accuses of tenaciously working to undermine the notion of *kalokagathia*. By redefining the idea as a concern with the betterment of *all* individuals, and even the human race, Socrates separated the value of excellence from its elitist, aristocratic core. In Burckhardt's view, this sullied the exalted and once noble value of personal excellence, which consequently fell into serious disrepute

[35] Indeed, Burckhardt remarks upon the low social standing of many competing artists (GK, 8.129).

(GK, 8.206). As a result, agonal competition devolved into a base oral contest – one chiefly fixated on the vulgar end of establishing who could most effectively fawn to public caprice: "indeed the whole practice of democracy gradually became a *pseudo* agon [*unechter Agon*], in which scurrilous gossip, sycophancy etc. occupied the foreground" (GK, 8.203; emphasis mine).[36] For Burckhardt, then, once popularity supplanted the goal of noble excellence (*Edeltrefflichkeit*), the culturally dominant form of contest in ancient Greece no longer qualified as an authentic instance of agonal competition.

Within this new *pseudo* agon, overrun by celebrity demagogues, the conditioning element of *measure* or *restraint* disappeared: "The power of personality no longer showed itself [. . .] in great examples of competitive achievement, that is, in victory over one or several peers [*Ähnliche*], but absolutely" (GK, 8.204). Modesty no longer found a place in ancient Greek society, and individuals ceased to compete for transitory, agonal victory over their semblables. Instead, they began to pursue *absolute* victory, over *everyone* – otherwise put, they endeavored to establish themselves as *tyrants*. Needless to say, this had detrimental repercussions for the traditional, aristocratic agon. For Burckhardt, the superiority of the ancient Greeks was founded on their ability to measure themselves against their peers and exercise their will to distinction without resorting to violent means – all of which they achieved by virtue of their agonal ethos. Congruent with this, he remarks upon the rarity of inter-polis war during the agonal age (GK, 8.159). However, with the rise of arrogant celebrity-statesmen (which was exacerbated by victory in the first Persian War), and the associated wither-ing of the agon, the Greeks lost their nonviolent means of self-measurement. With this the seeds of the Peloponnesian War were sown, and the fate of the agonal age was sealed.[37]

Burckhardt's approbation for the aristocratic elements of genuine agon is therefore not to be confused with a restriction of agon to the landed, hereditary aristocracy. What he rather maintains is that the *sine qua non* of agonal conflict is the pursuit of the aristocratic value of excellence among one's equals. And he conceives this inclusive mode of agon to have been the fountainhead of ancient Greek brilliance – so long as it was prevented from degenerating into a clamorous jostle for democratic celebrity. Indeed, the value of excellence is, in his account, ultimately parasitic on the continued political hegemony of the nobility. Burckhardt's agon should therefore be

---

[36] See also GK, 8.183ff.

[37] See GK, 8.259: "Ambition and vanity were no longer satisfied by the proclamations and applause for agonal victors; there was a need for direct self-assertion outwards, against other poleis, other groups who were very easily provoked, and in extreme cases might have to be destroyed."

conceived as *dependent upon*, but *not limited to*, an aristocratic social stratum. And so we find ourselves presented with two species of agon: one that was socially inclusive, and general to Greek society, and another that was exclusive, and essentially aristocratic in nature, namely, the official sporting agon, which was *de facto* the preserve of the landed aristocracy. Crucially, the cultural fertility of the inclusive agon feeds off the vitality of its exclusive counterpart. Finally, though Burckhardt considers the society-wide diffusion of agonal conflict to be *possible*, he certainly does not endorse its manifestation within the political sphere. Having ascertained the defining features of Burckhardt's standpoint, we should now examine how this background bears upon Nietzsche's own distinctive view.

2.2.2   The Inclusivity of Nietzsche's Early Agonism

Among Nietzsche's preparatory notes for HC, we find a text which at first blow seems to support a strong aristocratic reading of the Nietzschean agon: "The contest [*Wettkampf*]! And that which is aristocratic [*Aristokratische*], hereditary [*Geburtsmäßige*], noble [*Edle*] for the Greeks" (KSA 7:16[9], 396). This fragment appears to show that Nietzsche's conception of agon is directly associated with hereditary (*geburtsmäßig*) aristocracy. Against this supposition, however, we are now going to see that what Nietzsche, much like Burckhardt, likely has in mind here is the *origins* and structuring values of the agon, not its social inclusivity.

The text that most readily lends itself to a socially inclusive reading of Nietzsche's agonism is HC, in which he affirmatively invokes "Hesiod's" (or rather, the Hesiodic rhapsode's) commercial, agrarian and generally banausic conception of the *Wettkampf*. This in itself implies that he concurs with Burckhardt regarding the idea of a community-wide agon. Henning Ottmann, however, pertinently rejects this line of interpretation. He contends that although Nietzsche's reference to the proem of *Works and Days* may very well reveal that he thinks agon *possible* in a wider socially inclusive sense, he cannot be said to *sanction* such an expansive conception of the practice. What Nietzsche vaunts, claims Ottmann (1999, 50), is "the glory of the state, education, culture. [. . .] The ethos that Nietzsche [seeks is] that of heroes, not workers or townsfolk." Ottmann theorizes that Nietzsche is implicitly *critical* of the inclusive, Hesiodic notion of agon; indeed, for Ottmann, the Nietzschean *Wettkampf* is in essence both Homeric *and* heroic. But does this heroic interpretation bear scrutiny? Or does Nietzsche uphold the sharp distinction that we saw Burckhardt draw between the heroic and agonal ages?

To be sure, we find numerous texts in which the early Nietzsche openly rebukes the pursuit of material gain (*Geldgewinn*) as boorish and philistine, and hence generally antagonistic to the goal of cultural enrichment.[38] Yet Nietzsche is by no means necessarily contradicting himself in celebrating the inclusive, Hesiodic conception of the good Eris. What is affirmed in the proem to *Works and Days* is the idea of agonal contest as a struggle for *Wohlstand* (HC, KSA 1.786), a term that signifies prosperity, health and well-being (i.e., *Wohlfahrt* or *Wohlergehen*), none of which are reducible to material wealth.[39] Nietzsche, like Burckhardt, evidently considers this struggle for prosperity to be a manifestation of the general impetus to enhance oneself, and therefore as much more than a base struggle for monetary gain. What is more, he is perfectly at ease with categorizing this as a species of *Wettkampf* (without even making the qualification, which we find in Burckhardt, that it represents a mere "parallel" of the true, noble *Wettkampf*).[40]

So is Nietzsche's agon necessarily limited to "that which is aristocratic, hereditary, [and] noble" (as is suggested by the note with which we began this section)? In HC itself, one cannot help but remark that he has suppressed the adjectives "aristocratic" (*aristokratisch*) and "hereditary" (*geburtsmäßig*). It is only "noble" (*edle*) that remains. Thus, Nietzsche opens HC declaring that the subject matter of the piece will be the human "in his highest and most noble [*edelsten*] forces" (HC, KSA 1.783). He then closes HC with a description of the *Wettkampf* as the "most noble [*edelsten*] of Hellenic principles" (HC, KSA 1.792). But this is not to say that he believes that the ancient Greek agon was confined to the hereditary aristocracy. The NWB entry for "edel" reveals that although the term is bound up with noble social class, "(high) birth is not a *conditio sine qua non*" governing Nietzsche's use of the adjective. Rather, according to his usage, the term denotes adherence to a set of values that are typically *associated* with nobility, such as strength (*Stärke*), measure (*Maß*) and self-mastery (*Selbst-Beherrschung*) (NWB, 698).[41] His decision to use the term "noble" instead of "aristocratic" or "hereditary" strongly suggests a desire to

---

[38] See KSA 7:10[1], 346; GSt, KSA 1.774; FEI, KSA 1 1.667; SE 5, KSA 1.379; D 175; D 308.

[39] See DWB, entry for "Wohlstand."

[40] For an example of Nietzsche apparently sanctioning the agon of the *banausoi*, see KSA 7:16[8], 396. See also Strong (1988, 151): "In Nietzsche's reading, Hesiod [...] in his contest with Homer, manages to establish an agon that is purely human and no longer tied to the immortal gods. By emphasizing the human nature of the *agon*, Hesiod opens the contest up to potentially much richer variations." Müller (2020, 95) and Jensen (2008, 328) also advance socially inclusive interpretations of Nietzsche's early agonism.

[41] See also entry for "Adel" (NWB 42): "nobility [*Adel*] is characterized by psychological features and habits, just as much as by social position."

link the *Wettkampf* to certain values *originating* in the ancient Greek aristocracy, but without implying that participation in the *Wettkampf* was limited to
the nobility.

Further disproving the idea that caste-pedigree represents an entry requirement of the Nietzschean agon, we see that Nietzsche, like Burckhardt,
only emphasizes *equality* as a necessary condition of *Wettkampf*, but says
suggestively little about the social standing of his ideal agonal adversaries.
Thus, already in ST, he submits that "as soon as two equally qualified
leading actors stand opposed to one another, there arises, in accordance
with a deeply Hellenic drive, contest [*der Wettkampf*]" (KSA 1.545).
Coherent with this, in Nietzsche's citation of *Works and Days* in HC,
the listed agonal adversaries are defined by a symmetry of *métiers* ("potters
harbor grudges against potters," etc.). And if we look forward to WS 29, the
condition of *equality* (*Gleichheit*) is postulated as a prerequisite of the envy
that elicits *Eris* (and, by the same token, agon). Resounding with
Burckhardt, in WS 226 Nietzsche further remarks how this requirement
of equality was reflected in the institutional Greek agon: "the Greek state,"
he writes, "sanctioned the gymnastic and musical contest [*Wettkampf*]
between equals [*innerhalb Gleichen*]." Texts such as these imply that for
Nietzsche *Wettkampf* can take place between *any* individuals of approximately
equal ability, irrespective of their social caste.

Before we rest satisfied with this conclusion, however, we ought to
consider Hannah Arendt's (1958, 41) observation that equality had a far
narrower meaning in antiquity than it does now: "To belong to the few
'equals' (*homoioi*) meant to be permitted to live among one's peers," in the
"public realm itself, the *polis*, [which] was permeated by a fiercely agonal
spirit." On Arendt's reading, it was but a minority of individuals in the
Greek polis who enjoyed the status of "equals," and who were therefore
able to participate in the public struggle for victory and predominance.
Perhaps, then, Nietzsche's conception of agonal equality is restricted to the
highest echelons of ancient Greek society – namely, that of *citizens*, the
elite minority allowed to engage in the public sphere of action.

Nietzsche, though, cannot be said to share Arendt's views. For one, his
citation in HC of the proem to *Works and Days* indicates that even beggars
could engage in agonal competition (among themselves that is). And in
HGL, he intimates that in ancient Greece, agonal conflict (here referred to
as *Wetteifer*) was a relation reserved for equals of *any* caste:

> The Greeks communicate with their gods *as a lower caste with a higher,*
> *nobler and more powerful caste* [. . .]. One lived together with them and did

everything one could to make this co-existence beneficial to oneself: the usual means being to love what they love, hate what they hate, *but never to enter into competition [Wetteifer] with them* [. . .]. (HGL III, KGW II/5, 519; emphasis mine)

We should read this in conjunction with a related note, in which Nietzsche maintains that among themselves, the Greek gods enjoyed agonal relations. He thus describes the Trojan War as "a competition [*Wettspiel*] of the Hellenic gods" (KSA 7:2[6], 46). Taken together, these two texts suggest that Nietzsche actively refrains from positing aristocratic social class as a precondition of engaging in nobly measured, agonal conflict. Both humans and the pantheon of gods could engage in agonal struggle *within the bounds of their distinct groups*.

This emphasis on caste would appear to set Nietzsche apart from Burckhardt, since the latter expressly states that the emergence of the Hellenic agon depended upon the partial effacement of the boundaries that divided social strata. But as we turn away from the relation of the ancient Greeks to their gods, and toward the specifically human agon, it becomes increasingly doubtful whether Nietzsche considers equality of social class as a condition of *Wettkampf.* Like Burckhardt, he differentiates between the Greeks and the caste-based societies of the "Orientals"; moreover, he claims that Greek educational institutions – which, as we saw above, he takes to be agonal in kind – were concerned with *individuals* rather than castes: "Oriental peoples have *castes*. Institutions such as schools [. . .] do not serve classes, but rather the individual" (KSA 7:16[26], 404). Lastly, the fact that Nietzsche considers the political tête-à-tête of Themistocles (of low birth) and Aristides (of aristocratic lineage) to be a *Wettkampf* indicates that he had no qualms about categorizing conflicts between individuals of different castes as agonal in kind.[42] It is therefore likely that the sort of equality that characterizes the Nietzschean agon is an approximate equality of *ability*, and that we should read his reference to castes in HGL as a metaphor for the different "leagues" of contenders that stratify any domain of competitive practice. And yet, if we look deeper, we find that parallel to this socially inclusive view, he none-theless also espouses a socially *exclusive* species of agonism.

2.2.2.1   *The Aristocratic Values of Nietzsche's Early Agonism*
The early Nietzsche conceives agonal contest as being motivated by three aristocratic values: ascendancy (i.e., excellence), glory (*Ruhm*) and

---

[42] See KSA 7:16[35], 406.

education (*Erziehung, Bildung*). In the previous section, we analyzed his thesis that the agonal impulse for the first of these three values – ascendancy – can be generalized across society. But we should now consider how the latter two values – glory and education – are, in spite of what was established in the previous section, inextricable from a socially *exclusive* conception of agon. On Nietzsche's account, the pursuit of these values simply cannot be diffused across society in the same manner as the impulse for ascendancy.

Before we commence, however, it is worth noting that Nietzsche does not figure political power as a fundamental agonal value (*pace* his radical aristocrat and agonistic readers alike); and hence, although we are going to see him develop an elitist model of agonal contest, we should take care not to misconstrue this as *politically* aristocratic. There are two ways in which we might conceive agonal conflict in terms of a struggle for political power; first, we might take such contention to be a *direct* struggle for power, one that takes place within expressly political fora (such as a parliament, for example); second, as Burckhardt (and Curtius) suggest, agon might also take the form of an *indirect* struggle for political power – that is, one fought within nonpolitical arenas, where success yields a certain degree of political honor and influence for the victor.[43]

There is, to be sure, some indication that Nietzsche understood direct political contention as an instance of *Wettkampf*; for example, where he describes the "struggle [*Ringen*] of political parties and states with one another" as a manifestation of the omnipresent Hellenic "thought of contest [*Wettkampfgedanke*]" (PTAG 5, KSA 1.825); and in HC itself, he refers to Themistocles' "long rivalry [*Wetteifer*] with Aristides" and his "remarkable purely instinctive genius for political action" (HC, KSA 1.788). And in HC, Nietzsche further describes how the Greeks practiced ostracism in order to safeguard political *Wettkampf*: in exiling overly ambitious "politicians and party leaders," they prevented those individuals from resorting to violent means (HC, KSA 1.788–789). And in HGL he recounts how poets *indirectly* vied to "carry out their (political) plans" – namely, by means of achieving victory in artistic agonal contest (HGL III, KGW II/5, 292).

Bar these sparse and oblique references to political agons, however, the idea of the *Wettkampf* as a struggle for political power (be it direct or indirect) is largely absent from Nietzsche's early writings. But later in the

---

[43] See Curtius (1864, 9): "the individual state was also a palaestra of civic prowess, where power and honor were apportioned to those who proved themselves best."

1870s, Nietzsche breaks this near-silence regarding political agon; indeed, he now reveals himself to be openly hostile toward the idea. In WS 226, which was cited at length above, he conjectures that the agon was only promoted as a means of diverting the "desire for victory and pre-eminence" *away* from the political sphere, in order to minimize political strife and social unrest.[44] The institutional agon – the official games – thus circumscribed a space for the *apolitical* discharge of the drive for victory and ascendancy. The guiding idea underlying this thought, which recalls Burckhardt, is that political agon jeopardizes the body politic insofar as *Wettkampf* so easily decays into unmeasured, violent sedition (*stasis*).[45] So while Nietzsche admits that political agonism may be *possible*, it is simply too fraught with danger to be recommendable. We should also observe that the criterion that Nietzsche is using to distinguish between better and worse modes of agonism is the extent to which they foster or frustrate cohesive, cultural flourishing. All of this forcefully suggests that his ideal agon is embodied in *neither* democratic *nor* aristocratic struggles for political ascendancy. Harmonious with Burckhardt, Nietzsche is broadly disinclined toward the idea of political agon.[46] Yet, whereas Burckhardt prefers the physical, sporting agon over and against artistic modes of contest (which he largely neglects, and even maligns), Nietzsche distinctly favors the latter.[47]

In trying to unpack the guiding ends of the ideal agon, we should also consider Nietzsche's account of how the desire for power, or *influence*, motivated the artistic *Wettkampf*. In his view, competing artists sought to guide the behavior of others (particularly their opponents) not so much by exercising political command as by instituting their own aesthetic preferences as authoritative norms. They yearned to be imitated by their peers and sought to achieve this by means of agonal victory. Every Greek artist understood that "the example [*Vorbild*] of the great incites vainer natures

---

[44] However, see also KSA 8:5[179], 91, where Nietzsche maintains that the Greek state was actively hostile toward the artistic-cultural agon.

[45] On this conception of the agon as a means of channeling potentially seditious, disgregative energies into culturally productive modes of activity, see also KSA 8:5[146], 79; KSA 9:11[186], 514–515.

[46] Hence, we must reject Ottmann's thesis that what distinguishes Nietzsche from Burckhardt is that he "wants agonal culture, and he wants it *without exception*" (1999, 50).

[47] This is not to say that Nietzsche unswervingly esteems aesthetic contention. As Siemens (2015, 452) notes, in HGL "we read of the prevalence of degeneration in Greek art; of the stifling of talent at the hands of publics utterly incapable of sound aesthetic judgement ([HGL] III, KGW II/5, 322ff.); of the fear of innovation in art and the resistance to it through harsh repressive laws ([HGL] III, KGW II/5, 298); and how the agon repressed the emergence of individuals for a long time." In HGL III (KGW II/5, 290), Nietzsche also shows how the pursuit of public praise often caused the agon to degenerate into a farce of posturing and pretense.

to extreme imitation" (HH 158). As Nietzsche puts it in HGL, "it took power of personality to impose [...] innovations; if one did not triumph, one was punished; if one did triumph, one's innovation became the rule" (KGW II/2, 405). On some level, the Nietzschean agon therefore comprises a contest of norms, with individuals developing novel styles and striving to institute these as paradigms of excellent performance. Viewed from this standpoint, cultural contest is far more than a struggle to prevail according to some pregiven measure; rather, it further includes the endeavor to establish one's own standard as an accepted rule. This explains why Nietzsche holds that "only in competition [*Wetteifer*] did one come to know the Good" (KSA 8:23[132], 450). Indeed, by his lights, agonal contest constitutes a vital matrix for new values – one that continually generates novel guidelines for agency.[48]

But what is of particular interest with regard to our current inquiry is that Nietzsche does not think that anyone and everyone was welcome to participate in this struggle for cultural influence. His valorization of the aesthetic agon harbors an undeniably elitist streak. With an eye to bringing this streak into relief, we should examine the agonal value of glory (*Ruhm*), since it is precisely this value that marks out the forms of agon for which Nietzsche reserves his highest praise. Thus, he affirmatively recounts the jealous desire with which Plato and the ancient Greek poets sought to conquer Homer and "to step into the place of the overthrown poet and to inherit his glory [*Ruhm*]" (HC, KSA 1.789). Nietzsche also refers to this superior value in terms of honor (*Ehre*) (HH 170, HH 474), praise (*Lob*) and posthumous fame (*Nachruhm*). Regarding the latter two values, for example, he states the following:

> The poet overcomes the struggle for existence [*Kampf um's Dasein*] insofar as he idealizes it into a free contest [*Wettkampfe*]. Here existence, which is still being fought over, is existence in a state of praise [*Lob*], in posthumous glory [*Nachruhm*]. (KSA 7:16[15], 397)

We can extrapolate from this that the quest for glory is in Nietzsche's view incompatible with the struggle for existence, and, further, that his conception of the agon might be at odds with the banausic struggle to achieve predominance through the acquisition of property, wealth and even prosperity (i.e., *Wohlstand*). Certainly, there is ample evidence that he considers the authentic pursuit of glory to be limited to an elite, nonbanausic minority. For an apt example of this, we should turn to his unpublished essay "On the Pathos of Truth" (part of the same collection of essays as HC

---

[48] See also HH 170; KSA 7:16[6], 395; Tongeren (2002, 7).

and GSt). In this short piece he states that "glory [*Ruhm*] [. . .], as a desire, is linked to the rarest humans, and their rarest moments." The struggle for immortal fame is the preserve of these few superior individuals, who are only obstructed by "the habitual, the petty [and] the common." The majority merely "want to live – at any cost. Who among them would like to imagine the difficult torch relay, through which alone greatness lives on?" (KSA 1.756).

Evidently, the banausic struggle to excel one's neighbor by accumulating greater material wealth would not qualify as an instance of this higher form of *Wettkampf.* Nor do artists and poets represent Nietzsche's ideal pursuers of glory; rather "the most audacious knights among these glory-hungry individuals [. . .], must be sought among *philosophers*" (KSA 1.757).[49] In this quote, he associates glory (*Ruhm*) with a handful of noble, knightly (*ritterlich*) heroes – a chivalrous few devoted to the arduous quest for posthumous fame; yet at the same time, this discussion of knights is obviously figurative, insofar as it now refers to the pursuit of glory that takes place within the *cultural* realm, among an elite minority of philosophers.

Alongside this yen for glory, the value of cultivation (*Erziehung*) plays an equally leading role in distinguishing the highest Nietzschean agon from acquisitive banausic contest. This fundamental value is defined by the pursuit of excellence understood not simply as "being first" but as a process directed at the cultivation of one's highest capacities. He describes how the ancient Greeks interwove the practice of agon with a drive for self-enhancement, how they demanded that "every talent unfold itself in struggle" (HC, KSA 1.789); or again, how the envious sight of others' excellence spurred individuals to better themselves – and thus how "every great virtue sparks a new greatness" (HC, KSA 1.788). What is more, this state of affairs was by no means confined to the student population, since their "educators were in their turn in rivalry with one another" (HC, KSA 1.790).[50] According to Nietzsche, the Hellenic drive for agon was therefore melded with the value of self-cultivation – that is, over and against base values such as wealth and Arcadian bliss. Consistent with this view, he approvingly reiterates Schopenhauer's pessimistic conviction that "excellent and noble people [. . .] see that in the world there is instruction [*Belehrung*], but not happiness to be found" (KSA 8:6[31], 110). However, Nietzsche complains that on

---

[49] See also KSA 7:19[170], 471: "Philosophers are the noblest class of the great of spirit. They have no audience, they need *glory* [*Ruhm*]."

[50] On the connection of *Wettkampf* and *Erziehung*, see KSA 7:8[77], 251; KSA 7:8[80], 252; KSA 7:16[4], 394; KSA 7:16[14], 397.

account of the Socratic-Christian tenor of modernity, we automatically tend to denigrate ambition, struggle and genuine cultivation in favor of modesty, peace and bourgeois contentment; hence, "modern educators fear nothing more than the unleashing of so-called ambition" (HC, KSA 1.789).

Given Nietzsche's belief that the noble impulse for cultivation and glory is incompatible with the materialistic aspirations of the majority, it makes perfect sense that he favors the stratification of society. In HH 439, he thus argues that culture cannot flourish unless society is divided into a leisure class on the one hand, and a working- or even slave-class on the other: "A higher culture can come into existence only where there are two different castes in society: [. . .] the caste compelled to work and the caste that works if it wants to." Converging with Burckhardt, Nietzsche maintains that the pursuit of nonutilitarian values – what he refers to in GSt as a "new world of needs" (KSA 1.767) – is enabled by, *though foreclosed to*, the banausic working classes. Since the ends of *education* and *glory* fall into this noble category of value, we can assume that members of the working masses would be debarred from Nietzsche's higher agon.

So while the struggle for excellence can, according to Nietzsche, be generalized into a socially inclusive agon, he nonetheless circumscribes an exclusive form of *Wettkampf*, one inextricably tied to the elitist values of glory and self-cultivation. The pursuit of these higher cultural ends is, in his view, conditioned by social stratification and, moreover, parasitic on a class-based division of labor. Nietzsche thus advances a two-tier model of agonal contest, akin to that of Burckhardt. This said, for the most part, participation in the higher Nietzschean agon appears to be open to anyone willing to dedicate themselves to the noble ends of glory and self-cultivation, provided, of course, they enjoy the material means needed to pursue these ends – in other words, he does not stipulate aristocratic lineage as a prerequisite of higher agonal contest.[51] We can therefore distance, though not fully dissociate, the early Nietzsche's cultural aris-tocratism from an aristocratic political agenda. We should bear in mind, though, that Nietzsche's ideal agonal minority is not necessarily coexten-sive with the ruling *political* elite. Nor should this higher contest be conceived as an agon for political power. Indeed, we have established at length that the early Nietzsche largely dismisses, and sometimes actively criticizes, any mode of contest motivated by a desire for direct instru-mental (political) command over one's adversaries. What we now need to ascertain is how Nietzsche's position evolves as he becomes increasingly

---

[51] Though note that in HH 439 Nietzsche expresses misgivings regarding social mobility.

convinced that instrumental power is the true stake in *all* conflictual relations.

2.2.3   The Inclusivity of Nietzsche's Later Agonism

In 1881, *Wettkampf* and *Agon* practically vanish from Nietzsche's philosophical vocabulary. This should come as little surprise given that two of the defining features of his earlier notion of agon are rendered deeply problematic by his then-emerging theory of the will to power. According to this theory, the world is entirely composed of will-to-power organizations. Atoms, bacteria, human individuals, churches and nations, along with an infinitude of other phenomena, would all equally qualify as just such organizations (the underlying rationale for this thesis will be fleshed out in Chapter 4). These organizations *uninterruptedly* strive to command or "dominate" (*herrschen*) their counterparts. They are each and every one of them a will to "*direct*" (*dirigiren* [*sic*]) those wills that they deem to be serviceable and weaker than themselves, to form them into "property" (*Eigenthum*), "servants" (*Diener*) or "tools" (*Werkzeugen*) (KSA 11:35[15], 514).[52] This conception of life as will to power, however, would seem to deflate the idea of agon as a noninstrumental relation of approximate equals. So how are agonal relations possible if the world is ubiquitously characterized by will to power?

One potential solution to this predicament is to follow Nietzsche's hard readers and straightforwardly equate his later agonism with his aggressive formulations of the will to power.[53] Such commentators tend to take it for granted that for Nietzsche the political regime that best embodies the principles of the will to power is one of an aristocratic sort. They submit that on Nietzsche's later conception, agonal conflict denotes a violent species of political struggle, one by means of which an elite minority subdues the slavish masses.[54] Or alternatively, they conceive it as a nonviolent struggle for command that is tightly confined to members of the political elite. But even on this interpretation, the maintenance of this narrow agonal space is said to be dependent upon a sustained, unmeasured struggle to keep the majority in their proper, subjugated place.[55]

---

[52] See KSA 12:2[131], 132: "The will to power. [. . .] Order of rank as order of power: war and danger the presupposition for a rank to retain the conditions of its existence"; or Z II Overcoming (KSA 4.147): "All living is obeying." See also KSA 11:25[430], 126.

[53] See Dombowsky (2004, 93): "Nietzschean agonism is thought along with will to power, which says . . . that life operates on the basis of exploitation, and with order of rank."

[54] See e.g., Dombowsky (2004, 91).   [55] See e.g., Appel (1999, 140–147).

Nietzsche's softer, agonistic readers, however, offer a quite contrary solution. These readers tend to interpret his theory of the will to power in terms of his earlier conception of agonally measured contest. Hatab, for example, argues that "the will to power expresses an agonistic force-field, wherein any achievement or production of meaning is constituted by an overcoming of some opposing force." Since my Other plays a constitutive role in my own nature, Hatab continues, "the annulment of my Other would be the annulment of myself" (Hatab 1995, 68).[56] On the basis of this interpretation, Hatab (1995, 70) goes on to argue that politically affirming the world qua will to power "entails giving all beliefs a hearing" – that is, democratically welcoming the resistance generated by beliefs that conflict with our own.

These polarized readings are inadequate in two key respects. First, Nietzsche's later conception of *Wettkampf* cannot be collapsed into his theory of the will to power. Rather, agonal conflict represents a particular *mode* of will to power, and so the two notions are related in the manner of species and genus. Second, regarding the pertinent question of social *scope*, for the later Nietzsche fruitful agonal relations can obtain between individuals of any social standing so long as they are approximately equal in power – in this way, his later agonism is just as hostile toward aristocratic exclusivity as it is toward democratic openness.

With respect to this line of inquiry, KSA 9:11[134] presents us with an instructive point of entry. In this fragment from the *Nachlaß* of 1881, we can easily discern Nietzsche's embryonic conception of life qua will to power – that is, qua push for the incorporation and exploitation of weaker entities. What is of particular interest in this fragment is that within the aforementioned conception of biological life, he clearly demarcates a viable space for agonal relations. Thus, "the lowest animated being"

> seeks to incorporate [*einzuverleiben*] as much as possible [. . .]. Growth and generation follow from the unlimited *drive for appropriation* [*Aneignungstriebe*]. – This drive leads [the organism] to the exploitation [*Ausnützung*] of the weak, and to competition [*Wettstreit*] with those of similar strength [. . .]. (KSA 9:11[134], 491)[57]

Nietzsche is describing the way in which plastidules greedily strive for nutrition and growth by means of assimilating weaker entities. This process of exploitative incorporation is distinctly unmeasured insofar as the consumed entities are first catabolized and then anabolized into new,

[56] See also Hatab (2005, 17); Connolly (1988, 146).   [57] See also KSA 12:7[3], 257; cf. KTO, 107.

utilizable compounds. Yet Nietzsche indicates that within this environment of rapacious struggle, measured relations do nonetheless arise,
namely, under conditions of approximate equality, where the drive for
appropriation cannot be immediately satisfied through the incorporation
of the other. Thus, when "those of similar strength" enter into struggle
with one another, it is competition (*Wettstreit*), not exploitation
(*Ausnützung*), that ensues. What is more, this *Wettstreit* would appear to
occur under *any* conditions of approximate equality. As we shall now see,
in 1883, when Nietzsche revisits the topic of the ancient Greek agon, he
begins to weave these early threads into a more substantive social theory.

2.2.3.1   *Nietzsche's Appropriation of Schmidt (1883)*

In 1883, Nietzsche's interest in the topic of *Wettkampf* undergoes a sudden
revival. This newfound concern was likely caused, at least in part, by his
discovery of Leopold Schmidt's *The Ethics of the Ancient Greeks*. In this
embracing philological study, Schmidt postulates that ancient Greek culture was propelled by individuals' ardent desire for honor (*Ehre*) and
prestige (*Geltung*). In his view, it was by means of agonal contention that
Greek individuals sought to validate their lofty self-estimations (EAG,
1.193–194). Indeed, Schmidt recounts the disdainful attitude of the ancient
Greeks toward those who opted for a life of solitude. This antipathy
stemmed from their belief that the duty to "know oneself" could only be
fulfilled by testing oneself in competition with others (EAG, 2.394–398).
Insulating oneself from public contest meant running the risk of falling
into a condition of either vanity or undue modesty, both of which were
commonly disparaged as vices. The impulse to validate oneself, and in so
doing achieve honor (*Ehrliebe* or *philotimo*), was thus vaunted by the
ancient Greeks – that is, so long as it did not exceed certain ethical
boundaries and descend into wanton self-pursuit (EAG, 2.394).

Schmidt explains how the ancient Greeks' love of honor had an important limiting effect on their drive for self-validation. In short, he claims that
it was precisely this love that discouraged individuals from damaging the
honor of others. This is what Schmidt variously calls *Aidos, Ehrfurcht,
Ehrebietung* and *Ehrgefühl* (all of which we might translate as "reverence"):
"the endeavor [*Streben*] not to harm others who are for whatever reason
revered [*denen* ... *Ehrerbietung gezollt wird*]" (EAG, 1.168). Schmidt distinguishes this noble reverence from what the Greeks held to be the baser,
though likewise limiting, affect of *Aischyne* ("shame" or in German,
Schamgefühl): "the dread of drawing criticism" from one's superiors.
Schmidt further discriminates between these two affects by pointing to

the way in which *Aidos* "is rooted in reflection on the feeling of another" – that is, of one's adversary – whereas *Aischyne* is rooted in reflection "on one's own feeling," which is to say in *self*-concern (EAG, 1.168).

In Schmidt's respective conceptions of *Aidos* and agon, we uncover a tension between social inclusivity and exclusivity, one that recalls both Burckhardt and the early Nietzsche. On the one hand, Schmidt describes the desire to prove oneself in *Wettkampf* as having "permeated the consciousness of all layers of the Greek people," regardless of their social standing (EAG, 1.190). But, on the other hand, his depiction of *Aidos* is conspicuously more equivocal. Unlike the feeling of shame, which is in his view an affect that only arises in relation to one's superiors, he claims that for the Greeks, *Aidos* "can also be directed toward those of equal standing, indeed, it can even be turned toward the helpless and unfortunate [. . .] and is thus even synonymous with pity [*Mitleid*]" (EAG, 1.169). For Schmidt's Greeks, then, the desire to avoid harming the honor of another can arise in relation to one's equals, and even subordinates, in addition to one's superiors. And yet, in Schmidt's analysis, it remains an exclusive affect. Certain groups of individuals are decidedly unworthy of *Aidos*. For instance, in *The Odyssey*, *Aidos* is pronounced "not appropriate" for beggars (EAG, 1.177). As such, while it is considered appropriate to feel *Aidos* toward the "helpless and unfortunate," this does not appear to include those who belong to the most abject strata of society.

Under the unmistakable influence of EAG, Nietzsche attempts to integrate a number of these ideas into a project aimed at cultivating a super-dominant minority of overmen.[58] KSA 10:16[51], a preparatory note for the third book of Z, gives a clear impression of what Nietzsche now intends to encourage by means of agon: "The *transition* from *free-spirit* and hermit to *having to rule*: [. . .] *The tyranny of the artist initially as self-compulsion and - hardening!*" (516). In this note, Nietzsche disavows the Epicurean isolationism that permeates his free-spirit trilogy; moreover, in so doing, he emphatically imbues his ideal agon with a new political purpose.[59] His overmen can no longer simply close themselves off from social life (regardless of how much they might desire to do just that). The future of humanity requires that they *return* from their hermitage and readily

---

[58] See for example, KSA 11:35[72], 541: "There must be many overmen: all goodness [*Güte*] only develops among equals. [. . .] A *commanding race*. On 'the masters of the earth.'" See also KSA 11:35[73], 541; or Z III Tablets 21 (KSA 4.263): "For the best should rule, my brothers, and the best also *want* to rule! And wherever the teaching says differently, there – the best are *missing*."

[59] See e.g., D 323; D 485; D 491; GS "Prelude," §33.

grasp the tiller of political life. Hence, dissatisfied with the isolationist
tendencies of Zarathustra (such as we see, e.g., in Z I Flies), he invokes
Schmidt's vision of the agon as a forum for public agency:

> To convoke to the contest [*Wettkampf*] for power precisely those who would
> gladly hide and live for themselves – also the wise, pious, silent in the land!
> Scorn for their *enjoyable* loneliness!
> All *creative* natures wrestle [*ringen*] for influence, even if they live alone –
> "Glory" [*Nachruhm*] is just a false expression for that which they desire.
> The tremendous task of the ruling, who educate themselves – the type of
> humans and people [*Volk*] over whom he wishes to rule, must be *prefigured*
> [*vorgebildet*] in him: there must he first become master! (KSA 10:16[86],
> 529)[60]

This appeal for a contemporary *Wettkampf* is quite obviously exclusive in
nature. Nietzsche is selectively summoning the diaspora of higher individuals that he believes to be cached in self-imposed isolation. It is this select
group, and this select group *alone*, that he wishes to draw into the public
arena.[61] But whereas Schmidt lays emphasis on the motivational force of
honor (*Ehre*) and glory (*Ruhm*), Nietzsche conceives this ideal form of
public struggle as being fought for the sake of *power* (*Macht*). Furthermore,
he even seeks to expose the quest for glory, which is so central to his earlier
conception of *Wettkampf*, as a mere front for the pursuit of *influence*
(*Einfluß*). It is worth our while remarking that these considerations are
underpinned by his conviction that a community built upon an ethos of
elite contest is likely to be a flourishing, noble one, akin to that of the
ancient Greeks.[62]

He would therefore appear to confine his endorsement of agonal contest
to the minority of individuals whom he deems worthy of ruling, and whom
he seeks to draw into society and to subject to selective pressure. And yet in
other texts we find him advocating a far more inclusive brand of
Wettkampf – for example, in the following *Nachlaß* note, where he brings
Schmidt's notion of *Aidos* directly to bear on the concept of agon:

> [...] *Aidos* is the impulse and dread not to offend gods, humans and eternal
> laws: therefore, the instinct for *reverence* [*Ehrfurcht*] as habitual among the
> Good. A kind of *revulsion* toward the *harm* of those worthy of reverence
> [*Ehrwürdigen*].

[60] See also KSA 10:15[21], 485.   [61] See KSA 10:15[21], 485; KSA 10:8[15], 339.
[62] See KSA 10:16[50], 515: "New nobility [*Adel*], through breeding [*Züchtung*]. ... The contest
[*Wettkampf*] as principle. / [...] 'Ruling' is taught, practiced, hardness just as much as mild-
ness.[...]"

> The Greek aversion to *excess* [*Übermaß*] in the joyful instinct of hybris, to
> the transgression of *one's* boundaries, is *very genteel* [*vornehm*] – and *noble*
> [*altadelig*]! The violation of *Aidos* is a terrifying sight for someone accus-
> tomed to *Aidos*. [. . .] The *free, measured ones* [*Mässigen*] invented the *contest*
> [*Wettkampf*] as the ever-growing refinement of that need to express power.
> [. . .]. (KSA 10:7[161], 295)

Though Nietzsche may appear to be merely describing ancient Greek
culture, his account has an unmistakably normative agenda; indeed, it is
reasonable to infer that he is picking out the elements of Greek agonal
culture that he believes ought to be recuperated by modern society.
Notably, in his eyes, it is prima facie only a select group who are capable
of limiting themselves in the manner required for agonal conflict. These are
the "Good," who are "accustomed to *Aidos*." However, there is little
evidence to suggest that this group is in any way identical with the
aristocratic social classes. Certainly, Nietzsche stresses the aristocratic
origins of *Aidos* and *Wettkampf*, describing the former as "noble" (*altadelig*),
and claiming the latter to have been "*invented*" by "the free, measured
ones"; but he in no way claims that these customs must *remain* confined to
the nobility. As in his early writings, then, Nietzsche's supposition that
agonal virtues *originate* in the nobility should not be confounded with the
claim that *Wettkampf* did not, or could not, proliferate beyond the boundaries of this social caste. And in BGE, as we will now see, he continues to
further develop this position.

2.2.3.2 *Agonal* Aidos *in* Beyond Good and Evil

While neither *Wettkampf* nor *Agon* are explicitly mentioned in BGE, the
kinds of struggle that Nietzsche delineates in aphorisms 259 and 265 satisfy
many of the defining criteria of agonal conflict. Furthermore, in BGE 259
Aidos is present in all but name, that is, as the noble ethos of "[m]utually
refraining from injury, violence, and exploitation"; likewise, in BGE 265,
this noble disposition is readily apparent in his affirmative description of
"finesse and self-limitation in dealing with [one's] equals." What is of
further interest is that proponents of the radical aristocrat reading adduce
these aphorisms in order to corroborate their claim that the Nietzschean
agon is stringently restricted to an aristocratic minority.[63] But do the
aphorisms in question genuinely permit such a reading?

The case for a socially exclusive interpretation of these texts runs as
follows. First, Nietzsche asserts that "life itself is *essentially* appropriation,

---

[63] See e.g., Appel (1999, 141).

injury, overpowering that which is foreign and weaker, oppression, hardness, the imposition of one's own form, incorporation, and at the least, at the mildest, exploitation" (BGE 259). From this it follows that if self-restraint, the treatment of others as one's equals and the renunciation of exploitation are to be life-enhancing, they *cannot* universally pertain, even within the boundaries of a given body politic – in other words, they cannot be inscribed as "fundamental principle[s]" of social organization (as socialists, Christians and utilitarians would have it). For Nietzsche, those who strive for the aforementioned values in a universal manner push to suppress life's essential characteristics – as such, universalism of this kind betrays a "will to *deny* life" and constitutes a "principle of disintegration and decay." Thriving life is in Nietzsche's view conditioned by the struggle for exploitation; and consequently, the sphere of agonal restraint must itself be kept within healthy bounds – measure must itself be measured:

> Even a body within which [. . .] particular individuals treat each other as equal (which happens in every healthy aristocracy): if this body is living and not dying, it will have to treat other bodies in just those ways that the individuals it contains refrain from treating each other. It will have to be the embodiment of will to power, it will want to grow, spread, grab, win dominance [. . .]. (BGE 259)[64]

Naturally, this is not to say that conflict is absent within such bodies composed of equals. For Nietzsche, the vitality of any body is in part a function of *inner* contention (as we will see in Chapter 4). Taken together, these ideas point to an important consideration: since the struggle between the mutually dependent equals that compose certain bodies can be neither destructive nor exploitative, there seem to be clear grounds for classifying this an *agonal* mode of conflict. What we now need to establish is whether, at a social level, these mutually dependent equals are necessarily members of a political aristocracy.

Nietzsche's rationale for limiting reverence to noble-minded, higher individuals should now be transparent.[65] In connection with this, we should observe that during this phase of his thought, he maintains that such individuals are very much in the minority, "for everything that stands out [*hervorragt*] is, according to its essence, rare[. . .]" (KSA 12:7[70], 321). But from this it does not necessarily follow that he takes agonal reverence to be restricted to the aristocratic classes. The conditions for agonal

---

[64] See also GM II 11, KSA 5.312.

[65] N.B. in BGE 263, Nietzsche refers to a form of *Ehrfurcht* that he deems appropriate for superior objects.

limitation stipulated in BGE 259 are simply "that the individuals have genuinely similar quantities of force and measures of value, and belong together within a single body." The claim that such conditions obtain "in every healthy aristocracy" is absolutely *not* to be confused with the claim that such limitation *only* occurs within healthy aristocratic social bodies. An aristocracy is just one instance of such a body; indeed, a guild of tradesman would seem to qualify equally well. So although we still see Nietzsche taking a special interest in the noble agon practiced by the aristocratic castes, he nonetheless keeps agonal conflict subtly open to all those willing to cultivate the requisite noble virtues.

This line of thought is elaborated in BGE 265, where, having once again stressed the necessity of exploitation, he recounts how the "noble [*vornehme*] soul"

> admits to itself, under certain circumstances [. . .], that there are others with rights equal to its own. As soon as it is clear about this question of rank, it will move among these equals and equally-entitled [*Gleichberechtigten*] with an assured shame [*Scham*] and a gentle reverence [*Ehrfurcht*] equal to that with which it treats itself, – in accordance with an inborn, celestial mechanic that all stars know so well. This is just one *more* piece of its egoism, this finesse and self-limitation in dealing with its equals – every star is an egoist of this sort. And the noble soul honors *itself* in them and in the rights that it grants them; it has no doubt that the exchange of rights and honors likewise belongs to the natural state of things, as the *essence* of all interaction.

What is noble, then, is the ability to exercise self-restraint toward one's equals out of complete egoism; one merely views one's relation to one's peers as analogous to one's own *self*-relation. In other words, one sees oneself mirrored in one's peers. While the vital limiting effect that Nietzsche attributes to reverence in this aphorism is immediately reminiscent of Schmidt, he has in fact significantly modified Schmidt's account of ancient *Aidos*. It is no longer, as in EAG, primarily other-oriented, in opposition to the self-oriented feeling of shame (*Schamgefühl*); instead, Nietzsche presents *both* "shame and gentle reverence" as self-relating affects. Both are in his view motivated by conscious egoism, and are therefore quite distinct from our conventional understanding of mercy or pity.

In order to illustrate his claim that *Ehrfurcht* is limited to equals, in BGE 259 and 265 he draws an analogy between three distinct ontological domains: the biological, the social, and the (astro)physical. Thus, he tells us that agonal self-restraint inheres within a "living, and not a dying [*absterbender*] body" (BGE 259); between equal individuals; and between stars, all in accordance with an "inborn, celestial mechanic" (BGE 265). The biological thesis draws on his reading of Roux, who theorized that organisms are composed of a dynamic equilibrium (*Gleichgewicht*) of competing bodily parts (see Chapter 4 of this book). The astrophysical thesis appears to be a celestial reinterpretation of Heraclitus' belief that properties exist in a state of dynamic equilibrium with one another. And finally, the social thesis draws upon his earlier representation of the agon as a nonexploitative conflictual practice reserved for those of approximately equal ability.

Regarding the astrophysical thesis, Nietzsche's claim that inanimate entities (such as stars) can act with reverence and shame toward one another may strike us as somewhat odd, if not as a flagrant case of anthropomorphic fallacy.[66] Since we will be returning to this issue in the final section of this chapter, for now we should merely observe how, in drawing these analogies, Nietzsche is gesturing toward the fact that *locally* checking the expression of the will to power need not entail a denial of nature. Indeed, in his view, such restraint is manifest in nature itself.

But how, if agonal conflict is nonexploitative, could it possibly qualify as an expression of will to power? As we have seen, direct command and instrumentalization are essential to the activity of will to power. If we cast our minds back to Nietzsche's Mayer-inspired conception of will to power (outlined in Chapter 1), we can straightforwardly resolve this query. The key is recognizing that will to power does not merely express itself as the *accumulation* and organization of force, but also as the *discharge* of this force, a process that does not necessarily have to generate direct exploitative relations over others. According to this dynamic, there are three ontologically coherent spaces for agonal conflict. First, power can be released purely for the sake of the pleasurable sensation of relieving pent-up force and experiencing the degree of command that one has over *oneself* (i.e., over one's "release apparatus" [*Auslösungsapparat*]) – as is often the case in vigorous sport. Thus Nietzsche conceives the ancient Greek penchant for "the 'useless' [*unnütze*] squandering of force (in agon of every kind) as ideal" (KSA 10:8[15], 336).[67] Second, agonal discharge may be motivated by

---

[66] Indeed, in the following note, Nietzsche concedes that restraint in conflict is specific to interpersonal relations: "How *can* the state *undertake* revenge! [. . .] *For it is not a person* [emphasis mine], let alone a noble person: therefore [it] is further unable to demonstrate its noblesse and self-cultivation in *moderation* [*Maßhalten*] (in [situations of] 'equal with equal')" (KSA 10:7[55], 259).

[67] See also BGE 260: "The capacity and duty to experience extended gratitude and vengefulness – both only among one's equals –, finesse in retaliation, [. . .] a certain need to have enemies (as flue holes, as it were, for the affects of jealousy, irascibility, arrogance, – basically, in order to be a good *friend*): all these are characteristic features of noble morality [. . .]." Note that friend and foe are not

the desire to ascertain, and showcase, how much force one has accumulated relative to others – to establish pre-eminence, without exercising any actual instrumental power over those whom one excels. As Nietzsche says of the Greek agon in TI Ancients 3, "in their festivals and arts they only wanted to feel that they were in a position of *superiority*, to *show* that they were in a position of strength: these are ways of glorifying oneself." The accent here is on *feeling* and *showing* oneself "superior" (*obenauf*), and not on the *exercise* of one's dominance (i.e., by directly controlling the behavior of one's vanquished adversaries). Finally, he conceives agonal conflict as a means of strengthening and training oneself, or one's agonal community, for the exploitative struggle against others. As such, we might think of the form of restraint inherent to the agon in the same way that Nietzsche thinks of law in GM II 11, namely, as a "means" (*Mittel*) in the exploitative, unmeasured "struggle [*Kampf*] of power-complexes" (KSA 5.313). As he claims in TI Ancients 3, Greek agonal institutions allowed "tremendous inner tension [to discharge] itself externally in fearsome and ruthless enmity." Such institutions did not simply negate exploitative conflict; rather, they enabled it *to be more effectively channeled* toward alterity. In multiple different respects, Nietzsche's later conception of agonal conflict is therefore perfectly consistent with his notion of the world as will to power.

The will to power can manifest itself variously in agon, destructive conflict and the struggle for exploitation. It is in no way necessarily agonal, and any agonal unity enjoyed by a particular social group must always be local, and thus can never be extended across an entire community (without causing total decay and disintegration). As such, we should not conceive Nietzsche's ideal agon in the manner of his agonistic readers – that is, as being founded upon the democratic principle of "open, fair opportunity for all citizens to participate in political contention" (Hatab 1995, 120). To do so would be to overinflate agonal equality into a "fundamental principle of society," a move that Nietzsche resolutely abjures. Accordingly, the strong should refrain from exercising agonal restraint toward those whom they perceive to be significantly weaker. Such behavior would, from a Nietzschean perspective, constitute a symptom of decline. And yet, *pace* Nietzsche's hard readers, this conception of agonal struggle is once again perfectly compatible with his conviction that *any* social group of equals (i.e., equal in terms of capacity, as opposed to class) can fruitfully

---

mutually exclusive notions for Nietzsche: "In one's friend one should have one's best enemy. In your heart, you should be closest to him when you struggle against him" (Z I Friends, KSA 4.72).

engage in agonal conflict. This said, he nonetheless portrays the vitality of agonal relations as being conditioned by social stratification. Any social group of agonal equals can, in his view, only sustain internal equality on the basis of exploiting other members and groups of society (BGE 259); further, the virtue of restraint remains an originally and predominantly noble virtue. As was the case in his earlier philosophy, Nietzsche's later agonism once again harkens back to Burckhardt in being socially inclusive, while, at one and the same time, being dependent on social stratification.

2.3   On the Sources of Agonal Measure

This leaves us with the third interpretive dispute that we found to be threatening the viability of Nietzsche's agonism. This concerns how measure is concretely imposed on the evil Eris, which is to say, on the primal disposition to engage in unmeasured, physically destructive behavior. As we established above, agon channels a range of the affects and drives that would otherwise propel *Vernichtungskampf*: for example, envy, ambition and the "once so terribly present drive" for "struggle and the pleasure of victory" (HC, KSA 1.785–786). Yet, even once these have been bridled and canalized into culturally productive agon, they none-theless continue to push toward excess (*Übermaß*). Indeed, Nietzsche tells of how the ancient Greek agon stimulated the ambition and envy of competitors to such an extent that in their struggle to excel their adver-saries, these competitors were often tempted to resort to illicit, unmeas-ured means that were antithetical to the intrinsically measured ethos of agonal conflict.

The chief risk was that super-dominant competitors would strive for the unmeasured goal of permanent victory and, in achieving this, tyrannize over the contest. This eventuality is what Nietzsche designates *Alleinherrschaft* (absolute, individual domination). If an individual virtuoso has sufficient talent to enduringly dominate a given contest – to become *hors de concours* – the competition dries up due to the fact that potential adversaries are no longer motivated to compete. As such, in the first place, measure represents a *sine qua non* of agonal conflict because approximate equality must be maintained in order to arouse the agonal affects of envy and ambition. Without constant measured tension, Nietzsche believes that Hellenic society slides back into *Vernichtungskampf*, and with this disintegrates.

> Without envy, jealousy and competitive ambition, the Hellenic state, like Hellenic man, deteriorates. It becomes evil and cruel, it becomes vengeful

and godless, in short, it becomes "pre-Homeric" – it then only takes a panicky fright to make it fall and shatter. (HC, KSA 1.792)

Since the ancient Greeks required *Wettkampf* as a vent through which they could release their competitive energies, it figures that with the loss of this agonally measured, nonviolent means of discharge they lapse into violently unmeasured forms of opposition. This explains why the moderate agonal ethos "loathes a monopoly of predominance" (HC, KSA 1.789).

The second threat is that of individuals who directly resort to violent means in their attempt to secure victory. Thus, Nietzsche speaks of "the obvious danger" that plagued the ancient Greeks – namely, "that one of the great contending politicians and party leaders might feel driven, in the heat of battle, to use harmful and destructive means and to conduct dangerous *coups d'états*" (HC, KSA 1.789).

At the same time, though, Nietzsche maintains that while "the contest unleashes the individual: [it] likewise *bounds* [*bändigt*] him in accordance with eternal laws" (KSA 7:16[22], 402; emphasis mine).[68] How, then, does Nietzsche think that the ancient Greeks were able to effectively guard against the two aforementioned dangers? How did the agon constrain individuals while simultaneously unleashing them?

The most prominent limiting mechanism discussed in HC is that of ostracism – the practice by which the ancient Greeks exiled superdominant individuals from the polis (HC, KSA 1.788–789). However, as commentators quite rightly remark, ostracism represents an auxiliary fallback option within Nietzsche's idealized vision of ancient Greek society – a failsafe, employed only in cases where the primary sources of agonal measure prove ineffective.[69] This said, commentators remain sharply divided regarding the nature of this primary source of restraint.

Proponents of what I will be referring to as the *respect* reading argue that agonal contestants are marked out by their capacity for self-restraint. According to this interpretation, the respect that competitors grant their adversaries motivates them to voluntarily play fair, and even altogether withdraw from the contest should they become excessively preeminent. William Connolly, for example, invokes Nietzsche in his sketch of a democratic ethos able to safeguard social pluralism. Connolly (1991, 185) glosses this ethos as one of "agonistic care and self-limitation". In explaining why we might reasonably adopt this ethos, he cites KSA 12:9[151], which states that "[t]he will to power can manifest itself only *against resistances*"

---

[68] See also KSA 7:21[14], 526.   [69] See Siemens (2001, 521).

(Connolly 1988, 146). On the basis of this text, he contends that the identity of the modern subject is dialectically constituted through its struggle with those elements of itself and society to which it stands opposed (156). It is the modern subject's "refus[al] to accept difference in itself and others," coupled with its wish to evade and deny this irreducible state of strife, that tempts it to assert its identity in a universalizing, intolerant and even aggressive manner (158). Connolly holds that this will to conquer, convert, exclude or eliminate otherness lies at the heart of modern suffering. This encapsulates his particular understanding of what Nietzsche calls *ressentiment*. Such eliminatory struggle causes hardship on account of its inherent futility – after all, *ex hypothesi*, we are each of us inherently conditioned by otherness. As a means to alleviating this suffering, Connolly recommends an allegedly Nietzschean ethic, one enjoining us to "come to terms with difference and [. . .] seek ways to enable difference to be" (161). This ethical stance flows from what he considers an "acceptance of [Nietzsche's] ontology of resistance," an ontology that Connolly thinks radically "calls into question the project of perfecting mastery of the world" – that is, insofar as this ontology demands that we acknowledge resistance as ineffaceable (161). The resulting ethical attitude is one of "agonistic respect for difference" (166). Moreover, in order to remedy the problem of *ressentiment*, he entreats us to adopt an ironic stance toward our personal values. Instead of asserting these values dogmatically, he instructs us to acknowledge their contingency, and to resist our counter-ideals *without seeking their eradication* (165; 1991, 183). Connolly believes that in so doing we cultivate healthy forbearance and "convert an antagonism of identity into an agonism of difference" (1991, 178).

Hatab, like Connolly, places KSA 12:9[151] center stage. Hatab's contention is that by genuinely acknowledging the will to power as that which "can manifest itself only against resistances," we are compelled to cultivate a "civic attitude" of "agonistic respect." As mentioned above, Hatab maintains that in conceding the necessity of resistance, we come to appreciate that when we negate our Other we thereby forfeit the constitutive ground of our own existence. The sense of respect generated by this realization demands that we hold others in "equal regard" to ourselves. And yet, distancing himself from Connolly, Hatab (1995, 188–189) warns that this attitude is not to be confused with a positive regard of compassion (for one's adversaries). Hatab's notion of respect merely requires the affirmation of others' equality of *opportunity* (i.e., to agonally compete). In spite of this discrepancy, Hatab (2002, 142) and Connolly (1991, 165) similarly argue that agonistic respect demands that we actively *raise inferior parties up to our level* (i.e., instead of seeking their exploitation, exclusion and eradication). Given that we are constituted in relation to our adversaries, we should, they submit, desire that our inferiors become our agonistic opponents.

What we can conclude from this precis is that advocates of the respect reading take agonal moderation to be grounded in an endogenous shift of disposition on the part of the agonal adversaries.[70] By contrast, proponents of what I will be calling the *counterbalancing* reading argue that agonal contestants are motivated by the very same aims and attitudes as those who are engaged in struggles of a destructive or tyrannical sort: all likewise vie for absolute domination. On this interpretation, it is the overarching structure of the contest that imposes limitation on the behavior of the involved contestants: agonal contest is fashioned in such a way as to establish a balance of powers whereby aspiring tyrants mutually frustrate one another's autocratic designs.[71] The key source for this interpretation is the passage in HC where Nietzsche states that agonal culture "desires, as [a] protective measure against genius – a second genius" (HC, KSA 1.789; see Honig 1993, 71; Siemens 2002, 83–112, 90, 104). In other words, an agonal culture must endeavor to balance multiple forces against one another in order to foreclose the stagnation that accompanies enduring hegemony. On this understanding of agonal measure – that is, in terms of reciprocal restraint – contestants retain their tyrannical ambitions; but so long as these adversaries remain roughly equal in ability and therefore able to counteract one another, none will be able to gain the upper hand, and tyranny will be kept at bay (temporarily at least). The counterbalancing reading therefore construes agonal measure as exogenous in kind, since each contestant is reciprocally kept in check by the external force of their opponent(s).[72]

In order to clarify Nietzsche's understanding of agonal moderation, Bonnie Honig (1993, 70–71) invokes Machiavelli's vision of the dynamic tension that inheres between the people and their nobility in the ideal civic republic:

> Because the nobles in a republic are always moved by their ambition to dominate the people, and the people moved always by their desire to secure

---

[70] Though Hatab and Connolly principally ground the respect reading in later texts, it is worthwhile remarking that other commentators (e.g., Acampora 2013, 35) have also sought to use this reading to elucidate Nietzsche's earlier theory of agonal moderation. Note, however, that Acampora (2003, 379) also highlights how the Nietzschean agon is upheld exogenously by institutions; furthermore, she expresses skepticism toward Hatab's and Connolly's interpretations.

[71] See e.g. Siemens (2002; 2013); Honig (1993, 69ff.).

[72] This model echoes the political systems of checks and balances advocated by Locke and Madison.

their liberty, their struggle is perpetual. The perpetuity of their struggle, and the institutional obstacles to its resolution, prevent any one party from dominating and closing the public space of law, liberty and *virtù*.

Likewise, Siemens (2001b, 521) describes Nietzsche's notion of agonal measure as "the result of a given equilibrium of forces." What is more, he directly opposes this conception to the idea that Nietzsche endorsed a policy of *self*-restraint. In support of his reading, Siemens (2002, 105) cites fragments such as KSA 9:4[301], where Nietzsche declares that "the equality of citizens is the means to hindering tyranny – their reciprocal surveillance and suppression" (175).[73] Siemens (2013, 91) thus concludes that "the measure or limit on action is determined *not* by the players' goals, interests or dispositions; rather it is the contingent result of dynamic relations that emerge between social forces competing for supremacy."

The disagreement between the respect and counterbalancing readings boils down to a pressing ethical question: Should we be expected to restrain ourselves, or is ensuring social restraint the responsibility of overarching social structures? Whereas Kantians famously come out on the side of self-restraint, Marxists tend to take the contrary position. What we now need to establish, though, is where Nietzsche sits in this debate. To give a preview, in what follows, we will see that while Nietzsche does indeed consider agonal self-limitation to be essential, this disposition is in his view a product of civic institutions. Consequently, the aforementioned opposition in the critical literature will turn out to be a false dilemma: agonal measure emerges from a peculiar combination of endogenous restraint *and* exogenous, structural limitation.[74]

2.3.1 Equality and the Agon

Some notion of equality is fundamental to both the counterbalancing and respect conceptions of agonal moderation. But we find a striking difference between the two notions of equality respectively at play in these opposed

[73] In support of his exegesis, Siemens also quotes KSA 8:5[146], 78–79; KSA 7:23[1], 537; KSA 8:6[7], 99; and HH 261. We might also cite PTAG (KSA 1.108), where Nietzsche asserts that "every Greek individual fought *as though he alone were right*" (emphasis mine). Also, note how the counterbalancing reading generally resounds with Nietzsche's agonal interpretation of Heraclitus in PTAG, which conceives opposed properties as standing in a relation of mutual restraint toward one another (see Introduction).

[74] We should note that proponents of the respect reading often present their interpretations as selective *appropriations* of Nietzsche's thought – namely, for the worthy end of developing a viable conception of agonistic democracy – rather than as strictly representative exegeses. See Hatab (1995, 53) and Connolly (1988, 175).

interpretations. For instance, Siemens (2013, 91) characterizes agonal equality as follows:

> By "equality of power," Nietzsche does not mean a quantitative measure of objective magnitudes, nor a judgement made from an external standpoint, but the expression of an estimated correspondence between powers, where each power judges itself (as equal) in relation to another power. Unlike the measure of equality, however, the concept of "equilibrium" can *not* be understood from the subject-position, the standpoint of the single antagonists [. . .] as their conscious goal. For the antagonists do not *aim* at equilibrium; rather, each strives for supremacy (*Übermacht*) – to be the best.

In this account, then, it is therefore the *apparent* competitive ability of each contestant that needs to be balanced if agonal struggle is to be at all possible. And yet it seems odd that the agon's measure should at one and the same time be based on the *judgment* of the opposed contestants without this judgment in some way altering their subjective aims and dispositions. How does this judgment of parity bring measure to the conflictual state of affairs if not by modifying the competitive intentions of those making the judgment? I might interpret my adversary as roughly equal in strength to myself, but unless I subsequently relinquish the goal of *Alleinherrschaft*, this judgment is void of practical significance. Duels are an apt example of a situation in which mutually perceived approximate parity in no way entails moderation.[75] Given that Siemens's account is based on the work of Volker Gerhardt, it behooves us to make a brief survey of Gerhardt's conception of "equilibrium." This will leave us better placed to assess the legitimacy of Siemens's exegesis.

2.3.1.1   *Perceived Parity and the Dawn of Culture*

We ought to begin by remarking that Nietzsche does not directly refer to either *Wettkampf* or *Agon* when delineating his theory of "equilibrium" (*Gleichgewicht*) in HH and WS. In HH 92, for example, Nietzsche's explicit concern is with deflating the ideas of transcendent justice and natural rights. The notion of justice, he contends, arises when "parties of approximately equal power" come face-to-face with one another in the state of nature. Where each party deems their counterpart to be of roughly equal power, and where there is therefore "no clearly recognizable superiority of force and a contest would result in mutual injury producing no

---

[75] As Nietzsche himself states: "Equality among enemies – first presupposition of an honest duel. You cannot wage war against things you hold in contempt" (EH Wise 7). See also GS 13; KSA 10:8[9], 331.

decisive outcome, the idea arises of coming to an understanding and negotiating over one another's demands." Gerhardt (1983, 117) underscores how the notion of equality under consideration in these texts – namely, a perceived equality of ability *to do harm*, redolent of Hobbes's conception of natural equality – should not be mistaken for *objective* parity. Instead of being "established from the standpoint of a neutral observer," this particular breed of equality is based on the mutual evaluation that each opponent makes of their counterpart.

Eager to escape the dangerous stalemate of equilibrium, each party renounces the goal of physically overpowering their opponent, hoping to thereby ensure their own preservation: "Justice goes back naturally to the viewpoint of an enlightened self-preservation, thus to the egoism of the reflection: 'to what end should I injure myself uselessly and perhaps even then not achieve my goal?'" (HH 92).[76] So, *pace* Siemens, it turns out that the kind of equilibrium (*Gleichgewicht*) at issue in Gerhardt's account *does* in fact lead to the exercise of self-control. Contestants consciously adjust their aims and dispositions – namely, insofar as they respectively renounce the goal of physically destroying their counterpart, preferring to compromise instead. According to Nietzsche, this compromise then grounds, and grows into, a system of institutional justice. In other words, his position is that juridico-political equality is necessarily grounded in *natural* parity (HH 92; WS 22). Reading these aphorisms in conjunction with HC, Gerhardt (1983, 124–125) interprets this as a pivotal moment in the prehistory of humankind, one that instigates a monumental transition out of the state of nature and into a specifically agonal form of civilization. Thus, he claims that equally opposed parties (e.g., states, social classes or individuals) continue to strive "for supremacy" upon entering this condition of justice; the only difference is that now "power augmentation is sought in a transferred manner, in self-mastery, in playful contest [*Wettkampf*] and generally in the production of culture and art."

Though Gerhardt sheds interesting light on the possible relation of HH to HC, his synthesis remains highly speculative. Moreover, we should observe that Nietzsche openly rejects the idea – suggested by Gerhardt – that adversaries invariably aim for the goal of supremacy. Indeed, he submits that sometimes rivals do in fact actively pursue the end of equilibrium. However, contrary to the respect reading, Nietzsche does not believe that such equilibrium is pursued by stronger parties in order to fashion "adversaries worthy of agonistic respect" (Connolly 1991,

---

[76] See also WS 22.

165). Rather, in his account, it is only *weaker* powers that sometimes pursue this goal vis-à-vis stronger opponents – thus, a comparatively weak community "prefers to bring its power of defense and attack up to precisely the point at which the power possessed by its dangerous neighbor stands and then to give him to understand that the scales are now evenly balanced: why, in that event, should they not be good friends with one another?" (WS 22).

In these texts, Nietzsche's broader aim is to demonstrate that the mutual self-control and compromise that condition justice and legal order simply do not obtain between unequal parties. Accordingly, law and self-restraint will inevitably collapse where sustained inequality arises: "if one party has *become* decisively *weaker* than the other: then subjection enters in and law *ceases*" (WS 26) (or, we might add, law becomes at best nominal). This indicates that Nietzsche would likely reject the idea (central to the respect reading) that we have good prudential reasons to elevate weaker parties into a state of equality with ourselves, that is, instead of seeking their exploitation or exclusion.

2.3.1.2   *The Dual Function of Equality Within an Agonal Culture*
But what about specifically *agonal* conflict, which normally takes place *within* the bounds of legally ordered collectives? Is it, as in the state of nature, equality qua equilibrium (i.e., mutually perceived equality of competitive ability) that prevents *these* adversaries from establishing monopolies of power? To be sure, Nietzsche maintains that within the "natural order of things" some form of counterbalancing does indeed serve this purpose – that is, "there are always *several* geniuses to incite each other to action, just as they keep each other within certain limits, too" (HC, KSA 1.789). The ideal situation is one in which no single contestant is able to tyrannize over the contest because their opponents are always strong enough to remain, on the whole, neck and neck with them. But contrary to Siemens's formulation of the counterbalancing model, it is *de facto*, as opposed to mutually perceived, equality that is central to Nietzsche's description of the agon. Despite striving maximally for predominance, contestants are unable to prevail conclusively due to the approximately equal prowess of their adversaries. In this case, one's *perception* of one's counterpart as approximately equal exerts no limiting force. By way of illustration, we might turn to the artistic struggle analyzed in HH 158. And we should note that in a preparatory fragment for this aphorism (KSA 8:5[146], 79), Nietzsche expressly describes this form of contention as "agonal" in kind.

[...] [A]ll great talents have the fatal property of suppressing many weaker shoots and forces and as it were laying nature waste all around them. The most fortunate thing that can happen in the evolution of an art is that several geniuses appear together and keep one another in bounds; in the course of this struggle the weaker and tenderer natures too will usually be granted light and air. (HH 158)

In this passage there do not appear to be any conditions under which the artist checks their pursuit of glory. In the transgenerational contest of artists, there is no mutual assessment and subsequent adjustment of goals such as we saw was occasioned by the equilibrium that sometimes obtains in the state of nature. Agon arises when multiple artists are incapable of monopolizing critical acclaim *despite striving maximally to do so* (i.e., while obeying the rules that define that particular artistic practice). This contest is in no measure kept in check by any sense of what we might call *moral* equality. That is to say, it is not portrayed as being limited by the mutual respect of the contestants for one another's rights qua fellow human beings (e.g., their right to participate in the contest).

On Nietzsche's view, each contestant inevitably perceives himself to be *superior* (not equal) to his rivals, and therefore duly entitled to "step into the shoes of the overthrown poet himself and inherit his fame" (HC, KSA 1.788). One function of contest is precisely to settle such otherwise irreconcilable claims to superiority. As Nietzsche himself states, "it is by means of a contest [*Wettkampf*] that the contestants' right to these claims is determined" (KSA 8:20[8], 363–364). The form of equality at issue is therefore a *de facto* equality of the adversaries' relative ability to win the favor of their judges and audience.[77] Artistic contest is consequently prone to being stifled by the emergence of super-dominant individuals.[78] It is merely "the most fortunate thing," a rare and happy event, when "multiple geniuses mutually hold one another within bounds [*in Schranken halten*]." To a certain extent, this vindicates the counterbalancing model: agonal moderation *is* founded on the counterbalancing of approximate equals; however, the operative form of equality is *not* that of mutually perceived equality but rather that of *de facto* equality.

---

[77] Nietzsche stresses the importance of third-party judgment in a number of notes. See e.g., KSA 7:16[22], 402, where he describes the contest (*Wettkampf*) as a "struggle before a tribunal"; or KSA 7:16[21], 401: "The contest among artists presupposes the right public."

[78] Indeed, Nietzsche portrays the history of art as a succession of tyrants, reserving particular criticism for Homer, who "flattened" the aesthetic contest by the fact that he "always triumphed," even after his death (KSA 8:5[146], 78).

In HC, however, equality of ability is by no means conceived as the contingent result of happenstance. Indeed, Nietzsche recounts how the ancient Greeks employed the practice of ostracism as a means of actively ensuring equality. In the first place, he conceives ostracism in broadly Aristotelian terms; that is to say, as an institutional mechanism by which a community rids itself of those members whose dominance jeopardizes law and order.[79] As we saw above, Nietzsche's view is that the ancient Greeks employed ostracism when they feared that a given politician might resort to violent, seditious means in order to seize tyrannical power (HC, KSA 1.788–789).

But Nietzsche then claims that this conception of ostracism – that is, as a means of *curtailing* the pursuit of superiority – only emerged later in Greek history: the "original sense [*Sinn*] of this strange institution is [...] not that of a safety valve but that of a stimulant: the preeminent individual is removed so that a new contest of forces can be awakened" (HC, KSA 1.789).[80] Nietzsche is thus now referring to a form of equality that *arouses* the competitive affects. Adversaries must feel themselves capable of worsting their peers if they are to experience envy and entertain earnest ambitions of victory. They need to reckon themselves approximately equal to their opponents in the sense of belonging to the same competitive league, which is perfectly compatible with their rating themselves superior to those opponents.[81] In making these observations, it is imperative that we recall that for Nietzsche the standards of excellence at play in this mutual act of measurement are in no way fixed or objective; rather, they are both determined and continually revised in the contest itself.[82]

This enlivening conception of approximate equality is comparable to the notion of equality qua equilibrium insofar as both are grounded in mutually perceived parity. However, far from viewing this enlivening form of perceived equality as *curbing* the competitive affects, Nietzsche construes it as *fomenting* them. The notion of equilibrium sketched in Gerhardt's interpretation of HH and WS is therefore nowhere to be found in Nietzsche's early writings on the agon itself. We can at most infer that such equilibrium (i.e., a contingently occurring form of natural

---

[79] For Aristotle's account of ostracism, see *Politics* (1991c, 1283a23–1284b34).

[80] For a more expansive survey of Nietzsche's thoughts concerning ostracism, see Acampora (2013, 24–25) and Tuncel (2013, 224–226).

[81] We find a similar idea in Aristotle's *Rhetoric* (1991d, 1387b21–1388a28): "It is clear also what kind of people we envy; [...] we envy those who are near us in time, place, age, or reputation. [...] Also our fellow-competitors, [...] [are not] those whom, in our opinion or that of others, we take to be far below us or far above us."

[82] As Acampora (2013, 24) and Owen (1995, 139–146) respectively observe.

parity) plays an *enabling* role with respect to the agon – namely, insofar as it enables the formation of culture.

From the above we can conclude that Nietzsche's early conception of agonal struggle is conditioned by three distinct species of equality:

1. Equilibrium (*Gleichgewicht*), which *enables* (agonal) culture. This is a mutually perceived equality *of ability to do physical harm*, which occasionally obtains in the state of nature. It encourages opposed parties to (a) renounce the goal of violently overpowering their counterparts and (b) establish a common legal order.
2. A *de facto* equality of competitive ability. This *limits* agonal struggle and obtains when agonal opponents striving maximally within the rules of a given contest are unable to conclusively defeat one another.
3. A mutually perceived equality of competitive ability. This *provokes* agonal struggle and obtains when agonal opponents perceive themselves to be capable of defeating an adversary whom they consider worthy – that is, once again, while obeying the rules of the contest in which they are engaged. This elicits individuals' competitive affects.

Note that for Nietzsche, ostracism primarily represents a means of safeguarding both the *de facto* species of parity (2) *and* the enlivening breed of mutually perceived equality (3).

The counterbalancing model therefore obfuscates the fact that *self-restraint* is a necessary *enabling* condition of the agon (i.e., insofar as it extricates us from the unmeasured state of nature); but furthermore it neglects the fact that *de facto* (as opposed to mutually perceived) equality represents a necessary condition of agonal moderation. Nonetheless, we should not prematurely conclude from these considerations that ostracism and *de facto* equality are the only available sources of agonal moderation. Certainly, as it stands, self-restraint seems to do little more than deliver us from the violent state of nature. But we should now ask whether, within the norms of a given agonal practice, self-restraint is as irrelevant for Nietzsche as advocates of the counterbalancing model would have us believe.

2.3.2 *Piety and the* Heimatsinstinkt*: The Foundations of Agonal Self-Restraint*

So just how essential is self-restraint within Nietzsche's account of agonal moderation? In trying to answer this question, we should begin by examining the conceptions of agonal moderation put forward by Nietzsche's contemporaries. Contextualizing his thoughts in this way will provide us with the foil that we need in order to fully appreciate Nietzsche's thesis that civic institutions are fundamental to agonal self-restraint.

2.3.2.1   The Institutional Roots of Continence

In his essay "Der Wettkampf," Ernst Curtius (1864, 9) writes of how the ancient Greeks would often descend into bloody civil war. These lapses were in his view precipitated by an overabundance of agonal ambition: "the flame of enthusiasm, kindled by contest, became a fire that prematurely destroyed the blossoming state in a conflagration of civil war [*Bürgerkriegs*]." But despite their intermittent loss of continence, Curtius maintains that the ancient Greeks were "far from allowing the drive that excited contest to exist in its natural state, in which it does more harm than good." Indeed, they had a distinct preference for what we have already seen him calling "regulated contests" (*regelmäßige Wettkämpfe*). He writes of how the ancient Greeks "tamed," "civilized" and "ennobled" their "wild drive" for contest, chiefly "by making it subservient to religion" (12). Religious belief propagated a sense of deference toward the godhead of the polis. This in turn served to dampen the perilous egoism enflamed by contest. In this way, the drive for competition was rendered serviceable – and not just to the polis, but to Hellas as a collective whole. Curtius adds that this explains why official agonal games were usually located at sites of religious significance. In competing, a contestant was thereby meant to be paying tribute to the gods – showcasing how proficiently he'd managed to cultivate his mind and body, both of which he conceived as divine endowments (13). Consistent with this belief, contestants were required to bequeath their prizes to the gods during specially organized religious ceremonies. Failure to observe this rite was thought to incur divine wrath and transgressors were accordingly punished (indeed, as severely as temple robbers) (14). Pertinent to our inquiry into agonal self-control, Curtius further claims that contestants were required to "willingly submit to" and "ceremoniously pledge to uphold" these humbling religious norms (15). As such, religious belief spurred people to engage in self-cultivation (in order to win divine favor), but simultaneously quelled their egoism (by instilling a deterrent fear of divine punishment).

In contrast to Curtius, Burckhardt locates the source of agonal measure in ancient Greek education. He tells of how gymnastic education in particular had a cultivating effect on the agonal Greeks, allowing for military training to be replaced by the "development of the body to the highest perfection of beauty" (GK, 8.83); yet, in order to achieve this, "each individual had to submit to a methodical discipline just as severe as training

in the arts, denying himself any personal manifestation of 'genius'" (ibid.).
In this way then, the strength of agonal education consisted in its ability to
concurrently cultivate *and* constrain individual competitors.

Finally, in his *History of Greece*, George Grote argues that it was the
individual Hellene's feeling of allegiance to their native polis, combined with
their collective subscription to a common moral framework, that motivated
their self-restraint. He begins by narrating the horrors of the Corcyrean
revolution as reported by Thucydides in his *History of the Peloponnesian War*.
Grote (1851, 377) describes the bloody week of revolt as a "deplorable
suspension of legal, as well as moral restraints." Instead of giving a merely
historical report however, Grote frames the event as archetypical of a certain
species of anarchy into which he believes humans recurrently descend, citing
the French Revolution as one of its more recent instantiations. This pathological social condition is marked, he tells us, by a complete "loss of respect
for legal authority," and an "unnatural predominance of the ambitious and
contentious passions, overpowering in men's minds all real public objects."
This is a condition in which constitutional maxims cease "to carry authority
either as restraint or as protection," and which is characterized by "the
superior popularity of the man who is most forward with the sword, or
runs down his enemies in the most unmeasured language[. . .]" (380). Grote
warns that societies are condemned to revert to this savage paradigm "unless
the bases of constitutional morality" are firmly laid.

The inverse of this chaotic state of affairs is, according to Grote,
epitomized by Athenian democracy. In ancient Athens, citizens were
able to exercise their combative instincts and voice their potentially
seditious discontent via institutionalized debate. One thus bears witness
to

> how much the habit of active participation in political and judicial affairs, –
> of open, conflicting discussion, discharging the malignant passions by way
> of speech, and followed by appeal to the vote – *of having constantly present to
> the mind of every citizen* [. . .] *the conditions of a pacific society, and the
> paramount authority of a constitutional majority* – how much all these
> circumstances [. . .] contributed to soften the instincts of intestine violence
> and revenge, even under very great provocation. (382)

Moderation is therefore, on the one hand, said to be grounded in
cathartic juridical and political institutions, but also, on the other, in
individual self-restraint – it falls on each member of the polis to subdue
his aggressive instincts, exercise respect for collective norms and voluntarily prioritize the interests of pacific society.

Curtius, Burckhardt and Grote place paradigmatic emphasis on the limiting power of civic institutions, a power which they take to be based in the capacity of these institutions to modify the dispositions of competing individuals – or in other words, to promote self-imposed moderation. For Curtius, Greek religion impeded citizens' egoism by inspiring fear of divine wrath. For Burckhardt, stringent educational institutions kept contestants' pretensions of grandeur in careful check. And lastly, for Grote, participation in political and juridical life inculcated a profound sense of care for the commonweal.

Note that respect for one's adversary is conspicuously absent from these distinct portraits of agonal moderation. Of course, respect is nonetheless of instrumental importance – particularly for Curtius and Grote; but the respect at issue is one reserved for the *commonweal* and *religious or juridical authority*, as opposed to being directed toward one's adversary. Let us now examine whether comparable ideas are to be found in Nietzsche's own unique conception of agonal measure.

2.3.2.2 *Nietzsche on Agonal Respect*

There is plenty of textual evidence that Nietzsche acknowledged the limiting function that myth and religion served within agonal Greek culture.[83] Moreover, his treatment of myth pertinently elaborates the views held by Curtius. An illuminating example of this can be found in the following fragment:

> The mythical inclination runs contrary to the contest: that is, it hinders the selfishness of the individual. [According to the mythic perspective,] the individual only comes into consideration on account of his ancestry: in him the past is honored. To what means did the Hellenic will turn in order to prevent naked self-interest in this struggle, and to place it at the service of the whole. The mythical.
> Example: Aeschylus's *Oresteia* [. . .].
> This mythical spirit [*Geist*] also explains the way in which artists were allowed to compete: their self-interest was purified [*gereinigt*] insofar as they felt themselves to be a medium: as the priest was without vanity when he appeared as his god. (KSA 7:8[68], 248)

From this somewhat broken text we can discern three different ways in which Nietzsche thinks religious myth served as a brake on the agonal ambition of the ancient Greeks. First, such myth reminded contestants of

---

[83] In his notes for a series of lectures that Nietzsche gave between 1875 and 1876 (RSG), we find him reiterating many of Curtius's views. See e.g., RSG, KGW II/5, 424–425: "All prizes, which were won in the contests [*Agonen*] had to be bequeathed by the victor to the [national] god."

the sanctity of the past (*Vergangenheit*) and, by extension, their own ancestry – it reminded them that they were competing not for the sake of their own glory, but for that of their forebears; and hence they understood the reputation of their entire line to be at stake.

Second, mythological narratives served a *deterrent* function. In Aeschylus's Oresteian trilogy, the overweening political ambitions of Clytemnestra and Aegisthus – which culminate in the latter murdering Agamemnon – are brutally punished, with Apollo himself ordering Orestes to kill the usurpers. This cautionary tale thus warns against the dangers of hubris.

Finally, religious sensibility served to moderate *artistic* ambition. The pious artist tended to conceive his creative agency as a product of divine inspiration. Hence, artists were not inclined to think of themselves as strictly responsible for the work that they produced, nor as personally meriting any plaudits occasioned by this work. As such their egos were kept in healthy check.[84]

In each of these examples, Nietzsche depicts religious myth as modifying the dispositions of agonal contestants. In their consideration of myth, the Greek individual was encouraged to temper their ambitions, which were thereby corralled into the "service of the whole." For a more lucid articulation of this idea, we might also turn to HC, where Nietzsche writes of how

> The Greek is *envious* and does not experience this characteristic as a blemish, but as the effect of a *benevolent* deity [. . .] [.] Because he is envious, he feels the envious eye of a god resting on him whenever he has an excessive amount of honor, wealth, fame and fortune, and he fears this envy; in this case, the god warns him of the transitoriness of the human lot, he dreads his good fortune and, sacrificing the best part of it, he prostrates himself before divine envy. (HC, KSA 1.787)[85]

Like Curtius, then, Nietzsche understands religious belief as having both a stimulating and limiting effect. Nietzsche's agonal Greeks only felt themselves permitted to affirm and act upon their envy to the extent that it was bestowed upon them by a "benevolent deity." At the same time though, they lived in dread of divine envy, and often curbed their own hubristic ambitions in an effort to avoid the scourge of nemesis. Myths such as those of Thamyris, Marsyas and Niobe (all discussed in HC) thus served to ingrain a moderating angst in the ancient Greek psyche.

---

[84] In RSG, Nietzsche also states that in the case of musical contests, "the victorious individual was regarded as an incarnation of the god [Apollo] [and] deferred to the god" (KGW II/5, 299). Note that this clashes with his comments in HH 158, where he implies that the only available cap on artistic ambition is mutual limitation.

[85] See also WS 30.

Consequently, the god-fearing ethos of the ancient Greeks was, for Nietzsche, fundamental to their prudence and self-restraint.[86]

Beside myth and religion, Nietzsche ascribes an important limiting role to the feeling of civic allegiance. In an early *Nachlaß* note, for example, he lists the "instinct for one's homeland" (*der Heimatsinstinkt*) as one of the most effective means in the struggle "*against the measureless self-pursuit of the individual*" (KSA 7:16[16], 398). Or, as he puts it in another note: "[W]hat is it that brings the powerful drives in line with the commonweal? In general, *love.* The *love for one's native city* girds and restrains [*umschließt und bändigt*] the agonal drive" (KSA 7:21[14], 526). In HC Nietzsche expands upon this thought, advancing an account of agonal education that resonates with Burckhardt, Curtius and Grote combined:

> [F]or the ancients, the aim of agonal education was the well-being of the whole, of state society. For example, every Athenian was to develop himself, through competition, to the degree to which this self was of most use to Athens and would cause least damage. It was not a boundless and indeterminate ambition like most modern ambition: the youth thought of the good of his native city when he ran a race or threw or sang; he wanted to increase its reputation through his own; it was to the city's gods that he dedicated the wreaths which the umpires placed on his head in honor. From childhood, every Greek felt the burning desire within him to be an instrument for bringing salvation to his city in the contest between cities: in this, his self-pursuit was ignited, as well as harnessed and restrained [*gezügelt und umschränkt*]. (HC, KSA 1.789–791)

Contestants were thus driven to compete out of love, both for the commonweal and the godheads of their polis; and yet it was this very same love that served to cool their ambitious enthusiasms. According to Nietzsche, their keen awareness of these higher entities (i.e., the commonwealth and its representative gods) unequivocally modulated the goals for which agonal contestants tended to strive. From this we can surmise that individuals would, *of their own accord*, rein in their personal ambitions in the event that these came into conflict with the greater good of the polis. This implies comprehensive submission to the moral authority of the state, an idea that reprises Grote's thesis that the ancient Greek democratic agon relied on there being "*constantly present, to the mind of every citizen* [. . .] *the conditions of a pacific society,*" that is, in addition to a thoroughgoing respect for "constitutional morality." This is not to say that the Greeks did not often

---

[86] Acampora (2013, 30) also remarks how myth and the practice of mythologizing victors served the function of "reiterating and restoring" the agonal order by transmitting key agonal values.

want to tyrannize over the particular contests in which they were engaged, or even society as a whole; rather, it merely requires that in the event of a clash of values, an individual's egoistic impulses would yield to their sense of civic allegiance.

Insofar as these findings demonstrate the persistent importance of self-limitation within Nietzsche's early conception of agonal moderation, they plainly contradict the counterbalancing reading. This said, it would be unduly hasty to conclude that our study therefore vindicates the respect reading. While our exegesis has described a dynamic in which subjects adjust their personal aspirations, this is not due to contestants acknowledging a particular ontology of difference and accordingly respecting their opponents' right to participate. It is rather a mode of self-restraint grounded in institutionally inculcated values and dispositions; and although Nietzsche can be said to conceive this self-restraint in terms of respect, it is respect *for one's community and the religious norms of that community* that he has in mind, not respect *for one's adversary*. His early understanding of moderation is in this way founded upon a synthesis of endogenous *and* exogenous limitation. What we now need to ascertain, though, is whether or not such a synthesis persists in his later conception of agonal opposition.

2.3.3   *The Later Nietzsche on Agonal Equality and Self-Restraint*

At first glance, the idea of self-restraint might seem to be inconsistent with Nietzsche's characterization of the world as will to power. This particularly applies to BGE 22, where he reduces all natural processes to the "tyrannically ruthless and inexorable [*unerbittlich*] execution of power claims." His thesis that "every power draws its final consequences at every moment" would seem to leave little or no ontologically viable space for agonal self-restraint. The only possible source of moderation would appear to be approximate *de facto* equality of power. But in BGE 265 he indicates that where equal forces are opposed, they *do* in fact exercise self-restraint toward one another. This is what we have already seen Nietzsche describe as the "inborn, celestial mechanic" according to which even a star acts with "finesse and self-limitation [*Selbstbeschränkung*] in dealing with its equals." But how can there possibly be an egoistic "exchange of rights and honors [that] belongs to the natural state of things"? Is this not, as was mentioned above, a manifest case of anthropomorphic fallacy? With an eye to untangling this issue, and deciphering Nietzsche's somewhat abstruse comments, we should take a closer look at BGE 22 and 265.

In BGE 22 Nietzsche seeks to reconceptualize nature as a plurality of active forces. In so doing he endeavors to contest the idea of natural law that informs the mechanistic worldview – that is, the idea that all natural events "obey" preordained natural laws. By contrast, he conceives nature as a plurality of actively striving power organizations (and nothing besides).[87] Though these organizations obey no law, in maximally striving against one another Nietzsche maintains that they nonetheless exhibit both necessity (*Notwendigkeit*) and predictability (*Berechenbarkeit*).

What BGE 265 reveals is that a will-to-power organization does not strive to overpower opposed organizations that it perceives to be roughly equal in strength to itself – hence the apparent celestial order. Nietzsche theorizes that heavenly bodies *actively* restrain themselves. But this recognition of the equality of their counterparts should not be conceived as a *concession* made in the face of an insurmountable obstacle. Nietzsche presents it as a positive expression of reverence, whereby an entity recognizes and honors its *own strength* in its semblables: "it honors *itself* in them and in the rights that it grants them." Rather than generating a pacific relation devoid of tension, this process issues in a mode of nondestructive and nonexploitative contest – a *Wettstreit* of opposed forces (KSA 9:11[134], 491). Even at the cosmological level, then, agonal contention is in Nietzsche's view conditioned by some form of self-imposed measure, which he considers to be grounded in a breed of mutually *perceived* equality (*Gleichgewicht*) of opposed entities.

The empirical verifiability of this hypothesis is not what is of philosophical import to Nietzsche (indeed, in Chapter 4 we will see that his conception of the will to power is in no way postulated as a falsifiable theory). As he sees it, what really matters is whether it can account for the same observable phenomena just as effectively as – or even better than – the passive, mechanical model of nature. And certainly, he believes it can do just that.[88] Given a choice between these two hypothetical views, he thinks it worth our while opting for the *active* vision, since the reactive notion of mechanism lends surreptitious support to a cluster of philosophical prejudices that negatively impact upon our practical lives. For instance, on account of the fact that the mechanistic worldview projects universal "equality before the law" onto nature (BGE 22), he charges this worldview

---

[87] See KSA 11:40[42], 650: "the sole *force* that exists is of the same sort as that of the will: a commanding of other subjects, which consequently transform themselves."

[88] See e.g., BGE 36.

with giving clandestine naturalistic support to the Christian-democratic ethical framework.

In de-moralizing nature, and thereby de-naturalizing the idea of universal equality (before the law), Nietzsche believes that we can free up a logical space of possibility for radically novel modes of social agency.[89] In his own attempt to envisage alternative modes of collective life, he seeks to formulate a political outlook that could fully embody his hypothetical view of the world as will to power. And his efforts in this direction are germane to our current line of inquiry insofar as they disclose a novel social conception of agonal moderation.

To unpack how his abstract theory of will to power cashes out in practical terms, we need to turn our gaze back to the blond beasts. Although we must take care not to read Nietzsche as advocating the murderous behavior of these figures (as was demonstrated in Chapter 1), his approving depiction of their social stability sheds important light on his own later conception of agonal moderation. Thus, he describes the community of blond beasts as being composed of individuals who are

> [...] so strongly restrained [*in Schranken gehalten*] by custom, reverence [*Verehrung*], habit, gratitude and even more through spying on one another and through jealousy *inter pares*, who, on the other hand, behave towards one another by showing such resourcefulness in consideration, self-control [*Selbstbeherrschung*], delicacy, loyalty, pride and friendship. (GM I 11, KSA 5.274)

Toward those excluded from their community, however, the blond beasts act with full, unbridled force. But what are the sources of measure that enable the blond beasts to socially cohere and effectively displace their aggressive pathos onto those whom they consider foreign? In GM I 11, it is equality that stands out as serving these all-important ends. In the first place, we can extrapolate that the society of the blond beasts is structured by a type of equality analogous to the equilibrium described in HH and BGE: thus, members mutually perceive, or *recognize*, one another as *pares*, and, like the stars in BGE 265, actively exercise *self*-restraint toward their apparent equals. But Nietzsche also portrays these individuals as *mutually* bounding one another: it appears that despite the prevalence of self-limitation, they are nonetheless forever pushing to overstep their bounds. However,

---

[89] Recalling Fichte, Nietzsche states the following in KSA 12:7[54], 313: "Becoming as inventing, willing, self-negation, overcoming oneself: no subject, rather a doing [*Thun*], positing [*Setzen*], creative, no 'cause and effect.' [...] Impracticality of mechanical theory – [it] gives the impression of senselessness."

thanks to the prevalence of "jealousy *inter pares*," they are able to detect and actively thwart one another's tyrannical aspirations in timely fashion.[90]

In keeping with his description of the will to power, this idea of acting with a customary reverence (*Verehrung*) toward one's equals is not construed by Nietzsche as a heteronomous act of subordination to the mores of one's society; it is rather conceived in active, egoistic terms. Observing the customs (*Sitte*) of one's society is not the same as ethicality (*Sittlichkeit*), in the sense of passive or automatic submission to the moral doxa of one's milieu.[91] This is manifest in his character-ization of the sovereign individual, whom, in GM II 2, he describes as "the autonomous, supra-ethical [*übersittlich*] individual," adding that "'autonomous' und 'ethical' ['*sittlich*'] are mutually exclusive":

> The "free" man, the possessor of an enduring, unbreakable will, thus has his own *standard of value* [*Werthmaass*] in the possession of such a will: viewing others from his own standpoint, he honors [*ehrt*] or despises [*verachtet*]; and [...] he will necessarily respect his peers [*die ihm Gleichen*], the strong and the reliable (those with the prerogative to promise) [...]. (KSA 5.294)

We might be tempted to equate this portrait with the Kantian ideal of autonomy; however, there are some critical differences. In the first place, Nietzschean sovereignty is not principally grounded in rational reflection, as is conformity to the categorical imperative; it is rather the culmination of a lengthy prehistory of social conditioning, which leaves humans disposi-tionally inclined to treat their peers with reverence. – that is, without any need of external compulsion: "with the help of the ethicality of custom [*der Sittlichkeit der Sitte*] and the social straitjacket, man was *made* truly predictable" (KSA 5.293). But it should be underscored that the sovereign individual leaves this passive condition of *Sittlichkeit* behind. What he usefully inherits from it, though, is the stable inclination to respect the minority of persons whom he actively affirms as his equals. What is more, this freedom is *embodied* – it is "quivering in every muscle" – as opposed to being of an intellectual sort. And finally, for Nietzsche, sovereign responsi-bility is not something that issues from the counteraction of man's instincts; rather, "*responsibility*, the consciousness of this rare freedom and power over himself and his destiny, has penetrated [the sovereign

---

[90] Nietzsche's portrait of *local* peace recasts Kant's (PP, 8.367) vision of a *universal*, cosmopolitan peace, "created and guaranteed by an equilibrium of forces and a most vigorous rivalry."

[91] See also KSA 12:9[145], 419, where Nietzsche directly associates *Sittlichkeit* with passivity and obedience: "The *inability to acquire power*: its *hypocrisy* and *shrewdness*: as obedience (subordination, pride in duty, morality [*Sittlichkeit*] ...); as submission, devotion, love."

individual] to his lowest depths and become an instinct, his dominant instinct" (KSA 5.294). It is by means of custom, legal institutions and disciplinary practices that this tenacity of will has been stamped into the human animal. Instead of being a mere slave to his momentary desires, the sovereign individual, the fruit of a protracted labor of breeding, can now resist his impulses. His drives are coordinated and stable, enabling him to make good on his promises without being driven off course by the whim of his caprice.[92] But whereas Nietzsche previously valorized discipline insofar as it enables individuals to better serve the higher goals of their community (as in GSt, or HH 477), he now exalts this aptitude on account of the way in which it allows sovereign individuals to realize their *own* projects (i.e., promises). We should add that this type of individual is in no way answerable to the moral authority of the community; instead, he fully satisfies Nietzsche's edict that one be "answerable to oneself, and proudly, too, and therefore [that one] have the prerogative to *say 'yes'* to oneself" (GM II 3, KSA 5.294–295).

Nietzsche further departs from the Kantian notion of moral autonomy insofar as he censures Kant for demanding that one treat everyone as equal to oneself (BGE 187, 188).[93] By contrast, the sovereign individual's comportment toward others is determined by his particular evaluation of the specific individual under consideration. He honors (*ehrt*) those whom he considers to be his equals, and despises (*verachtet*) those he deems inferior.[94] Furthermore, the honor that he grants these equals is born of neither fear, nor passive submission to an external moral authority; it is the product of a purely personal, active and affirmative assessment of other individuals according to his own criterion of valuation (*Werthmaass*).

Although it may seem as though mutually perceived equality is sufficient to induce agonal self-restraint according to Nietzsche's later agonism, this is not in fact the case. Agonal continence is based in a sentiment of reverence or veneration toward one's equals, and the disposition to experience this sentiment in response to the perception of equality is impressed by means of custom (*Sitte*, *Brauch* or *Gewöhnung*) and, again, institutional inculcation. The perception of equality on its own in no way entails self-restraint. As mentioned above, perceived approximate equality can just as easily lead to destructive conflict (e.g., duels). This is where the cosmological notion of an "exchange of rights and honors" diverges most radically from his respect-oriented vision of agonal society. At the cosmological level there is no need for the institutions and cultural mores that condition social moderation. Echoing Schmidt's picture of the ancient Greeks, the

---

[92] On this point, see Gemes (2009, 37).   [93] See Bailey (2013, 151).   [94] See also GS 13.

later Nietzsche frames the social virtue of reverence as one that must be *cultivated*: "To educate for [*erziehen*] reverence [*Ehrfurcht*], in this plebeian age, which is plebeian even in its worship, [and] usually intrusive and shameless" (KSA 11:26[244], 214).[95] And as we saw in a fragment already cited above, he tellingly accounts for the ancient Greeks' disdain for hubris as follows: "The violation of *Aidos* is a terrifying sight for someone *accustomed* [*gewöhnt*] to *Aidos*" (KSA 10:7[161], 295; emphasis mine). Reverence, then, is a question of both education (*Erziehung*) and habituation (*Gewöhnung*).[96] And Nietzsche is clear that institutions are essential to this process of *Bildung*, since it is they that instill the virtues of *continence* and *tenacity* (as components of *responsibility*) into members of the polity.[97]

Though ostracism drops out of the picture, Nietzsche's later conception of agonal measure is thus defined by a mélange of self-restraint, education and conventional morality that resonates with his earlier reflections on ancient Greece. By the same token, his later writings jar with the counterbalancing reading in much the same way as his earlier writings. By virtue of educational practices, individuals actively moderate their goals and dispositions when faced with those whom they acknowledge as their equals. But contra the respect reading, this continence is in no way evoked by a sense of equal opportunity or positive regard for one's Other; rather, in honoring their semblables, individuals egoistically honor *themselves*: that is to say, "the noble soul honors *itself in them*" (BGE 265; emphasis mine).

2.4 Conclusion

We have now rebutted the idea that Nietzsche's social philosophy of conflict can be reduced to an endorsement of murderous struggle. In both his early and later writings, he persistently valorizes agonal contention, which we have found to be an expressly measured species of conflict. However, there were three obstacles that faced us in our endeavor to elucidate his unique understanding of agonal struggle. First, it was unclear whether such conflict is in his view intrinsically measured at all. There

---

[95] See EAG, 1.173, where Schmidt recounts how Democritus "treats the awakening and entrenching of *Aidos* as the essential goal of childrearing."
[96] See also BGE 259, where Nietzsche states that "[m]utually refraining from injury, violence, and exploitation, placing your will on a par with the other's" can "*become good custom*" (*zur guten Sitte werden*).
[97] In this respect, see also TI Skirmishes 39, where Nietzsche traces *responsibility* (*Verantwortlichkeit*) back to social institutions: "The West in its entirety has lost the sort of instincts that give rise to institutions, that give rise to a *future* .... People live for today, people live very fast, – people live very *irresponsibly* [*unverantwortlich*; emphasis mine]."

seemed to be grounds for supposing agon to include violently unmeasured modes of struggle. Second, the social inclusivity of Nietzsche's endorsement of agon remained deeply ambiguous; prima facie, it could be construed in either democratic or aristocratic terms. Finally, supposing the Nietzschean agon to indeed be measured, it was unclear *how* this measure was to be concretely achieved; there were apparent grounds for conceiving it in terms of either self-restraint or mutual limitation, though these two interpretive options seemed to be mutually incompatible.

With respect to the first problem, we determined that *Wettkampf* is indeed inherently measured, and therefore conceptually distinct from destructive violence. But despite this relation of *conceptual* disjunction, we nonetheless unearthed a *genetic* relation between these two antithetical species of struggle. Thus, agon is born out of *Vernichtungskampf* insofar as it yokes the very affects that would otherwise fuel destructive violence. And contrariwise, we can all too easily slip back into *Vernichtungskampf* if we fail to actively uphold the measure that sustains agonal relations. There is a serious point at stake in these considerations: If we elide the distinction that Nietzsche draws between *Wettkampf* and *Vernichtungskampf*, we run the risk of losing sight of the taxing work that we need to perform *on our destructive inclinations* in order to reap the cultural fruit of agonal contest. Fascistic readings of Nietzsche's agonism – that is, as an endorsement of war – neutralize this transformative project before it even gets off the ground – the reason being that they confound the starting point of this project (i.e., *Vernichtungskampf*) with its goal (i.e., *Wettkampf*).

We resolved the second problem, regarding the inclusivity of Nietzsche's ideal agon, by cleaving his conception of *Wettkampf* in two. On the one hand, we found that he recommends a socially open brand of agonal conflict, one characterized by the pursuit of excellence and, correspondingly, self-improvement. On the other hand though, we found him advocating an elite species of agon, one in which glory constitutes the principal stake. This was seen to be reserved for a minority of individuals endowed with exceptional creative talent. But while this *is* a socially exclusive form of agon, we also established that it is by no means aristocratic in the sense of being restricted to individuals of noble birth, nor does Nietzsche conceive it as being fought for the sake of political power. And yet this elite agon is nonetheless parasitic on oligarchic political organization, on a social regime ensuring a strict division of labor. It can only subsist if participants are able to exploit the surplus produced by a subordinate working class. There remains, then, an indirect, practical link between this elite agon and traditional aristocratic order. This conclusion has significant ramifications for us today. In our advanced industrial, and even postindustrial, societies – in which an ever-increasing number of individuals are liberated from the struggle for life's necessities – there seems to be no reason why this elite agon cannot become correspondingly more inclusive and detached from its oligarchic political roots.

Crucially, in Nietzsche's early writings we found that neither of these two forms of agon was motivated by an impulse for direct instrumental power. By contrast, we discovered that the later Nietzsche postulates power and command as the chief incentives of agonal conflict. Yet, notwithstanding this shift, he continues to distinguish agonal contention from situations in which rival entities struggle to instrumentalize one another. Indeed, on this later picture, we saw that agonal conflict only arises when adversaries judge themselves to be *incapable* of profitably overpowering their counterpart(s). Within his theory of the world as will to power, agon thus becomes a means for opposed entities to discharge excess force, strengthen themselves and experience a feeling of power without directly instrumentalizing or eradicating their opponent(s). The idea of the world as will to power is thus *compatible* with, but not reducible to, the idea of agonal conflict. But although we should take care not to conflate *Wettkampf* with the will to power, which often assumes destructive or instrumentalizing forms, it was nonetheless found to be indissociable from unmeasured or exploitative species of conflict. Agonal measure can only ever *locally* inhibit violence and exploitation. These insights therefore cast serious doubt on the extent to which democratic agonists can lay claim to a Nietzschean heritage, particularly if they have cosmopolitan proclivities.

With respect to our third obstacle, we identified various different sources of moderation, including mutually perceived equality, *de facto* equality of ability, and ostracism. But we also found that socially ingrained continence was of particular import, both for the early and the later Nietzsche. In conceiving agonal struggle as based upon a combination of ostracism and counterbalanced forces (à la Siemens), we risk overlooking the indispensable function of *self*-limitation in sustaining the agon. What is more, we are liable to underestimate the instrumental value of educational institutions, which represent an essential source of agonal continence. Defenders of the respect reading are then, by contrast, in danger of neglecting the fact that agonal moderation might be cultivated by means of instilling respect for one's *community* – a far simpler and more realistic approach to fostering agonism than that of pushing for the acknowledgment of a complex ontology of difference and the corollary respect for other individuals.

In Nietzsche's early writings, the limiting force of mutually perceived equality principally consisted in its ability to elicit envy; in his later writings, though, we saw that mutually perceived equality of power played a far greater limiting role, namely, insofar as it occasions *reverence*. In both cases, however, perceived equality *of ability* represents a *sine qua non* of agonal engagement. Against the respect reading, then, Nietzsche holds the realist position that without perceived equality *of ability*, the kind of conflict that arises is one that naturally tends toward exploitation, exclusion or annihilation. This has severe implications for those who invoke Nietzsche in order to promote the "agonistic respect" of weaker minority groups. It is unrealistic, in Nietzsche's view, to expect healthy individuals or social groups to agonally relate to their inferiors, since the condition of perceived equality of ability simply does not obtain. But this is not to say that such minority groups are disqualified from Nietzsche's agonal project; on the contrary, it encourages them to cultivate agonism *among themselves* and thereby raise themselves up to, or beyond, the level of their superiors.

The fundamental role of equality presents a further, more trenchant issue for those who wish to read Nietzsche as a predominantly agonistic thinker. As we move into the 1880s, he begins to emphasize just how seldom relations of equality actually occur: "In nature, a fragile equilibrium [*Gleichgewicht*] arises as infrequently as two congruent triangles" (KSA 9:11[190], 516).[98] It therefore stands to reason that agonal conflict is going to account for a minute fraction of the net total of conflictual relations that structure reality at any given moment. And consonant with these considerations, the later Nietzsche becomes increasingly interested in the forms of struggle that arise under conditions of *in*-equality – specifically, as we will now see, the struggle to form and maintain thriving hierarchical organizations.

---

[98] See also D 112: "The 'man who wants to be fair' is in constant need of the subtle tact of a balance: he must be able to assess degrees of power and rights, which, given the transitory nature of human things, will never stay in equilibrium [*Gleichgewichte*] for very long but will usually be rising or sinking [...]." And KSA 9:11[132], 490: "Disparity [*Verschiedenheit*] rules in the smallest things [...] – equality [*die Gleichheit*] is a great delusion."

PART II

The Struggle for Organization

CHAPTER 3

Conflictual Unity in the Untimely Meditations

Over the course of the previous two chapters, we examined Nietzsche's thoughts regarding two conceptually distinct forms of conflict – namely, *Vernichtungskampf* and *Wettkampf*. However, this division implies a dichotomy that is at variance with Nietzsche's rejection of binary oppositions. As he states in BGE 2, "we can doubt [. . .]whether opposites even exist."[1] Consistent with this doubt, in the following two chapters, scrutiny is going to reveal that his thoughts on conflict cannot be split into a neat dichotomy. Probing the gap left by the previous chapters is going to expose a third fundamental species of struggle – one that we will not be able to classify under the headings of either *Wettkampf* or *Vernichtungskampf*.

The previous chapter established that according to Nietzsche, agonal conflict presupposes the approximate equality of the relata at variance; yet we also remarked that he takes such equality to be an exceptional rarity. If for Nietzsche, as for Schopenhauer and Heraclitus, "all occurrence is a struggle [*alles Geschehen ist ein Kampf*]" (KSA 12:1[92], 33), we therefore have to ask ourselves: What type, or types, of conflict does Nietzsche think can obtain under conditions of *in*-equality? And moreover, what kinds of conflict does he think *should* ideally define such relations? In light of his critique of *Vernichtungskampf*, and the very limited conditions under which he endorses such conflict, it would be surprising if he were to recommend destructive struggle. These considerations point to the probable existence of categories of conflict that do not fit the *Vernichtungskampf-Wettkampf* dyad that he constructs in HC.

For some indication as to the types of conflict that Nietzsche thinks arise under conditions of inequality, we might look to KSA 10:7[86], where he states the following: "struggle [*Kampf*] with destruction [*Zerstörung*] *or*

---

[1] See also BGE 24, where Nietzsche speaks of how language "cannot get over its crassness and keeps talking about opposites where there are only degrees and multiple, subtle shades of gradation." See also KSA 12:9[91], 384; KSA 12:9[121], 406; WS 67; Müller-Lauter (1999, 10f.).

assimilation [*Assimilation*] of those that are weaker" (272; emphasis mine). And later, in 1886, he submits that in situations of inequality, when "two different power-quanta collide, the stronger encroaches on the weaker, which it progressively weakens until finally subjugation, adaptation [*Anpassung*], integration, incorporation occurs" (KSA 12:5[82], 221). The type of conflict that takes place in lieu of destroying inferior forces is therefore one directed at "overpowering the alien and the weaker, oppressing, being harsh, imposing your own form, incorporation, and at least, the very least, exploitation" (BGE 259). The principal claim that I defend in the following two chapters is that in formulating alternatives to detrimentally unmeasured conflict, Nietzsche posits a measured species of struggle that cannot be called agonal in kind. This *sui generis* species of measured opposition is what I will be referring to as *incorporative* conflict – a nondestructive form of struggle aimed at organizing opposed entities into an instrumental hierarchy.

In addition to this thesis, I defend a further, related claim: Though Nietzsche conceives incorporation in categorically measured terms, it is nonetheless necessarily conditioned by an *unmeasured* form of struggle; and yet we will see that this conditioning species of conflict, though unmeasured, cannot be subsumed under the heading of *Vernichtungskampf.* This conditioning mode of conflict is broadly directed toward the elimination, excretion, excision or repulsion of that which cannot be profitably incorporated. We can discern this species of conflict, for example, in his calls for a form of cultural "struggle" (*Kampf*) that begins with the "excretion [*ausscheiden*] of foreign elements that have been forcibly grafted [onto culture]" (BT 23, KSA 1.149); or again, later, in his classification of the "drive [*Trieb*] to repel something [*etwas zurückzustoßen*]" as a fundamental drive of nature (KSA 11:36[21], 560); or at the end of his working life, in his belief that a thriving society must, just like any organism, "cut out" (*ausschneiden*) its "degenerate parts" (KSA 13:23[1], 600). I will be referring to these closely related processes as instances of *exclusionary* conflict, since the verb "exclude" can signify both the act of shutting out external entities and that of expelling those that are already internal.[2] This struggle is unmeasured to the extent that for Nietzsche it is in no way motivated by an interest in the continued existence of that which is excluded.[3] In the English language, the

---

[2] See entry for "exclude, v.," OED.
[3] This applies even in cases where the products of excretion are bequeathed to others as fertilizing dung (see e.g., KSA 9:11[134], 492).

measureless aspect of exclusionary struggle is neatly captured by the double sense of the verb "eliminate," which can signify "expel or remove from the body," but also "remove entirely, get rid of, do away with."[4]

The *combination* of these two forms of opposition – that is, incorporative (measured) and exclusionary (unmeasured) conflict – is what I will then refer to with the overarching term *organizational* struggle. This label is fitting since both of these conflictual processes are in Nietzsche's eyes similarly directed toward the enhancement and expansion of the internal hierarchy that constitutes any living organization. Although organizational conflict is most pronounced in Nietzsche's later writings, in this chapter we will be analyzing the way in which it already plays a pivotal role in his early period, specifically that of his *Untimely Meditations* (1873–1876).

This chapter thus reconstructs Nietzsche's grounds for affirming organizational struggle in UM. What we are going to find is that he presents this species of conflict as the most effective remedy to an internecine breed of antagonism that he sees threatening modern man. In his own words, in modernity, "everything is hostile to everything else and all noble forces [are engaged] in a mutually destructive war of annihilation [*Vernichtungskrieg*]" (KSA 7:30[8], 734). His diagnosis, however, remains obscure and difficult to parse. This opacity is then exacerbated by the fact that during this period of his thought, his complaints regarding the problem of disgregation are not limited to *social* disgregation, but are refracted across a spectrum of different ontological domains. For example, we find him discussing such conflict at the axiological level of our ethical and aesthetic values; the psychological level of our affects and behavioral dispositions; and the political level of individual social agents. Accordingly, with a view to better understanding how Nietzsche sees organizational struggle functioning as a remedy, we should begin by dissecting his multidimensional diagnosis of the crisis of disintegration.

Having explicated the problem with which Nietzsche is concerned, we will then turn to his proposed solution. Insofar as in UM he conceives modernity as a maelstrom of reciprocally destructive forces (i.e., a *Vernichtungskrieg*), we might want to draw an analogy between this and the *Vernichtungskampf* that he disparages in HC. Given this apparent symmetry in diagnosis, we might reasonably expect a corresponding symmetry in remedial prescriptions. That is, we might expect UM to follow HC by prescribing *Wettkampf* as the antidote to an absence of measure. This is all the more appealing given that commentators frequently argue that Nietzsche conceives agon as a means of

---

[4] See entry for "eliminate, v.," OED.

sociocultural *unification*.[5] And as we saw in the previous chapter, the agonistic democrats claim that Nietzsche promotes an "agonistic" mode of social organization – in other words, a society that instead of dominating or suppressing dissonant ethical views, is characterized by a respectful, egalitarian contest of values.[6] Analogously, with respect to the psychological plane, commentators often describe Nietzsche's normative ideal as one in which the various drives that comprise the self are held in a state of contention comparable to his vision of the ancient Greek agon.[7] Finally, UM itself has been read by many as an example of Nietzsche agonally contending with modernity, and, moreover, inciting his readers to follow his lead.[8] Over the course of the following two chapters, however, we will see that these agonal interpretations of Nietzsche's philosophy of organization are ultimately inadmissible. The real stumbling block for these readings is not merely a lack of textual evidence, but the additional fact that his vision of vibrant holism is structured by forms of instrumentalization and exclusion that are flatly incompatible with his understanding of agonal conflict. Contrary to the agonistic reading, we will discover that he consistently recommends an ongoing struggle to establish, sustain and renew *instrumental hierarchies* –

---

[5] Acampora (2006, 327) emphasizes how, for Nietzsche, "competitive relations serve as an organizing force of culture by bringing together diverse elements [and] coordinating heterogeneous interests." David Owen (1994, 77) has also argued that the agon unifies communities insofar as it generates shared norms and standards of excellence. See also Müller (2020, 96); Tuncel (2013, chap. 6). There *is* one note that supports this reading, and which many of these commentators cite, namely, KSA 7:16[22], 402 (a preparatory note for HC), in which Nietzsche minimally states the following: "The panhellenic festivals: unity of the Greeks in the norms of the contest [*Wettkampf*]." However, he otherwise refrains from ascribing the agon any unifying quality. Rather, as we saw in the previous chapter, he often emphasizes the socially centrifugal force of ancient Greek contest. To my mind, commentators tend to grant the aforementioned note far too much weight, particularly since many of his influences persistently highlight the unifying quality of the agon. Thus, when read in context, he appears to have actively suppressed this idea from his writings. For Curtius (1864, 11), for example, the dramaturgical agon gathered the Greek people (not just those from a single polis) and thereby helped generate a national identity amidst bitter inter-polis conflict (19). And he hoped that cultivating a similar agon within German academia would further the project of German unification. Similarly, for Burckhardt, Panhellenic contests actively fostered the formation of a unitary Greek identity by offering a neutral locus where ordinarily hostile tribes could socially interact (GK 8.93–94). And according to Schiller (2010, Brief XV, 62–64), it was through nonviolent, agonal play that the Greeks managed to synthesize their physicality and their love of law and form.

[6] See e.g., Owen (1995, 161–162): "[F]or Nietzsche, tolerance for other views, a willingness to engage with them in an open and fair-minded way, is a condition of claiming to hold one's own beliefs to be true. [. . .] [T]his position commits citizens to a form of society which is characterized by the cultivation of the conditions of honest and just argument between free and equal citizens."

[7] See Burnham (2015, 16): "[S]ince the individual self is comprised of a multiplicity of drives, an agonistic 'society' is also found within the self"; Gemes (2009, 56; see also 49–52); Hatab (2008a, 173); Honig (1993, 229).

[8] Vanessa Lemm (2007, 14) has argued that in SE Nietzsche's vision of freedom is inherently public and characterized by "a public struggle (*agon*) between the individual and society." Siemens (2001a, 101) and Acampora (2013, 39) also advance agonistic interpretations of HL.

that is, a decidedly un-agonistic, organizational form of conflict, by means of which he thinks we can resolve the ontologically diverse problem of disintegration.

The first part of this book exposed the way in which Nietzsche's respective conceptions of destructive struggle and agonistic conflict undergo a seismic shift, both as he repudiates Schopenhauerian metaphysics, and, in reaction to this, develops his conception of the world as will to power. This latter part of the book will reveal that much the same holds for his understanding of organizational conflict. Thus, his early theory of organization is, as we will presently see, heavily influenced by, and even grounded in, Schopenhauer's metaphysical *Weltanschauung*. The question is, then, what happens when he disavows this framework? The contention of the final section of this chapter is that this repudiation irreparably undermines the model of organizational conflict that he advances in UM. This conclusion generates the guiding question of Chapter 4: Can Nietzsche formulate a theory of organizational conflict without appealing to these untenable metaphysical foundations? But if we are to appreciate the full weight of the challenge contained in this question, it is imperative that we first obtain a clear view of the flaws in his earlier synthetic project. With this end in mind, let us begin by reconstructing his early diagnosis of the crisis of disintegration, which his synthetic project in UM aspires to remedy.

3.1   The Crisis of Cultural Disintegration

In his opening meditation, "David Strauss, the Confessor and the Writer," Nietzsche censures the Germans for their complacent belief that military victory in the Franco-Prussian War had been followed by a corresponding cultural triumph. He thus upbraids them for supposing "that struggle and bravery are no longer required" (DS 1, KSA 1.161). But to what kind of cultural struggle is Nietzsche rallying his compatriots, most of whom he pejoratively labels "cultural philistines" and "barbarians" (DS 2, KSA 1.166)? In trying to address this question, we ought to recall his definition of barbarism as a "lack of style or a chaotic jumble of all styles," and, contrariwise, true culture as a "unity of artistic style in all the expressions of the life of a people" (DS 1, KSA 1.163). In calling Germans barbarians, then, Nietzsche is accusing them of lacking precisely this kind of unity, of being a fragmented "modern fairground motley" (DS 1, KSA 1.163) characterized by "atomistic chaos" (SE 4, KSA 1.367).[9] We

---

[9] In this respect, Nietzsche follows thinkers such as Goethe, Schiller and Wagner in pronouncing Germans and German culture to be pathologically lacking in human wholeness. Schiller (2010, Brief

can surmise from this that they (and indeed *we*) must therefore struggle *for* harmony and *against* discord. Before we take a closer look at the precise nature of his ideal, though, first we ought to dissect what Nietzsche means by fragmentation.

For Nietzsche, one of the root causes of German barbarism lies in its decadent approach to education, which he indicts for being superficial and encumbered by an excess of historical learning. As a result, Germans have become mere "walking encyclopedias" (HL 4, KSA 1.274). But amassing knowledge does not intuitively seem to be harmful or disintegrative per se. So why then does Nietzsche deem it pathological? And how does it cause fragmentation? In DS, Nietzsche's chief allegation is that philistinism obstructs authentic agency, especially that of an aesthetic or ethical sort. With respect to aesthetics, he complains that due to the excessive study of sundry languages, literary expression has deteriorated into a "soulless mosaic of words," with writers clumsily employing an awkward amalgam of Latin and French styles (DS 11, KSA 1.222). Consequently, these authors lack the "natural basis" and capacity for "artistic evaluation" needed "to become even a mediocre and tolerable writer" (DS 11, KSA 1.220). Nietzsche thus scorns this disarray of styles on account of the fact that it leaves potential artists in want of fixed rules and evaluative criteria, which he takes to be essential for coherent artistic practice.

He also condemns the German proclivity for accumulating inordinate quantities of knowledge. In his view, this gluttonous attitude has had the effect of thwarting *ethical* agency. The problem is that one simply cannot implement all the ethical models that one has ingested from past cultures. This is due to their mutual incompatibility. For example, in SE he criticizes the to-ing and fro-ing (*Hin und Her*) generated in the individual by the conflicting ideals of Christianity and antiquity. The struggle of these value systems "engenders a restlessness, a disorder in the modern soul which condemns it to a joyless unfruitfulness" (SE 2, KSA 1.345). In presenting the individual agent with incompatible maxims and models for action, such discordance tends to generate a condition of paralysis reminiscent of Buridan's ass.

VI, 22), for instance, speaks of how within German culture, "The inner union [*Bund*] of human nature was torn apart, and a pernicious struggle divided its harmonious forces [. . .]." Schiller's target in this letter is the division and specialization of the sciences, as well as the division of labor and the stratification of the social classes. Wagner (1850a) comparably laments the way in which the German *Volk* has been divided against itself by egoism and the pursuit of luxury. He further claims that science has become divorced from life (§2), and that the various domains of art have "splintered" apart from one another. Only his tragic artwork of the future can, he proclaims, reunite them (14). It should also be borne in mind that Germany was, at the time of Nietzsche's writing UM, still undergoing an arduous and protracted process of political unification.

The second form of harmful disintegration indexed by Nietzsche concerns the chasm he identifies between the inner (i.e., private and intellectual) and outer (i.e., public and practical) aspects of the individual's life. In HL 4, he recounts how, as a result of their inner havoc, the modern individual simply abandons the toilsome task of practically implementing their acquired knowledge. In lieu of doing so, they simply turn inward, disregarding the need to make authentic decisions as to how to intercourse with others and present themselves to the outside world (HL 4, KSA 1.274; HL 5, KSA 1.280). In their effort to circumvent the difficulty of practically applying this internal bedlam of ethical and artistic models, modern Germans simply defer to convention, and focus on imitating others as best they can: "[N]o one dares to appear as he is, but masks himself as a cultivated man, as a scholar, as a poet, as a politician" (HL 5, KSA 1.280). To the extent that they thereby fail to exteriorize their personal inner life, Nietzsche maintains that Germans suffer from a "weakness of personality" (HL 10, KSA 1.281). What is most harmful about the resulting atmosphere of conformism, however, is the way in which it impedes the cultivation of genuine individuals: any nascent true individuals are forced to suppress, rather than nurture, their uniqueness out of "fear of [their] neighbor, who demands conventionality" (SE 1, KSA 1.337). This, then, is why Nietzsche takes such emphatic issue with *"the antithesis of form and content, of inwardness and convention"* (HL 4, KSA 1.278).

The third species of fragmentation fostered by philistine culture is more social in kind. The sheer quantity of history ingested by the erudite barbarian evokes a destabilizing sense "of the fluidity of all concepts, types and species, of the lack of any cardinal distinction between man and animal." Nietzsche describes this view of existence as "true but deadly" (HL 9, KSA 1.319). In his eyes, the disorienting experience of existing in a state of pure flux, devoid of higher purpose, breeds a pernicious strain of cynicism vis-à-vis the world of action (HL 5, KSA 1.279). Moreover, this attitude issues in a socially divisive form of egoistic immoralism as individuals fall back on the one thing of which they are certain: their own personal life-needs. Needless to say, once the rapacious pursuit of personal gain becomes the social norm, the community "falls apart [*zu Grunde geht*] and ceases to be a people [*Volk*]" (HL 9, KSA 1.319).

In UM, Nietzsche's general concern with the pathology of disintegration can therefore be expressed as a preoccupation with the following triad of specific disorders:

a. The anarchic discordance of models guiding agency;
b. The diremption of our interior, intellectual life from our external comportment, which is consequently governed by convention;
c. The socially divisive egoism engendered by cynicism.

We ought to recall that the evaluative criterion that dominates Nietzsche's thought during this period is the extent to which phenomena aid or obstruct "an evolving culture and the procreation of genius – which is the goal of all culture" (SE 3, KSA 1.358). In their own fashion, each of the aforementioned species of disgregation undercuts the social and individual conditions of coordination *that are necessary for genius to arise*. In contrast to the Hegelian belief that modern Germans have already achieved a "completion of world-history" (HL 8, KSA 1.308), or Hartmann's whiggish conviction that progress is guaranteed by an automatic "world-process" (*Weltprozess*) (HL 9, KSA 1.311), Nietzsche warns that the amelioration of our condition is wholly contingent upon our actively fighting for it: "[T]hat ideal condition will not be created by dreaming, *it must be fought and struggled for [erkämpft]*" (HL 9, KSA 1.317; emphasis mine). But what kind of fight does Nietzsche have in mind exactly?

3.2   The Paths to Unity

Nietzsche volunteers a number of intertwined solutions to the three forms of disunity delineated in the previous section. One of the key ways that these remedies are related is in their paradigmatic appropriation of Schopenhauer's conception of healthy purposive organization. Before we can properly reconstruct Nietzsche's view, we therefore need to make a detour through *The World as Will and Representation*.

3.2.1   *Incorporation and Eradication: The Twofold Root of Organization*

Schopenhauer inherits his concern with purposive organization (*Zweckmäßigkeit*) from Kant, whose most lucid treatment of the topic is to be found in his *Critique of Judgment*. Here Kant asks how we can explain the existence of self-organizing beings – that is, *organisms* – within which interdependent parts are neatly coordinated to serve the interests of the whole (what Kant calls *inner* purposiveness). Kant further asks how we can explain the harmonious holism of nature: How is it that all the flora and fauna of nature seem to mutually support one another (as is evidenced by food webs)? And how is it that all of this taken together serves to support rational human culture, which stands at the apex of this grand system (what Kant calls *outer* purposiveness) (CJ, 5.377ff.)? Since the interdependence of such parts means that they could not have independently pre-existed the wholes to which they belong, Kant argues that we simply cannot conceive of how either outer or inner purposiveness could arise in a purely mechanistic universe, by force of sheer coincidence (CJ, 5.376). His response is to suggest that we are forced to make recourse to the concept of teleological causality as a principle of reflective judgment – that is to say, failing a better explanation, we must provisionally think "as if" such phenomena were the product of intelligent design (CJ, 5.397ff.).

Schopenhauer, by contrast, arrives at a markedly more dogmatic conclusion – namely, that purposiveness can only be explained by the fact that the unity of an entity is grounded in the substantial unity of its Platonic Idea, the timeless prototype that determines the development of all individual instantiations of any given natural kind.[10] Schopenhauer describes these Ideas as being engaged in an unrelenting zero-sum struggle over matter, which they require in order to become fully manifest phenomena; indeed, "each only has what it has torn away from another" (WWR 1, 2.364).

This "universal struggle [*Kampf*]" (WWR 1, 2.175) is then, for Schopenhauer, the turbulent matrix out of which ever-higher Ideas enter the world – a process culminating in man, whom he crowns the "clearest and most perfect objectivation" of the noumenal world-will (WWR 1, 2.182). Yet, in order for the Idea of man to become manifest, Schopenhauer asserts that it must be "accompanied by the stepwise descent through all animal forms, through the plant kingdom, and down to the inorganic" (ibid.). The reason that man, the ultimate end of nature, needs the existence of this complete, internally conflictual system in order to become manifest is that it is precisely this system that provides the materials requisite for human life.

Whereas outer purposiveness emerges from the conflictual relations *between* individual phenomena, Schopenhauer theorizes that inner purposiveness emerges from the conflict *within* individual phenomena –

---

[10] Young (2005, 129–133) persuasively argues that Schopenhauer's understanding of Ideas cannot be equated with that of Plato, the reason being that Schopenhauer does not reify Ideas in the manner of his predecessor. Indeed, we may want to think of Schopenhauer's Ideas as having more in common with Aristotelian essences, which inhere within objects like blueprints governing the development and activity of those objects. For a comprehensive account of Schopenhauer's theory of Ideas, see Atwell (1995, 129–153).

specifically, within organisms. Every organism, aside from being constituted by a single Idea, supervenes on a *hierarchy* of Ideas (e.g., those of organs, cells, molecules, atoms, etc.). Higher Ideas are only able to prevail in the aforementioned universal struggle by pressing lower Ideas into the service of their higher purpose. By way of example, Schopenhauer cites the way in which the human body vies to digest organic matter, and to control its various conflicting humors.

> The appearance of a higher Idea will emerge from this conflict [*Streit*] and overpower all the less perfect Ideas that were there before, in such a way that it lets their essence continue to exist in a subordinate manner by taking an analogue of them into itself. (WWR 1, 2.172)

This exploitative, instrumentalizing struggle to establish hierarchical relations represents the constitutive ground of every phenomenon: "No victory without a struggle: since the higher Idea or objectivation of the will can come forward only by overpowering the lower Ideas, it encounters resistance on their part" (WWR 1, 2.173). Like Kant, Schopenhauer denies that we can explain organismic unity with reference to exclusively mechanical laws. But diverging from his predecessor, Schopenhauer dogmatically asserts that the only adequate explanation is that Ideas are engaged in a mutual struggle for "*overwhelming assimilation [Assimilation]*" (ibid.).

What is more, on Schopenhauer's account, once lower Ideas have been co-opted, conflict nonetheless persists insofar as subjugated Ideas constantly vie to reassert their independence. Health (*Gesundheit*) then consists in the capacity of an organism to subdue this rebellious inner conflict and keep lower Ideas subordinated to its higher purpose (WWR 1, 2.174).[11] Death often results from the inevitable success of lower Ideas in their relentless push for independence, since this process drives organismic disintegration. But destructive struggle is also necessitated by the fact that Ideas can only make themselves manifest by means of consuming other Ideas. Just as a victor in battle might sack and enslave a defeated city, the triumphant Idea disbands the opposed organization, instrumentalizing the Ideas and matter previously organized therein; hence, "every animal can maintain itself in being only by constantly destroying another" (WWR 1, 2.175).

From the above, we can ascribe the following defining criteria to the assimilative struggle envisioned by Schopenhauer:

---

[11] This idea finds precedence in Goethe (1948–1960, 56), for whom "[t]he subordination of the parts indexes a more perfect creature." Note that this conception of organisms as hierarchies of internal elements is also present in Leibniz's *Monadology*.

1. Its contending relata (i.e., Ideas) are principally aimed at subjugating their counterparts into an instrumental hierarchy;
2. Its telos, instrumental hierarchy, is associated with health;
3. It is conditioned by unmeasured struggle. In order to achieve the subjugation described in (1), relata must first destroy certain of their counterparts – that is, in order to separate, seize and instrumentalize their utilizable constituent parts;
4. It continues *within* the instrumental hierarchies that it tends to generate.

In terms of its structure, this struggle of higher Ideas to instrumentally dominate their lower counterparts has remarkably little in common with the agonal contest described in HC. First, it takes place under conditions of inequality; second, it generates instrumental, hierarchical relations; and finally, it is ineluctably married to unmeasured, destructive struggle. If we now examine how Schopenhauer's account informs Nietzsche's early theory of incorporation, we will see that Nietzsche's position is equally unagonal in kind.

3.2.2   *Plastic Force*

In DS, as in HC, Nietzsche explicitly disavows the idea of militarism as a viable path to true, unified culture. Contrary to militaristic readings of his philosophy, he plainly states that "[s]tern military discipline [*Kriegzucht*], [. . .] unity and obedience in the ranks, are elements *that have nothing to do with culture*" (DS 1, KSA 1.160; emphasis mine). But despite this overlap, HC and UM do not share a corresponding concern with the *Wettkampf* as a constructive social alternative. Indeed, not once does Nietzsche mention either *Wettkampf* or *Agon* in UM, a text in which he is overtly responding to the problem of disintegration. Rather, insofar as his solution seems to be structured by Schopenhauer's theory of assimilation, it is conspicuously unagonal in nature.[12] Since the Schopenhauerian dimension of UM is particularly salient in HL, it is with this text that we should now commence our inquiry.

In HL Nietzsche takes arms against the disunity caused by overaccumulating historical knowledge. This is not to say, however, that he

---

[12] This resonance does not appear to be a product of mere coincidence. Surveying texts from the period during which Nietzsche was writing UM, we find strong evidence that he was well acquainted with, and even assented to, Schopenhauer's description of the world as a universal struggle for purposive organization. See e.g., his citation of the relevant passages of WWR 1 in PTAG (KSA 1.826). This undermines Hill's claim (2003, 75) that Nietzsche abandoned Schopenhauer's notion of purposiveness as of 1868.

censures historical knowledge per se; on the contrary, he posits such knowledge as a necessary condition of health. As he emphatically remarks: "[*T*]*he unhistorical and the historical are necessary in equal measure for the health of an individual, of a people and of a culture*" (HL 1, KSA 1.252). But this prompts the question of how historical knowledge can remedy the disintegration to which its excess originally gave rise. In order to answer this question, we first need to unpack why Nietzsche divides historical practice into three interrelated categories – that is, monumental, antiquarian and critical history.

Nietzsche's tripartite analysis commences with *monumental* history. This mode of historical practice glorifies past individuals and thereby conscripts them as exemplars for future action. First and foremost, monumental history serves the great man of action, "who fights a great fight [*einen grossen Kampf kämpft*], who needs models, teachers, comforters and cannot find them among his contemporaries" (HL 2, KSA 1.258). We might think of Schiller's idealization of the Greeks as epitomizing this kind of history insofar as he mines the past in order to provide his present with models for future action.[13] By looking into the past, one can identify the potential, and set a standard, for greatness in the future. But in order to render the past serviceable to the present, monumental historians must carefully omit anything that makes an exemplar particular to their given historical context; hence, the monumental historian must always *distort* the past:

> How much of the distinct would have to be overlooked if it was to produce that mighty effect, how violently the individuality of the past would have to be forced into a universal form and all its sharp corners and hard outlines broken up in the interest of conformity! (HL 2, KSA 1.261)

Despite the overtone of disapprobation contained in these remarks, Nietzsche is *not* campaigning against historical distortion *tout court*. Such distortion is, in moderation, a necessary condition of fruitful monumental history. But Nietzsche warns that monumental history is susceptible to excess, whereby it dangerously distorts the past for violent, seditious ends, or advocates a strain of atavism that detrimentally impedes progress. It is thus liable to hinder "those who are becoming and desiring," who yearn to evolve (HL 2, KSA 1.263).[14]

Thankfully, antiquarian history, which is principally concerned with faithfully documenting the past, can act as an antidote to the disfiguring

---

[13] For evidence that Nietzsche thought of Schiller in just this way, see KSA 7:29[117], 684.
[14] Note that the chief target of these critical remarks is Rousseau.

excesses of its monumental counterpart. The antiquarian serves life in his own, more obviously conservative manner: "By tending with care that which has existed from of old, he wants to preserve for those who shall come into existence after him the conditions under which he himself came into existence" (HL 3, KSA 1.265). Nietzsche describes this as an act of "clinging to one's own environment and companions, one's own toilsome customs " (HL 3, KSA 1.266). However, the myopic and reverent study of one's own past comes with its own attendant dangers:

> The antiquarian sense of a man, a community, a whole people, always possesses an extremely restricted field of vision; most of what exists it does not perceive at all, and the little it does see it sees much too close up and isolated; it cannot measure [*messen*] and it therefore accords everything it sees equal importance and therefore to each individual thing too great importance. There is a lack of that discrimination of value and that sense of proportion which would distinguish between the things of the past in a way that would do true justice to them [. . .]. (HL 3, KSA 1.267)

In stressing that *everything* is valuable within this narrow range of focus, antiquarian history ends up distorting the past in its own peculiar fashion. It artificially flattens history by emptying it of what we might call its *variability in value* (*Werthverschiedenheit*). As Catherine Zuckert (1976, 61–62) laconically puts it, the problem is that "antiquarian preservation changes the very past it would retain."[15] Moreover, this fetishistic piety toward traditions and cultural roots eventually means that antiquarian history is, like its monumental counterpart, liable to constrict growth and progress: it "knows only how to *preserve* life, not how to engender it; it always undervalues that which is becoming" (HL 3, KSA 1.268). Finally, when this mode of historical praxis extends beyond one's own national roots, it easily descends into "the repulsive spectacle of a blind rage for collecting, a restless raking together of everything that has ever existed" (ibid.) – at which point, it comes to embody the very quintessence of philistinism.

This brings us to *critical* history, which Nietzsche presents as an iconoclastic corrective to the antiquarian's conservatism: "in order to be able to live, man must possess and from time to time employ the strength to break up and dissolve [*zerbrechen und aufzulösen*] a part of the past" (HL 3, KSA 1.269). Critical history denudes the *unjust* origins of social constructs that

---

[15] Indeed, according to Nietzsche, all history can be said to have a distorting effect insofar as "all recollection is comparison, i.e., equation [*Gleichsetzen*]" (KSA 7:29[29], 636). For more on this point, see Salaquarda's instructive analysis of critical history (1984, esp. 20).

have grown constrictive or simply obsolete. For example, it might subvert "a privilege, a caste, [or] a dynasty" by showing how these were established through morally egregious violence. In demolishing the unquestioned authority of such constructions, critical history clears the ground for the creation of new social orders and traditions. It thereby allows us to supplant an embedded part of our "first nature" with a new "second nature" (HL 3, KSA 1.270).[16] This said, Nietzsche has misgivings about the feasibility, and indeed prudence, of this destructive enterprise.

> If we condemn these aberrations and regard ourselves as free of them, this does not alter the fact that we originate in them. The best we can do is to bring about an antagonism [*Widerstreite*] of our inherited, hereditary nature and our knowledge, and through a new, stern discipline combat our inborn heritage and implant in ourselves a new habit, a new instinct, a second nature, so that our first nature withers away [*abdorrt*]. It is an attempt to give oneself, as it were *a posteriori*, a past in which one would like to originate in opposition to that in which one did originate: – always a dangerous attempt because it is so hard to know the limit to denial of the past and because second natures are usually weaker than first. (HL 3, KSA 1.270)

The critical approach, when indulged to excess, runs the risk of deteriorating into a botched attempt at self-deracination. And Nietzsche underlines just how difficult it is to place a limit on the destructive animus inherent to critical history.[17] He thus avers that "men and ages which serve life by judging and destroying [*richten und vernichten*] a past are always dangerous and endangered men and ages" (ibid.). But caveats and qualifications notwithstanding, Nietzsche nonetheless sanctions this destructive act of radical critique – that is, the unmeasured struggle to empty a tradition of its cachet by means of divulging its ignominious origins.

These, then, are the potential uses of history for life, which is to say, for preservation (secured by antiquarian history) and flourishing (enabled by critical history and realized by monumental history). As we saw above, Nietzsche does not think man can survive without distorting and exploiting the past for his own purposes. And echoing Schopenhauer's account of assimilation, he describes this process of pressing history into the service of one's life-needs as one of *incorporation* (*Einverleibung*):

---

[16] Nietzsche first describes critical history as the means by which "the human" fulfills his desire "to free himself from necessity [*Noth*]" (KSA 7:29[115], 683).

[17] This emphasis on the fact that we often originate (*abstammen*) from the very elements of our culture that we wish to destroy can be seen as a step away from the position that he defends in BT 23 (KSA 1.149), where he suggests that Roman influences should be excised from German culture as a failed graft should be amputated from an otherwise healthy tree.

> The stronger the innermost roots of a man's nature, the more readily will he
> be able to appropriate or incorporate [*sich aneignen oder anzwingen*] the
> things of the past; and the most powerful and tremendous nature would be
> characterized by the fact that it would know no boundary at all at which the
> historical sense began to overwhelm it; it would draw toward, and into itself
> all the past, its own and that most foreign to it, and as it were transform it
> into blood. (HL 1, KSA 1.251)

The ability to *exploit* history in order "to transform and incorporate
[*einzuverleiben*] into oneself what is past and foreign, to heal wounds, to
replace what has been lost, to recreate broken molds" is what Nietzsche
refers to as "the *plastic force* [*Kraft*] of a human, a people, a culture" (HL 1,
KSA 1.251). He takes this force to have been maximally embodied by the
pre-Socratic ancient Greeks, who drew their knowledge of foreign cultures
together and subsequently *applied* it to their real needs (*ächte Bedürfnisse*).[18]
The Greeks' sharp understanding of their authentic needs endowed them
with a standard according to which they were able to regiment the tumult
of foreign influences that suffused their rich culture: "The Greeks gradually
learned to *organize the chaos* by following the Delphic teaching and
thinking back to themselves, that is, to their real needs, and letting their
pseudo-needs die out" (HL 10, KSA 1.333).

This gives us some indication as to how we might keep monumental and
antiquarian history within productive bounds. And indeed, Nietzsche
counsels that exemplars from past or foreign cultures – our models and
standards for aesthetic and ethical agency – should only be conserved and
transmitted to later generations if, and only if, they can be *implemented* as
expedients in the face of current obstacles. Thus, that which a vibrant
individual or culture "cannot subdue it knows how to forget" (HL 1, KSA
1.251). The dynamic of forgetting is therefore a necessary correlate to the
process of historical incorporation.

At a stroke, this strategy promises to resolve both (a) and (b). First, by
implementing utilizable knowledge, and forgetting that which is redundant, one brings into being a synthesis of influences tailored to one's true
aesthetic and ethical needs. Second, by making sure that one *applies* one's
knowledge, one reconnects one's inner life (of knowledge and belief) with
one's external being (in *praxis*). What this overview discloses is that the
struggle that Nietzsche recommends in HL is profoundly incompatible
with his abstract notion of agonal conflict. The primary reason for this is
that in HL he endorses a mode of struggle aimed at the direct

---

[18] See PTAG (KSA 1.807): "Whatever [the Greeks] learned they wanted to live through, immediately."

instrumentalization of that which is overpowered. As Vanessa Lemm (2013, 6) puts it, according to Nietzsche's ideal in HL, "the human being appropriates, dominates and rules over the past."

Another way that HL resists agonistic readings is in its persistent valorization of *unmeasured* conflict. For one, this is readily discernible in Nietzsche's approbation of critical history. But perhaps more pertinently, we have also just witnessed him exhorting us to forget expendable knowledge and let our "pseudo-needs die out," thereby ridding ourselves of their debilitating effects. The organizational struggle that Nietzsche propounds is therefore defined, on the one hand, by the struggle to *include* useful knowledge within the horizon of our true needs and, on the other, by the fight to conclusively *exclude* obsolete knowledge and what prove to be our mere pseudo-needs. Furthermore, this latter struggle is not one that aims to maintain a conflictual relation with that which has been excluded; its telos is complete annihilation – any excluded or forgotten datum of knowledge "*no longer exists*, the horizon is rounded and closed" (HL 1, KSA 1.251; emphasis mine).[19]

It should be added that while this process of elimination recalls the exclusive practice of ostracism described in HC, this does not warrant our labeling it agonal in kind. First, the eliminatory species of struggle denoted by ostracism should not itself be described as agonal; rather, ostracism represents a *non*-agonal safeguard of agonal contest, and should not be confounded with the species of conflict which the ancient Greeks contrived it to ensure. Second, as we saw in HC, Nietzsche frames ostracism as a fallback mechanism, one that the ancient Greeks only called upon if and when alternative sources of measure happened to fail, though such failure was by no means inevitable. As such, ostracism is not a *necessary* component of agonal culture in the way that exclusionary struggle is with respect to the dynamic of organizational conflict.

At the end of HL, Nietzsche reiterates his affirmation of unmeasured struggle in petitioning the "*youth*" – "that first generation of fighters and dragon-slayers" – to execute the urgent task set forth in the body of the essay. In dubbing them "dragon-slayers" and defending their right to "coarseness and immoderation [*Unmässigkeit*]" (HL 10, KSA 1.331), he blocks any hint of analogy with the form of measure endorsed in HC. This is a struggle to destroy (*zerstören*) the beliefs that frustrate the project of cultural renewal. And we can destroy such beliefs, according to Nietzsche, by subjecting them

---

[19] Drawing on BGE 188, Müller-Lauter (1999, 31) refers to this as "the healthy tendency to eliminate what could disturb the 'healthy closedness' of the horizon [...]."

to "mockery and hatred" (ibid.) – that is, through a process of *devaluation* or *radical critique.*

But what distinguishes the forms of unmeasured conflict that Nietzsche advocates from those that he so often rebukes as culturally injurious – such as, for example, the struggles of annihilation that he denigrates in HC? Apart from being nonphysical, the elimination sanctioned in HL *promotes* both life and culture by enabling creativity, agency and individuality. Nietzsche states that the great productive spirit only aims to "condemn" (*verurtheilen*) "what to him, as a living being and one productive of life, is destructive and degrading" (HL 4, KSA 1.278). What we may doubt is whether Nietzsche's attempt to harness this destructive force is immune to the dangers that he ascribes to critical history: Will Nietzsche's youthful dragon-slayers be able to set a limit on their own destructive activity? But moreover, are we moderns even *able* to supplant the exclusively antiquarian model of education that drives the crisis of disintegration? Or is this malignant growth simply inoperable, being too deeply rooted in our first nature to be removed without causing mortal damage?[20] While it remains a moot point whether Nietzsche's own project can overcome these obstacles, this should not leave us disaffected. No course of action could be more perilous than that of *inaction.* By Nietzsche's lights, in passively allowing knowledge to expand its dominion over life, we effectively condemn ourselves to death.

Regardless of their viability, Nietzsche's appeals for destructive action clearly mirror Schopenhauer's belief that elimination invariably attends the struggle for assimilation. Indeed, so far, our analysis has shown that Nietzsche's theory of organization reprises three defining features of his predecessor's conception of assimilative struggle:

1. It is aimed at subjugation (i.e., of the various data of knowledge to a person's or culture's true life-needs).
2. Its telos, instrumental hierarchy, is associated with health.
3. It is conditioned by unmeasured struggle (i.e., for the omission of redundant knowledge, the radical critique of counterproductive conventions, and the eradication of individuals' pseudo-needs).

One notable difference, however, is that whereas Schopenhauer merely *describes* the struggle for assimilation as a naturally occurring process,

---

[20] Nietzsche registers this problem in SE 6 (KSA 1.401–402): "The difficulty, however, lies for mankind in relearning and envisaging a new goal; and it will cost an unspeakable amount of effort to exchange the fundamental idea behind our present system of education, which has its roots in the Middle Ages [...], for a new fundamental idea."

Nietzsche's depiction of such conflict has an unmistakably normative objective. For Nietzsche, healthy organization requires that we *consciously* struggle for both incorporation and exclusion. We might be tempted to infer that the absence of the fourth criterion of assimilative conflict – that such conflict continues within the instrumental hierarchies which it tends to establish – is indicative of further divergence from Schopenhauer; yet, if we now turn to the question of self-knowledge as it is worked out in the latter two meditations, we will see that this criterion is indeed satisfied by Nietzsche's broader synthetic project.

3.2.3 *Knowing Thyself*

Self-knowledge represents a *sine qua non* of the organizational struggle that we unearthed in HL. One must know one's true needs in order to synthesize one's historical influences. Such knowledge provides the metric by which one is able to separate the wheat (to be incorporated) from the chaff (to be eliminated) – hence Nietzsche's emphasis on the "Delphic teaching," that is, the maxim: "know thyself" (HL 10, KSA 1.133). Self-knowledge is likewise fundamental within Schopenhauer's account of *subjective* organization – and indeed, in a manner germane to our current inquiry, since the conception of self-organization that Nietzsche develops in the latter two meditations (though especially in SE) is one that strongly recalls a great deal in Schopenhauer's account.

Notwithstanding the title of the second meditation – "Schopenhauer as Educator" – commentators are wont to claim that Schopenhauer is "scarcely present in the text" (Cavell 1990, 53), or even that the ideas advanced in SE plainly "contradict Schopenhauer's own philosophical views" (Conant 2001, 202). However, we should take care not to misread a lack of explicit mention of Schopenhauer for a lack of *presence*. Indeed, we have already had a preview of the formative influence that Schopenhauer seems to have exerted on UM, in spite of also turning up some fundamental points of divergence. In line with this, I will now defend the claim that Nietzsche's conception of psychological, agential organization is one that he largely inherits from Schopenhauer, and which is correspondingly committed to a number of Schopenhauerian metaphysical presuppositions. It is vital that we acknowledge this inheritance since it reveals just why the solutions Nietzsche presents to (a)–(c) become unsustainable in his later period (i.e., because he comes to reject their Schopenhauerian metaphysical premises).

Schopenhauer tells us that each person possesses their own distinctive character, or what he calls their unique "complete personality" (WWR 1,

2.155). Again recalling Kant, he initially informs us that an individual's character, or what he also refers to as their "individual will" (WWR 1, 2.344), has two sides: one that *appears* to us (our *empirical* character) and one that remains imperceptible (our *intelligible* character). Like all objects within the Kantian *Weltanschauung*, an individual's character is undetermined to the extent that it exists outside of space and time (qua *intelligible* character) as a thing in itself, exempt from the laws of causality. However, one's character appears as one's *empirical* character when one makes decisions and acts in the spatiotemporal world of representation. Crucially, Schopenhauer claims that one's character is in essence fixed. Just like any natural kind, an individual's character is defined by its own unchanging Platonic Idea (WWR 1, 2.265). One's character is thus determined at birth (WWR 1, 2.346), or as he puts it elsewhere, "inborn and unalterable" (Schopenhauer 2009, 106). When presented with a given conflict of motives and a given degree of knowledge about how best to pursue these motives, an individual will therefore only ever resolve upon one particular course of action. As such, their behavior is, according to Schopenhauer, determined with iron necessity.

Schopenhauer goes on to identify a third species of character – namely, *acquired* character. He describes how man finds in himself "the tendencies to all the various human aspirations and abilities"; yet, if one is to profitably follow a directed line in life instead of running in a "zigzag all over the place without getting anything done," some impulses "must be entirely repressed." In order to achieve this, "a human being must also *know* what he is willing, and *know* what he can do" (WWR 1, 2.358). By reflecting on our actions, he thinks we are able to glean a progressively more comprehensive picture of our unique empirical character. By virtue of this insight into our empirical character – and in particular our unique strengths and weaknesses – we learn which of our impulses we need to suppress in order to follow the path in life most suited to our personal aptitudes.

Nietzsche is openly skeptical toward Schopenhauer's account of acquired character. Indeed, he opens SE by casting doubt on the very possibility of self-knowledge. Man, he maintains, "is a thing dark and veiled" who can never say to himself "this is really you, this is no longer outer shell" (SE 1, KSA 1.340). But if this is the case, how could we ever be certain that we have obtained insight into our *true* needs and abilities and not those that merely *appear* so (i.e., our pseudo-needs and -abilities)? What sense does it make to speak of a core, essential self if we have no means of ever obtaining an assured vision of such a thing? Deepening this problem, elsewhere in SE Nietzsche openly rejects essentialist conceptions of the self. He thus maintains that while each individual may be a kind of "unicum," this in no way entails their being unified in any substantial sense; rather, echoing Hume's bundle theory of the self, he theorizes that we are each "a so strangely variegated [*buntes*] multiplicity [*Mancherlei*] gathered into a unity [*Einerlei*]" (SE 1, KSA 1.337). Moreover, even in 1865, he explicitly criticizes Schopenhauer's notion of empirical character, arguing that conceiving character as something fixed and determined negates the possibility of doing normative philosophy, which is by its very nature aimed at *changing* individuals.[21]

But this should not distract us from the strong undercurrent of essentialism that runs through UM. In WB, for instance, Nietzsche appears to openly concur with Schopenhauer's notion of character, albeit with certain modifications:

> It would be strange if that which a man can do best and most likes to do failed to become a visible presence within the total formation of his life; and in the case of men of exceptional abilities their life must become not only a reflection [*Abbild*] of their character, as is the case with everyone, but first and foremost a reflection of their intellect and of the capacities most personal to them. (WB 2, KSA 1.435)

So, character *is* realized with absolute necessity and automaticity for Nietzsche. One's life is the inexorable imprint of one's character, and thus any attempt to change or shape this character is entirely in vain. Further recalling Schopenhauer, in the above text Nietzsche sketches a rudimentary theory of *acquired* character. In his view, in order to unlock this supplementary dimension of the self we must first discover something beyond our basic character – namely, our *intellect* and "the capacities most personal to [us]" (our *eigenste Vermögen*), of which our life can *also* be a reflection, though it is not necessarily so. But whereas for Schopenhauer acquired character is something enjoyed by anyone who has harkened their calling in life, and correspondingly abstained from dilettantism, for Nietzsche it is an accomplishment reserved for only the most exceptional individuals.

Elsewhere in WB and SE we bear witness to Nietzsche conceiving the self in more clearly essentialist, Schopenhauerian terms. For example, where he speaks of the "core [*Kern*] of [one's] essence [*Wesens*]" (SE 3, KSA 1.359) and even simply of a person's "true essence" (*wahres Wesen*) (SE

---

[21] See KGW I/5, 276: "One criticizes Schopenhauerian ethics on account of its lack of imperative form: The thing that philosophers call character is an incurable sickness. An imperative ethic is one that deals with the symptoms of sickness, and while it fights [*kämpft*] against this, has the belief that it is getting rid of [*beseitigen*] the unitary basis [of the symptoms], the original disease."

1, KSA 1.341). And in SE 5 he acclaims the way in which Schopenhauer was governed (*waltet*) by his "Platonic Idea" (KSA 1.376). Finally, he declares that our true educators should enlighten us to precisely this essentialist facet of our deeper self: they should "reveal to you that the true, original meaning and basic stuff of your nature is something completely incapable of being educated or formed [*Unerziehbares und Unbildbares*] [. . .]" (SE 1, KSA 1.341).[22]

What is more, although Nietzsche harbors doubts regarding the possibility of self-knowledge, he nonetheless follows Schopenhauer in considering such knowledge to be an essential condition of self-organization. This is succinctly borne out in the following passage:

> [W]hat have you truly loved up to now, what has drawn your soul aloft, what has mastered it and at the same time blessed it? Set up these revered objects before you and perhaps their nature and their sequence will give you a law, the fundamental law of your actual [*eigentlichen*] self: Compare these objects one with another, see how one completes, expands, surpasses, transfigures another, how they constitute a stepladder upon which you have clambered up to yourself as you are now [. . .]. (SE 1, KSA 1.340)

Nietzsche hypothesizes that recollecting and comparing our highest joys reveals an inner law that describes the ideal trajectory of our self-development. This, he thinks, endows us with an idea of our higher self toward which we can determinately aim. Note that, in contrast to Schopenhauer's conception of empirical character, this fixed inner law is one that directs a continual process of *development* – it never describes us *as we are*. We might think of it as being analogous to the algebraic formula that describes the pattern underlying a numerical series. Such a formula, while lacking any determinate content of its own, nonetheless allows us to deduce how the series should continue for higher values.

The extrapolation of this inner trajectory is of interest to Nietzsche because, recalling HL, such self-knowledge forms the basis for organizing the self into a "harmonious whole" (*harmonische Ganzheit*) or "polyphonic harmony" (*vielstimmigen Zusammenklang*) (SE 2, KSA 1.342). Self-knowledge functions as a lynchpin, the discovery of which radiates order into the surrounding self. It enables the individual to become one of those rare types

> in whom everything, knowledge, desire, love, hate, strives toward a central point, a root force, and where through the compelling and commanding

---

[22] Other commentators have also remarked on Nietzsche's essentialist notion of the self in UM (e.g., Miner 2011, 339ff.).

supremacy [*die zwingende und herrschende Uebergewalt*] of this living center, a harmonious system is constructed here and there, above and below. (SE 2, KSA 1.342)

This idea is also apparent in Nietzsche's characterization of Wagner, whom he praises for the "severity and uniformity of purpose he imposed upon his will" (WB 9, KSA 1.496):

> [F]rom the moment when his ruling passion became aware of itself and took his whole nature in its charge [. . .], there was an end to fumbling, straying, to the proliferation of secondary shoots, and within the most convoluted courses and often daring trajectories assumed by his artistic plans there rules a single inner lawfulness [*Gesetzlichkeit*], a will, by which they can be explained [. . .]. (WB 2, KSA 1.435)

Once the ideal trajectory of the self has been deduced, or becomes "aware of itself," it functions as what Nietzsche describes as a "root" or "cardinal force," that is, a "middle point" under and around which all of our other capacities can then be coordinated.[23] Consonant with Schopenhauer's account of acquired character, ascertaining our calling in life is said to give us the fundamental criterion we need in order to synthesize our "knowledge, desire, love, [and] hate" into a stable and coherent system. We engender such holism by assessing how each subjective force can serve our authentic calling, and by then ordering them accordingly.[24] We should observe that Nietzsche not only construes this central point as the cornerstone or fulcrum of self-organization but, in addition to this, as the organizing force itself.

This brief overview brings to light the multifarious ways in which Nietzsche envisions the ideal self in UM: as a quasi-Schopenhauerian Idea, a quasi-Humean bundle, and a quasi-Aristotelian developmental law (or *entelechy*). Nietzsche manifestly vacillates over this issue, as he does vis-à-vis the possibility of self-knowledge. Determining his ambiguous relation to Schopenhauer's essentialism in UM, however, is not necessary with respect to our principal objective, which is to illuminate the unagonistic impetus of the text. It suffices to remark that Nietzsche consistently posits the existence of a deeper self that he believes ought to govern that individual psyche in a consistently centralized manner. This is problematic for agonistic readings of UM for two reasons. Firstly, because

---

[23] See KSA 7:30[9], 734: "Harmony is present when everything is related to a middle point, a cardinal force, not when numerous weak forces simultaneously play with one another."

[24] Although it is my contention that Nietzsche presents self-organization as a conscious process in UM, we should bear in mind that he explicitly rejects this position in later texts (as we will see in Chapter 4). See e.g., EH Clever 9.

the struggle for self-governance that Nietzsche is promoting is categorically directed at the *instrumentalization* of our serviceable subjective forces. Secondly, the notion of a "living center" that enduringly reigns over the hierarchy of the self is incompatible with the fluid pluralism of approximately equal powers that characterizes Nietzsche's agonism. In HC, his idealized agonal community is defined by decentered constellations of mutually limiting powers – what he calls a "contest of forces" (*Wettspiel der Kräfte*) – from which any hegemon is forcibly removed by means of ostracism (HC, KSA 1.788–789).

Aside from controverting the agonistic reading, this analysis of Nietzsche's campaign for instrumental hierarchy further vindicates the idea that we should read UM in terms of Schopenhauer's notion of assimilation. And there are yet further reasons as to why we might favor a Schopenhauerian interpretive framework. For Nietzsche, the struggle to coordinate our inclinations into a functional hierarchy is necessarily accompanied by an unmeasured struggle of *eradication*, a struggle for "the removal of all the weeds, rubble and vermin that want to attack the tender buds" of a burgeoning culture (SE 1, KSA 1.341). Nietzsche's sights are firmly set on the dross conventions that hinder the fruition of genius. He thus speaks with approbation of how Schopenhauer assailed "those aspects of his age that prevent[ed] him from being great," and did so with the aim of recovering "the health and purity native to him" (SE 3, KSA 1.362). Once again, note that *what* are being destroyed (*zerstört*) are, according to Nietzsche, *doxai*, and *how* they are being destroyed is by means of radical critique, or *denial* (*Verneinung*) (SE 4, KSA 1.364; SE 4, KSA 1.372). The false belief Nietzsche thinks that Schopenhauer most effectively dispelled is the idea that happiness constitutes the goal for which we should all strive. According to Nietzsche, Schopenhauer exposed the futility of pursuing happiness – showing it to be driven by ignorance of the fact that all such striving ever yields is a never-ending cycle of painful yearning, momentary satisfaction and boredom.[25] Schopenhauer debunked such beliefs by denuding their foundations in myopia and naïveté. Indeed, we might view Nietzsche's Schopenhauer as launching a distinctly unmeasured assault on the belief in, and impulse for, enduring happiness.[26]

---

[25] See KSA 7:35[12], 812, where Nietzsche speaks of "[t]he philosopher [...] as the destroyer of all apparent and seductive happiness and everything that promises such happiness [...]." In SE 4, KSA 1.373 he then quotes Schopenhauer as stating that "[a] happy life is impossible: the highest that man can attain to is a *heroic one*."

[26] See SE 4, KSA 1.372: The Schopenhauerian man "will, to be sure, destroy his earthly happiness through his courage; he will have to be an enemy to those he loves and to the institutions which have produced him; he may not spare men or things."

Like Schopenhauer, Nietzsche takes the discovery of our inner self to be a key source of increased efficacy and purposiveness; but whereas Schopenhauer merely emphasizes the way in which this revelation provides the basis necessary for suppressing (*unterdrücken*) diverting impulses, Nietzsche accents how it can act as an Archimedean point around which our psychological forces can be synthesized and *stimulated*. The ideal educator, Nietzsche stresses, should not merely engender the harmonious ordering of their pupil around a dominant "central root"; they should also "foster and nourish all available forces" (SE 2, KSA 1.342). Only wholly recalcitrant impulses should be eradicated in Nietzsche's view. As such, the ordering Nietzsche seeks is not one that simply forces our inclinations into passive submission to our core selves; this order is rather the very means by which subaltern forces can be fomented and held in ever-increasing degrees of mutual tension. This is forcefully illustrated by Nietzsche's characterization of Wagner and Wagner's music, in both of which, he tells us,

> storm and fire take on the compelling force of a personal will. Over all the individuals realized in sound and the struggles their passions undergo, over the whole vortex of opposing forces, there soars in the supremist self-possession an overwhelming symphonic intelligence which out of all this conflict brings forth concord: Wagner's music as a whole is an image of the world as it was understood by the great Ephesian philosopher [i.e., Heraclitus]: a harmony produced by conflict [...]. (WB 9, KSA 1.494)

Ideally, then, the passions should continue to struggle in their coordination, forming a dynamic balance like the opposed qualities described by Heraclitus.[27] And we should therefore not construe the dominating center of which Nietzsche speaks as having an exclusively suppressant effect on the subaltern forces of the self. Rather, it maximizes their mutual conflict, while constantly struggling to maintain order and keep psychological tension within beneficial limits. With this, we can affirm that the struggle proposed by Nietzsche as a solution to individual disintegration fulfills the fourth and final criterion of Schopenhauer's model of assimilative struggle – namely, that such struggle persists within the instrumental hierarchies that it tends to generate.

3.2.4   Common Purpose

We have so far been concerned with Nietzsche's remedies for individual disintegration. But what remains to be seen is how he proposes we

---

[27] See Introduction, §1.1.

counteract fragmentation at the level of the collective. In HL, he suggests that the solution to the problem of disintegrative egoism, which was seen to be caused by excessive historical learning, is what he calls "the suprahistorical" (*das Überhistorische*). Drawing on Schopenhauer, he theorizes that art and religion grant us metaphysical insight into the truth of reality, and thereby give us the existential foothold that we require in order to prevent ourselves from sliding into the stream of becoming and, with this, into disillusioned egoism. Myth and art (especially *mythological* art) are framed as antidotes to the excessive consumption of historical knowledge, namely, by virtue of the fact that they "bestow upon existence [*Dasein*] the character of the eternal and the stable [*Gleichbedeutenden*]" (HL 10, KSA 1.330).[28] Nietzsche was certainly probing the unifying properties of religion and art during this period of his thought – stating at one point that "art and religion are suitable for organizing the chaotic [*Chaotischen*]" (KSA 7:29-[192], 708).[29] However, while they appear to counteract existential disenchantment and its socially divisive implications, in UM it remains unclear how they actively serve to bind the community together.[30]

In SE, Nietzsche seeks to found cultural coherence on quite different, though nonetheless metaphysical bases. He summons his readers to a "struggle for culture" (*Kampf für die Kultur*) (SE 6, KSA 1.386) – a struggle to synthesize society into a thriving cultural unity. As will become evident, this cultural *Kampf* is aimed at the hierarchical organization of society around a higher, metaphysically grounded objective: the "generation of genius" (SE 3, KSA 1.358). What we need to ascertain is how Nietzsche's proposals resonate with Schopenhauer's conception of assimilative conflict.

Nietzsche insists that when one acknowledges one's need to strive for a higher (integrated) self, this commits one to duties that

---

[28] Nietzsche is here drawing on Schopenhauer's conception of "the metaphysical need," a notion with which he was certainly familiar (see e.g., letter to Gersdorff, April 7, 1866 [KGB I/2, 120]). Schopenhauer argues that humans require, as consolation for their knowledge of death and "the consideration of the suffering and distress of life" (WWR 2, 3.175ff.), some form of metaphysical explanation and justification for these hard realities. Since ordinary people lack the requisite time for philosophy, religious dogma leads them, by a shorter route, to the same ethical and metaphysical convictions. Religion thus grants ordinary people an insight into a higher realm of existence, one that transcends, and gives meaning to, that of fleeting appearance.

[29] N.B. Wagner (1911, 22) appropriates Schopenhauer's notion of the metaphysical need and tries to show how religious belief can help the state achieve its purpose (*Zweck*) – i.e., *stability* – by propagating the "most unshakeable, deeply blissful tranquility."

[30] In this connection, see Young's communitarian interpretation of Nietzsche. Young (e.g., 2010, 113–119) emphasizes the overlap between Nietzsche's and Wagner's accounts of how mythology (and the art that conveys that mythology) contribute to social unity.

are not the duties of a solitary; on the contrary, they set one in the midst of a mighty community *held together, not by external forms and regulations, but by a fundamental idea* [emphasis mine]. It is the fundamental idea of culture, insofar as it sets for each one of us but one task: *to promote the production of the philosopher, the artist and the saint within us and without us and thereby to work at the perfecting of nature.* (SE 5, KSA 1.381–382)

According to Nietzsche, collectively recognizing our duty to engender genius therefore functions as the primary foundation for social organization.[31] What we should now ask, however, is whether we can categorize this collective struggle – that is, the "struggle for culture" – as agonal in kind.

   In trying to elucidate the kind of contention that Nietzsche has in mind here, we should begin by underlining the deep equivocation in his conception of genius. Since genius represents the final end of his overarching cultural program, resolving this ambiguity is of paramount importance. On the one hand he adopts the Kantian understanding of genius as a "talent" (*Talent, Naturgabe*) or "the innate mental aptitude (*ingenium*) *through which* nature gives the rule to art" (CJ, 5.307). Needless to say, on this conception, the talent characteristic of genius is only enjoyed by a minority of innately gifted individuals. Let us call this *elite* genius. Those who read Nietzsche as a radical aristocrat – such as Rawls, for example – are inclined to argue that in SE Nietzsche exclusively promotes *this* form of genius. Rawls (1971, 325) thus reads SE as campaigning for an elitist species of perfectionism, according to which "it is the sole principle of a teleological theory directing society to arrange institutions and to define the duties and obligations of individuals so as to maximize the achievement of human excellence in art, science, and culture."[32] On this interpretation, the majority of individuals are expected to sacrifice their personal self-development for the sake of cultivating a minority of elite geniuses. And certainly, there are passages that unmistakably support this interpretation – for instance, where Nietzsche asks his readers: "[H]ow can your life, the individual life, receive the highest value, the deepest significance? [. . .] Certainly only by your living for the good of the rarest and most valuable exemplars, and not for the good of the majority" (SE 6, KSA 1.383–384).

---

[31] Nietzsche's solution is no doubt based on Wagner's Rousseauian definition of a "people" (*Volk*) as "those who feel a common need [*gemeinschaftliche Noth*]" (Wagner 1850b, 8; see also, 20–22, 214–215). Further, the image of the genius as a socially unifying figure is a conspicuously Emersonian trope (see Miller 1953).

[32] For a more recent defense of this position, see Hurka (2007, esp. 17–22).

On the other hand, alongside this, following Romantics such as Emerson and Byron, Nietzsche also employs a more global conception of genius qua the capacity for originality and authenticity, a capacity enjoyed by all, and in equal measure, without exception. Thus, Emerson (2000, 375) proclaims to *all* of his readers that "Genius is the power to labor better [. . .]. Deserve thy genius; exalt it." Let us call this the *global* conception of genius. Cavell, and following in his wake, James Conant, both reject Rawls's reading, contending instead that Nietzsche prioritizes the cultivation of this global type of genius: "[T]he 'something higher and more human' in question is not [. . .] that of someone *else*, but a further or eventual position of the self now dissatisfied with itself" (Cavell 1990, 52).[33] And to be sure, we can adduce passages from SE that seem to corroborate this reading – for example, where Nietzsche declares that "culture is the child of *each* individual's self-knowledge and dissatisfaction with himself" (SE 6, KSA 1.385; emphasis mine).

What, then, is the *one* goal that is meant to be binding us together, and for which we are meant to be striving – the cultivation of *my* global genius, or the cultivation of *others'* elite genius? In fact, as we will now see, Nietzsche views these as mutually complementary undertakings – the cultivation of genius "outside us" and "within us" represent "*one* task" (SE 5, KSA 1.382). In the final sections of SE, he proffers two arguments for why we ought to endeavor to cultivate the elite genius of others. The first argument is premised on little more than the realization that we must each strive to become elite geniuses ourselves. According to this line of reasoning, he suggests that it is in our own personal interest, as aspiring elite geniuses, to create a social environment that fosters this type of genius in others. First, our personal struggle to achieve elite genius demands the aid of other elite geniuses. We need exemplars who can illuminate, and spur us toward, higher goals – "we have to be lifted up" (SE 5, KSA 1.380). Second, in fashioning an environment in which elite geniuses are able to achieve *their* highest potential, Nietzsche thinks that we simultaneously create an environment in which *we* can independently strive to attain *our* highest potential. In struggling against the social forces that prevent elite geniuses such as Schopenhauer from emerging, we also "unwearyingly combat [*ankämpfen*] that which would deprive us of the supreme fulfillment of our existence by preventing us from becoming such Schopenhauerian men ourselves" (SE 5, KSA 1.160). This argument thus implies a fairly straightforward compatibility of egoistic and collective ends.

---

[33] See also Conant (2001, 203, 225).

But what about those individuals who know themselves to be wholly incapable of attaining the stellar heights of elite genius – "second- and third-rate talents" as Nietzsche calls them (SE 6, KSA 1.403)? How can he persuade such individuals – who might quite reasonably take their egoistic interests to be incompatible with those of the elite genius – to devote themselves to this higher, cultural goal?

In order to convince such middling types, Nietzsche declares that *generating elite genius represents the highest end of nature*, and so it is only by collectively pursuing this end that the mediocre can realize their highest calling. Otherwise put, it is only in contributing to the procreation of elite genius that the majority can maximize their own global genius. Nietzsche's argument hinges on the supposition that "[n]ature needs knowledge [of itself]" in order to attain redemption (*Erlösung*) (SE 5, KSA 1.379), and it can only achieve this enlightenment by means of the elite genius, who therefore constitutes nature's highest goal. Although elucidating this rather esoteric claim – which is grounded in an admixture of Hegel, Kant and Schopenhauer – would undoubtedly be illuminating, doing so would take us too far from our main line of inquiry. What is worth mentioning, however, is that Nietzsche follows Schopenhauer in viewing nature as *vainly* pressing toward its goals. This conception of nature is perhaps most conspicuous in Schopenhauer's portrait of the artistic genius:

> [A]ctual objects are almost always very deficient exemplars of the Idea presented in them: hence the genius needs imagination [*Phantasie*] in order to see in things not what nature actually created, *but rather what it was trying unsuccessfully to create*, a failure due to that struggle between its forms [. . .]. (WWR 1, 2.220; emphasis mine)

Analogously, Nietzsche considers nature to be incapable of achieving its goal of producing ideal humans (i.e., elite geniuses) unaided: we see "nature pressing toward man and again and again failing to achieve him" (SE 6, KSA 1.386). Consequently, Nietzsche deems it necessary "to replace that 'obscure impulse' with a conscious willing" (SE 6, KSA 1.387). This is what he describes as the "*metaphysical significance* [*Bedeutung*] *of culture*" (SE 6, KSA 1.401). Culture's true *raison d'être* is to aid nature in its otherwise futile endeavor to realize elite genius: "[E]verything calls to us: come, assist, complete, bring together what belongs together, we have an immeasurable longing to become whole" (SE 6, KSA 1.386).

The basic structure of this argument can therefore be summarized as follows: given that nature's highest goal is the production of elite genius, it is *our* goal to assist nature in achieving this, *even if we are without hope of becoming elite geniuses ourselves.* Contrary to Cavell's interpretation, Nietzsche demands the sacrifice of our egoistic goals for the sake of elite geniuses – that is, "on behalf of *another individual [Einzelner]*" (SE 6, KSA 1.384; emphasis mine).[34] Crucially, this gives us further cause to reject agonistic readings, insofar as the social order that Nietzsche is advocating with such arguments is one unquestionably characterized by entrenched inequality and instrumental social relations. Yet we must take care not to misinterpret the nature of this instrumentalization. Contrary to Rawls's reading, it is not conceived as an oppressive social arrangement. Instead, Nietzsche stresses that lesser individuals stand to *gain* by acquiescing to their metaphysical duty, since it is only in so doing that their lives come to "possess significance and a goal" (SE 6, KSA 1.403). It is only by *voluntarily* serving elite genius that we realize nature's highest purpose and with this, our own highest capacities. In striving to attain this external end, we therefore concurrently work toward maximizing our own inner, global genius.[35]

It should by now be apparent that *neither* the reading of Rawls *nor* that of Cavell stand up to scrutiny – the entire either/or approach is misguided. Both err in assuming that Nietzsche is operating with one or the other of the aforementioned definitions of genius. In actuality, though, we find him invoking *both* conceptions, and, furthermore, arguing that when taken as cultural goals, they are not just compatible, but *mutually complementary*.

In formulating these collective ends, Nietzsche proves himself to be fulfilling what he designates as the ideal cohesive function of the philosopher qua "physician of culture" – namely, to "bind everyone through a common goal *[Ziel]*" (KSA 7:30[8], 734).[36] Nonetheless, it should be restated that he principally strives to establish this cohesion by cajoling large swathes of society into an enduring position of subservience.[37] This is pertinent because it is on these grounds that we must rebut agonistic conceptions of Nietzsche's struggle for culture in SE.

As we turn to some of Nietzsche's more concrete recommendations as to how we might achieve cultural renewal, we unearth yet more obstacles for the agonistic reading, and, simultaneously, further support for our

---

[34] See also KSA 7:30[8], 733.

[35] Andrew Huddleston (2014, 135–160 [see esp. fn.3]) draws a similar conclusion.

[36] See also KSA 7:30[7], 732.

[37] Note that Jeffrey Church (2015) does not view Nietzsche as persuading (i.e., pressuring or manipulating) his readers into making this voluntary sacrifice to elite genius: "Rather than coercing individuals, Nietzsche draws on the power of shame that excellent individuals can arouse in the majority" (257). *Pace* Church, though, I find it difficult to view this kind of shaming as anything but psychological coercion.

Schopenhauerian line of interpretation. We should first examine Nietzsche's call for the creation of a sequestered social space for cultivating elite geniuses, one vigilantly shielded from any pressures extraneous to this goal, be they the needs of the economically or politically powerful, or even the elite genius's own material needs (they should have "no necessity for bread-winning") (SE 8, KSA 1.411). Nietzsche commends the "small band" who view cultural institutions as a bulwark (*Schutzwehr*) protecting elite geniuses from the vulgar utilitarian demands of society (SE 6, KSA 1.402).[38] With respect to *philosophical* genius, one way that Nietzsche envisions this being realized is by means of completely purging philosophy from the sphere of academia. He complains that universities have rendered philosophy ridiculous by allowing it to be subordinated to the base ends of the state. It is therefore a "demand of culture that philosophy should be deprived of any kind of official or academic recognition [. . .]. Let the philosophers grow untended" (SE 8, KSA 1.422). In this way, Nietzsche incites his readers to a distinctly unagonal fight for the complete abolition of academic philosophy.[39]

Nietzsche's struggle for culture is indissociable from a "hostility towards those influences, habits, laws, institutions in which he fails to recognize his goal [*Ziel*]: the production of the genius" (SE 6, KSA 1.386). But, as we have just seen, this hostility is far from entirely measured in kind. Indeed, Nietzsche avows the fact that "the genius must not fear to enter into the most hostile relationship [*feindseligsten Widerspruch*] with the existing forms and order" (SE 3, KSA 1.351). He thus advocates *superlative* hostility toward cultural orders that stymie the birth of genius. This initial purge must then be followed, he instructs us, by a process of "continual purifica-tion [*Läuterung*]," whereby any encroachment of extraneous demands into the cultural refuge of the elite genius is promptly thwarted (SE 6, KSA 1.403). Consequently, even if we managed to establish the hierarchy necessary for genius, this would not entitle us to declare a final victory. The battle is *never* conclusively won. Nietzsche's struggle for culture demands that we relentlessly endeavor to maintain this ideal hierarchy by combatting the emergence of social formations that are inimical to the flourishing of elite genius.

Having demonstrated that for Nietzsche perpetual strife represents a necessary condition of purposive social organization, we can now soundly

---

[38] Nietzsche refers to this as the "refuge of culture" (KSA 7:30[7], 733).

[39] See FEI Preface, where Nietzsche states that "between you and the present lies the destruction of the gymnasium, perhaps even the destruction of the university" (KSA 1.648).

conclude that his struggle for culture instantiates the key structural features of Schopenhauer's model of assimilative conflict. Thus:

1. It is directed toward subjugation (of the majority to the needs of elite genius);
2. The hierarchy for which it strives is associated with (cultural) health;
3. It is conditioned by unmeasured conflict (toward social conventions that hamper elite genius);
4. It continues within the hierarchies that it tends to generate (as a struggle to maintain this hierarchy through "continual purification").

We now have a comprehensive picture of how Nietzsche proposes to remedy the three pathological forms of disintegration that were enumerated above. Against the self-fragmentation that hindered agency (a), we found him recommending that we *instrumentalize* the utilizable knowledge, habits and values that we have acquired from other cultures. By subordinating these to our true life-needs, we shape them into an integrated whole which is able to facilitate agency. At the same time, he enjoins us to eliminate redundant cultural influences that fail to serve our life-needs. Through this dual struggle he believes that we can resolve the pathological diremption of our inner and outer lives (b). By forging our myriad habits, beliefs and values into a coherent unity – one dominated by our life-needs – we render these psychological influences on our agency *externally applicable* (i.e., implementable in our quotidian practical lives). Finally, as a corrective to the social division Nietzsche associates with cynical egoism (c), he recommends that we collectively subscribe to the metaphysically grounded goal of cultivating elite genius.

By virtue of its analogy with Schopenhauer's model of assimilation, Nietzsche's struggle for culture is manifestly incompatible with his notion of agonal conflict. Although this campaign for assimilation may be considered measured insofar as it aims to preserve that which proves useful, we have also seen Nietzsche persistently emphasizing the need for *unmeasured* confrontation. Thus, he calls on us to root out the habits, opinions, traditions and institutions that impede the urgent task of self- and social-unification. We should further observe that eradication and measured incorporation represent two halves of a single dynamic, the ultimate goal of which is *coordination* – hence my treating both processes under the single rubric of organizational struggle. In misconstruing Nietzsche's prescriptions in UM as agonal in kind, previous commentators have tended to occlude the decisive value that he identifies in hierarchical organization, instrumentalization and eradication. These considerations indicate that we would do well to exercise great caution when analyzing Nietzsche's wider philosophy through the interpretive prism of HC.

Our secondary objective was to illuminate the significant structuring influence of Schopenhauer on Nietzsche's thought in UM, which should now be beyond reasonable doubt. But we should take care not to mistake this structuring influence for a wholesale avowal of Schopenhauer's viewpoint. Nietzsche significantly modifies various aspects of Schopenhauer's account of purposive organization. Most obviously, he gives Schopenhauer's purely descriptive treatment of organization a strikingly normative coloration, urging us to conceive healthy unity as an accomplishment contingent on our conscious efforts. This, however, should not cause us to neglect the fact that he construes both the self and nature in patently Schopenhauerian terms, the import of which cannot be overstated. In denuding this influence, we have simultaneously laid bare the two key metaphysical fundaments of Nietzsche's synthetic project in UM. First, we discovered that knowledge of the unchanging, essential dimension of our unique character is imperative for the goal of self-organization. Second, we witnessed Nietzsche invoking a teleological vision of nature as striving (and largely failing) to spawn elite geniuses. And recall that the force of his demand that we foster elite genius in others depends on our buying into this speculative theory of natural teleology. Yet, as we established in Chapter 1, Nietzsche was growing disaffected with Schopenhauer's metaphysics as early as the 1860s, and by the time of HH this disaffection had evolved into outright rejection. Before we examine his later theory of organization, we should briefly survey how his rejection of Schopenhauerian metaphysics undermines the foundations of his synthetic project in UM.

3.3   Nietzsche's Attack on the Foundations of Organization

In Chapter 1, we analyzed the way in which Nietzsche denies the possibility of legitimately ascribing any positive properties to the world in itself. In "On Schopenhauer" (1868) (KGW I/4, 417–426), for example, we saw that he rejects Schopenhauer's description of the noumenal world as an eternal, unified and free will. For Nietzsche, such speculative, metaphysical predication constitutes a flagrant transgression of the Kantian critical ban. We are cognitively barred from the world in itself, if indeed there even exists such a world from which to be barred. This promptly rules out the idea that Nietzsche floats in HL, namely, that religion, myth or art might grant us a suprahistorical refuge by putting us in touch with some a priori metaphysical truth of reality.[40] But what really interests us here is how he specifically undermines the metaphysical conceptions of the self and nature that condition his synthetic project in UM.

A convenient place to begin trying to unpick Nietzsche's rejection of the Schopenhauerian self is with his nominalist objections to Platonic idealism. In criticizing idealism, Nietzsche thereby commits himself to rejecting Schopenhauer's metaphysical understanding of character qua Idea. Already in TL, written in the same year as DS (1873), he refutes the claim that natural kinds have any objective existence, that is, beyond the specifically human picture of the world. Closer inspection of nature, he contends, discloses nothing more than a conglomeration of irreducibly *unique* cases. Humans then abstract from the differences between roughly comparable cases to create so-called natural kinds. Omitting the discrepancies between the unique members of these man-made groups then

> awakens the idea that, in addition to [individual] leaves, there exists in nature the "leaf," something like an original model [...]. We obtain the concept, as we do the form, by overlooking what is individual and actual; whereas nature is acquainted with no forms and no concepts, and likewise with no species, but only with an X which remains inaccessible and undefinable for us. For even our contrast between individual and species is something anthropomorphic and does not originate in the essence of things [...]. (TL, KSA 1.880)[41]

For Nietzsche, the belief that there exist "originary forms" (*Urformen*) in nature is a fallacious inductive inference. Individual objects are not inferior copies of an ideal prototype; they are unique instances, even if they often happen to exhibit points of resemblance with other objects.[42]

Although the later Nietzsche takes exception to the epistemically "dark" and "uncertain" nature of Schopenhauer's Ideas (CW, KSA 6.36), his general grievance with idealism becomes far more focused on its practical ramifications. For instance, in GS 372, entitled *"Why we are not idealists,"* he rejects the "cold realm of 'Ideas,'" less on account of its questionable

---

[40] See also HH 10, in which Nietzsche exclaims that *"a religion has never yet, either directly or indirectly, either as dogma or as parable, contained a truth."* Elsewhere, he suggests that although religion may once have fulfilled the human need for consolation, and even facilitated social organization (HH 472), these needs can (and should) "be weakened and exterminated [*ausrotten*]" (HH 27). See also HH 145, 146, 150.

[41] See also HH 14, where Nietzsche states that "so often, the unity of the word is no guarantee of the unity of the thing [*Sache*]."

[42] See KSA 7:41[59], 592: "A thing [*Ding*] to which a concept precisely corresponds would be *without* origin. Plato's error of the *eternal Ideas*." See also KSA 9:3[124], 87.

verisimilitude, so much as by reason of the harm that it so often wreaks on our sensual existence. The injury stems from the fact that all idealism devalues the senses as vehicles of knowledge. Nietzsche's rejection is therefore no longer premised on the *falsity* of Ideas, understood as their lack of correspondence to a purportedly real world. The crux of his attack rather lies in his conviction that they are simply more misleading than the senses: "*Ideas* are worse seductresses than the senses." And as we read on, we discover that Nietzsche is more perturbed by the way in which Ideas lure us away from *life* than with their lack of objective reality. Ideas, he warns, desensualize people, steadily making them "*grow paler.*" As we saw in the Introduction, however, Nietzsche maintains that Plato forged his realm of Ideas as an expedient means of tightening the reins on his *over*-powerful senses, thereby counteracting their tendency to excess. By contrast, however, the average modern suffers from a badly starved sensuality, and is therefore perhaps "not healthy enough *to need* Plato's idealism." Where the Ideas offered Plato a salubrious psycho-physiological check, for us they merely serve to deepen our impoverishment.

In light of these criticisms, it should now be plain why Nietzsche could no longer maintain that Schopenhauer was able to synthesize himself by means of discovering his unique "Platonic Idea" – the metaphysical kernel of his self (SE 5, KSA 1.376). Nor could Nietzsche coherently uphold his implicit conviction that the elite genius embodies the ideal form of human, which nature is forever clumsily struggling to make manifest (SE 6, KSA 1.386–387). But we should remark that Nietzsche makes a number of more direct attacks on the essentialist notion of the self. In HH 41, for example, he pointedly contests the Schopenhauerian concept of "unchangeable character" as a false inference from the relative stability of an individual's personality across a single lifetime; and elsewhere he discourages us from treating ourselves as a "rigid, unchanging [*beständiges*], single individuum" (HH 618).

In stark opposition to Schopenhauer's notion of the unitary "individual will," Nietzsche argues that humans subject the numerous unique experiences that they have of their own personal will to the very same process of simplification that generated the illusory Platonic forms.[43] For Nietzsche, scrutiny reveals acts of willing to be comprised of a *complex* constellation of psychological and physiological processes, which we then misconstrue as a simple unity. Thus, in BGE 19, he rebuts Schopenhauer's conception of

---

[43] See AOM 5, where Nietzsche speaks of "the word 'will,' which Schopenhauer remolded as a common designation for many different human states [. . .]." See also HH 14 and 18, and D 115.

the individual's will as a simple phenomenon, arguing that willing is "above all, something complicated, something unified only in a word."[44] Hence, he deflates the Schopenhauerian dogma that the activity of willing discloses a single, essential or core self.

In D Nietzsche then campaigns against the notion of moral responsibility by demolishing the idea of a stable subject to which such responsibility could possibly be ascribed.[45] What we variously call the "subject," "self," "ego" or "I" is merely a multiplicity of interrelated drives. A drive, or *Trieb*, roughly designates an ingrained appetite or behavioral disposition. In this period alone, Nietzsche designates a panoply of such drives: for example, a drive "for calm" (D 109), "for distinction" (D 113), "to attachment and care for others" (D 143), "to knowledge" (D 429); and there is then a "sex drive" (KSA 9:11[16], 447), a "property drive [*Eigenthumstrieb*]," a "nutritive drive" (KSA 9:11[47], 459) and a "drive for revenge" (GS 49). According to Nietzsche, it is a fluid confederation of just such drives "which constitute[s] one's essence [*Wesen*]" (D 119). Against proponents of the "doctrine of the unchangeability of character," Nietzsche maintains that we are each of us free to give shape to this confederation – presumably, in accordance with our higher-order desires (D 560). However, here is not the place for a detailed reconstruction of Nietzsche's drive psychology; for now, suffice it to say that he conceives the self as an amalgamation of such drives – a position that he maintains throughout the later period. Hence, he refers to the soul in BGE 12 as a "social construction [*Gesellschaftsbau*] of drives and affects."[46]

Although Nietzsche's deflationary attacks on the notion of a unified, atomistic self are often simply asserted without argumentation, he insists that the composite nature of both the will and the self is revealed by "more cautious" self-observation (BGE 19).[47] Thus, in BGE 17, he takes issue with the Cartesian "proof" of the self qua *res cogitans*, contending that we are only aware of the "process" or "activity" of thinking and that the existence

---

[44] See also GS 127.   [45] See e.g., D 115.

[46] See also BGE 6, 9, 19. For an adroit critique of Nietzsche's fictionalist account of the self, see Gardner (2009, 2–5).

[47] Nietzsche's critique of subjectivity bears many parallels with that of Hume. As Nietzsche theorizes in KSA 12:10[19], 465: "'The subject' is the fiction that many *equal* [*Gleiche*] states in us are the effect of one substratum: but it is *we* who first created the 'equality' [*Gleichheit*] of these states; our adjusting them and making them similar is the fact, not their similarity (– which ought rather to be denied –)." Compare Hume (1739, 168): "The identity, which we ascribe to the mind of man, is only a fictitious one, and of a like kind with that which we ascribe to vegetables and animal bodies. It cannot, therefore, have a different origin, but must proceed from a like operation of the imagination upon like objects." As Gardner (2009) convincingly argues, however, Nietzsche does not seriously consider Kant's rejoinder to Hume in CPR.

of a self or "I" *doing* this thinking is no more than a dubious inference. The idea of an underlying "I" is in his view "a supposition, an assertion," "a *falsification* of the facts" (BGE 17).[48] This rules out the possibility of one being able to look back over one's past joys and thereby discover "the fundamental law of [one's] actual self" (SE 1, KSA 1.340), which we found to be fundamental to the synthetic project sketched in SE.

There is no self external to our impulses and appetites that we could call our "actual" or "true" self. And when we believe ourselves to be resisting the force of an overbearing drive, we *never* do so from the position of some core, authentic part of our self: "While 'we' believe we are complaining about the vehemence of a drive [*Trieb*], at bottom it is one drive *which is complaining about another*" (D 109).[49] This means that there is no way one could possibly organize oneself from the standpoint of some impulse that could be considered authentically one's own, the reason being that according to Nietzsche there *is* no impartial self that stands over and above one's drives. Thus, he tacitly disavows his earlier conviction that our struggle to order the various influences on our agency should be orchestrated from the perspective of our "actual self."

But why, we should ask, have we constructed the fiction of a unitary self? Briefly put, Nietzsche believes that our survival depends upon the illusion of subjective stability. The simplification of our self-experience represents a "condition of life" (*Lebensbedingung*) (KSA 11:38[3], 526) insofar as it renders the chaotic multiplicity of (interior) reality manageable.[50] By virtue of the fact that this enables our survival, Nietzsche considers it to be both "useful and important" (KSA 11:40[21], 639). The problem is that this pragmatically postulated self has been hypostatized, and thereby transformed from a useful fiction into an allegedly real metaphysical entity. Nietzsche deems this act of reification to be pernicious insofar as it constitutes "the fundamental presupposition" (*Grundvoraussetzung*) of life-denying systems of morality, and especially, "Christian doctrine"

---

[48] See also KSA 12:7[60], 315, where Nietzsche states that the idea of the substantial self "is not something given, it is something added and invented and projected behind what there is."
[49] See also BGE 117.
[50] In KSA 12:9[144], 148, Nietzsche suggests that such processes of simplification are a precondition of human existence: "One should not understand this *compulsion* to construct concepts, species, forms, purposes, laws ('*a world of identical cases*') as if they enabled us to fix the *true world*; but as a compulsion to arrange a world for ourselves in which *our existence* is made possible – we thereby create a world which is calculable, simplified, comprehensible, etc., for us." See also KSA 9:11-[270], 545.

(BGE 54). After all, a fixed subject is needed to ground the religious concepts of guilt and sin that are so anathema to Nietzsche.

He also becomes increasingly skeptical toward the kind of self-knowledge that we previously found him advocating in UM. In SE we saw that he already casts doubt on the possibility of discerning an essential, core self; but we also established that he nonetheless instructs us to ascertain the ideal direction in which our self both wills and develops (its "inner lawfulness"). This project is undone by a number of later texts however. In D 115, for example, entitled "*The so-called 'I*,'" he argues that we only have consciousness of, and words for, the extreme states of our self. Its breadth of fine nuance forever eludes observation and articulation (we might, on this interpretation, compare the extreme states of the self to the narrow portion of the electromagnetic spectrum visible to the naked human eye).[51] Due to this blinkering of our introspective view, Nietzsche concludes that "[w]e are none of us that which we appear to be in accordance with the states for which alone we have consciousness and words [. . .]" (D 115). In D 119, he then foregrounds the practical ramifications of this self-opacity:

> However far a man may go in self-knowledge, nothing however can be more incomplete than his image of the totality of *drives* [*Triebe*] which constitute his being. He can scarcely name even the cruder ones: [. . .] *above all the laws* [*Gesetze*] *of their nutriment remain wholly unknown to him* [emphasis mine].

Nietzsche's skepticism regarding the possibility of self-knowledge and -cultivation further deepens in GS 354. In this aphorism he theorizes that (self-)consciousness only evolved to the extent that it helped humans identify, communicate and ensure what the collective needed to survive. Everything that we can become conscious of is, according to Nietzsche, "finely developed only in relation to its usefulness to community or herd"; and therefore, he continues, "each of us, even with the best will in the world to *understand* ourselves as individually as possible, 'to know ourselves,' will always bring to consciousness precisely that in ourselves which is 'non-individual,' that which is 'average.'" He concludes from this that we only have access to the "shallowest, worst part" of ourselves.

These objections unequivocally deny the possibility of obtaining the kind of self-knowledge required for the synthetic project that Nietzsche proposes in UM. In the first place, Nietzsche refutes the *existence* of the kind of

---

[51] See also D 212.

essential self that he presupposes in UM – there simply is no "kernel," "Platonic Idea," "personal will," "inner lawfulness" or "actual self" that we could possibly identify. But second, even if there *were* such a unique, "true, original meaning and basic stuff of [our] nature [*Wesen*]" (SE 1, KSA 1.341), no prospective educator, however gifted, could ever lead us to consciousness thereof since it would lie beyond our epistemic reach.

3.3.1 Debunking Natural Teleology

But what about the second cornerstone of Nietzsche's early synthetic project – that is, natural teleology? Unfortunately, this does not fare any better than its counterpart. Already in 1868, in a plan for a dissertation he intended to write on Kant's conception of teleology, he argues that "outer purposiveness is a deception [*Täuschung*]" (KGW I/4 62[12], 553). According to Nietzsche, "[t]he purposiveness of the organic, the lawfulness [*Gesetzmäßigkeit*] of the inorganic is brought into nature by our intellect [*Verstande*]" (KGW I/4 62[7], 551).[52] Indeed, "there is no order and disorder in nature" (KGW I/4 62[19], 555), "purposiveness is our idea" (KGW I/4 62[34], 562). Like Empedocles before him, Nietzsche submits that "chance [*der Zufall*] can find the most beautiful melody" (KGW I/4 62[12], 553). So, even prior to UM, he privately holds that pure mechanism and brute causal coincidence *can* sufficiently account for the emergence of organisms in all their melodious, interwoven complexity.[53] Since, contrary to Kant, this *is* conceivable, there is no real need to posit teleological causality as a principle of reflective judgment.[54] Purposiveness is therefore illegitimately inferred: in nature, "we see *existence* and its means, and conclude that these means are purposive" (KGW I/4 62[15], 554).

In HH, however, the idea underlying these disjointed preparatory notes is worked into a more coherent refutation of teleological causality. For instance, in HH 2 Nietzsche criticizes philosophers for depicting the human type as an unchanging *aeterna veritas*; and, furthermore, he derides their mistaken assumption that we can deduce the purpose of any given nonhuman object by referring it to man as he currently exists: "the whole

---

[52] In making this argument, Nietzsche draws on Schopenhauer's criticisms of outer purposiveness in WWR 2 (3.372ff.). See Crawford (1988, 105–127). On Nietzsche's critique of teleology, see Hatab (2005, 61–63); Abel (1998, 133–140, 439–441).

[53] See KGW I/4 62[27], 559: "Mechanism combined with casualism provides this possibility."

[54] Nietzsche theorizes in KGW I/4 62[27], 559, that "it is only necessary to demonstrate a coordinated possibility in order to eradicate the *compelling element* [*das Zwingende*] of Kant's idea."

of teleology is constructed by speaking of the man of the last four millennia as of an *eternal* man toward whom all things in the world have had a natural relationship from the time he began." Nietzsche, however, spurns the idea of man as a fait accompli, preferring to construe him as something enduringly protean. From this perspective, one cannot conclude that nature's final purpose is to eternally engender geniuses according to a single, ideal mold. Humans as we know them will, in time, evolve into some quite distinct form of life.[55] The relevant implication of these remarks is that the ideal Schopenhauerian, whom Nietzsche exalts in UM, cannot in fact be conceived as nature's highest goal.

Nietzsche pursues a similar line of argument in GS 109, where he claims that the order that we identify in the immediately surrounding world is most probably a mere product of local coincidence, and that we therefore cannot extrapolate from this that the universe and nature form an ordered, end-orientated whole. On the contrary,

> The total character of the world [. . .] is for all eternity chaos, not in the sense of a lack of necessity but of a lack of order, organization, form, beauty, wisdom, and whatever else our aesthetic anthropomorphisms are called.

The ordered world in which we happen to live is merely an "exception," and he expressly adds (in what might be read as an allusion to SE) that "the exceptions are not the secret goal [*Ziel*]." To suggest that nature "strives" [*strebt*] toward some hidden end is to commit an anthropomorphic fallacy; defenders of outer purposiveness illegitimately project agency, ends and values that are peculiar to humans onto nature. In point of fact, though, "there are no ends" in nature; all we really find is necessity (*Notwendigkeit*).[56]

Though the later Nietzsche does on occasion slip back into a teleological register when discussing nature, he broadly maintains this denial of natural teleology.[57] The critical thesis of GS 109 is even quite clearly recapitulated in TI, where he states that "[p]eople are *not* the products of some special design, will, or purpose, they do *not* represent an attempt to achieve an

---

[55] See also HH 38, in which Nietzsche states that both *Wissenschaft* and nature know "no regard for final ends [*letzte Zwecke*]." Consequently, as Abel (1998, 137) remarks, Nietzsche begins to stress that humans need to posit their *own* goals.

[56] With respect to this point, as well as Nietzsche's general rejection of Schopenhauer's veiled teleology, see KSA 9:4[310], 177; D 122.

[57] For an example of Nietzsche reverting to teleological language, see GM II 1, KSA 5.291: "To breed an animal with *the prerogative to promise* – is that not precisely the paradoxical task which nature has set herself with regard to humankind?"

'ideal of humanity' [. . .]. We have invented the concept of 'purpose': there are no purposes in reality" (TI Errors 8). In these remarks, Nietzsche vitiates the teleological vision of nature that we discovered to be fundamental to his early synthetic project. He has divested himself of the means by which he proposed to persuade "second- and third-rate talents" to relinquish their egoistic aspirations and subordinate themselves to the collective enterprise of generating elite genius. Consequently, he now lacks a convincing account of how we can combat the pernicious egoism that drives social disintegration (c).

3.4   Conclusion

In the first two sections of this chapter, we delineated the type of struggle that Nietzsche prescribes to remedy the crisis of disintegration. The notion of organizational struggle brought to light by this analysis was found to be dichotomous, consisting of both measured and unmeasured conflict – though the measured component of this struggle was found to be of a distinctly unagonal sort, being geared toward the instrumentalization of weaker, or inferior elements. We also identified how Schopenhauer's theory of assimilation paradigmatically structures Nietzsche's prescriptions in UM. And this was seen to be equally true of Nietzsche's recommendations regarding our organization of knowledge, the ordering of society and the synthesis of our psychological aptitudes and behavioral dispositions. But Schopenhauer's influence proved to be more than merely structural; indeed, we found that Nietzsche builds the following two substantive Schopenhauerian theses into the foundations of his synthetic project:

A.   There is an essential component to the self (to which we have epistemic access);
B.   Nature proceeds in accordance with pre-given ends (albeit inefficiently).

Yet in the final section of this chapter, we exposed how he roundly undermines each of these two premises. Having compromised these fundaments, Nietzsche must accept that the early model of organization that he designed in response to the crisis of disintegration itself disintegrates. We can do little more than speculate why Nietzsche granted these two metaphysical suppositions such a fundamental role, given that he had already begun to undercut them long before the publication of UM. I suggest that we read UM as his last attempt to salvage the Schopenhauerian *Weltanschauung*. However, around the time of his departure from Basel and final break with Wagner

(1876), he comes to fully accept the futility of this endeavor. In HH he then publicly pulls the temple down upon his earlier synthetic project. But this act of demolition leaves two resounding questions hanging in the air: Does the crisis of disintegration disappear from Nietzsche's later writings? If not, then on what alternative fundaments does he construct his new synthetic project?

CHAPTER 4

Organizational Struggle in the Later Nietzsche

We concluded the previous chapter by asking whether disintegration remains a pressing concern for the later Nietzsche. We saw that if this concern does indeed persist then he needs to concoct a novel remedy, since his earlier solution was found to be premised on metaphysical suppositions that he himself comes to abjure. And what we discover is that while Nietzsche's thought undergoes many permutations between his earlier and later writings, social and individual disintegration remain high on his agenda. In Z, for example, he laments the fact that he "walk[s] among human beings as among the fragments and limbs of human beings" (Z II Redemption, KSA 4.178); in A 41, he similarly complains of how the instincts of modern individuals "contradict, disturb, destroy [*zerstören*] each other"; and in BGE 208 we find him still fervently engaged with the issue of *political* disintegration, diagnosing modern Europe as suffering from a debilitating condition of "democratic multi-willing [*Vielwollerei*]."

But how can we resolve this condition of widespread fragmentation? By what means should we struggle to foster a healthy condition of holism? On the one hand Nietzsche appears to rally his readers to a *measured* form of struggle – one in which we abstain from destroying any of the discordant elements that drive disintegration. To this end, he advocates a "spiritual-ization of *enmity*" and censures those who seek the "destruction [*Vernichtung*] of their enemies" (TI Morality 3); likewise, he reprimands Christians for endeavoring to "castrate," rather than bridle, their bother-some impulses (TI Morality 1).

But on the other hand, he oftentimes incites his readers to a distinctly unrestrained campaign against the sources of disintegration. Thus, he instructs us to "destroy" (*vernichten*) certain drives (KSA 12:1[81], 31);[1] and

---

[1] See also KSA 11:25[349], 104.

he stresses that we ought to annihilate degenerate values and moralities (particularly Christianity).[2] Finally, he sanctions another, apparently physical, form of eradication, calling for the "destruction [*Vernichtung*] of millions of failures" (KSA 11:25[335], 98), where by "failures" he appears to be denoting a particular set of individuals – a statement that some quite justifiably read as an endorsement of eugenics (e.g., Detwiler 1990, 113). How, though, can we square this insistence on unmeasured struggle with his disapprobation of destructive conflict?

Prima facie, Nietzsche's normative outlook appears to be riven by an irresolvable contradiction. How can he coherently recommend both measured *and* unmeasured struggle? The reason commentators have so far failed to resolve this apparent *aporia* is that they tend to grasp only one of the two horns of the dilemma, while discounting, or entirely ignoring, the other. That is to say, they read the later Nietzsche as a proponent of *either* measured *or* unmeasured struggle. For instance, at the level of the self, interpreters are inclined to fixate on his prescription of measured, incorporative struggle, arguing that he entreats us to *sublimate* our troublesome impulses instead of seeking their outright elimination (e.g., Kaufmann 1974, 218ff.; Gemes 2009; Richardson 1996, 25). With respect to the critical literature on Nietzsche's later political thought, which of the two horns commentators are inclined to grasp is usually determined by their exegesis of the will to power. As we saw in the introduction to Chapter 2, the agonistic democrats take his theory of the will to power to affirm measured, and only measured, struggle. On the political plane, they then claim that his will-to-power thesis translates into an egalitarian regime founded upon an agonistic ethos of respectful, democratic contest. They correspondingly tend to disregard Nietzsche's later aristocratism, branding it inconsistent with the tenor of his wider philosophy. By contrast, interpreters who read the later Nietzsche as a radical aristocrat are wont to grasp the *unmeasured* horn of the dilemma. On their reading of the will to power, he portrays thriving life as an entirely unrestrained struggle for dominion: power is, and should be, secured by *whatever* means necessary. These interpreters then claim that the radically aristocratic vein of Nietzsche's

[2] He also speaks of his "[i]nterest in the *destruction* [*Vernichtung*] of *morality*" (KSA 10:7[37], 254). See also KSA 10:7[29], 548: "*The evil one* [*der Böse*] [is] venerable as a destroyer [*Zerstörer*] – destruction [*das Zerstören*] is *necessary.*" In KSA 11:25[211], 69, he calls for "[t]he destruction [*Vernichtung*] of slavish values." And referring to "the Christian-nihilistic measure of value," he proclaims that "[...] there can be no peace *treaty*: here one must exterminate [*ausmerzen*], destroy [*vernichten*], wage war [*Krieg führen*]" (KSA 13:14[6], 220).

later political thought is continuous with his vision of life as will to power.[3]

In this chapter, I contend that the dilemma presented by the critical literature is in fact false and can therefore be sidestepped. The aforementioned aporia dissolves once we appreciate how the later Nietzsche, in developing an alternative remedy to the crisis of disgregation, prescribes much the same species of conflict as in UM – namely, organizational struggle. Since this form of struggle coherently synthesizes measured and unmeasured contention, it enables us to reconcile his apparently incompatible prescriptions. Though there is to this extent a definite similarity between his early and later normative views, we will see that this similarity should not be mistaken for identity. There are two reasons for this.

First, Nietzsche needs to purge his conception of organizational struggle of its earlier metaphysical flaws. In trying to achieve this, he draws upon the work of Wilhelm Roux, someone who preceded Nietzsche in trying to formulate a naturalistic model of organization.[4] In his magnum opus, KTO, Roux gives an account of how purposive integration emerges from the internal struggle that takes place between the parts of an organism, and he does so without presupposing the existence of either essences or natural teleological forces. Although in fashioning his theory of the world as will to power – that is, his own abstract model of organization – Nietzsche abandons much in Roux's account, he nonetheless retains Roux's explanation of organized unity in terms of a combined struggle for measured incorporation and unmeasured exclusion. We are therefore going to need to reconstruct Roux's account in order to obtain a comprehensive picture of the unique, general model of organization that Nietzsche develops in his later writings.

The second major discontinuity between Nietzsche's early and later theories of organizational conflict concerns his diagnosis of the crisis of disintegration. Whereas the early Nietzsche blames disintegration on philistine education, in his later writings he posits racial mixing as the dominant cause of this malaise. And in response to this new etiology of the malady at issue he makes significant modifications to his remedial notion of organizational struggle. If we wish to obtain a comprehensive understanding of his later theory of organization, we must therefore begin by delineating how he reconceives the crisis of disintegration.

---

[3] See, e.g., Detwiler (1990, 43–44).
[4] See Müller-Lauter (1999, chap. 9; 1978). My reading of Roux's impact on Nietzsche is heavily indebted to Müller-Lauter. On this impact, see also Moore (2002, 37–39).

4.1   Reconceiving the Crisis of Disintegration

Nietzsche pejoratively dubs the town into which Zarathustra descends "The Motley [*bunte*] Cow," clearly recalling his description of German culture as a "fairground motley [*buntheit*]" in UM (DS 1, KSA 1.163).[5] Lamenting the disintegrated condition of modern man, Zarathustra proclaims himself dedicated to the task of resynthesizing him into a balanced whole: "And all my creating and striving [*trachten*] amounts to this, that I create and piece together into one, what is now fragment and riddle and grisly accident" (Z II Redemption, KSA 4.179). He further maintains that since modern individuals are a mere hotchpotch of clashing convictions, they are unable to meaningfully commit themselves to any *particular* beliefs: "how should you be *capable* of believing, you color-speckled ones [*Buntgesprenkelten*] – you who are paintings of everything that has ever been believed!" Echoing UM, this discordance is said to leave moderns both "infertile" (*unfruchtbar*) and mired in pessimism (Z II Education, KSA 4.154).

In Z, however, the problem of disintegration remains much the same as in UM; Nietzsche continues to attribute this cultural ill to philistine education (*Bildung*).[6] But in 1884 a decisive shift occurs: he begins to single out racial mixing as the primary motor of fragmentation. While he already thematizes the problem of racial mixing in D 272 (entitled "*Purification of the race*") he puts the issue on ice until 1884–1885, at which point its presence in the *Nachlaß* becomes persistent and pronounced.[7] Not long after, the idea then begins to surface in his published writings. In BGE 208, for example, Nietzsche blames racial mixing, not philistine education, for the emergence of skepticism, which in his view "originates whenever races or classes that have been separated for a long time are suddenly and decisively interbred."

It should be underscored that one of the crucial differences between D 272 and Nietzsche's later conception of race (*Rasse*) is that the earlier focus on "physical features" (*Körperformen*) fades into the background by the time we reach BGE. In contrast to thinkers such as Gobineau, Nietzsche's mature conception of *Rasse* cannot be equated with the dominant modern conception of race – that is, understood as a distinct set of humans grouped according to physical resemblance (e.g., of skin color). For the later

---

[5] Nietzsche is also alluding to Plato's critique of democracy in the *Republic* (1992, 558b). See also, entry for "bunt", in NWB.

[6] See e.g., Z II Education, KSA 4.154.

[7] See e.g., KSA 11:25[211], 69: "The destruction [*Vernichtung*] of the degenerate races. Europe's degeneration"; KSA 11:26[376], 250. For Nietzsche's celebration of racial purity, see e.g., KSA 11:25[234], 74; KSA 11:25[382], 112; KSA 11:25[407], 118; KSA 11:25[413], 120.

Nietzsche, a race is a group of people defined by a particular unicity in their "ways of living" (*Lebensweisen*), and the distinct behavioral compulsions and values that sustain these ways. Accordingly, as in BGE 208, Nietzsche often elides the distinction between social classes and races: "classes always indicate differences in descent and race as well" (GM III 17, KSA 5.378).[8] It is therefore the discordance of our drives, instincts and values that he now wishes to rectify:

> Thanks to this mixture [of classes and races], the past of every form and way of life, of cultures that used to lie side by side or on top of each other, radiates into us, we "modern souls." At this point, our instincts are running back everywhere and we ourselves are a type of chaos –. (BGE 224)[9]

In BGE 200, he further articulates the problem as that of "conflicting [...] drives and value standards that fight [*kämpfen*] with each other and rarely leave each other alone."[10] Of course, he does not hold racial mixing to be the *sole* cause of modernity's fractured condition. As we read on in BGE, we discover that he also holds democracy responsible for accelerating racial mixing, which he accordingly refers to as the "*democratic* mixing of classes and races" (BGE 224; emphasis mine). At other times, he blames *morality* for driving this descent into racial discord: "the morality of the common people has triumphed. You might take this victory for blood-poisoning (it did mix the races up)" (GM I 9, KSA 5.269). From 1884 onward, then, we find that the disintegration of our impulses stands in a causal nexus with racial mixing, the Enlightenment democratic movement and a certain species of morality. In order to get a firmer handle on why Nietzsche thinks disintegration represents such an urgent threat, we should now examine this nexus in greater detail.

4.1.1 Individual Disintegration and the Poisoned Chalice of Ascetic Morality

With a view to determining why exactly the later Nietzsche characterizes the disintegrated will as pathological, we should begin by adumbrating how he conceives its contrary: the healthy, integrated individual. This will grant us an illuminating point of comparison. An apt text for this purpose

---

[8] As Gerd Schank (2000, esp. 29–30) has shown at length, "race" (*Rasse*) more frequently signifies something akin to "people" (*Volk*) or "social class" (*sozialer Stand*) for Nietzsche. For an overview of Nietzsche's relation to Gobineau, see Schank (2000, 426–441); Ottmann (1999, 246–249).
[9] See also HH 475, where Nietzsche talks about the mixing of *geographically* distinct cultures, attributing this to the mobility facilitated by trade, industry and other factors that have rendered modern life nomadic.
[10] See KSA 11:34[63], 441.

is BGE 19, where Nietzsche clearly associates the healthy will with hierarchical order:

> the one who wills takes his feeling of pleasure as the commander, and adds to it
> the feelings of pleasure from the successful instruments that carry out the task,
> as well as from the serviceable "under-wills" or under-souls – our body is, after
> all, only a society constructed out of many souls –. *L'effet c'est moi*: what
> happens here is what happens in every well-constructed and happy community:
> the ruling class identifies itself with the successes of the community. (BGE 19)

So for Nietzsche the healthy or strong will is structurally analogous to the well-
ordered, which is to say *hierarchically* ordered, society. There must be "a
commanding thought" which is able to govern the plurality of one's drives
and bodily parts. Only when such a thought commands in a sufficiently stable
manner can it make itself manifest in agency. Stable hierarchical organization
allows for the successful performance of intended actions, which in turn elicits
a pleasurable feeling of power. This coordination "under the predominance of
a single impulse" issues in the "precision and clarity of direction" that
Nietzsche takes to be symptomatic of the "strong will" (KSA 13:14[219],
394).[11] By contrast, he denigrates *akrasia* in the following terms: "The multitude and disgregation of impulses and the lack of any systematic order among
them result in a 'weak will.'" This anarchic psychological condition is characterized by "oscillation and a lack of center of gravity" (ibid.). In Nietzsche's
eyes, this crippling state of impotence is intrinsically negative in value.

Closer inspection reveals that for Nietzsche this weakness (or in current
scientific parlance, poor *executive functioning*) takes two distinct forms –
namely, exhaustion (*Erschöpfung*) and caprice (*Willkürlichkeit*). We might
usefully think of this in terms of the distinction that Aristotle draws (1991a,
1145a–1152a) between weakness (*astheneia*) and impetuosity (*propeteia*),
which he designates as the two principal species of *akrasia* (literally meaning "lack of command").[12] BGE 208, in which Nietzsche discusses the
relation of skepticism to "paralysis of the will" (*Willenslähmung*), neatly
illustrates the first of these two species of pathology:

[11] In associating health with hierarchy, and in describing pathology in terms of disgregation, the later
Nietzsche moves away from the influence of Schopenhauer, Goethe and Leibniz and toward that of
various natural scientists – e.g., Théodule Ribot (esp. 1888; on this relation, see Cowan 2005); Paul
Bourget (see Campioni 2009, 313ff.); and J. R. Mayer (1893; recall from Chapter 1 that Mayer
associated a well-ordered "release apparatus" with health). Wilhelm Roux, to whom we will shortly
come, is also key in this regard.
[12] Ribot (1888, 53–55), another of Nietzsche's influences, similarly distinguishes between two chief
pathologies of the will: a malfunctioning "mechanism of impulsion," which leads to "weakenings of
the will" (*aboulia* or a depressive state of inaction); and a malfunctioning mechanism of "inhibition"
(*arrêt*), where reasoned plans cannot be carried out due to the capricious anarchy of one's impulses.

> Skepticism is the most spiritual expression of a certain complex physiological condition which in layman's terms is called weak nerves or a sickly constitution. It originates whenever races or classes that have been separated for a long time are suddenly and decisively interbred. In the new generation, which has as it were inherited varying standards and values in its blood, everything is in a state of restlessness, disorder, doubt, experimentation. The best forces have inhibitory effects, the virtues themselves do not let each other strengthen and grow, both body and soul lack equilibrium [*Gleichgewicht*], a center of gravity and the assurance of a pendulum. But what is most profoundly sick and degenerate about such hybrids is the *will*: they no longer have any sense of independence in decision-making, or the bold feeling of pleasure in willing. (BGE 208)

No single impulse (*Kraft*) is strong enough to allow this akratic individual to commit to a particular position in any given debate; they are consequently forced to assume the skeptical position and abstain. Such individuals, Nietzsche thinks, then try to masquerade their impotence as an *active virtue*, namely, by presenting their skepticism as an expression of "good taste" (ibid.).[13] In addition to tacitly disparaging this state of vacillation per se, he also describes it as an intrinsically *unpleasurable* experience – one antithetical to the pleasant feeling of successfully commanding the various parts of oneself and thereby carrying an action through to completion.

On the other hand, Nietzsche contends that disgregation of the will can express itself as *caprice*, a condition in which *all* of one's instincts are able to express themselves to some extent. For an aesthetic representation of this unhealthy inner state, Nietzsche thinks that we can turn to the works of Richard Wagner, which are characterized by "multiplicity, overabundance, caprice [*Willkür*] [and] uncertainty in things spiritual" (KSA 13:15[6], 407). Nietzsche avers that Wagner's caprice is manifest in his pastiche abuse of historical references.[14] This is what, in BGE 224, he criticizes under the heading of the "historical sense," which he takes to be a consequence of both the "democratic mixing of classes and races," and, more specifically, the "mixing" of our instincts. Although he praises the fact that this instinctual chaos enables modern individuals to relate to, and imitate, a diverse range of past cultures, he censures the way in which this leaves us with an indiscriminate (and therefore *ignoble*) "taste and tongue for everything" (KSA 11:29[393], 254). (Recall that it was precisely this kind of

---

[13] See also BGE 209.

[14] On Wagner's art as an instance of modern disgregation, see Cowan (2005, 67ff.) and Hamacher (1986, 322–324).

unscrupulousness that defined antiquarian history.) The undesirable upshot of this eclectic historical sense is that

> [...] it is only poorly and haltingly, only with effort that we are able to reproduce in ourselves the trivial as well as greatest serendipities and transfigurations of human life as they light up every now and then: those moments and marvels when a great force stands voluntarily still in front of the boundless and limitless –, the enjoyment of an abundance of subtle pleasure in suddenly harnessing [*Bändigung*] and fossilizing, in standing fast and establishing yourself [*Feststehen und Sich-Fest-Stellen*] on ground that is still shaking. *Measure* [*Maass*] is foreign to us, let us admit this to ourselves; our thrill is precisely the thrill of the infinite, the unmeasured [*Ungemessenen*]. (BGE 224)

The problem is once again framed in terms of creative impotence – our lack of stable values makes it difficult for us to select and imitate (*nachbilden*) exemplary forms of human life, all of which are marked by an ability to *harness* (*bändigen*) plurality and stand fast in its midst. In a word, we lack the capacity for *measure* (*Maass*).

Aside from this imitative–historical caprice, disintegration also causes what we might call *altruistic* caprice, a condition in which

> [...] one loses one's power of *resistance* against stimuli, – one comes to be conditioned by accidents: one coarsens and enlarges one's experiences tremendously – "depersonalization," a disintegration of the will –
> – example: one whole type of morality, the altruistic one which talks much of pity: the essence of which is weakness of the personality, so that it *resonates* [*mitklingt*], and like an overstimulated string continually vibrates . . . an extreme irritability . . . (KSA 13:17[6], 527–528)

Caprice manifests itself as an inability to inhibit one's actions and *resist* stimuli. According to Nietzsche, embracing altruism exacerbates caprice because one thereby cultivates a pathological hypersensitivity to others' feelings – one allows oneself to sympathize far too readily, quickly losing the power to do otherwise, which results in a psychological state of "extreme irritability." Nietzsche thinks the capriciously altruistic individual suffers from a weakness of personality insofar as their thoughts and actions are – like the skin color of a chameleon – little more than *re*-actions induced by their milieu. Altruism is therefore indicative of *décadence* for Nietzsche – it represents an inferior fallback ethic, one that we are liable to adopt when we lack the power of will needed to determine the kinds of agency that are good for us *personally*. What is more, in Nietzsche's view, this process of altruistic "depersonalization" commonly devolves into a more embracing rejection of life:

> Disintegration of the instincts! – People are done for when they become altruistic . . . – Instead of naively saying "*I* am not worth anything anymore," the moral lie in the decadent's mouth says "nothing is worth anything, – *life* isn't worth anything" . . . At the end of the day, a judgment like this is very dangerous, it is infectious, – it quickly grows in society's morbid soil into a tropical vegetation of concepts, now as religion (Christianity), now as philosophy (Schopenhauerianism). (TI Skirmishes 35)

So in addition to breeding manic irascibility, altruism fosters a harmful strain of self-neglect, and even full-blown pessimism.[15] In this passage, Nietzsche also reveals himself to be concerned with the way in which this pessimism further fuels the growth of Christianity, which then in turn promotes further altruism, forming a morbidly vicious circle.

Nietzsche's chief grievance is that the suffering caused by inner disgregation impels people toward harmful palliatives that ultimately "hasten exhaustion" (KSA 13:17[6], 527) – particularly Judeo-Christian morality and its secular derivatives (e.g., Kantian and Schopenhauerian ethics, socialism and utilitarianism).[16] He accuses modern individuals of failing to proactively organize themselves, and in place of this simply seeking to suppress the painful inner turmoil of their drives – for instance, by trying to stamp out bothersome, but at bottom indispensable, instincts.[17] For the individual who follows this course of self-treatment,

> His most basic desire is for an end to the war [*Krieg*] that he *is*. His notion of happiness corresponds to that of a medicine and mentality of pacification (for instance the Epicurean or Christian); it is a notion of happiness as primarily rest, lack of disturbance, repletion, unity at last and the "Sabbath of Sabbaths." (BGE 200)

In terms of concrete ethical practice, this hankering for escape becomes a lust for inner tranquility, and for a community founded upon the principle of altruism, one therefore free of interpersonal friction. In the domain of philosophy, Nietzsche believes this impulse commonly takes the form of a predisposition for idealism – that is, an Anaximandean desire to flee from the world of "appearance" into an ideal world of pure objective knowledge

---

[15] On the connection of weakness of will and pessimism, see KSA 13:11[228], 89.

[16] See KSA 11:25[407], 118: "All our religions and philosophies are *symptoms* of our bodily health: – Christianity's triumph was the consequence of a general feeling of displeasure and a mixing of the races (i.e., of a confusion and opposition [*eines Durch- und Gegeneinanders*] within the organism)."

[17] See e.g., TI Morality 2.

(KSA 13:14[83], 262). And in art, Nietzsche identifies this impulse with the proclivity for disinterestedness (i.e., the idea of "*l'art pour l'art*") (BGE 208).[18]

By impelling people toward Christianity, psychological disintegration indirectly initiates a wave of knock-on pathological effects. In the third essay of GM, Nietzsche expands upon this at length, making a detailed study of the "epidemic" of "weariness and heaviness" plaguing modern Europeans. One of the more popular strategies of combatting this affliction, he tells us, involves the provocation of "an *excess of feeling*" (GM III 19, KSA 5.385) – in particular, "*the feeling of guilt.*" This emotional response, which Nietzsche also dubs "bad conscience," consists in the unhealthy *internal* discharge of one's instinct for "animosity [and] cruelty." The sick are prone to adopt this self-mortifying therapeutic because they are often too weak and disempowered to discharge their strength *externally*, in open contention with others (GM II 14, KSA 5.321). The morbid excitement of scouring one's own self for the cause of one's pain, and subsequently contriving ingenious ways of punishing oneself for the sins turned up in this hunt, provides some welcome respite from lethargy. Life becomes "*very* interesting again: awake, eternally awake, sleepless, glowing, burned out, exhausted and yet not tired" (GM III 20, KSA 5.390–391). But Nietzsche is quick to add that this toxic course of treatment leaves people with "a shattered nervous system," and "under all circumstances *sicker*" (GM III 21, KSA 5.391).[19] Indeed, it can result in "terrible paralyses and long-lasting depressions" – of not just individuals, but even entire communities (GM III 21, KSA 5.392). While such frenzy may, by virtue of its distracting qualities, allow sufferers to *endure* the agony elicited by their disintegrated will, the hangover caused by these electrifying palliatives leaves patients ever more exhausted, and ever less capable of redressing their malaise.

But Nietzsche indexes another far more deleterious side effect of these pseudo-remedies. In short, the harmful ascetic values that are associated with these therapies turn out to be highly "*contagious*" (*ansteckend*), thus imperiling the wider health of European man (TI Skirmishes 35; GM III 21, KSA 5.392). As Alexander Nehamas (1985, 125) observes, "[t]he ascetic ideal

---

[18] See Introduction (pp. 6–14); KSA 12:9[35], 351: "The strength of the spirit may be worn out, exhausted, so [...] that the synthesis of values and goals (on which every strong culture rests) dissolves and the individual values wage war against each other: disintegration / whatever refreshes, heals, calms, numbs emerges into the foreground in various *disguises*, religious or moral, or political, or aesthetic, etc."

[19] See also TI Socrates 9.

does not rest content with ordering the lives of those who may actually need it" – it attacks and infects the healthy, the noble, and actively stifles the emergence of "rare cases of spiritual and physical powerfulness" (GM III 14, KSA 5.367). Owing to their sickness, the weak are filled with hatred at the sight of the healthy and the strong ("the sight of the victorious man is *hated*"). In order to disguise this animosity, they conceive *themselves* as the "the good and the just," demonize the strong, and express their hatred as *righteousness (Rechtschaffenheit; Gerechtigkeit)* (GM III 14, KSA 5.369).[20] The sick then proceed to subject the strong to bitter, unrelenting judgment. Eventually this drives the strong and healthy to "start to be ashamed of their happiness and perhaps say to one another: 'It's a disgrace to be happy! *There is too much misery!*'" (GM III 14, KSA 5.371). And so the noble fall prey to a great nausea (*Ekel*), which in turn provokes them to embrace compassion for their fellow men – in other words, they are drawn into the vicious circle of altruism that we identified above.[21] The yearning of the weak to dominate and avenge themselves on the strong is what Nietzsche refers to as their "*ressentiment*" (GM III 14, KSA 5.370), which is characteristic of what he describes as the "slave revolt in morality" (GM I 10, KSA 5.270).

We have therefore isolated four key reasons why the later Nietzsche warns against psychological disintegration. In the first place, it encourages depression and caprice, which, aside from being intrinsically unpleasurable, impede proactive agency. Second, by promoting the historical sense, it prevents us from constructing effective exemplars. Third, it propels us toward counterproductive pseudo-remedies; and finally, this condition of disorder is highly contagious in nature, propagating an aggressive attitude of *ressentiment* toward those who are healthy and still capable of greatness, which consequently threatens the health of humanity at large. In light of this final observation, we should now consider the later Nietzsche's account of *collective* health.

4.1.2   Collective Disintegration

Nietzsche's vision of communal vitality structurally mirrors his account of the healthy individual will. Like Plato before him, he compares the healthy subject to a "social construction" (*Gesellschaftsbau*) (BGE 19), and describes

---

[20] On this demonization of the strong and their values, see GM I 7; BGE 260; and A 5.

[21] This is why Nietzsche states that morality is both a symptom *and* a cause: "morality as result, as symptom, as mask, as tartuffery, as sickness, as misunderstanding; but also morality as cause, remedy, stimulant, inhibition, poison" (GM Preface 6, KSA 5.253).

"our subject-unity [. . .] as regents at the head of a commonwealth [*Gemeinwesens*]" (KSA 11:40[21], 638). As such, for Nietzsche, rank order is a precondition of the strong polity. Without this, a collective is at risk of decaying and even altogether perishing. Yet this rank order does not merely ensure the continued existence of society. It also facilitates its highest creative function – the generation of higher individuals: "Every enhancement so far in the type 'man' has been the work of an aristocratic society" (BGE 257). The creation of higher individuals is a collective enterprise that requires (according to Nietzsche) a form of hierarchical organization analogous to that which enables individual agency. Since we will be further exploring this ideal vision of collective health later in this chapter, we should for now focus on establishing how Nietzsche thinks *décadent* societies fall short of this ideal.

Nietzsche is above all troubled by the way in which social disintegration propagates harmful strains of morality. Furthermore, he indicts these moralities for exacerbating the very pathologies they pretend to cure. An apt example of this can be found in BGE 262, where he recounts what happens when societies deteriorate into an atomistic chaos of amorally self-interested individuals. Under such conditions, each member of society cleaves to their own set of idiosyncratic values, while simultaneously growing fearful of those who hold views at variance with their own. The xenophobic fear that people once harbored toward foreigners is thus displaced "onto the neighbor or friend, onto the street, onto one's own child." In order to maintain law and security, the default course of action usually taken by such aggregates of individuals is to enact a blanket *suppression* of social conflict. This end is achieved by promoting moralities that generate homogeneous mediocrity. Hence, the preachers of morality seductively proclaim that mediocre humans "are the people of the future, the only survivors: 'Be like them! Be mediocre!'"[22] The moralities that Nietzsche has in mind are those that promulgate "equal rights" (BGE 44), "dignity and duty and neighborly love" (BGE 262), as well as those that buttress the Enlightenment democratic movement.[23] He remonstrates that such moralities militate against healthy social tension, thereby mediocritizing humankind in the name of pacific homogeneity. On these grounds, he inveighs against Kantian ethics, with its ideal "kingdom of ends" (KSA 11:25[437], 128; KSA 11:35[31], 522; BGE 188); socialist *libres-penseurs* such as Rousseau, who campaign for democracy and equal rights for all (BGE 44;

---

[22] See KSA 9:11[130], 488 and KSA 9:11[182], 511–512, in which this thought is clearly prefigured.
[23] See also KSA 11:34[176], 478–479; KSA 11:26[282], 224.

KSA 12:7[46], 310; KSA 12:9[3], 340–341; TI Skirmishes 48); and utilitarians such as Bentham, Mill and Spencer (KSA 11:25[242], 75; KSA 11:35[34], 523–524; BGE 228, 258).

Nietzsche criticizes these moralities for having tamed the human animal. In recommending universal values, for example, they erode the difference between individuals that originally gave rise to social struggle. It is for this reason that he disparagingly calls such moralists "levelers" (*Nivellirer*; BGE 44). Indeed, he warns that this moral program propels us toward the dystopian society of the "last man" – a community homogenously dominated by a tame and feeble breed of human. According to Nietzsche, these "last men" readily conform to a universal morality of altruism:

> Beware! The time approaches when human beings will no longer give birth to a dancing star. [. . .]
> Behold! I show you the *last man*. [. . .]
> They abandoned the regions where it was hard to live: for one needs warmth. [. . .]
> A bit of poison once in a while; that makes for pleasant dreams. And much poison at the end, for a pleasant death. [. . .]
> No shepherd and one herd! Each wants the same, each is the same, and whoever feels differently goes voluntarily into the insane asylum.
>
> (Z Preface 5, KSA 4.19)

The community of the last man is in Nietzsche's view wholly unable to carry higher men ("stars") to term.[24] In order to anesthetize themselves, these tame herd animals routinely imbibe poison (*Gift* – i.e., morality).[25] Moreover, they are eager to create a social condition free of danger and difficulty. They yearn for "the universal, green pasture happiness of the herd, with security, safety, contentment, and an easier life for all" (BGE 44). Redounding of social Darwinists such as Spencer, Nietzsche maintains that such egalitarian and altruistic moralities negate the very conditions under which great individuals arise and thrive. By Nietzsche's lights, "the plant 'man' has grown the strongest" under conditions of tremendous "danger," since it is these that drive the cultivation of his highest capacities, particularly those of a *spiritual* kind: man's "power to invent and dissimulate (his 'spirit' –) has had to develop under prolonged pressure and compulsion into something refined and daring"

---

[24] For Nietzsche's opposition of the last man and the *Übermensch*, see Z IV Higher Man 3, KSA 4.358: "these small people: *they* are the greatest danger to the overman!" See also KSA 10:4[171],162; BGE 62; KSA 9:11[44], 458.

[25] Echoing Marx, Nietzsche explicitly refers to Christianity as an "opiate" (KSA 12:2[144], 138) and "narcotic" (GM Pref 6, KSA 5.253).

(BGE 44).[26] In robbing people of the opportunity for struggle and resistance, herd morality denies them the chance to exercise their individual wills and enjoy the attendant feeling of pleasure and freedom. What is more, the society of the last man entirely disavows the figure symbolized by the shepherd (*Hirt*), who stands above the multitude, coordinating it into an organized whole (KSA 11:37[8], 581). This antipathy for "everything that dominates and wants to dominate" is what Nietzsche brands *"misarchism"* (GM II 12, KSA 5.315). So, in driving people toward egalitarian morality, social disgregation causes those people to undermine the very conditions – of struggle, command and hierarchy – that enable higher forms of collective and individual agency.

As we saw in our analysis of individual disgregation, the moral stance that proliferates in response to social chaos does not merely negate the conditions under which greatness is able to emerge; for Nietzsche, it is also actively hostile toward existing higher individuals. For one, it brands them *evil*.[27] Indeed, Nietzsche calls *"moral judgment"* the *"chief means"* in the struggle of the many against the exceptional few (KSA 12:2[168], 152). Moreover, socialist and democratic movements, in sanctioning class mixing, give rise to a debilitating form of *"social mishmash*," which unleashes the hostile forces of *ressentiment* that were previously confined to lower social strata:

> With this, the bearers of the instincts of decline (of *ressentiment*, discontent, the drive to destroy [*Zerstörer-Triebs*], anarchism, and nihilism) [...] in those orders that have *long* been kept *down*, mingle with the blood of all classes: two, three generations later the race is no longer recognizable – everything *has become mob* [*verpöbelt*]. (KSA 13:14 [182], 367)

The push for political emancipation topples the superordinate, structuring elements of society, and hence aggravates the lack of social structure. This culminates in what Nietzsche calls an *"anarchy* of elements" (KSA 12:9[8], 343), which explains why he scorns the democratic movement as "a decadent form [*Verfalls-Form*] of political organization" – one that

---

[26] Nietzsche's botanical metaphor echoes Kant's account of why humans ought to live in competitive society with one another: "In the same way, trees in a forest, by seeking to deprive each other of air and sunlight, compel each other to find these by upward growth, so that they grow beautiful and straight" (IUH, 8.22).
[27] See BGE 201: "Everything that raises the individual over the herd and frightens the neighbor will henceforth be called *evil* [...]." See also KSA 13:11[153], 72–73.

promotes the "diminishment," "mediocritization" and even the *complete degeneration of man*" (BGE 203).[28]

Nietzsche further criticizes democracy on account of its favoring the "short-sighted and swift-handed" (BGE 256) – otherwise put, he disdains the inherently *capricious* character of democratic politics. Short-term governments strive for correspondingly short-term goals.[29] And he complains of how this impetuous democratic outlook has more generally infiltrated the modern psyche: "people live for today, people live very fast, – people live very irresponsibly: and this is precisely what people call 'freedom.'" He refers to this condition as a form of "nervousness" (TI Skirmishes 39). The practical consequence of this impetuous social caprice is that it badly hampers the search for higher forms of humanity, leaving communities incapable of anything more than "*bungled [mißrathen]*," "rash and arbitrary attempts [*willkürlichen Versuchens*]" (KSA 12:1[236], 62). Handicapped by the democratic ethos, all we can do is erratically grope for the meaningful enhancement of humanity. And yet, in spite of such unpropitious conditions, great individuals *have* nonetheless emerged: "This more valuable type has appeared often enough already" (A 3). Nietzsche's point, however, is that their realization has hitherto been too fitful, too accidental: "only as a stroke of luck, as an exception, never as *willed*" (ibid.). This is one sense in which modern Europeans suffer from what he calls "democratic multi-willing [*Vielwollerei*]" (BGE 208) – that is, because they are unable to commit to long-term, transgenerational goals, precisely what is needed for the deliberate creation of higher forms of humanity: "the breeding of a *stronger race*" (KSA 12:9[153], 425).[30] The democratic will is neutered by short-term governments and fragile coalitions. Yet, in BGE, Nietzsche's antipathy toward nationalism indicates that his political objective is not to empower individual nation-states. His sights are rather set on the synthesis of a pan-European will: "nationalist nonsense has alienated and continues to alienate the peoples of Europe from each other" (BGE 256).[31] He scathingly refers to nationalist politics as "petty provincialism" (*Kleinstaaterei*) and the "politics of dissolution," and insists that Europe must "*acquire a single will*" (BGE 208).

[28] For an informative survey of Nietzsche's multifaceted critique of democracy, see Siemens (2009, 20–37; 2008, 231–268). As Siemens notes, Nietzsche makes a number of positive appraisals of democracy.
[29] This concern is foreshadowed in HH 472.
[30] This need for a transgenerational project, which will be examined in greater detail later in the chapter, is most clearly expressed in KSA 11:37[8], 581–583 and GS 356. See also TI Skirmishes 39 and KSA 13:11[31], 17–18. Regarding Nietzsche's emphasis on the need to cultivate a long-term will, see BGE 212.
[31] See also GS 377.

Regarding society, then, Nietzsche warns of two poles of disorganization, which together reflect the two key pathologies that he diagnosed in his analysis of the individual will. The first pole is that of anarchic disorder, where tensions are over-enflamed and the component parts of society lack a higher organizing force. As a result, impulses mutually frustrate one another, and the capricious body politic is left incapable of concerted agency. The second pole is that of collective depression – a torpid homogeneity characterized by the wholesale loss of tension. In his view, these pathological extremes vex agency and thereby render humankind impotent, particularly with respect to the goal of generating higher forms of humanity. What is more, these extremes impel the afflicted toward pseudo-therapies that only serve to aggravate their plight.

While Nietzsche fruitfully deploys this distinction as a heuristic tool, it is vital to note that in reality he sees modern society as being stricken with an admixture of these two opposed pathologies:

> Paralysis everywhere, exhaustion, numbness or hostility and chaos: *both* becoming increasingly conspicuous the higher you climb in the forms of organization. The whole does not live at all any more: it is cobbled together [*zusammengesetzt*], calculated, synthetic, an artifact. (CW 7, KSA 6.27; emphasis mine)

For Nietzsche, then, these polarized extremes represent conditions of mere *aggregation* (*Zusammensetzung*), in contrast to which he seeks to generate a form of holistic cohesion (or *Ganzheit*) – a species of unity that navigates a path between the many-headed Scylla of anarchy and the Charybdis of depression. In the following two sections, our task is to explore in greater depth how Nietzsche pictures this condition of healthy measure and, decisively, how he thinks that it can be achieved.

But before we embark on this task, we first need to consider an objection to my account of the crisis of disintegration: Perhaps there is no real need to strive for organization at all, since Nietzsche repeatedly suggests that societies have a built-in negative feedback loop, such that the malady of disintegration generates its own cure.[32] Gerd Schank (2000, 440) contends, for example, that far from being critical of the mixing of races, Nietzsche is to be distinguished from racist thinkers such as Gobineau insofar as he believes that "the mixture of peoples contributes to the enhancement of the human." The melee of psychological impulses

---

[32] See e.g., KSA 11:35[10], 512: "The same conditions that hasten the evolution of the herd animal also hasten the evolution of the leader animal."

engendered by such mixing furnishes the strong individual with precisely the conditions he needs in order to cultivate a taught, hale and efficacious self. And he is able to accomplish this because, unlike most, he possesses "genuine proficiency and finesse in waging war with himself, which is to say, self-control [...]" (BGE 200). Moreover, the weakness of will so widespread among others provides these superior individuals with a pliable social mass ripe for instrumental organization. As such, "the democratization of Europe is at the same time an involuntary exercise in the breeding of *tyrants*" (BGE 242).

However, Nietzsche is more often than not openly critical of disintegrative processes, which he describes as "very unhealthy" (KSA 13:14[157], 342).[33] As Paul van Tongeren (1989, 148) notes, Nietzsche does not conceive the overcoming of slave morality as an "automatic process." The prognosis is at best uncertain; as Nietzsche warns, his higher types "could fail to appear, or simply fail and degenerate" (BGE 203).[34] Herd morality constitutes a very real danger, "our greatest danger" even (GM I 12, KSA 5.278): "this brutalizing process of turning humanity into stunted little animals with equal rights and equal claims is *possible*, there is no doubt!" (BGE 203; emphasis mine).

The task of realizing higher forms of humanity is therefore one that can only be achieved by means of "artificial and *conscious* breeding of the opposite type [to the herd animal] and its virtues" (KSA 12:2[13], 73; emphasis mine);[35] further, in order to attain this end, Nietzsche stresses that we need to "invoke immense countervailing forces" (BGE 268). His optimistic moments therefore give no reason for complacency. Rather, they should imbue us with the *hopeful* sense that there remains a real possibility of our being able to raise "a *stronger* species" out of the "cosmopolitan chaos of [our] affects" (KSA 13:11[31], 17).[36] It is nonetheless essential that we acknowledge the corresponding possibility of failure. While this may fill us with disgust for the present condition of humankind, Nietzsche believes that it summons us to "a new *task* as well! ..." (BGE 203) – namely, that of enhancing humanity. But how does Nietzsche think that we can accomplish this task? In order to answer this question, we should begin by examining his abstract theory of organization.

---

[33] See also KSA 13:14[83], 262–263. [34] See also BGE 242. [35] See also KSA 12:9[153], 425.
[36] However, cf. KSA 11:26[117], 181, where Nietzsche doubts whether we should consciously struggle for the realization of higher individuals, which he considers to be "a thousand times too complicated, and the probability of failure *very great*: [...] – skepticism." On this skeptical vein of Nietzsche's thought, see the conclusion to this book.

4.2 A Non-Metaphysical Account of Organizational Struggle

Let us recall that Nietzsche's earlier solution to the crisis of disintegration is no longer serviceable. As we saw in the previous chapter, it turned out to rest on what the later Nietzsche considers to be untenable metaphysical foundations. We therefore now need to ascertain how he reformulates his proposed remedy, purging it of its earlier metaphysical flaws – that is, we need to establish how he overhauls his earlier theory of organizational struggle. To this end, we ought to begin by making a study of Wilhelm Roux's KTO, which had a conspicuous influence on Nietzsche's later theory of organization.[37]

4.2.1 *Roux on the Sources of Purposiveness*

KTO, which is relevantly subtitled *A Contribution to the Completion of the Mechanistic Doctrine of Purposiveness*, represents an attempt to construct a naturalistic-scientific theory of how the inner purposiveness of organisms can arise from purely mechanistic causal processes (a possibility that we saw both Kant and Schopenhauer likewise deny). For Roux, organisms are characterized by pervasive internal struggle. As was the case for Schopenhauer, it is through such struggle that organisms emerge as complex purposive unities, striving for particular ends in a coordinated fashion. In KTO, Roux takes issue with Darwin's (and Wallace's) thesis that the primary motor of evolution is best conceived as natural selection, understood as the struggle for existence (*Dasein*) fought *between* organisms (KTO 3–4). Roux objects that Darwin's account overlooks the significance of struggle *within* the individual organism. An organism, Roux tells us, should be construed as a "confederation" (*Bund*) or "society" (*Gesellschaft*) of relatively independent parts. As proof of this relative independence, he adduces Virchow's discovery that cells can be transplanted from one organism into another.[38] However, Roux supplements Virchow's observations by making the further claim that within any given organism these semi-autonomous parts are engaged in a fierce selective struggle for existence *with one another* (KTO 65).

---

[37] Note that in the wake of UM, Nietzsche almost completely drops "incorporation" (*Einverleibung*) and "assimilation" (*Assimilation*) from his philosophical vocabulary. The significance of Roux for Nietzsche's later theory of organization is intimated by the fact that only after reading KTO for the first time (in 1881) does he reprise these long-sidelined concepts.

[38] Nietzsche notes this independence in KSA 10:7[92], 274.

The second polemical target of KTO is the idea of teleological causality –
in other words, the Kantian thesis, which we examined in the previous
chapter, that the only way to make sense of the origin of organic organizations is to presuppose that they have been "desired" (*gewollt*) by nature.
Much like Nietzsche in 1868, Roux sides with Empedocles, rejecting the
notion of a natural force "forming [nature] in accordance with preconceived
goals."[39] Against this speculative theory, Roux seeks to defend the idea that
inner purposiveness (*Zweckmäßigkeit*) is "*not teleological, but natural historical*," having emerged "*in a mechanical manner*" – that is, out of the selective
struggle in which both organisms and their individual parts are respectively
engaged (KTO 1–2).

Roux claims that the intra-organismic dimension of this selective struggle takes place at four different levels: among (intracellular) molecules;
among cells; among tissues; and among organs – with, he adds, "each unity
only struggling [*kämpfend*] with its equals [*Ihresgleichen*]." Thus, recalling
Nietzsche's conception of *Wettkampf,* Roux maintains that this internal
conflict only takes place *inter pares*, that is, between entities belonging to
similar orders of complexity. In this way, cells struggle with cells, organs vie
with organs, and so on throughout the various levels of the organism.
Crucially, there is no such struggle *between* these orders (KTO 72).[40] The
equality that conditions this contention, however, is only ever approximate, temporary equality, and therefore never *absolute* equality (KTO
79–80).[41] According to Roux, organismic parts principally compete for
space and nutrition, and selective competition only arises by dint of the fact
that these "parts are not perfectly equal to one another" (KTO 68). After
all, where there is no *difference* there can be no meaningful competition,
nor anything to meaningfully select between.

Roux characterizes this struggle of organismic parts in different ways
depending on the physiological order in question. Of the four orders of
complexity, he begins at the bottom, with the struggle of molecules.
Within cells, he tells us, there are molecules that serve the function of
producing energy. Roux is referring to what are now termed "plastidules" –
mitochondria in particular. He then states that we find variation in the
efficiency with which these molecules are able to assimilate nutrients from
their surroundings. It is by means of this capacity for assimilation that they
replace the energy which they expend in striving to regenerate (i.e., grow

---

[39] On Nietzsche's early proximity to Empedocles, see Chapter 3 (Section 3.3.1).
[40] However, Roux suggests that there is some mobility between these orders – e.g., cells can develop
into tissues through extended use (KTO 72).
[41] As Nietzsche notes in KSA 10:7[93], 274. See also KTO 69.

and reproduce). The efficiency with which the different molecules assimilate nutrients is then positively correlated with their relative sensitivity to what Roux calls "trophic stimuli." These stimuli – which can take the form of warmth, nervous stimulation or different wavelengths of light – promote assimilation and growth (KTO 79–80). Roux postulates that molecules which exhibit greater efficiency in this struggle reproduce at a greater rate than their less-adaptive counterparts; consequently, given the finite space within an organism, those lacking the advantageous traits are edged out of existence (KTO 73, 75). Between molecules that share a similar function, and that respond to similar stimuli, this struggle is annihilatory in kind. In Roux's own words (which notably echo Nietzsche's agonal vocabulary), the strongest competitors achieve *"Alleinherrschaft"* – absolute, individual domination. This said, new variants, which are continually emerging, quickly challenge any established hegemony (KTO 76).[42]

By contrast, the struggle between types of molecules that respond to *different* trophic stimuli does not tend toward elimination; since these competing molecules are unable to exploit the same stimuli, each occupies a distinct environmental niche. By virtue of this environmental diversity, various types of molecules, ever more adapted to specific stimuli, are continually generated by the inter-molecular struggle described by Roux. Once again resonating with Nietzsche's agonal register, Roux maintains that these distinctly specialized molecules exist in a state of dynamic "equilibrium" (*Gleichgewicht*) with one another – though they similarly compete for space and nutrition, they are nonetheless unable to eradicate one another (KTO 82). The resulting functional differentiation and improved efficiency then serve to strengthen the organism in which this struggle takes place. It should be underscored, however, that for Roux such enhancement arises without the parts having "any concern for the special purposiveness of the organism as a whole" (KTO 86).

We encounter a similar dynamic within Roux's account of the higher levels of intra-organismic struggle. Conflict within these strata more consistently involves functionally differentiated units; now, however, the survival of each of these parts is requisite for the survival of the organism as a whole. This applies not only to the struggle between different types of cells, but also to the struggle among distinct organs and tissue types. Thus, stronger organs cannot simply force their less efficient counterparts out of existence. This would amount to a Pyrrhic victory, since it would bring about the death of the organism as a whole (and therefore, *a fortiori*, the

---

[42] For evidence of Nietzsche having appropriated this idea, see KSA 10:7[86], 272.

victorious organ). Any part that develops a variant that renders it disproportionately aggressive, to the detriment of other necessary parts, will
either outright kill the organism, or weaken it in its Darwinian struggle
against other organisms such that the maladaptive variant is eventually
edged out of existence. By way of example, Roux cites the adverse effect
that excessive fatty tissue has on the heart (KTO 57). To a limited extent we
might consider this process comparable to the practice of ostracism,
whereby unduly dominant individuals (i.e., variants) are removed for the
sake of the commonweal; however, this measure is now effectuated by
virtue of a natural selective mechanism, as opposed to (collectively)
intended agency (KTO 103).[43] As such, these biological parts will automatically tend to fall into relations of harmony, even if this state of concord is
subject to continual disruption and adjustment on account of the ongoing
emergence of novel variants (KTO 98) and environmental changes. Within
these higher strata, then, the struggle over space, nutrition and trophic
stimuli must be defined by a certain degree of equilibrium (if the organism
is to thrive, that is).[44]

Roux claims that this condition of equilibrium can, within certain
bounds, be *actively* maintained by the higher functions of the organism.
This is because the capacity for growth exhibited by a given part is
determined by what he calls "functional stimuli." These are a species of
nervous stimulation that facilitates assimilation and growth: the more
stimulation received by a given part, or the more responsive that part is
to that particular type of stimulation, the more nutrients it can assimilate
and the more it can therefore grow. Since according to Roux *use* increases
stimulation, the brain apportions this functional stimulus in such a way as
to make growth neatly tailored to use. Roux argues that regulated growth
can therefore be explained without reference to either internal entelechies
or conscious intentions. An organism naturally generates a balance among
its organs suited to its specific needs (KTO 113). This is what Roux calls
"self-regulation" (*Selbstregulierung*) (KTO 112). Nonetheless, each organ
and tissue type is constantly pressing to assimilate and grow as much as it
possibly can. As soon as one of these receives an increase in stimulation, it
starts to grow at the expense of its rivals, thereby improving its relative
standing in the intra-organismic struggle of parts. By way of illustration,
Roux adduces the example of a breastfeeding woman whose bones suffer as

---

[43] Compare Aristotle's claim (1991c, 1284b4–1284b34) that the strongest individual in a human
collective must often be removed for the sake of the whole, just as "the ship-builder [will not]
allow the stern or any other part of the vessel to be unduly large."
[44] For evidence that Nietzsche was aware of this thesis, see KSA 10:7[190], 302–303.

a consequence of her enlarged breast tissue (KTO 106). In this way, the struggle for space and nutrition is constant and the equilibrium of an organism's bodily parts is dynamic, perpetually shifting in response to the changing requirements of the organism as a whole.

Roux mistakenly defends the Lamarckian idea that organisms pass on to their progeny the characteristics which they acquire by virtue of this inner struggle. Following on from this, he also theorizes that the complexity of organs and bodily systems is a result of their increased *use* and activity across successive generations (KTO 61).[45] In his account, inner conflict thereby generates the fittest Darwinian organisms in a non-teleological manner. Constant variation among the struggling parts, coupled with the fact that the equilibrium of higher-order parts is being continually tested in the external environment of inter-organismic competition, means that organisms will naturally evolve a complex and functionally integrated form of holism, although untold numbers of poorly coordinated organisms must inevitably perish in the process.

Having dissected the general features of intra-organismic struggle, we should now focus on Roux's specific conception of assimilation. According to Roux, assimilation takes two distinct forms. The first is of a catabolic, nutritive kind. Thus, he claims that in order to survive, an organism needs to maintain a certain degree of "durability" (*Dauerfähigkeit*) – that is, it needs to consume more energy than it expends. Its efficiency in this respect is determined by its "capacity for assimilation" (*Assimilationsfähigkeit*): its ability "to uniformly transform foreign objects within itself, to uniformly regroup different groupings of atoms within itself, and thus to qualitatively appropriate foreign entities, and to produce that which is necessary when only the raw materials are available" (KTO 216).

Recalling Nietzsche's notion of "plastic force," this process is one by which the foreign is transformed into the familiar. With respect to our current line of inquiry, we should note that Roux's conception of assimilation, much like that of Schopenhauer, has a necessarily destructive component. It involves the attraction and catabolism of existing foreign unities into their constituent groups of atoms, followed by the selective incorporation of those groups that the organismic part in question can leverage to compensate for its energetic losses (KTO 56). This process then issues in growth (*Wachsthum*) and reproduction (*Fortpflanzung*). Yet Roux states that what defines an organism is not its capacity to merely compensate, but rather to *over*-compensate, for its energetic losses (KTO 216–217).

---

[45] See also KTO 24.

This constitutes the foundation of an organism's durability, since *under*-compensation results in diminution and death, and *mere* compensation does not allow for periods of nutritional privation, or indeed any other unanticipated environmental pressures (KTO 217).[46] We should also remark that while Roux describes assimilation as being motivated by a form of hunger, in this context, hunger does not signify a form of psychologically represented craving, but rather a strong *affinity* for nutrition (KTO 222).

Alongside this species of assimilation, Roux considers the organic function of *excretion* (*Beseitigung*) to be equally imperative for the survival and competitive success of any given intra-organismic part. This process, which he considers to be a "vital general condition of life," involves the removal of the catabolic byproducts generated by assimilation, or in other words, those elements of the foreign that cannot be exploited and whose "accumulation would be harmful" (KTO 95). Those parts of the body that are more efficient at eliminating such byproducts are then favored in the intra-organismic struggle of parts because the accumulation of waste impedes assimilation and growth. At the level of functionally similar cells and molecules, those variants which eliminate with relatively less efficiency will therefore be edged out of existence by their superior rivals.

Although this catabolic process certainly represents the dominant mode of assimilation in Roux's account, he also mentions another model. The catabolic mode of assimilation just outlined represents what he calls an *indirect* form of conflict, one in which parts only compete against one another insofar as they vie for the same space and nutrition. In contrast to this, he submits that it sometimes occurs that parts exhibiting novel traits "triumph in *direct struggle* with the old parts and propagate themselves insofar as the latter are either directly destroyed or get used, assimilated by the new" (KTO 87).[47] In this *direct* struggle of molecules, weaker competitors are usually simply destroyed (*zerstört*); however, this is sometimes not the case, and instead the inferior molecules are *assimilated*, intact, by their superior opponents. This type of assimilation results in what contemporary biologists refer to as "endosymbiosis," where an existing biological unity is preserved after being incorporated. This allows the stronger, assimilating unity to exploit the activity of its new subaltern.

Though it may have dated badly, Roux offers a naturalized account of how complex organisms come into existence. His model of organization in

---

[46] Nietzsche's familiarity with these passages is evinced in KSA 10:7[95], 274.
[47] Nietzsche transcribes this excerpt in KSA 10:7[86], 272.

no way presupposes metaphysical entities such as Aristotelian essences, Platonic Ideas or the idea of such organismic complexity contained in the mind of a divine creator (à la Kant). The way in which a given organization will develop over the course of generations through this process of internal conflict is wholly *contingent* – that is, upon its interior, partite variation and, moreover, its particular environmental conditions. For Roux, inner purposiveness is therefore emphatically *not* determined by some metaphysically pregiven blueprint.

We should also recapitulate that this is in large part a *measured* process: certain nutritive materials, or exploitable cells, are selected from the environment and subsequently incorporated. Measure is also present insofar as the struggle of functionally differentiated parts is characterized by a species of equilibrium (*Gleichgewicht*). On the other hand, though, this struggle is conditioned by processes of a distinctly unmeasured sort: organismic parts must catabolize unities in order to extract nutrition therefrom; and furthermore, they need to eliminate the harmful metabolic byproducts generated by the struggle for assimilation. What remains to be determined, though, is how Nietzsche assimilates this naturalistic theory of purposiveness into his own mature theory of organization.

4.2.2 *Exploitation Not Preservation*

We can tell from Nietzsche's *Nachlaß*, and his heavily annotated copy of KTO (NPB 511), that he was intimately familiar with Roux's vision of organismic unity. Indeed, in his middle period, Nietzsche initially accedes to Roux's model of healthy organization, almost without reservation; he then seeks to straightforwardly apply this model to the problem of social and psychological organization. Notwithstanding, Nietzsche consistently rejects KTO's pretensions to scientific realism.[48] To reiterate what was stated in the Introduction, he rejects the idea that one can legitimately apply the language of struggle to nonhuman entities, the reason being that struggle presupposes specifically human forms of consciousness.[49] In spite of its lack of objective truth, however, Nietzsche nevertheless takes Roux's "*manner of speaking*" (KSA 9:11[128], 487) about organisms (i.e., in terms of *Kampf*) to represent a valuable heuristic tool. Its value, according to Nietzsche, lies in its capacity to render obscure organic processes at least partially comprehensible. Provided that we keep in mind the metaphorical

---

[48] See Müller-Lauter (1999, 165); KSA 9:11[128],487; KSA 9:11[241], 532.
[49] Introduction, pp. 22–23.

character of our discourse, interpreting the world through the language of conflict remains an illuminating enterprise. And to be sure, between 1881 and 1883, Nietzsche routinely avails himself of this *Bilderrede* ("image-language"; ibid.) in his effort to shed light on the nature of both the self and society.[50] In 1884, however, he begins to reject significant portions of KTO. Accordingly, in seeking to reconstruct Nietzsche's mature account of organization, we should begin from this point in his philosophical trajectory.

So, what does Nietzsche come to reject in KTO? Above all, Roux's conviction that intra-organismic struggle is structured by the following three teloi:

a. *Survival (Erhaltung)*. The idea that "uninterrupted durability [*Dauerfähigkeit*] is the first precondition of the organic" (KTO 214), and that "the parts live purely for their own preservation" (KTO 220).
b. *Nutrition*. The idea that intra-organismic parts principally compete for sustenance.
c. *Overcompensation*. The idea that assimilation can be defined as a struggle for the "replacement and over-compensation of that which has been used" (KTO 238).

To begin with (a), already in Z II Self-Overcoming (KSA 4.149), Nietzsche attacks the idea that self-preservation represents the defining telos of living beings. With this critique, his aim is to refute the existence of a Spinozistic *conatus* or Schopenhauerian will to live. But it was only after reading William Rolph's *Biological Problems* in 1884 that he began to formulate a more thoroughgoing refutation of the logic of preservation.[51] Aside from contesting Schopenhauer and Spinoza, Nietzsche's critique of preservation (*Erhaltung*) as the ultimate end toward which all life (either consciously or unconsciously) tends is, like Rolph's, (mistakenly) framed as a critique of Darwin and (less mistakenly) Spencer.[52]

---

[50] Indeed, Nietzsche conceives nation-states as the "highest [organisms] known to us – very imperfect organisms" (KSA 9:12[163], 604; see also KSA 9:11[316], 563). For Nietzsche's early application of Roux to social issues, see e.g., KSA 9:11[132], 490; KSA 9:11[134], 490–492. See also KSA 9:11[130], 487–488; KSA 9:11[182], 509–512; GS 118.
[51] Evidence of Nietzsche's having read BP can be found in NPB (504). On the impact of Rolph on Nietzsche's thought, see Moore (2002, esp. 47–53; 1998, 535–551).
[52] See Richardson (2004, 16). On the flaws in Nietzsche's critique of Darwin, see Richardson (2004, 20–26). Moore (2002, 51, fn.42) also remarks that Rolph attacks a straw-man Darwin. However, the notion of a drive for self-preservation is certainly present in Spencer's *The Data of Ethics* (1882, 135), which Nietzsche was reading in the early 1880s (NPB 565–566).

Rolph conceives the tendency toward accumulation (what he calls the "force of attraction" or *Anziehungskraft*) as an original and fundamental force of nature (BP 59). In his view, growth is a function of this process of attraction, as we can see from not just organisms (as they consume nutrition and grow), but also from the growth of *in*organic organizations, such as crystals. While Rolph claims that both the organic and inorganic are likewise characterized by this "drive" (*Trieb*) to accrue, he argues that it is only in the case of organic entities that this impulse is "insatiable" (*unersättlich*) (BP 61). One might object to Rolph's conception of the organic in terms of "insatiable acquisition" (*unersättliche Aufnahme*) on account of the fact that many organisms only grow during the adolescent phase of their life span. This would indicate that for many species, the process of excessive consumption halts at a certain stage in their development. Rolph responds, however, that the division of single-celled organisms demonstrates that once an organism reaches the "boundary" of its "capacity for acquisition" (*Aufnahmfähigkeit*), it discharges its accumulated surfeit by *reproducing*: "two young cells emerge, which now begin the game anew" (BP 67).[53] For Rolph, the idea of a "drive for self-preservation" (*Selbsterhaltungstrieb*) is unable to explain organic processes, given that assimilation consistently outstrips the survival needs of the organism: "from its gains, the creature also accomplishes the function of procreation, which in no way pertains to [the function of] self-preservation" (BP 92).

Rolph also rejects the Darwinian-Malthusian view of nature qua unrelenting struggle over limited resources. However, he mistakenly reads Darwin as suggesting that *this* constitutes the primary motor of evolution.[54] It is only in times of environmental dearth, says Rolph, that the brutal "Darwinian" picture corresponds to reality. Interestingly, Rolph thinks that under such conditions of privation, certain species of bacteria satisfy their urge for assimilation through a quite distinct form of activity: what Rolph calls "conjugation," where an impoverished male cell tries to unite with a healthy (and therefore understandably reluctant) female cell. The male's aim is to materially benefit from fusing together into a new single cell, which is stronger than the original male but weaker than the

---

[53] With higher-order organisms that reproduce sexually, Rolph theorizes that this process of division is displaced to the sexually reproductive organs, where "procreative substances" (*Zeugungsstoffe*) build up and generate discomfort in the organism. Such organisms are then driven to discharge this either through the act of copulation (in the case of the male) or through parturition (in the case of the female) (BP 168–170). Compare KSA 11:25[179], 62: "Drive for excretion [*Ausscheidung*] (love) (to which regeneration also belongs) [. . .]."

[54] See above, Introduction, fn.52.

original female. Rolph describes this as a process of self-consumption, or *isophagy*. It pools the accrued energy of two cells, though the resulting sum is now only needed to sustain one cell, and so this cell is left with a consumable excess (BP 136–138). Although Rolph mischaracterizes conjugation – which was discovered in the 1950s to be a means by which cells transfer genetic information rather than a form of isophagy – the theory is nonetheless relevant insofar as it indicates that Nietzsche would have been aware of a type of biological assimilation that is symptomatic of *declining* health, and by which relatively weaker unities seek to exploit their stronger counterparts.

This conjugational mode of assimilation is, in Rolph's view, contrary to the process of reproduction that drives evolution. Indeed, Rolph claims that evolutionary progress only occurs under conditions of plenitude – that is, when a species is *not* engaged in a depleting struggle for survival. It is only when environmental pressure is relaxed, Rolph claims, that variation is able to proliferate (otherwise less efficient variants are quickly edged out of existence). Rolph takes the rich variety of well-adapted flora and fauna that surround us today as proof that species must, more often than not, enjoy such conditions of plenitude. Since organisms will invariably struggle to over-accumulate wherever possible, Rolph takes this to be the truly fundamental organic drive; thus, organic life is not defined by a "struggle for the 'acquisition of the most indispensable life-necessities,' but rather a struggle for increased acquisition [*Mehrerwerb*]" (BP 97).[55] On these grounds, Rolph claims that life should be conceived as a struggle to further "propagate life" (*um Lebensvermehrung*), for "perfection" (*Vervollkommnung*) and "growth" (*Wachsthum*), rather than a relentless battle for survival. Animals are only ever *temporarily* forced to engage in a defensive struggle (*Vertheidigungskampf*) for preservation, under rarely obtaining conditions of environmental hardship (BP 97).

Nietzsche appears to draw on Rolph quite directly in contesting the idea that preservation represents the guiding telos of assimilation. This line of influence is readily apparent in GS 349, though Nietzsche nonetheless differentiates himself from Rolph in this aphorism by designating *power* (*Macht*) as the guiding end of all living beings:

> To wish to preserve oneself is a sign of distress, of a limitation of the truly basic life-instinct, which aims at the *expansion of power* and in so doing often enough risks and sacrifices self-preservation. [...] [I]n nature, it is not distress which rules, but rather abundance, squandering – even to the point of absurdity. The struggle for survival is only an *exception*, a temporary

---

[55] See also BP 114.

restriction of the will to life; the great and small struggle revolves everywhere around preponderance, around growth and expansion, around power and in accordance with the will to power, which is simply the will of Life.[56]

Nietzsche understands nature as being for the most part bountiful and profligate.[57] Under such conditions, living beings struggle for *growth*. Consequently, he characterizes the "fundamental life-drive" as a drive for growth and power augmentation – desiderata for the sake of which animals and individuals will often risk their own survival. This said, for Nietzsche, the impetus toward power nonetheless often *coincides* with the goal of self-preservation, insofar as power augmentation often indirectly promotes survival (or endurance – *Dauer*).[58] This is why to the myopic observer it can appear as though survival constitutes the motivating telos of *all* life, when in point of fact this tendency for preservation is either epiphenomenal, or merely indicative of a *particular* mode of pursuing power expansion (i.e., under conditions of scarcity).

At other times, though, Nietzsche takes the drive for growth to be entirely at variance with the drive for self-preservation. For example, according to Nietzsche, the protoplasma of a cell

> takes into itself absurdly more than would be required to preserve it: and, above all, it does *not* thereby "preserve itself," it *falls apart* . . . The drive that rules here has to explain precisely this desire [of the cell] *not* to preserve itself [. . .]. (KSA 13:11[121], 57)

In making this point, Nietzsche clearly borrows from Rolph, who claims that single-celled organisms consume to a point at which they are forced to relinquish their individual unity (and therefore in a certain sense *die*), and split into a pair of newborn cells. At the specifically human level, Nietzsche points to various circumstances under which the impetus toward power reveals itself to be antagonistic vis-à-vis the end of survival. This discrepancy is particularly salient in "strong races," who *"mutually decimate* one another: war, greed for power, adventure; their existence is costly, short [. . .]" (KSA 13:14[182], 369). Indeed, those who are proficient at pursuing power are often grossly inefficient when it comes to preserving themselves. We might also cite Nietzsche's earlier analysis of martyrs, who, in their

---

[56] See also TI Skirmishes 14.
[57] Elsewhere, he also reiterates Rolph's thesis that variation only occurs under conditions of plenitude. See e.g., BGE 262: "[. . .] species with overabundant diets [. . .] will immediately show a striking tendency towards variations of the type [. . .]." See also KSA 11:35[22], 516–518.
[58] See also A 6: "I consider life itself to be an instinct for growth, for endurance, for the accumulation of forces, for *power*."

ardent desire to possess the truth, and the attendant "feeling of power" (*Machtgefühl*), gladly sacrifice their own lives (GS 13).[59]

In this way, he launches a deflationary attack on the idea of a fundamental (conscious or unconscious) drive for self-preservation. As he exclaims in an earlier note: "there is no drive for self-preservation!" (KSA 9:11[108], 479). Cementing this position, he then states the following in BGE 13, discernibly echoing Rolph's (and also Mayer's) discharge model of the organism, albeit now with an emphasis on *power* that is totally absent in Rolph:

> Above all, a living thing wants to *discharge* its strength – life itself is will to power –: self-preservation is only one of the indirect and most frequent *consequences* of this. – In short, here as elsewhere, be cautious of *superfluous* teleological principles![60]

Elsewhere, though, Nietzsche refrains from altogether rejecting the telos of survival, and suggests instead that organisms *do* sometimes directly (and in the case of humans, *consciously*) strive for self-preservation (see e.g., GS 349); however, in such texts, this condition is still framed as an exceptional state, only arising when organisms are in a position of weakness and their existence is under immediate threat.

But the chief way in which Nietzsche distinguishes himself from both Rolph and Roux is in his rejection of (b) – the idea that *nutrition* constitutes a fundamental telos of the struggle that defines life. For Nietzsche, this struggle is fought over *power*: any living organization vies to overwhelm foreign unities and assimilate them into its power structure – in a word, to *command* them. And as we saw in Chapter 1, this tendency is endlessly plastic, and assumes an infinitude of distinct forms. The struggle for nutrition is then just one of the many different ways that this "fundamental life-drive" manages to express itself: "the will to power specializes itself as will to nutrition, to possession, to *tools* [*Werkzeugen*], to servants – obeying and commanding: the body. – the stronger will directs the weaker" (KSA 11:35[15], 514).[61]

---

[59] See also D 262; Z II Self-Overcoming, KSA 4.148: "[. . .] truly, wherever there is decline and the falling of leaves, behold, there life sacrifices itself – for power!"

[60] See also KSA 11:26[277], 222–223; KSA 12:2[68], 92.

[61] Katsafanas (2016, 170), has argued that the will to power is "not a drive but the form drives take"; however, Nietzsche frequently refers to it as a drive, the *fundamental* drive, even. See e.g., KSA 12:9 [151], 424: "'Hunger' is only a narrower adaptation, by which the fundamental drive [*Grundtrieb*] for power acquired a more spiritual form." KSA 12:1[30], 17: "The desires [*Begehrungen*] always further specialize themselves: their unity is *the will to power* (to take the expression from the strongest of all drives [*Triebe*], which has hitherto directed all organic development)." See also TI Ancients 3.

Congruent with this, competing bodily parts are in Nietzsche's account first and foremost concerned with *commanding* their rivals. Of course, higher organisms *are* at times motivated by the sensation of hunger; but Nietzsche maintains that this "[h]unger is a specialized and later form of the drive [for power], an expression of the division of labor, in the service of a higher drive that rules over this division" (KSA 13:11 [121], 58). The struggle for nutrition is only ever a specific manifestation of the more general push for power augmentation (KSA 12:5[64], 209). Returning to the example of the single-celled organism, Nietzsche describes how it "stretches out its pseudopodia in order to seek that which resists it – not from hunger but from will to power. Thereupon it attempts to overcome, appropriate, incorporate that which it encounters" (KSA 13:14[174], 360). Nietzsche thereby seeks to refute the Schopenhauerian supposition that willing is inherently motivated by pain and a feeling of lack, a supposition reiterated by Rolph in BP (169–170, 177, 181).[62] By contrast, Nietzsche understands willing as an expression of accumulated *excess*. In the act of stretching out its pseudopodia, of trying to increase its power, a single-celled organism is *discharging* its pent-up power. And as we saw above, exercising one's will elicits a pleasurable sensation of freedom. As Deleuze remarks (1983, 85), for Nietzsche, the process of willing is therefore best characterized as "joyful."

This brings us to Nietzsche's rejection of (c) – the idea that energetic over-compensation constitutes a fundamental organic end. As Nietzsche sees it, thinking of assimilation as being "directed towards 'compensation' ['*Ersatz*'], towards 'overcompensation' even, contains a deep and danger-ous misunderstanding."[63] The expression of power is, in Nietzsche's view, always an act of striving to *increase* power – that is, in relation to another resisting power. As such, we should not define it as an impulse to *replace* expended energy or force.[64] Nietzsche thus takes exception to the termin-ology of "compensation" used by Roux, opting instead for Rolph's vocabu-lary of "insatiability"; hence, he asserts that the will to power is "a will to overcome that has in itself no end" (KSA 12:9[91], 385).

---

[62] See Moore (2002, 75 [fn.25]). At other times, Nietzsche also indicates that pain is a constitutive part, or necessary condition, of pleasure. See KSA 11:35[15], 514: "[. . .] pain is immanent to all pleasure"; KSA 10:16[15], 505; KSA 12:5[64], 209; KSA 12:7[18], 302–303; KSA 13:11[71], 33–34; KSA 13:14[173], 358; KSA 11:25[378], 111. Another pertinent note, in which Nietzsche contests the hedonistic, utilitarian conception of pleasure qua fundamental (human) telos, is KSA 13:14[174], 360: "Man does *not* seek pleasure and does *not* avoid displeasure [. . .]. Pleasure and displeasure are mere consequences, mere epiphenomena – what man wants, what every smallest part of a living organism wants, is an increase of power. Pleasure or displeasure follow from the striving after that."

[63] Quoted in Müller-Lauter 1978, 207.   [64] See Aydin (2007, 26); KSA 13:14[82], 261–262.

This figuration of the will to power is wholly at odds with what we found to be the non-instrumentalizing character of the Nietzschean agon. To bring this further into relief, we should examine the remainder of the note that Hatab and Connolly cite – though in strategically truncated form – as evidence for their agonistic reading of the will to power:

> The will to power can manifest itself only *against resistances*; therefore it seeks that which resists it – this is the primeval tendency of the protoplasm when it extends pseudopodia and feels about. Appropriation and incorporation are above all a desire to overwhelm, a forming, shaping and reshaping, until at length that which has been overwhelmed has entirely gone over into the power domain of the aggressor and has increased the same. (KSA 12:9[151], 424)[65]

Since this note forcefully asserts the necessity of instrumental domination, invoking it as evidence that Nietzsche held an agonal conception of nature does significant interpretive violence to the letter of the text. What we can further discern from this fragment is that although Nietzsche rejects Roux's description of survival, nutrition and over-compensation as fundamental organic tendencies, he nonetheless retains one of the core ideas of KTO: that incorporative struggle represents an essential feature of life.

4.2.3   Pathos Not Mechanism

Nietzsche's general theory of organization diverges from KTO in a number of other important respects. For one, he denies the mechanistic presuppositions that structure the argument of KTO. Recall that for Roux bodily parts are *not* affective agents; rather, they are purely physical entities, partaking in a particular set of mechanical processes. For Nietzsche, by contrast, when he describes living entities as willing – as "*seeking resistance*" – he is unequivocally attributing some form of sentience to them. After all, according to Nietzsche, "willing" is merely an "*affect* of command" (BGE 19; emphasis mine). He speculates that the parts of the body have some form of affective, agential awareness – that the body as a whole is suffused with the affect or *pathos* of command: "here the supposition is made that the whole organism thinks, that all organic entities partake in thinking feeling willing [*Denken Fühlen Wollen*]" (KSA 11:27[19], 280).[66] And in Z II Self-Overcoming, he writes that every living thing that is commanded is fundamentally characterized by a "desire" (*Lust*) to instrumentalize weaker entities

---

[65] See Chapter 2, Section 2.3, above.

[66] See KSA 13:14[79], 259: "[T]he will to power [is] not a being [*Sein*], not a becoming [*Werden*], rather a *pathos* is the elementary fact." See also KSA 11:34[124], 462.

(KSA 4.148). We should further recall how in BGE 19 he compares the body to "a social construction [*Gesellschaftsbau*] of many souls." In the *Nachlaß*, he floats a number of potential empirical proofs for his claim that all purposive unities engage in "thinking feeling willing." In his published works, however, we find that he opts for a nonempirical, nondeductive proof. It is worth our while devoting some attention to these proofs, since his understanding of the will to power is integral to his later conception of organizational struggle.

In the *Nachlaß*, then, Nietzsche's view is that for a living unity to bring foreign entities under its command (i.e., incorporate them), it needs to be able to *evaluate* these entities. Only by means of such evaluation can it determine whether to seek their incorporation or exclusion. He calls this "an assessment [*Abschätzen*] relating to incorporation or excretion [*Einverleibung oder Abscheidung*]" (KSA 10:24[14], 651). He then makes the further argument that living unities need to be able to communicate with any entities that they wish to command (KSA 11:14[21], 638). In other words, there must be "mutual understanding [*sich verstehen*]" – as Nietzsche points out, "a rock cannot be commanded" (KSA 12:2[69], 92).[67] The simultaneity and reciprocity exhibited by the parts of any coordinated unity are incompatible with mechanical explanation, which construes nature as a series of diachronic relations taking the form: A causes B; B causes C; and so on (KSA 11:34[124], 462). Expanding upon these considerations, he further maintains that such organized entities need to practice certain "virtues" (*Tugenden*) toward one another: "[I]n the relation of the organs to one another, all *virtues* must already be practiced – obedience, diligence, helpfulness, watchfulness – the character of machine is completely *absent* from all matters organic (self-regulation)" (KSA 11:25[426], 124).[68] Any organized body must, Nietzsche writes, be governed by a moral order that is simply incompatible with the mechanistic representation of the body as a machine. This is why he conceives "morality as a doctrine of the power relations under which the phenomenon of 'life' arises" (BGE 19).

Nietzsche then extends a number of these claims to *inorganic* unities. Even inanimate organizations – such as atoms, for example – must, in his view, be able to distinguish between that which they need to attract (i.e., assimilate) and that which they need to repel:

---

[67] See also KSA 11:34[124], 462; KSA 11:34[123], 461; Wotling (2011). Moore (2002, 39) persuasively argues that Michael Forster was a key influence in this respect.

[68] See also KSA 11:37[4], 578.

[. . .] the will to power is that which also directs the inorganic world, or
rather, there is no inorganic world. [. . .]
    [. . .] [I]n order for this will to power to be able to express itself, it must
perceive those things which it attracts; [. . .] it *feels* when something assimil-
able approaches it. (KSA 11:34[247], 504)[69]

Nietzsche is advancing an inferential (*modus ponens*) argument of the following
sort: Given that atoms behave in a particular way (i.e., actively attracting and
repelling other atoms), they must *necessarily* be endowed with perceptual
awareness and endogenous force.[70] On the one hand, this elides the
organic–inorganic distinction insofar as it denies the possibility of truly inanimate matter.[71] On the other, it rejects mechanistic ontologies, which figure the
external world as an aggregate of corpuscular bodies each of whose motions are
exclusively caused by the impacts they passively receive from other corpuscular
bodies (in the manner of colliding billiard balls). The upshot of Nietzsche's
view is that existence must be conceived as a mass of organizations engaged in
direct conflict with one another, where each opposed organization strives to
incorporate or exclude its counterparts; this explains why Nietzsche conceives
"[a]ll events, all motion, all becoming, as a determination of degrees and
relations of force, as a *struggle* [*Kampf*] . . . " (KSA 12:9[91], 385).[72]

    But how can we possibly *know* that on the inside *all* things are in reality
thinking, feeling and desiring? Is Nietzsche not blatantly transgressing the
Kantian ban (on describing the world in-itself) – the very same ban that we
saw him indict Schopenhauer for breaching?[73] Is he not hypocritically courting
dogmatism? To be sure, his multifarious private efforts to empirically ground
his panpsychic speculations are far from satisfying. Fortunately, in the published works he frames his argument in a different and somewhat more rigorous
manner. In BGE 22, he thus argues that the idea of the world as will to power is
merely plausible – that is to say, ontologically possible. In contrast to those who
suppose the natural world to be a mechanistic aggregate of atomistic units
governed by natural law,

    somebody with an opposite intention and mode of interpretation could
    come along and be able to read from the same nature, and with reference to

[69] See also KSA 11:35[58], 537; KSA 10:12[27], 404–405.
[70] On the need to explain the activity of inorganic organizations with reference to an endogenous
source of motion (rather than merely conceiving such organizations as being reactively propelled),
see KSA 12:1[30], 17.
[71] See KSA 2[172], 153; KSA 11:36[21], 560; KSA 11:25[356], 106.
[72] Harking back to Schopenhauer (and Nietzsche's reading of Balfour Stewart in KSA 8:9[2], 183), in
KSA 11:43[2], 702, Nietzsche explicitly claims that this struggle takes place at the level of atoms.
[73] On Nietzsche's critique of Schopenhauer in this regard, see Chapter 1.

the same set of appearances, a tyrannically ruthless and pitiless execution of power claims. (BGE 22)

Here the will to power is offered as an explanatory model that is just as capable of accounting for observable phenomena as its rival, the mechanistic model. The subtext of this aphorism is that what tips the scales in favor Nietzsche's will-to-power hypothesis is that it refuses to interpret nature in a way that would naturalistically vindicate democratic values (especially the idea of universal "equality before the law" [BGE 22]), which for reasons expounded above, he takes to be severely detrimental.

In BGE 36, Nietzsche likewise refrains from arguing for the objective truth of his vision of the world as will to power. Rather, he indicates that his account is *"enough* to render the so-called mechanistic (and thus material) world comprehensible."[74] On this reading, we can legitimately assent to the hypothesis that the world is will to power on the grounds that in comparison with the mechanistic worldview, it is *theoretically* just as ·possible, while in *practical* terms being decidedly preferable (as is claimed in BGE 22).[75] Nietzsche's conviction that his will-to-power hypothesis is pragmatically superior to all other competing possible worldviews is, to my mind, somewhat dubious. In the interests of charitably reconstructing his outlook, however, I suggest that we suspend our disbelief and provisionally acquiesce to his controversial point of view.

So, if we assume that every entity is hypothetically a will-to-power organization, how does this bear upon the issue of *Zweckmäßigkeit?* According to Nietzsche's account, the component parts of any living organization exhibit a certain function with respect to the whole because they were once *perceived* by the superordinate forces of that organization to be in some way useful – and therefore not because they were divinely designed to serve said organization. These parts were then overpowered and finally incorporated – that is to say, shaped to fulfill that perceived use:

> – The individual itself as a struggle between parts (for food, space, etc.): its development tied to a *victory, predominance* of individual parts, to an *atrophy,* "becoming an organ" of other parts.

[...]

---

[74] Nietzsche thus defends the will-to-power thesis on the grounds of its explanatory parsimony. However, for the sake of brevity, I have bracketed much of this argument out of my analysis.

[75] In this way, my interpretive approach gainsays ironic readings of BGE 36 (i.e., the claim that Nietzsche does not actually adhere to the proposition that he is ostensibly defending in the aphorism – namely, that the world is *actually* will to power). See e.g., Clark and Dudrick (2012, 242); Loeb (2015). For a rebuttal of the ironic reading, see Janaway (2007, 153–163).

– The *new* forms molded from within are not formed with an end in view; but in the struggle [*Kampf*] of the parts a new form is *not* left long without being related to a partial usefulness and then, according to its *use*, develops itself more and more completely. (KSA 12:7[25], 304)

In this way, the ascendant force and the subjugated organ enter into a new "order of means and ends," "an order of *rank*" (KSA 12:9[91], 386). So whereas for Roux the mainspring of organizational development is principally *indirect* struggle – over space and nutrition, and receptivity to functional stimuli – for Nietzsche it is instead *direct* struggle *for instrumental command.*

But what kind of exploitative command defines healthy organization for Nietzsche? In the first place, he rebuts the idea that such organization should be conceived in terms of centralized, monarchic order. That is to say, ideal coordination is not structured pyramidically under the command of a single ruling entity. Instead, he asks the following question: Should we not rather assume that "dominion resides in a kind of *aristocracy* of 'cells'? To be sure, [an aristocracy] of equals [*pares*], used to ruling jointly and understanding how to command?" (KSA 11:40[42], 650).[76] In order to clarify how Nietzsche envisions this aristocratic order, it is worth our while making a close reading of KSA 11:40[21], where he describes the human subject in a manner that sheds useful light on his general conception of functional unity:

> We gain the correct idea of the nature of our subject-unity, namely as regents at the head of a commonwealth (not as "souls" or "life forces"), also of the dependence of these regents upon the ruled and of an order of rank and division of labor as the conditions that make possible the whole and its individual parts. In the same way, how living unities continually arise and die and how the "subject" is not eternal; in the same way, that the struggle also expresses itself in obeying and commanding, and a fluctuating determination of the limits of power is part of life. The relative *ignorance* in which the regent is kept concerning individual activities and even disturbances of the commonwealth is among the conditions under which rule can be exercised. In short, we also gain a valuation of not-knowing, of seeing things on a broad scale, of simplification and falsification, of the perspectival. (KSA 11:40[21], 638–639)

There are three key points that should be highlighted in this note. First, Nietzsche does not think of healthy hierarchy as being analogous to political

[76] See also KSA 11:40[38], 647, where Nietzsche states that the affects "are a multiplicity, behind which it is not necessary to insert a unity: it suffices to conceive them as a regency [*Regentschaft*]."

regimes dominated by a rigid hereditary nobility. Rather, it has far more in common with flexible oligarchy – where the ruling group is never entirely segregated from its subordinates; where membership in this group is ideally porous; and where the boundaries of power remain fluid and defeasible.[77] If we look elsewhere, we find that Nietzsche further understands the units that compose a living organization as being just as fluid as the whole of which they are a part: "these tiniest living beings, which constitute our body, do not count as soul-atoms, but rather as something growing, struggling [*Kämpfendes*], self-enlarging, and again dying away" (KSA 11:37[4], 577). Every commanding unit is therefore in its turn likewise a fluid power organization.[78] We are left with a world devoid of metaphysical substance – a world that is will to power all the way down, so to speak. Furthermore, since the locus of power lacks any fixed being, and is relatively flexible, we can assume that Nietzsche affirms the idea of subordinate units climbing up to participate in executive command, and, vice versa, commanding units suffering demotion.

The units that contingently happen to be in command of any given organization at any particular time impose a function on the subordinate parts and thereby establish an order of means and ends. Yet, and this is the second point of note, due to the complexity of any given organization, its ruling units are forced to govern in partial ignorance, delegating much of their formative power to auxiliary overseers. Consequently, no commanding unit could ever *intentionally* organize the entire hierarchy of parts since they could not possibly *know* (or "feel") the totality of these parts. There is simply too much information to process – an infinitude of actions and relations.[79] Nietzsche marshals this argument to reject the Schopenhauerian thesis that we have to assume that the *Zweckmäßigkeit* of an organism is determined by a single "end-conscious being" (*zweckbewußtes Wesen*) – a Platonic Idea, for example.[80]

The third point that merits our attention is that Nietzsche does not limit conflict to the separate orders of a purposive organization, as is the case in both KTO and Nietzsche's own stratified vision of agonal struggle. On the

---

[77] See also KSA 11:34[123], 462; KSA 12:9[98], 391.
[78] In making this argument, Nietzsche draws on Boscovich's critique of atomism (Poellner 1995, 46ff.). As an alternative to atomism, Boscovich posits extensionless "centers of force" that either repel or attract other centers of force. Nietzsche fuses this idea with observations in cellular biology that cells can divide and unite, and hence appear to have no fixed atomistic essence. See KSA 11:43[2], 701; Moore (2002, 49).
[79] This applies to human consciousness in particular (see KSA 11:34[131], 464).
[80] See KSA 11:26[60], 164; compare, however, KSA 10:24[16], 654, where Nietzsche suggests that there exists an unconscious intellect ordering the body.

contrary, he depicts organizational struggle as a type of conflict that principally occurs *between* the various orders of a given functional unity. Subaltern forces, in addition to trying to command those still weaker than themselves (Z II Self-Overcoming, KSA 4.148), continue to struggle upward in resisting their commanders: "the struggle also expresses itself in obeying and commanding." The process by which these hierarchical relations are established (*festgestellt*) is described by Nietzsche as

> [. . .] a struggle [*Kampf*], assuming that one understands this word wide and deep enough to understand even the relation of the ruler to the ruled as a struggle [*Ringen*], and even the relation of the obeying to the ruling as one of resistance [*Widerstreben*]. (KSA 11:40[55], 655)[81]

Subordinate entities are usually able to successfully resist their superordinates since, as in Roux, the continued existence of the higher orders depends upon that of the lower orders – there is a "dependence of these regents upon the ruled." The dominant parties must therefore constrain their drive for exploitation and even actively ensure the vitality of their functionaries – that is to say, the rulers must in part satisfy, or *obey*, the demands of their subjects. As such, within these hierarchies, "the commander must provide everything that serves to preserve those who obey, and is thus *conditioned* by their existence" (KSA 11:34[123], 461).[82] Recalling Hegel's master–slave dialectic, Heidegger (1961, 265) describes the situation as follows: "insofar as the servant makes himself indispensable to the master as such, and so obligates and orients the master to himself (the underling), the underling dominates the master." In this way, then, the moral order of virtues that undergirds healthy power organization is anything but unidirectional. Nietzsche's ideal abstract commanders do not amorally determine said order from a downward-looking point of transcendence; rather, they are immanent to the organization that they endeavor to form, and must therefore practice certain virtues of reciprocal obedience vis-à-vis those whom they command. It is this reciprocal process of overcoming – of command and obedience – that Nietzsche refers to as the "contest" (*Kampfspiel*) that *is* the organism (KSA 11:36[22], 561).

---

[81] See KSA 11:26[276], 222: "*To rule* is to bear the counterweight of the weaker force, therefore a kind of *continuation* of the struggle [*Kampfs*]. *To obey* [is] likewise a *struggle* [*Kampf*]: just enough force to resist *remains*." See also KSA 11:36[22], 561.

[82] Indeed, Nietzsche repeatedly highlights the measured nature of incorporation – that is, how the unity of the subject "can transform a weaker subject into its functionary *without destroying it*, and to a certain degree form a new unity with it" (KSA 12:9[98], 392; emphasis mine). Compare, however, KSA 12:9[151], 424, where Nietzsche suggests that incorporation proceeds until "finally the overpowered has entirely gone over to, and increased, the power of the attacker."

> All unity is unity *only* as *organization and co-operation*: just as a human commonwealth is a unity: therefore the *opposite* of atomistic *anarchy*, as a *pattern of domination* that *signifies* a unity but *is* not a unity. (KSA 12:2 [87], 104)

The upshot of these claims is that the way in which a power organization expresses itself is a function of its relation to those parts of "itself," or alterity, which it is trying to command. It has no independent essence to speak of, and can only manifest itself in its contingent, reciprocal relations with other living unities. In this way, "the apparent *'purposiveness'*" which *all* (and not just organic) purposive organizations exhibit is "merely the consequence of that *will to power* which plays itself out in all events" (KSA 12:9[91], 386).

So while Nietzsche disavows Roux's mechanistic interpretation of the organism (in favor of positing active command as the primary driver of inner purposiveness), he retains Roux's conception of *direct* struggle – that is, endosymbiosis – as a measured mode of assimilation that tends to generate relations of interdependence. Having established this, we should now consider how the later Nietzsche further follows Roux in positing unmeasured, exclusionary conflict as a correspondingly vital life process.

4.2.4 Exclusion and Excretion

Nietzsche maintains that the organizational struggle that characterizes the will to power manifests itself through two fundamental processes: "The drive to approach [*sich anzunähern*] and the drive to repel something [*etwas zurückzustoßen*] are the bond, in both the inorganic and the organic world" (KSA 11:36[21], 560). In Nietzsche's later writings, the repulsive aspect of this activity, to which we should now direct our attention, takes a number of different forms. On the one hand, he echoes Rolph in theorizing that weaker power organizations perpetually seek to conjugate with those that are stronger, which must in turn strive to repel these parasitic inroads.[83] Exclusion is also integral to his account of the will to power qua interpretation. Nietzsche claims that a will-to-power organization be able to "reinterpret" the opposed entities that it overpowers. In order to exploit these entities, it needs to reconceive them as organs, to impose a new meaning and function on them, and thereby incorporate them into a new

---

[83] See KSA 11:36[21], 560: "The weaker presses to the stronger from a need for nourishment; it wants to get under it, if possible to become *one* with it. The stronger, on the contrary, drives others away; it does not want to perish in this manner [. . .]."

command structure: "The will to power *interprets: the formation of an organ is a matter of an interpretation*; it delimits, determines degrees, differences in power" (KSA 12:2[145], 139). This process demands the occlusion of those elements of the co-opted unity that are perceived as harmful or useless to the dominant power organization, what Nietzsche variously refers to as the eclipsing (*Verdunkeln*), thinking away (*Wegdenken*), obliterating (*Auslöschen*) and even elimination (*Elimination*) of previous interpretations (or parts of previous interpretations) that were imposed on the unity undergoing assimilation (GM II 12, KSA 5.314; KSA 12:5[99], 226–227).[84] Referring to the organic – though he also claims to be describing "the whole history of a 'thing'" – he states the following:

> [. . .] everything that occurs in the organic world consists of *overpowering, dominating*, and in their turn, overpowering and dominating consist of re-interpretation, adjustment, in the process of which their former "meaning" and "purpose" must necessarily be eclipsed or completely obliterated. (GM II 12, KSA 5.313–314)

With this insight into Nietzsche's vision of the necessity of exclusionary struggle, we can elucidate the hermetic logic of "self-overcoming." As a power organization grows, it is concurrently forced to reorder its own internal hierarchy – in other words, it has to deconstruct its own *self*-interpretation. As part of this reshuffling activity, the organization in question must further perform a process of separation (*Abscheidung*) and exclusion (*Ausscheidung*), allowing for the disappearance (*Verschwinden*) of those functions which, though previously serviceable, now fail to fit within the new command structure (KSA 12:7[9], 296–297; KSA 11:40[38], 647). As Nietzsche states in another note, "'*development*' in every sense is always a loss (*Verlust*), an injury (*Schädigung*)" (KSA 11:34[194], 486). On this view, then, development is inextricable from the unagonistic process of excluding elements that have become redundant or counterproductive. This is why "Life" tells Zarathustra that it is "that which must always overcome itself": "Whatever I may create and however I may love it – soon I must oppose it and my love, thus my will wants it" (Z II Self-Overcoming, KSA 4.148). A condition of possibility of an organization's growth is that it breaks out of its outmoded hierarchical organization in a manner comparable to ecdysis.[85]

---

[84] KSA 12:5[99], 226–227: "– the will, which *underlines* (and eliminates the rest) that which, in an object, serves *its being content and harmonious with itself* / [. . .] The *thinking away* of all harmful and hostile factors in the beheld thing."

[85] On the importance of ecdysis for Nietzsche, see D 573; GS 26, 307 and 371.

This is Nietzsche's own ontological conception of creative destruction – or what he also dubs his "Dionysian" view of reality.[86]

His commitment to the idea that will to power can only manifest itself against resistances does not entail that it cannot reject, exclude or even destroy *particular* entities or interpretations that present it with resistance. Rather, it means that resistance cannot be eschewed *absolutely*. Nietzsche's affirmation of exclusion and excretion starkly vitiates any reading of the will to power as a wholly nondestructive dynamic (e.g., of sublimation or agonal contention).

With this affirmation of exclusion, Nietzsche's later theory of incorporation satisfies almost all of the criteria that defined his earlier, Schopenhauerian conception of the struggle for assimilation:

1. The opposed relata (i.e., will-to-power organizations) strive to subjugate their counterparts;
2. Its telos is instrumental hierarchy, which is associated with health;
3. It is conditioned by unmeasured conflict (i.e., the exclusion of that which cannot profitably be incorporated);
4. It continues within the instrumental hierarchies that it tends to generate.

Pivotally, though, we have discovered that Nietzsche no longer grounds organizational struggle in essentialist metaphysical entities (such as, for example, Ideas). The actively striving wills to power that drive any given organizing process are *immanent* to reality, and there is nothing beyond or behind the plurality of relationally determined wills to power that compose the world in which we live. Having established this, let us now examine how Nietzsche recommends we *implement* this abstract conception of organization in our campaign against individual and collective disintegration.

4.3   Individual Organization

Our analysis of subjective disintegration found the problem to be rooted in the disorder of an individual's behavioral impulses or *drives* (*Triebe*). Since Nietzsche's use of the term "drive" is at first glance deeply ambiguous, we ought to begin by clarifying *what* it is exactly that he thinks we ought to reorganize. Furthermore, we should establish how his drive psychology instantiates the abstract principles of his theory of the will to power. Consonant with his account of thriving power organizations, we are going to see that he advances a program of self-cultivation that requires

---

[86] See GS 371; EH BT 3 and 4. We find an interesting precursor of this idea in AOM 323.

both a restrained, measured struggle to exploit serviceable drives, and an unmeasured push to exclude, eradicate or suppress any that prove redundant, injurious or intractable.

Given our preceding analysis of his abstract theory of organization, the idea that Nietzsche entreats us to adopt an eliminative or exclusionary stance toward certain of our behavioral impulses may not seem so controversial. It is worth highlighting, however, that this idea seems to be inconsistent with a number of key aphorisms in TI, in which he admonishes Christians for trying to extirpate their affects – particularly their sensual (i.e., *sexual*) desires (TI Morality 1–4). Likewise, in the following *Nachlaß* note Nietzsche clearly expresses his antipathy toward eliminatory approaches to self-cultivation.

> *Overcoming of the affects?* – No, if what is implied is their weakening and destruction [*Vernichtung*]. But putting them into service: which may also mean subjecting them to a protracted tyranny (not only as an individual, but as a community, race, etc.). (KSA 12:1[122], 39)[87]

On the basis of these (and other) texts, commentators have sought to read Nietzsche as a proponent of an exclusively measured mode of self-cultivation – what I will be calling the *sublimational* reading. On this interpretation, most famously advanced by Walter Kaufmann (1974, 226), Nietzsche accepts that order *can* be imposed on one's disgregated impulses "by thoroughly weakening the whole organism or by repudiating and repressing many of [these] impulses: but the result in that case is not a 'harmony,' and the *physis* is castrated, not 'improved.'" For Kaufmann's Nietzsche, therefore, "the impulses should be 'overcome': not by extirpation, but by sublimation" – "a sexual impulse, for example, [can] be channeled into a creative spiritual activity, instead of being fulfilled directly" (220). Because such channeling activity co-opts the problematic drive instead of amputating it, Ken Gemes (2009, 47–48) argues that for Nietzsche "sublimations involve integration or unification, while pathological symptoms involve splitting off or disintegration."[88]

But if our drives and affects are open to a "reduction [...] to the will to power" (KSA 12:6[26], 244), and, moreover, psychology is understood merely as a "morphology and *doctrine of development of the will to power*" (BGE 23), then surely we can expect Nietzsche's model of self-cultivation to involve an unmeasured struggle to exclude certain drives or impulses. Is

---

[87] See also KSA 13:16[7], 485; GS 47, 139.

[88] Other defenders of the sublimational reading include Jaspers (1981, 134f.); Nehamas (1985, 217f.); Schacht (1983, 323–326); and Richardson (1999, 25).

Nietzsche's view of human psychology simply inconsistent with his vision of the world as will to power? Or do these veins of his philosophy somehow cohere?

4.3.1   *The Self as Wills to Power*

In the first section of this chapter, we established that Nietzsche entreats his ideal readers to organize themselves hierarchically. But what *are* the component parts of the self that require organization? Nietzsche tends to use the terms "drive" (*Trieb*) and "affect" (*Affekt*) when referring to the constituents of the human psyche. But if one scrutinizes texts from 1883 onward, one cannot help but notice the conceptual overlap and woolliness in his use of these terms. Thus, he refrains from neatly analyzing the self into behavioral compulsions and emotions, since he often characterizes our affects as driving us toward particular forms of behavior. Furthermore, he frequently refers to emotions – for example, hatred – as both drives *and* affects.[89] The indeterminacy of the term "drive" is then exacerbated by the fact that he often employs it in close conjunction, or even interchangeably, with terms such as "feeling" (*Gefühl*),[90] "instinct" (*Instinkt*),[91] "desire" (*Begierde*)[92] and "inclination" (*Hang*).[93] Much ink has been spilled trying to ascertain what exactly Nietzsche means by drive. For instance, Peter Poellner (1995, 215) argues that Nietzsche's drives are akin to homunculi, with much the same kind of agency and consciousness as the higher self. Against this, Paul Katsafanas (2013, 745) contends that we can minimally describe a drive as that which generates a particular "evaluative orientation" within our mind, and he therefore concludes that we can account for them "without treating [them] as homunculi." John Richardson (2004, 78–85) then takes an evolutionary-biological tack, reading drives as genetically ingrained behavioral dispositions. He sharply distinguishes these from culturally acquired habits, customs and practices, which he argues Nietzsche treats "as less securely or solidly or deeply settled [...] than our animal inheritance; they can go as quickly as they came." Tom Stern (2015, 121), however, contests Richardson, demonstrating that Nietzsche

---

[89] See Stern (2015, 126). In BGE 23, for example, Nietzsche refers to the "affects of hatred, envy, greed, and power-lust" as drives.

[90] See KSA 11:25[413], 120: "The entire inner antagonism [*Widerstreit*] of the feelings [*Gefühle*], the consciousness of the superior drives [*Triebe*]."

[91] See KSA 13:14[92], 270, where Nietzsche speaks almost synonymously of "the ferocity of the drives" and the "ferocity and anarchy of the instincts." See Assoun (2003, 54–58) on the relation of drive and instinct.

[92] See KSA 10:17[81], 564.   [93] See KSA 11:25[460], 135; GS 294.

does in fact often equate drives with culturally inculcated habits. Stern goes on to reject the very possibility of defining a Nietzschean drive, remonstrating that Nietzsche's usage is simply too inconsistent.

Certainly, Nietzsche's frequent slippage between the term "drive" and related nouns, such as "affect," "inclination" and "instinct," means that this constellation of terms eludes sharp definition. Yet this does not mean that we have to resort to Stern's defeatism. Rather, we should think of a "drive" as a flexible heuristic device (i.e., a *Bilderrede*) that Nietzsche uses to discuss the often-obscure plurality of forces that together compose the self. Accordingly, I will be using the term "drive" to loosely index the power organizations that constitute the self. On my interpretation, drives broadly manifest themselves as ingrained impulses toward particular patterns of thought and behavior. Importantly, it is semantically irrelevant whether these impulses are biologically encoded or culturally inculcated – their being ingrained is sufficient for them to qualify as drives.

The quality that Nietzsche most consistently predicates to the drives is a tendency to promote a particular form of life: "[E]very drive is reared [*angezüchtet*] as a temporary *condition of existence*" (KSA 11:26[72], 167).[94] Crucially, though, the entity whose existence is furthered by a given drive is not necessarily the agent in whom that drive is embedded – it might also be the community or family of that agent that stands to gain (even at the expense of the agent themself).[95]

Nietzsche nonetheless distinguishes ingrained subjective forces from those that are only superficially embedded. And certainly, he tends to use the term "drive" (*Trieb*) when denoting the former. But this is not to say that drives are straightforwardly biological. As we can see from the semantic proximity of "inclination" (*Hang*) and "drive" (*Trieb*), there is not such a clear-cut line between drives and culturally acquired inclinations. In fact, Nietzsche suggests that there exists a relation of *continuity* between the two – culturally acquired habits can *become* drives as they grow increasingly inveterate: "First compulsion, then habituation, then need, then natural inclination (drive)" (KSA 11:25[460], 135).[96] He thus appears to use the term *Trieb* to signify an impulse that has passed a certain threshold of embeddedness. Richardson (2004, 79) presents Nietzsche as defending the Lamarckian thesis that once inclinations pass this threshold they thereby become biologically encoded.

---

[94] See also KSA 11:25[460], 135; KSA 11:27[29], 283.
[95] See KSA 11:26[72], 167: "There is a good whose purpose is the preservation of the individual; a good whose purpose is the preservation of one's family or one's community or one's tribe – a struggle can [thus] emerge within the individual, [that is, between these] two drives [*Triebe*]." See also GS 21, 116.
[96] See also D 248.

Richardson bases this claim on a literal reading of Nietzsche's statement in BGE 208 that we inherit cultural mores in our "blood" (they are "*in's Blut vererbt*"). But it is worth pointing out that in SE, the process of "taking into the blood" (*zu Blut umschaffen*) is very obviously intended to metaphorically signify *cultural* incorporation (SE 1, KSA 1.251). And indeed much the same could arguably be said of his statement in BGE. So, to reiterate my point, Nietzsche merely distinguishes between deeply ingrained behavioral tendencies – that is, *drives*, which may be culturally *or* biologically rooted – and those that are more superficial or malleable.

Since drives are described as will-to-power organizations – or as Nietzsche also puts it, "under-wills" (*Unterwillen*) – we can anticipate that he is going to ascribe some form of independent perceptual and affective awareness to them. In other words, "thinking feeling willing."[97] Every drive is a will-to-power organization that seeks to direct the perception, evaluation and physical activity of the organism – primarily by means of seizing control of its intellect – in such a way as to provide itself with what it needs in order to augment its power.[98] By commandeering the intellect, ascendant drives are able to steer the organism toward forms of behavior that facilitate their expansion – thus the sex drive impels us toward sexual activity, and the drive for truth presses for us to pursue truth, and so on. For Nietzsche, then, we cannot use rationality as an external means of controlling and organizing our impulses, the reason being that our capacity for ratiocination does not stand over and above our drives; indeed, it is more commonly described by Nietzsche as a *tool* of these drives.[99]

But our drives do not merely seek to control our intellect, they also strive to command *one another*. "Every drive is a kind of lust to rule; each has its perspective that it would like to compel all the other drives to accept as a norm" (KSA 12:7[60], 315).[100] According to Nietzsche, this command consists in a superordinate drive compelling a lower drive to act as an "impulse" (*Impuls*) or "stimulus" (*Reiz*) (KSA 11:27[59], 289). For instance, when a scholar takes himself to be exercising his disinterested, objective drive for

---

[97] This supports Poellner (1995, 215ff.). Of course, Nietzsche does not think that drive-awareness should be *identified* with human consciousness; rather, there is simply a degree of symmetry between the two.

[98] See KSA 10:26[72], 274: "The most general image of our essence is *an association of drives*, in perpetual rivalry, and individual alliances, with one another. The intellect [is the] object of the competition."

[99] As noted by Detwiler (1990, 158–159). Kaufmann (1974, 229–230) argues that rationality is the means to sublimation. On reason as a tool of the drives, see BGE 158, 191.

[100] See also BGE 6; KSA 9:11[119], 483.

truth, he might in reality be discharging his drive to hunt, or merely satisfying the interest he has in his "family, or earning money, or politics" (BGE 6).[101] And to be sure, our drives are in perpetual contention with one another in Nietzsche's view.[102] Just like the body's organs, they need to organize themselves into a tense and shifting hierarchy (*Rangordnung*) "expressed through commanding and obeying" (KSA 11:25[411], 119). As in Roux, if this inner struggle of impulses is kept within healthily measured bounds (i.e., *gebändigt*), it serves to strengthen the individual:

> The highest human would have the greatest multiplicity of drives, in the relatively greatest strength that can be endured. Indeed, where the plant "man" shows itself to be strong one finds instincts that drive powerfully *against* one another (e.g., in Shakespeare), but are restrained [*gebändigt*]. (KSA 11:27[59], 289)[103]

Ideally, then, the contention of our drives, and the mutual stimulation arising therefrom, transform us into potently active, creative agents. Such tense dynamism forecloses depression because it keeps our impulses vivacious enough to initiate action; but, at the very same time, the *ordering* of these impulses likewise keeps caprice firmly at bay.

In texts such as the above, Nietzsche tacitly entreats us to undertake a conscious struggle to organize our drives and to incorporate them into a vibrant hierarchy.[104] But *how* does he think that we can accomplish this task in practice? So far, our analysis appears to vindicate the sublimational reading. Properly functioning drives endeavor to *co-opt* their counterparts – that is, instead of seeking their suppression or destruction. It seems to follow that our active approach to self-cultivation ought to align with this dynamic, and therefore be correspondingly sublimational; in other words, that we ought to emulate the Greek genius, who, as we saw in Chapter 2, managed to sublimate his drive for conflict and victory by channeling it away from destructive violence and into culturally productive agon. And yet when we look elsewhere, we find Nietzsche recommending a conspicuously contrary approach to self-cultivation. Already in GS, for example, he overtly endorses the elimination of certain component parts of the self.[105] Thus, the art of self-cultivation

---

[101] Richardson (1996, 33): "Drive A rules B insofar as it has turned B towards A's own end, so that B now participates in A's distinctive activity." See also KSA 13:14[142], 326; GS 348.

[102] See also GS 333 for an account of how Nietzsche thinks conscious knowledge emerges from the unconscious fracas of our drives.

[103] See also KSA 12:1[4], 11; KSA 13:16[7], 485.

[104] Compare, however, EH Clever 9, which discourages conscious self-cultivation.

[105] As Huddleston (2017, 157) remarks.

is practiced by those who survey all the strengths and weaknesses that their nature has to offer and then fit them into an artistic plan [...]. Here a great mass of second nature has been added; *there a piece of first nature removed* [*abgetragen*] [...]. (GS 290; emphasis mine)[106]

Again, in D 202, he proposes that "[o]ne should place before [the criminal] quite clearly the possibility and the means of becoming cured (*the eradication* [*Ausrottung*], transformation, sublimation of [a burdensome tyrannical] drive)."[107] In Nietzsche's view, then, eradication evidently accompanies sublimation as an equally advisable means of controlling problematic drives.

This endorsement of elimination persists throughout Nietzsche's later writings. Thus, in BGE 36 he describes the life of our drives as being characterized by eliminatory processes such as, for example, that of "excretion" (*Ausscheidung*). From our analysis so far, we can identify a number of reasons why Nietzsche would posit elimination as a psychological necessity. First, we may have inherited, or been infected by, drives and instincts that are antagonistic to our flourishing. As was intimated above, we may have had drives foisted upon us that serve (or once served) the interests of a particular social group, but which are injurious to us as individuals. But further, as we also witnessed above, "every drive is reared as a *temporary* [emphasis mine] *condition of existence*," and Nietzsche tellingly adds to this that a drive "is inherited long after it has ceased to be [a condition of existence]" (KSA 11:26[72], 167). Impulses become ingrained because they promote human flourishing; but insofar as we grow, and the conditions of our flourishing change, many impulses end up redundant, vestigial and even counterproductive dross.

Regarding this last problem, in one text Nietzsche indicates that drives are *automatically* streamlined: the useless aspects of inherited drives simply wither away as a result of neglect: "A certain degree of [an inherited] drive is, insofar as it has preservation-potential in relation to other drives, always passed on; an opposed degree disappears [*verschwindet*]" (KSA 11:26[72], 168). At other times, though, Nietzsche contends that we should *consciously* perform this streamlining activity. The first guise in which we encounter such a recommendation is in his valorization of ascetic practices. As he declares in KSA 11:26[409]: "all the virtues and efficiency of body and soul

---

[106] See GS 304, however, where Nietzsche argues we should only deny our drives *unconsciously*.
[107] See also D 109, where Nietzsche states that one can combat "the vehemence of a drive" and thereby attain "[s]elf-mastery and moderation" by avoiding "opportunities for gratification of the drive," and making it thereby "wither away [*abdorren machen*]."

are acquired laboriously and little by little, through much industry, self-constraint, limitation, through much obstinate, faithful repetition of the same labors, *the same renunciations [Entsagungen]*" (KSA 11:26[409], 260; emphasis mine).[108] But while here Nietzsche is arguably only advocating *temporary* abstinence with a view to long-term control, at other times he openly affirms a more radical breed of asceticism. A case in point is TI Skirmishes 41, where having defined the modern individual as a "physiological self-contradiction" of instincts, he goes on to state the following:

> A rational education would have *paralyzed* at least one of these instinct systems with iron pressure so that another could gain force, become strong, take control. Today the individual would first need to be made possible by being *pruned [beschneidet]*: possible here means *complete [Ganz]* [...].

Sculpting the self into a holistic organization is evidently not, in Nietzsche's view, a matter of simply *controlling* the instincts and pressing them into the service of higher goals. Where those instincts are plainly harmful, we should endeavor to *paralyze*, and even *excise* them. And in the *Nachlaß* we encounter a number of further passages in which Nietzsche enthusiastically calls for an "eradication" or "destruction" of certain impulses:

> One day we will barely need *denial* and *slander* in order to deal with certain of our drives [*Triebe*] as *enemies*; [...] to destroy [*vernichten*] undisturbed and with godly eye. (KSA 12:1[81], 31)

> The eradication [*Ausrottung*] of the "drives" ["*Triebe*"]
>   the virtues which are not possible or the virtues which among slaves, dominated by priests, are most highly prized. (KSA 11:25[349], 104)

Though the shudder quotes in the second citation indicate that Nietzsche does not consider the life-denying impulses that he seeks to eradicate to be genuine drives, there are no such shudder quotes in the first of the two excerpts. And in any case, in both fragments, we find him unambiguously inciting us to adopt an eliminative attitude toward certain of our behavioral impulses.

This same destructive impetus is also present in the second essay of GM. In this text he advises that we turn our self-mortifying sense of guilt, or "bad conscience" – which he describes as an inwardly turned "[a]nimosity, cruelty, [...] pleasure of pursuing, raiding, changing *and destroying*

---

[108] This is reminiscent of GM II 3, where Nietzsche implies that the reliability of the sovereign individual (as described in GM II 2) is the fruit of many centuries of brutal punishment (as well as brutal *self*-punishment and asceticism).

[*Zerstörung*]" (GM II 16; emphasis mine) – onto our life-denying, "*perverse inclinations*" (*unnatürliche Hänge*) (GM II 24, KSA 5.335; original emphasis):

> For too long, man has viewed his natural inclinations [*Hänge*] with an "evil eye," so that they finally came to be intertwined with "bad conscience" in him. A reverse experiment should be possible *in principle* [...] – by this, I mean an intertwining of bad conscience with *perverse* inclinations [*Hänge*], all those other-worldly aspirations, alien to the senses, the instincts, to nature, to animals, in short all the ideals which up to now have been hostile to life and have defamed the world. (GM II 24, KSA 5.335)

Perverse inclinations are in Nietzsche's view those that have been imposed on humankind by *herd morality*. In the above passage, then, Nietzsche mobilizes one set of impulses that constitute the ascetic ideal against another set of impulses that belong to that very same ethical framework. He makes this move in the name of his own personal counter-ideal – that is, of "great health." This further illustrates how Nietzsche wishes to marry the process of sublimation to its contrary: the activity of eradication. He thus calls on us to isolate and master the *useful* impulses associated with our "bad conscience," but only in order to purge ourselves of inclinations that are entirely incompatible with his vision of the wholesome self. While he often (though not always) avoids labeling these life-denying dispositions "drives," it is nonetheless incontrovertible that he seeks the complete eradication of certain ingrained behavioral impulses.

Nietzsche's affirmation of eliminatory modes of self-cultivation faces three obstacles. First, as I have already indicated, this endorsement appears to be incompatible with the aphorisms in TI (1–4) in which he disparages the ascetic Christian method of controlling the passions (*Leidenschaften, Passionen*) – that is, "by cutting them off" (*Ausschneidung*), seeking their "eradication" (*Ausrottung*) or, in other more visceral terms, by means of self-castration (*Castratismus*). But if we examine what Nietzsche is *precisely* objecting to in these texts, the apparent inconsistency quickly dissolves. Thus, in TI Morality 1, he complains that the church

> never asks: "how can a desire be spiritualized, beautified, deified?" – it has always laid the weight of its discipline on eradication [*Ausrottung*] (of sensuality, of pride, of greed, of the thirst to dominate and exact revenge). – But attacking the root of the passions means attacking the root of life: the practices of the church are *hostile to life* ...[109]

---

[109] On Nietzsche's criticism of the church's destructive impulse, see also A 58; KSA 11:26[167], 193. On self-castration, see KSA 12:10[157], 545.

And in TI Morality 2, his criticism runs as follows:

> The same methods – castration, eradication – are *instinctively* [emphasis mine] chosen by people whose wills are too weak and degenerate to exercise any restraint in a struggle [*Kampfe*] against a desire: [. . .] they need some sort of definitive declaration of hostilities, they need a *gap* between themselves and the passion. Radical means are only indispensable for degenerates [. . .].

Prima facie, these texts seem to launch an unrestrained assault on unmeasured spiritual exercises. Closer scrutiny, however, reveals that Nietzsche is *specifically* criticizing the following three approaches to self-cultivation:

1. *Unreflectively* resorting to castration – that is, instinctively resorting to this drastic method *without first asking* "how can a desire be spiritualized" (which does not entail that it *can* be spiritualized).
2. *Exclusively* resorting to castration when faced with troublesome passions – that is, using this method in *all* circumstances, and thus treating it as "indispensable."
3. Eradicating impulses that are fundamental to life, such as the acquisitive drives (e.g., "greed"), and the sexual (or "sensual") passions, which are necessary for reproduction.[110]

Contrary to the generalized sublimational reading, the qualified nature of these criticisms strongly implies that there are legitimate conditions under which we might seek the eradication of a given drive – that is, upon arriving at the considered judgment that the drive in question is *not* necessary for life and *cannot* be sublimated into the overall economy of our impulses (though recall that the deliberating "I" making this decision is not an impartial, rational ego distinct from our impulses, but rather a dominant drive, or alliance of drives).[111]

The second issue is that Nietzsche fails to clarify how his particular brand of excision circumvents the risk of what Freud would call a "return of the repressed," a danger that Nietzsche himself flags in other texts. The problem is that entrenched impulses that we deny external release are prone to discharge themselves internally in surreptitious and harmful ways.[112] How can we ever verify whether we have successfully "excised" a drive, instinct system, or inclination (and not just inadvertently forced them to take a less perceptible, but nonetheless malignant guise)? We

---

[110] Compare, however, D 331. For a similar reading of TI Morality 2, see Huddleston (2017, 159).
[111] See BGE 117; D 109.
[112] See WS 83; GS 47; KSA 12:8[4], 334; Caro (2004, 124); Gemes (2009, 46).

might charitably speculate that Nietzsche would think his policy of amputation impervious to this risk due to the fact that it is only impulses that are *indispensable* to life that are forced to return, and these are expressly not his target. On the contrary, in a manner reminiscent of his limited endorsement of eradication in UM, he exclusively sanctions the destruction of life-*denying* impulses.

The final pressing issue with Nietzsche's model of self-cultivation concerns the degree of epistemic access that we have to our drives. As we saw at the end of the previous chapter, Nietzsche (in opposition to Descartes, for example) does not think that individuals enjoy complete self-transparency. Indeed, Nietzsche's drives should not be equated with the behavioral dispositions that we *consciously* feel. This is because the drives are often conceived by Nietzsche as *pre*-conscious. On this conception, drives present our conscious mind with motives much like carrots on the end of a stick (as we just saw, a scholar might *consciously* believe that the desire for truth is fundamentally propelling their behavior, when in reality this motive may just be a façade for the activity of deeper drives hidden from conscious view).[113] Confirming this, Nietzsche unambiguously declares that, "the household of our drives is [...] far beyond our insight" (KSA 10:7[268], 323); and that "self-consciousness is fictive!" (KSA 12:1[58], 25). How, then, can we hope to distinguish, sublimate and excise our impulses when they are so often obfuscated, both in themselves and in their entanglement with our various other drives?

4.3.2 Organization via Revaluation

We should not confuse limited epistemic access for no access whatsoever. Nietzsche often states that our drives *do* frequently manifest themselves to our consciousness. For example, we have found that he sometimes identifies drives with conscious affects.[114] But another important route via which Nietzsche thinks that we can gain a more penetrating view of our self is offered by our *values*. As he says in BGE 268, "[a] person's valuations (*Werthschätzungen*) reveal something about the structure of his soul and what the soul sees as its conditions of life, its genuine needs." Indeed, in line with this claim we are now going to see that for Nietzsche it is chiefly

---

[113] See KSA 12:1[20], 15: "[A]ll our conscious motives are surface-phenomena: behind them stands the struggle [*Kampf*] of our drives"; see also KSA 11:39[6], 621; KSA 11:27[26], 282; KSA 11:39[6], 621; GS 335: "Everyone is farthest from himself."
[114] Nietzsche also states that our conscious feelings and thoughts reflect the "overall condition" (*Gesamtzustand*) of our underlying drives (KSA 12:1[61], 26).

by means of our *values* that we are able to discern and organize the enshrouded household of our drives.

Our "valuations" (*Werthschätzungen*), Nietzsche writes, "correspond [*entsprechen*] to our drives [*Triebe*]" (KSA 11:40[61], 661); they are the "sign-language" of our affects (BGE 187). Drives express themselves at the level of our conscious mind as an evaluative stance toward the world: "[E]very 'drive' is the drive to 'something good' viewed from some standpoint; it is a valuation [*Werthschätzung*] only insofar as it has been incorporated" (KSA 11:26[72], 162).[115] Although they impel us toward "goods," it is only once a drive has been incorporated into the command structure of the self, that its "good" is recognized as an end for the individual and thereby becomes a (positive) "valuation."[116] We can therefore glean at least *some* insight into the underlying economy of our drives by analyzing our conscious values. Perhaps more importantly, though, as Nietzsche had already intimated in 1882, our (moral) values grant us a *practical*, as well as an epistemic, handle on our behavioral impulses: "[O]ur opinions, valuations [*Werthschätzungen*], and tables of what is good are certainly some of the most powerful levers in the machinery of our actions" (GS 335).

Contrary to moral objectivists, and sounding more like an expressivist, Nietzsche maintains that every value is the contingent expression of a particular power organization. Any given value can therefore be traced back to some organization's particular perspective on the world and to the specific conditions under which that organization flourishes. On this view, our values are irreducibly man-made; as he states in Z, "[h]umans first placed values [*Werthe*] into things" (Z I Goals, KSA 4.75), and they created these values to serve the power-augmenting needs of particular human organizations (e.g., individual, family, state, etc.).[117] Through the propagation of

---

[115] KSA 11:27[28], 283: "The varying feeling of value [*das verschiedene Werthgefühle*] with which we distinguish these drives is the consequence of their greater or lesser importance, [that is,] their actual ranking, with respect to our preservation [*Erhaltung*]."

[116] See D 38; and KSA 13:14[104], 282, where Nietzsche once again draws a similar distinction (i.e., between unincorporated and incorporated values): "Moral values as *pseudo-values*, compared with *physiological* values." See Schacht (1983, 403), who accordingly distinguishes between two orders of Nietzschean value.

[117] See KSA 11:26[119], 181: "all evaluation [*Werthschätzung*] is made from a definite perspective: that of the preservation of the individual, a community, a race, a state, a church, a faith, a culture." KSA 12:10[10], 459: "The *economical* denigration of former ideals. The law-givers (or the instinct of society) select a number of states [*Zustände*] and affects, whose activity guarantees regular achievement [...][.] Supposing that these states and affects strike [people] as ingredients of that which is painful, then a means must be found to overcome this pain through a value judgment [*Werthvorstellung*]: the pain must be made *valuable* [*werthvoll*], it must be felt as honorable, that is, pleasurable." See also BGE 224.

moral values, the dominant members of these organizations augment their power by regulating the drives out of which these federations are composed:

> Moralities are the expression of locally limited orders of rank in this multifarious world of drives, so man should not perish through their contradictions. Thus a drive as master, its opposite weakened, refined, as the impulse that provides the stimulus for the activity of the chief drive. (KSA 11:27[59], 289)

A given organization promotes a system of moral values that disparages, and thereby discourages, any drives that run counter to its power-augmenting needs. Contrariwise, this same system then esteems, and therefore encourages, any drives that facilitate the organization's pursuit of power. As such, moral values are akin to Roux's functional stimuli, ensuring that the various parts of the whole are kept in a healthy, balanced hierarchy – one that serves the organization's higher ends. The chief polemical target of this naturalization of values is herd morality, particularly what Nietzsche considers to be its sham altruism and its oppressive claims to universality. He argues that "altruistic" moral values are hypocritically grounded in selfish motives; and he casts doubt on the idea of a comprehensive, universal morality: if each individual and organization has their distinct and evolving needs, they therefore require, and tend to generate, their own distinct, self-serving morality (though this morality may happen to overlap with other moral orders).[118]

On Nietzsche's account, far from contradicting the logic of the will to power, the ostensibly altruistic and universalizing values that characterize herd morality are in fact posited by weaker individuals as part of a rearguard power-winning strategy. In this way, "the ascetic ideal springs from the protective and healing instincts of a degenerating life, which uses every means to maintain itself and struggles for its existence" (GM III 13, KSA 5.366).[119] As we saw in our analysis of the crisis of disintegration, it is by means of herd values that the weak (i.e., the slavish, oppressed masses) suppress both the dangerous social conflict associated with excessive individualism, and the painful inner havoc of their disordered drives. Universal moral values mitigate the pluralism that generates social struggle, and altruistic values encourage individuals to focus on others in a way that enables them to evade their own state of inner disgregation. Nietzsche thinks that slave morality therefore presents itself to the weak in times of

---

[118] See also KSA 12:10[154], 542 (which is *contra* hypocrisy) or BGE 43 (which is *contra* universality).
[119] See also A 10.

crisis as a prudent last resort, one that he sometimes compares to "hibernation" (*Winterschlaf*) (GM III 17, KSA 5.379).

In a similar vein, he describes the slavish desire to form a herd in terms reminiscent of Rolph's account of isophagy and conjugation. Within a herd, individuals are able to exercise their will to power and incorporation in a manner *internal* to the social whole – namely, by means of performing small acts of pity toward one another. This enables them to experience a feeling of power over others, in spite of their impotence ("[t]he happiness of the 'smallest superiority'") (GM III 18, KSA 5.383). With this purpose in mind, "[a]ll the sick and sickly strive instinctively for a herd-organization" (GM III 18, KSA 5.384). Just like Rolph's starving bacteria, humans therefore pursue power expansion in an abnormal fashion under conditions of weakness.[120]

Yet Nietzsche warns that such values are profoundly harmful when adopted indefinitely or imposed upon those who are not already sick (as he believes has happened on a grand scale in modernity). The problem, however, is not just that we have inherited and been infected by values that preserve the interests of the weak at the expense of the healthy, but that these values have become *ossified* and placed beyond question. This is why

> we need a *critique* of moral values, *the value of these values should itself, for once, be examined* – and so we need to know about the conditions and circumstances under which these values grew up, developed and changed [...]. (GM Preface 6, KSA 5.253)[121]

One of the first steps toward developing a general remedy to disintegration is to distinguish those values that *preserve pathological* organizations from those that promote the *flourishing* of *healthy* organizations. This, he conjectures, can be at least partially achieved by formulating a genealogy of the multitude of different moral orders of which we have knowledge. Such a genealogy is, importantly, not to be confused with a mere catalogue. Rather, it is a "rank order of 'higher' and 'lower' moralities ('more important, more essential, more indispensable, more irreplaceable')" (KSA 11:25 [411], 119).[122]

But against what criterion can Nietzsche establish such a rank order? In his own laconic words: "What is the objective measure of value [*Werth*]? Solely the quantum of *enhanced* and *organized power* ... "

---

[120] See also GS 119.   [121] See also BGE 186.
[122] See also GM Preface 3, KSA 5.249; KSA 12:7[42], 308; BGE 260.

(KSA 13:11[83], 40).[123] Nietzsche's conception of (thriving) life and the world as will to power acts as the new fulcrum around which the task of self-organization can proceed. But in contrast to the dogmatic metaphysical presuppositions of UM, the idea of the will to power represents a purely *immanent* keystone. Nietzsche is no longer appealing to fixed essences or natural ends built on a priori foundations and somehow transcending the lived world of flux and becoming. The will to power is a defeasible, pragmatic *hypothesis* – one established by means of a posteriori knowledge, and which expressly denies dogmatic notions such as fixed essences and natural purposes. It is in this sense that the will to power constitutes a non-metaphysical theory.[124] With this in mind, let us now inquire further into how Nietzsche's theoretical view translates into a practicable ethic of self-cultivation.

Since it is the human richest in (controlled) opposition who flourishes most vibrantly according to Nietzsche, he sets this individual as his benchmark: "[T]he greatest force, as command over opposites, sets the standard" (KSA 11:25[408], 119). But we should note that achieving this is not a question of simply identifying and eradicating those values that conflict with the principle of the will to power. *All* values are formulated as power-augmenting strategies, they are *all* expressions of the will to power, without exception – as we just saw, even slave morality represents a last-ditch stratagem employed by the weak in their desperate lust for power.[125] The task of the genealogist is therefore one of distinguishing between the values that respectively support weaker and stronger power organizations.

We have already explored in detail why Nietzsche deems universalizing, egalitarian and altruistic moral values to be degenerate, but it would be a mistake to interpret this as an all-out rejection of the concept of morality or moral values. For example, Nietzsche himself consistently valorizes (among other things) social exploitation (BGE 259); hierarchy, and the feeling of distance between the different strata of society and the self ("between human and human" [BGE 62] and "within the soul itself" [BGE 257]); the need for a plurality of moral orders suited to the different types of

---

[123] See KSA 12:5[71], 215: "There is nothing in life that has value (*Werth*) except the degree of power." KSA 13:11[414], 192: "What is good? – Everything that increases the feeling of power, the will to power, the power itself in humans." See also KSA 12:2[131], 132; KSA 9:4[104], 126.

[124] Though we may call it "metaphysical" in the very general sense of belonging to the "branch of philosophy that deals with the first principles of things" (OED, entry for "metaphysics, n.").

[125] The fact that *all* our values are expressions of the will to power contradicts Katsafanas's claim (2015, 189) that "the Nietzschean theory holds that values are legitimate insofar as they do not generate conflicts with will to power."

individual that coexist within society (thus, "never thinking about debasing our duties into duties for everyone" [BGE 272]); and finally, externally directed expressions of the struggle for power ("war, adventure, hunting, dancing, martial games [*Kampfspiele*]" [GM I 7, KSA 5.266]).[126] These values – which favor the pursuit of hierarchy and power augmentation by means of external discharge and organizational struggle – are the values associated with what Nietzsche sees as the vital (and often observable) properties of any healthy organization.[127]

But the values that Nietzsche advocates certainly cannot be said to amount to a complete morality. They represent an intentionally thin moral framework, meant to spur us to develop our *own* unique thick morality, which is to say a hierarchy of values that promotes the most empowering economy of impulses given our idiosyncratic set of drives and environmental context. But this raises yet another problem: In fashioning a new order of values and drives, are we not prohibited from invoking our rationality, since, as we saw above, our intellect is in Nietzsche's view simply the handmaid of our dominant drives?[128]

There is a case to be made that, in contrast to his conception of self-cultivation in UM, the later Nietzsche wants us to do very little conscious work beyond that of combatting degenerate herd values. In UM he charges Goethe with having failed to identify his guiding idea and consequently of suffering a dissipation of his forces (WB 3, KSA 1.442); this is in contrast to Wagner, who Nietzsche thinks managed to consciously channel his powers in accordance with his "inner lawfulness" or "will" (WB 2, KSA 1.435). EH Clever 9, however, shows how the later Nietzsche ends up defecting to a more Goethean model of self-cultivation:

> The whole surface of consciousness – consciousness *is* a surface – has to be kept free from all of the great imperatives. Be careful even of all great words, of all great attitudes. They pose the threat that instinct will "understand itself" too early. – – In the meantime, the organizing, governing "Idea" grows and grows deep inside, – it starts commanding, it slowly leads back from out of the side roads and wrong turns, it gets the individual qualities and virtues ready, which will at some point prove themselves indispensable as means to the whole, – one by one, it develops all the *servile* faculties before giving any clue as to the domineering task, the "goal" [*Ziel*], the "purpose" [*Zweck*], the "meaning" [*Sinn*].

---

[126] See also BGE 270.

[127] For a more comprehensive overview of Nietzsche's account of noble values, see Tongeren (1989, 151–172).

[128] See fn.99.

Whereas in UM, Nietzsche affirmed the Schopenhauerian conception of a worthy life as one that traces a straight line, he now makes a rather fitting U-turn. Life, he now claims, should trace what Schopenhauer pejoratively calls a *"zigzag"* (*Zickzack*) or *"surface"* (*Fläche*) (WWR 1, 2.358). To be sure, the coordination of one's impulses into a vigorous functional unity still represents the underlying goal. But this is no longer a question of discerning an essential aspect of oneself around which one then organizes one's impulses, thereby bringing an end "to fumbling, straying, to the proliferation of secondary shoots" (WB 2; KSA 1.435). It is vital that we remain open to what may strike us as digressions, diversions and distractions. This ethic of receptivity allows a guiding "instinct," "purpose" (i.e., a superordinate value) or ruling "Idea" to genuinely crystallize (though Nietzsche significantly places "Idea" in scare quotes in the above citation, thereby distancing himself from the Platonic elements of his earlier synthetic model). In BGE, this ethic of receptivity takes the form of a yen for experimentation, which is to say *a drive to explore the value of new values*. His ideal experimenters (*Versucher*, which can also be translated as *tempters*) (BGE 42) are philosophers "who possess a taste and inclination [*Hang*] that are somehow the reverse of those we have hitherto seen" (BGE 2); these exemplars work without "the certainty of value standards, the conscious implementation of a unity of method" (BGE 210).[129] Crucially, one's ruling "Idea" promotes an ideal order within oneself *without* the interference of the conscious, rational part of one's mind. All we need consciously do, according to Nietzsche, is *inhibit* our clumsy tendency to overmanage and prematurely determine our character.[130] Actively inhibiting the drive for self-knowledge is therefore a necessary condition of becoming who one is, which explains why Nietzsche approvingly quotes Goethe's maxim that "[o]ne can only truly admire those who do not *seek* themselves" (BGE 266).

This attitude, however, is not to be confused with an amoral policy of *laisser-aller*. In the first place, Nietzsche wants to generate new, relatively fixed standards of judgment – standards tailored to the complex variety of drives and environmental needs that characterize modern individuals; he wants to forge new values, future ideals and above all, a new *wozu*

---

[129] See KSA 12:9[93], 388, where Nietzsche calls for "an experiment [*Versuch*] in adventures and haphazard [*willkürlich*] dangers." BGE 256 commends those "with uncanny access to everything tempting, seductive, compelling, and subversive, born enemies of logic and straight lines, longing for the foreign, the exotic, the monstrous, the crooked, the self-contradictory."

[130] See GS 382; compare D 301.

("whither") for humanity (BGE 211).[131] Second, his ideal of experimentation is enabled by a set of core virtues – for example, *courage*.[132] And third, he maintains that his ideal experimenting philosophers are inextricably "woven into a strong net and shirt of duties"; moreover, he exhorts these philosophers to affirm this fact, and learn to "dance quite well in [their] 'chains'" (BGE 226).[133] As such, he in no way rejects moral order *tout court*.

Setting Nietzsche's ideal ethic of experimentation into motion clearly requires a conscious revaluation (*Umwerthung*) of the herd values that proscribe such deviance. But to what extent does this demand the *negation* of herd morality, and, with this, the impulse to behave as an ideal herd animal (i.e., Christian, utilitarian or Kantian, etc.)? KSA 12:10[117] shows that Nietzsche's declaration of war against Christian values is in a certain sense limited:

> I have declared war on the anemic "Christian ideal" (together with what is closely related to it), not with the aim of destroying [*vernichten*] it but only of putting an end to its *tyranny* and clearing the way for new ideals, for *more robust* ideals [. . .]: our drive for self-preservation wants our *opponents* to retain their strength – it only wants to become *master over them*. (KSA 12:10 [117], 523)

Nietzsche assures us that he only seeks to *dominate* Christian ideals (i.e., values). Since he envisions a society in which the slavish mass is preserved and exploited, and since herd morality is a condition of existence for this herd, he concludes that "[t]he ideas of the herd should rule in the herd – but not reach out beyond it" (KSA 12:7[6], 280).[134] What is more, he submits that higher individuals would do well to remain in conflict with slave morality as it subsists *within themselves*. The reason for this, as we have repeatedly seen, is that Nietzsche takes such inner struggle to be a necessary condition of health: "The price of fertility is to be rich in contradictions; people stay young only if their souls do not stretch out languidly and long for peace" (TI Morality 3). This explains why he holds higher culture to be defined by the struggle of slave and master morality, "inside the same person even, within a single soul" (BGE 260).

If we turn back to EH Clever 9, we get a clearer picture of the kind of psychological struggle that Nietzsche has in mind here. In this aphorism he

---

[131] Indeed, in A 57 and 58 he explicitly rebukes anarchism, and hopes that experimentation will lead to a stable set of laws able to sustain an enduring social order akin to the *Imperium Romanum*.

[132] See e.g., EH Books 3, where Nietzsche calls his perfect reader "a beast of courage."

[133] See also WS 140.

[134] See also KSA 11:35[9], 511–512; and KSA 12:10[2], 454, where Nietzsche describes himself as only struggling "against *the predominance of the herd instincts*."

vies to appropriate the Christian value of neighborly love (*Nächstenliebe*). By encouraging "forgetting yourself, misunderstanding yourself, belittling, narrowing yourself, making yourself mediocre," altruistic practices can distract us from ourselves, and in this way enable our drives to organize themselves organically without our counterproductive conscious interference. As such,

> neighborly love, living for other people and other things, can be a form of precautionary discipline for maintaining the toughest selfishness. Here I make an exception to my rule and conviction, and side with "selfless drives": in this case, they are working in the service of selfishness [*Selbstsucht*] and self-discipline [*Selbstzucht*].

So he condones the drive to care for others, even at the temporary expense of one's own well-being, as a long-term strategy for achieving the egoistic goal of self-cultivation. He thereby places an interpretation on the drive for, and valuation of, altruistic behavior that rids it of its unconditional status and subordinates it to the higher value of individual health. Some Christian values, and their corresponding impulses, *can* therefore be repurposed and retained within the healthy subjective economy provided we abolish their dominion over the value of health. By this act of revaluation, altruism is reconceived as instrumentally valuable – that is, it is valued *as a means to* health, which now represents the intrinsically valuable *summum bonum*.

This clarifies how we might approach the task of sublimating our herd impulses by means of revaluation. And yet there remain copious texts in which Nietzsche's conception of value critique appears to be far more destructive in kind. In A, for instance, he declares a "[w]ar to the death [*Todkrieg*] against vice," where "the vice is Christianity" ("A Law Against Christianity"). This is prefigured in Z, where he repeatedly goads his readers to demolish (what he considers to be) the ruinous Christian moral order: "Break [*zerbrecht*], break me these old tablets of the pious, my brothers! Gainsay me the sayings of the world slanderers!" (Z III Tablets). But even here Nietzsche is still not advocating the wanton nullification of degenerate values. What he is rather endorsing is *creative destruction*: that is, the unmeasured critique of life-denying values *only* insofar as this enables the construction of vibrant, life-enhancing moral orders:

> [W]hoever must be a creator in good and evil – truly, he must first be an annihilator [*Vernichter*] and break [*zerbrechen*] values. (Z II Self-Overcoming, KSA 4.149)

> [*I*]*n order for a shrine to be set up*, a shrine has to be destroyed [*zerbrochen*]: that is the law – show me an example where this does not apply! (GM II 24, KSA 5.335; emphasis mine)

> [N]egation [*Verneinen*] and destruction [*Vernichten*] *are conditions of affirmation*. (EH Destiny 4; emphasis mine)[135]

This prompts a number of questions – for instance: What could it possibly mean to "destroy" a value? And how might this be a prerequisite of creativity? And doesn't destroying moral values entail the suppression of the behavioral impulses associated therewith?

With respect to the first of these queries, the destruction that Nietzsche demands could be said to consist in merely negating the *unconditionality* of moral values. On this reading, it is only their tyrannous claim to transcendence and universality that ought to be nullified. If we are to imagine and form new normative hierarchies, then we need to reconceive our values as contingent and malleable. This is why Nietzsche asserts that "the unconditioned [*das Unbedingte*] cannot be the creative [*das Schaffende*]" (KSA 11:26[203], 203). His naturalization of values eradicates this veneer of unconditionality by denuding the *falsity* and even conceptual incoherence of the notion of absolute values.[136] And he further undermines such universality by highlighting its harmful practical consequences. The supposition of universality prevents us from adapting our values (and therewith our behavior) in order to meet our ever-changing, power-augmenting needs. In blocking adaptation, universal values therefore serve to hasten our demise:

> Were there an absolute morality, it would demand that the truth was followed unconditionally: thus, I and humankind [would] perish due to morality. – This is my interest in the destruction [*Vernichtung*] of morality. In order to be able to live and advance – in order to satisfy the will to power, every absolute command must be eradicated [*beseitigt*]. (KSA 10:7[37], 252)

Little wonder, then, that Nietzsche gives those who neglect the task of destructive struggle a rather blunt ultimatum: "Either abolish [*abschaffen*] your venerations or – yourselves!" (GS 346). On the logic of these texts, however, moral values, and the underlying drives sanctioned by those values, are not themselves entirely abolished; they are merely *qualified*;

---

[135] See also KSA 10:13[13], 462: "The truth should shatter [*zerbrechen*] the world in order for the world to be constructed!" GS 58: "Only as creators can we destroy."
[136] E.g., KSA 11:34[28], 429: "[S]uperstition: to believe in being [*das Seiende*], in the unconditioned, [...] *in absolute value*, in the thing in itself! Everywhere, these formulations conceal a *contradiction*" (emphasis mine).

thus, the creativity affirmed by Nietzsche would appear to be enabled by minimally negating a certain formal quality or modality predicated to those values.

This interpretation of the destructive aspect of Nietzsche's program of revaluation may on the face of things seem perfectly compatible with the sublimational reading. Yet it is difficult to read his remarks as anything but a *total* rejection of the value of universality and the impulse we have to make unconditional axiological claims. Moreover, other texts suggest that he seeks a far more substantive denial of herd morality (and the set of behavioral impulses fostered by such morality). In texts such as KSA 12:7[6], for example, he suggests that *no* part of slave morality can be rendered compatible with his model of thriving life:

> My insight: all the forces and drives [*Triebe*] by virtue of which life and growth exist lie under the ban of morality: morality as the instinct [*Instinkt*] to deny life. One must destroy [*vernichten*] morality if one is to liberate life. (KSA 12:7[6], 274)

Both morality (by which he means *herd* morality) and the underlying instinct to deny life must therefore be *wholly* negated if life is to be given any chance of flourishing. We can soundly assume that by this he means that the values that characterize herd morality must be subjected to *unrestrained* critique – that is, to the point of being entirely emptied of value – and that the behavioral impulses encouraged by these values should be indefinitely suppressed.[137]

Another way in which Nietzsche can be said to endorse elimination is insofar as he encourages his readers to quarantine themselves from the contagion of herd values. We discover this in BGE 230, for instance, where he describes the two fundamental drives that sustain the healthy human will. The first is marked by measured, exploitative struggle, "it wills simplicity out of multiplicity, it is a binding, subduing, domineering, and truly masterful will." The "opposite drive of spirit," however, presses for "a closing of [the will's] windows, an inner nay-saying to something or other, a come-no-closer, a type of defensive state against many knowable things." One must therefore stop one's ears to the siren song of herd morality, to its seductive, distracting and ultimately debilitating account of ideal human life; only then does Nietzsche think that one can gain an

---

[137] After calling for the destruction of morality in KSA 12:7[6], 273–283, Nietzsche then enumerates a variety of different ways in which he envisions this mode of radical critique proceeding; for example, by showing how such morality is a "work of error," "harmful to life" and a "work of immorality" (insofar as it relies on the very egoistic drives that it condemns).

empowering insight into the reality of the human qua will to power. On a similar note, in GM he emphasizes the need to *insulate* oneself from the contagious spread of altruistic values, which he likens to a plague: "And so we need good air! Good air! At all events, well away from all madhouses and hospitals of culture!" (GM III 14, KSA 5.371).[138] Again then, within Nietzsche's later writings, the outright exclusion of harmful values, along with the impulses sustained by those values, is clearly prescribed as a requirement of self-cultivation.

So although Nietzsche *does* promote measured conflict – namely, with those drives and values that can be incorporated into a renewed, healthy subjective organization – this should not be classified as agonistic in kind. First, the measured subjective struggle that he prescribes involves an entirely unagonistic struggle to *instrumentalize* that which has been overcome. But second, his affirmation of measured incorporation is married to a strident call for the full negation of certain embedded impulses.[139] Intriguingly, proponents of the sublimational reading have hitherto entirely suppressed this significant aspect of Nietzsche's ethics.

We have also seen how this affirmation of elimination neatly harmonizes with his vision of the will to power as organizational struggle – that is, as a combined struggle for the measured integration of that which is deemed serviceable *and* the unmeasured exclusion of that which is deemed obsolete or injurious. Indeed, this vision of organization represents the foundation stone of his later ethics of self-cultivation. In contrast to his earlier Schopenhauerian model of organizational struggle, he no longer postulates knowledge of our particular metaphysical essence as the lynchpin of individual synthesis; instead, it is now an entirely immanent appreciation of the world (and particularly the *self*) qua will to power, qua active organizational struggle, that serves this function. Acquiescing to this worldview should, Nietzsche thinks, encourage us to embrace and even stimulate (rather than spurn or suppress) psychological conflict as a condition of life, which should in turn enable us to avert both the risk of *aboulia* and the corollary danger of succumbing to the pseudo-therapy of herd morality. As opposed to his earlier, essentialist appeal to the notion of authenticity, in his later writings Nietzsche offers health and power augmentation as the guiding values of self-organization. By empowering these

---

[138] On Nietzsche's support of such prophylactic measures, see Appel (1999, 66).
[139] Note, however, that Nietzsche himself suggests that such ideological destruction is impossible. Thus "Ideas" (*Vorstellungen*) that are "overcome are not *annihilated* [*vernichtet*], only driven back [*zurückgedrängt*] or subordinated. There is no destruction [*Vernichtung*] in the sphere of spirit [*im Geistigen*]" (KSA 12:7[53], 312).

as intrinsic values we can assess the extent to which our various drives and valuations serve or obstruct these ends. And we can then, both consciously and unconsciously, organize our drives into a relatively stable functional hierarchy, which forecloses the pathology of anarchic caprice.

But Nietzsche's model of self-cultivation faces yet another obstacle. This stems from the fact that he reframes the crisis of disintegration as an issue of *race*, which implies that the problematically conflicting parts of the self are so deeply embedded as to be impervious to our best efforts at self-cultivation:

> What a man's forefathers liked doing the most, and the most often, cannot be wiped from his soul [. . .]. It is utterly impossible for a person *not* to have the qualities and propensities of his elders and ancestors in his body: however much appearances might speak against it. This is the problem of race. [. . .] With the help of the best education and culture, people will only just reach the point of being able to *lie* about a bequest such as this. (BGE 264)

He thus claims that there are parts of the self that we are entirely unable to cultivate: "at our foundation 'at the very bottom,' there is clearly something that will not learn, a granite of spiritual *fatum*, of predetermined decisions and answers to selected, predetermined questions" (BGE 231). Yet it would be incorrect to interpret this granite as evidence that Nietzsche has returned to his earlier essentialist conception of the self ("something completely incapable of being educated or formed [. . .]" [SE 1, KSA 1.341]); rather, he is merely referring to those parts of the self that are too inveterate to undergo transformation or elimination, those which exist beyond the reach of our best self-creative efforts.[140] This does not mean, however, that we ought to abandon the struggle to manage ingrained drives that we identify as harmful. As we will discover in the following section, even if we are unable to effectively manage these drives within *ourselves*, within our own individual lifetime, we can nonetheless endeavor to eradicate or sublimate such drives in *other*, future individuals.

4.4 Collective Organization

Given that Nietzsche reconceives the crisis of disintegration in terms of *race* – which is to say, as a pathology stemming from deeply rooted impulses – he needs to formulate a far longer-term program of treatment than that which

---

[140] Note that neither Nehamas (1985, chap. 7) nor Kaufmann (1974) adequately acknowledge this obstacle in their optimistic depictions of Nietzschean self-creation.

he prescribes in UM. An ethic of *self*-cultivation will simply not suffice. Cultivating the ideal human accordingly becomes a transgenerational project for Nietzsche, one that can only be pursued by means of a *collective* struggle to breed or cultivate this archetype; indeed, "the lifetime of a single man signifies virtually nothing in relation to the accomplishment of such protracted tasks and aims" (KSA 11:37[8], 581–582). But what mode of sociopolitical organization does Nietzsche think can most effectively enable this monumental project?

My contention is that his ideal commonwealth is one that politically embodies his abstract conception of healthy will-to-power organization. This said, it is far from clear how Nietzsche's general theory of organization translates into a concrete political regime. The critical literature presents us with two starkly contradictory accounts. On the one side, we have the agonistic democrats. As we saw in Chapter 2, these readers (mis)construe Nietzsche's theory of the will to power as an essentially agonistic vision of reality. We also saw how this group of readers takes the affirmation of the world as will to power to flow into a corollary affirmation of agonistic-democratic politics. To buttress their agonistic vision of the healthy social expression of the will to power, they often invoke TI Morality 3, in which Nietzsche explains how the "spiritualization of *enmity*"

> involves a deep appreciation of the value of having enemies [...]. The church has always wanted to destroy its enemies: but we, we immoralists and anti-Christians, think that we benefit from the existence of the church. Even in politics, hostility is becoming more spiritual, – much cleverer, much more thoughtful, much more *careful*. Almost every party knows that its self-preservation depends on its opposition not losing too much strength: and the same is true in power politics.

On the basis of this text, Hatab argues that Nietzsche's ontology of difference translates into a political ethos of democratic respect, which "forbids exclusion, [and] demands inclusion" (Hatab 1995, 69).[141] On this reading, traditional aristocratic regimes, in seeking to establish a monopoly of political power that excludes members of other social classes, exhibit "weakness in a Nietzschean sense" (122). Moreover, for Hatab, TI Morality 3 demonstrates that equality of opportunity is integral to perfectionist politics, and such opportunity is, Hatab submits, best enacted by representative democracy – an open "contest of speeches" (63), which generates a "temporary aristocracy" by meritocratically granting power to the

---

[141] See also Hatab (1995, 122). For Connolly's use of TI Morality 3, see Connolly (1993, 156–157).

victorious contestants (123). And yet Hatab recognizes that this is "not in keeping with Nietzsche's version of aristocratism," which Hatab rightly construes as being of a more traditional mold (125).[142]

Connolly attacks Nietzsche's "aristocratic solution" on the grounds that in condoning oppression, it "recreates the very resentment it seeks to redress" (1988, 160). He contends that the ethic of "letting be" – which by his lights follows quite obviously from the logic of the will to power – is more straightforwardly congruent with Nietzsche's denigration of *ressentiment*. It is agonistic-democratic politics that Connolly thinks are most consistent with Nietzsche's ethical (and ontological) outlook since it "provides the best way to incorporate the experience of contingency into public life," and furthermore, he maintains that rough equality of income would "relieve social causes of resentment" (171).[143]

Mark Warren follows a similar, and equally inventive, line of interpretation. He openly concedes that for Nietzsche the will to power translates into "neoaristocratic conservativism" (Warren 1991, 211). However, Warren rejects Nietzsche's claim that affirming the will to power necessarily commits us to aristocratic politics. He controversially reads the will to power as, above all, a human drive for "autonomy of the self" (141). At the level of the collective, he insists that the "will to power as an organized capacity for action is not inconsistent with social and political equality, simply because the universal motive identified by the concept of will to power is not domination but self-constitution" (232). On Warren's reading, such self-constitution is most effectively served by equitable political relations – more specifically, an agonistic society founded upon the principle of equal opportunity (72).

Nietzsche's radical aristocratic readers, however, ardently reject this agonistic interpretation of the will to power. For example, Bruce Detwiler and Fredrick Appel both invoke BGE 259 in order to defend the claim that Nietzsche's aristocratism gels perfectly well with his notion of the will to power. In this aphorism, Nietzsche theorizes that

> Even a body within which [. . .] particular individuals treat each other as equal (which happens in every healthy aristocracy): if this body is living and not dying, it [. . .] will have to be the embodiment of will to power, it will want to grow, spread, grab, win dominance, – *not out of any morality or immorality* [emphasis mine], but because it is *alive*, and because life is precisely will to power. [. . .] "Exploitation" does not belong to a corrupted

---

[142] For Hatab's exegesis of Nietzsche's aristocratism, see (1995, 39ff.).
[143] For Connolly's reasons as to why we need to embrace contingency, see Chapter 2.

or imperfect, primitive society: it belongs to the *essence* of being alive as a fundamental organic function; it is a result of genuine will to power, which is just the will of life.

Detwiler cites this text (among others) to argue that, *pace* Warren, the will to power is *not* purely oriented toward *self*-overcoming; it is rather, he continues, irreducibly geared toward the amoral domination *of others*; thus, the will to power "finds its highest expression in the artistic will to give form, whether to the self or the state" (60). Detwiler further contends that Nietzsche's "discussion of the political ramifications of life as will to power do indeed flow from the same ontology as his thoughts on self-constitution" (161). In line with Detwiler, Appel (1999, 31) then draws attention to the way in which BGE 259 approvingly paints the pursuit of political power as an *amoral* activity. Quoting BGE 44, he also claims that Nietzsche exalts individuals who exercise an "unconditional will to power," who revel in the "art of experiment and devilry of every kind."

Radical aristocratic readings portray Nietzsche as unequivocally favoring the idea that humans should, under ideal conditions, pursue power in a manner entirely free of moral constraints. Commanding individuals and social groups ought to govern with ruthless *sangfroid*, exploiting the masses without any consideration for their well-being. On this interpretation, it is only through such instrumentalization that the state is able to generate higher men, who stand as the ultimate goal of humanity.[144] To reinforce their account of ideal Nietzschean command, both Detwiler and Appel quote KSA 11:26[409], where Nietzsche champions military figures such as Napoleon and Cesare Borgia. From men such as these, Nietzsche tells us, "one gets some notion of a 'disinterested' work on one's marble, whatever the cost in men" (KSA 12:1[56], 24). Such comments certainly imply that Nietzsche envisaged ideal statecraft as an amoral aesthetic activity, according to which the masses ought to be treated as little more than disposable shards of marble.[145] Appel and Detwiler insist that for Nietzsche, this is the only way that one can sculpt a society capable of generating higher individuals.[146] In a similar vein, other interpreters read Nietzsche's apologies for slavery and exploitation as incontrovertible proof that he sanctions an undiluted strain of amoralism, if not outright *im*moralism.[147]

---

[144] See Detwiler 1990, 53f.; Appel 1999, 132, 147f.

[145] Nietzsche also employs the amoral marble metaphor in KSA 11:35[75], 542, where he condones "unconditional force" on the part of his political sculptors.

[146] Detwiler (1990, 53); Appel (1999, 120–126).

[147] Conway (1997a, 4); Dombowsky (2004, 140ff.).

So agonistic democrats read Nietzsche's ontology of will to power as inherently measured and therefore inconsistent with his brutally exploitative aristocratic politics. Likewise, they see his ethic of self-cultivation as being sharply at odds with his radical aristocratism. They claim that his ontological commitments and perfectionist aspirations are, *malgré lui*, far more consistent with an agonistic-democratic normative outlook. Nietzsche's radical aristocratic interpreters, however, counter that the world as will to power is marked by a callous lack of measure and therefore dovetails perfectly well with his aristocratic persuasions.

One possible response to this aporia has been ventured by Herman Siemens (2008). Siemens reads the will to power as a dynamic structured by the goal of "power augmentation" (*Machtsteigerung*), which Nietzsche takes to be fundamental to all life (267). The greatest threat to this goal is that of "equalization" (*Gleichmachung*), since this favors homogenous stasis at the expense of wholesome plurality and dynamism (235). Nietzsche then indicts certain forms of democracy for promoting just such homogeneity. According to Siemens, though, Nietzsche ultimately equivocates regarding the political conditions that best promote plurality and perfectionism. For example, in some texts Nietzsche prescribes that we should altogether refrain from consciously attempting to establish the social conditions that generate higher individuals (because, recalling his criticism of conscious self-cultivation, we are bound to botch the job).[148] Likewise, he sometimes avers that higher individuals should in no way sully themselves with the dirty business of ruling (KSA 10:7[21], 244). But elsewhere he actively encourages higher individuals to institute a pyramidic Platonic society within which they are able to mercilessly instrumentalize the masses (KSA 11:35[47], 533). Siemens (2008, 242) concludes that the plurivocality of these proposals "falsifies any attempt to ascribe a coherent, settled political vision to Nietzsche".

It is vital that we acknowledge the lack of univocity in Nietzsche's political writings, and that we duly refrain from ascribing an overly thick or concrete political ideal to his later thought. This said, we are nonetheless going to see that Nietzsche advocates a relatively consistent political ideal, albeit one of a remarkably thin sort. What is more, this thin political ideal harmonizes with his conception of the will to power qua organizational struggle (i.e., a balance of measured and unmeasured struggle). Against agonistic readings, his ideal commonwealth is therefore going to involve exploitation and exclusion. But against the radical aristocratic

---

[148] See e.g., KSA 11:26[117], 181.

interpretation, ideal Nietzschean rule will prove to be neither unconditional nor unidirectional, namely, because it should ideally *preserve* that which it commands; otherwise put, it should be *measured* in kind.

4.4.1   Aristocracy and Exploitation

We can obtain a preliminary impression of how Nietzsche conceives healthy collective organization by examining his idealized portrayal of real historical aristocracies, such as those of ancient Greece, the Roman imperium and the Italian Renaissance. In doing so, however, we must bear in mind that Nietzsche is no atavist; indeed, he openly scorns the idea of nostalgically returning to any past mode of political organization: "We 'conserve' nothing; neither do we want to return to any past" (GS 377).[149] Nonetheless, across these diverse historical accounts Nietzsche repeatedly spotlights certain abstract political principles that he deems to be essential to collective flourishing.

   The first defining feature of Nietzsche's ideal society is a commitment to elite perfectionism – that is, a prioritization of exceptional individuals. *This* should represent the ultimate goal (and justification) of any given polity: "[. . .] society cannot exist for the sake of society, but only as the substructure and framework for raising an exceptional type of being up to its higher task" (BGE 258).[150] These higher creative types are what Nietzsche sometimes refers to as "a species of overman" (A 4), in other words, the antithesis of the "last man." So when he declares that he wants to advance the "human type," we should avoid conflating this with a generalized concern with improving the conditions of all social strata of humanity. His overriding concern is rather with the *highest* fruit of society – that is, in the language of the previous chapter, *elite* genius. It is this that represents the ultimate touchstone of human achievement, the "highest possible power and splendor of the human type" (GM Preface 6, KSA 5.253). In one *Nachlaß* note, clearly informed by his discharge model of will to power, Nietzsche implies that a society should release its accumulated capital by producing overmen. Obviously drawing on Rolph's account of reproduction, he thus conceives the overman as an "excretion [*Ausscheidung*] of a *surplus of luxury* of humanity" (KSA 12:10[17], 462). The cultivation of overmen, it turns out, is the highest form of collective agency through

---

[149] See also TI Skirmishes 43.
[150] See also KSA 12:10[111], 520; KSA 12:10[17], 462f. Recalling his valorization of elite genius in UM (which we explored in Chapter 3), in BGE 126 he writes that "[a] people is nature's roundabout way of getting six or seven great men."

which a social organization can vent its accumulated power. But what mode of political organization does Nietzsche think best *enables* this process of collective efflorescence?

Nietzsche's partiality for great individuals (over and against the happiness of the greatest possible number) testifies to the inherently inegalitarian nature of his ideal body politic. And, in keeping with his notion of the will to power, he maintains that the political structure of any fecund society is invariably going to be hierarchical in kind:

> Every enhancement so far in the type "man" has been the work of an aristocratic society – and that is how it will be, again and again, since this sort of society believes in a long ladder of rank order and value distinctions between men, and in some sense needs slavery. (BGE 257)[151]

We should note that Nietzsche conceives aristocratic social order in remarkably minimal terms – that is, as a mode of organization in which individual members form a hierarchy (*Rangordnung*), both insofar as they are held to be of differential worth *and* insofar as each reliably obeys the directives of those stationed at higher rungs of the social ladder. And congruent with our reading of the will to power, in A 57 he suggests that sociopolitical hierarchy is in fact underwritten by nature itself: "*Caste-order*, the most supreme, domineering law, is just the sanction of a *natural order*, natural lawfulness of the highest order."

For Nietzsche, one of the chief attractions of aristocratic social order lies in its close association with the institution of slavery (*Sklaverei*), which he describes as "a condition of every higher culture, of every enhancement of culture" (BGE 239). In GS 377, he thus calls for "a new slavery: for to every strengthening and enhancement of the type 'man' there belongs a new species of slavery." The collective task of breeding higher individuals depends on this practice: "Slavery, in both the crude and refined senses of the term, seems to be the indispensable means of disciplining and breeding" (BGE 188). And as we have repeatedly seen, in BGE 259 he further justifies exploitative social relations on the naturalistic grounds that "life itself is *essentially* a process of [. . .] incorporation [*Einverleibung*], and at the least, at the mildest, exploitation" (BGE 259). From this standpoint, healthy society is ineluctably defined by a constant struggle for *incorporation*, understood as the overpowering, integration and subsequent *exploitation* of that which is useful. But why does Nietzsche take this to be the case? And what form should such exploitation take?

---

[151] See also KSA 12:2[76], 96–97.

One reason that Nietzsche posits slavery as a social necessity is that he takes it to be a *sine qua non* of cultivating tyranny over one's self, an idea borne out by BGE 257:

> Without the *pathos of distance* as it grows out of the ingrained differences between stations, out of the way the ruling caste maintains an overview and keeps looking down on subservient types and tools, [...] that other, more mysterious pathos could not have grown at all, that demand for new expansions of distance within the soul itself, the development of states that are increasingly high, rare, distant, tautly drawn and comprehensive, and in short, the enhancement of the type "man," the constant "self-overcoming of man" [...].[152]

Here Nietzsche considers the external "*pathos of distance*" (toward others) to be exigent insofar as it generates the feeling of distance within *oneself* – that is, to the extent that it functions as a means to *self*-exploitation. We might then argue that the need to enslave others has now, in modernity, been obviated; the abundance of *historic* slavery can provide the requisite basis needed to cultivate this interior distance.[153] It is now the serviceable aspects of the *self* that we need to master, not other individuals or social groups. Yet this interpretation accounts for only a fraction of the texts in which Nietzsche discusses slavery, and so we therefore ought to consider some of the further grounds on which he defends this controversial practice.[154]

Nietzsche's main argument in favor of slavery is of an economic sort. As we just saw, he figures the overman as the product of a collective "*surplus of luxury*." Recalling his account of genius in GSt, he maintains that an economic surfeit is required to satisfy the life-needs of potential overmen, since this enables them to dedicate their time and energy to higher cultural pursuits. In the absence of such provisions, they would be forced to invest their time in reproducing their material existence. In this way, overmen "stand upon" and "live off" the masses (*Menge*), who form an otherwise meaningless machine. This "higher form of aristocracy," Nietzsche proclaims, "is that of the future" (KSA 12:10[17], 463).

He further argues that this apex of higher individuals ought to make *direct* use of the masses – as opposed to simply creaming off the proletariat's economic surplus – in order to execute their creative plans. Pre-eminent figures such as Caesar and Napoleon thus required legions of conscripted

---

[152] See also BGE 188.

[153] This interpretation is prominent in Ansell-Pearson (1994, 204–205); and Owen (2002, 121).

[154] We should also observe that in the preparatory note for BGE 257 (KSA 12:2[13], 73), Nietzsche suggests that an expressly *Other*-oriented "new slavery" is exigent.

men in order to accomplish their imperial state-building projects, and they needed to be perfectly at ease with the attendant loss of human life (recall Nietzsche's marble metaphor for example).[155] Another legitimate way of reading the "pathos of distance" is therefore as a feeling of moral license that enables precisely this kind of dispassionate instrumentalization of others, an attitude encapsulated in BGE 258:

> [T]he essential feature of a good, healthy aristocracy is that it does not feel that it is a function [. . .] but instead feels itself to be the *meaning* and highest justification (of the kingdom or community), – and, consequently, that it accepts in good conscience the sacrifice of countless people who have to be pushed down and shrunk into incomplete human beings, into slaves, into tools, all *for the sake of the aristocracy*. (BGE 258)

Ill-placed empathy would, Nietzsche maintains, hinder the execution of higher political directives. It would impede functional organization, and thereby frustrate effective collective agency.

While this all stands in support of the amorally top-down, radical aristocratic reading, Nietzsche's position is in fact more nuanced than might so far seem to be the case. For one, he emphasizes that these modern aristocrats must also be willing to sacrifice their *own* lives for the sake of enhancing humanity (TI Skirmishes 38). And elsewhere he also vacillates regarding the degree to which his higher individuals in reality serve their subordinates.[156] Our quotation from BGE 258 illustrates how Nietzsche's higher humans conceive themselves as *providing for* the masses, imbuing the average plebeian's life with *meaning*, with justification and significance. And in KSA 12:10[17], he points out that if an economically productive and well-managed society lacks higher exemplars, it becomes little more than a smoothly operating machine, the existence of which is utterly devoid of *purpose*. Nietzsche is therefore not extolling purely economic exploitation per se. The overman endows this instrumentalizing apparatus with a sense of purpose: he fills the toilsome lives of the masses with existential significance – in short, by providing them with a higher *whither* (*Wozu*). In this way, then, overmen should be understood as serving those whom they ostensibly exploit.[157]

---

[155] See also KSA 11:25[105], 38.

[156] Siemens (2008, 258–267), highlights the later Nietzsche's equivocation regarding who is really exploiting whom (or even whether there is perhaps equitable reciprocity).

[157] This recalls his vision of the mutual complementarity of elite and global genius in UM (see Chapter 3).

A further relevant point is that Nietzschean slavery should not be conflated with *chattel* slavery. Indeed, his conception of enslavement is remarkably broad, denoting any situation in which we find "man as tool [*Werkzeug*]" (KSA 11:25[238], 74). This encompasses a wide range of professions that we would not usually categorize as cases of enslavement: "In truth there *is* always slavery – whether you want it or not! E.g. the Prussian civil servant. The scholar. The monk" (KSA 11:25[225], 72).[158]

Consonant with his account of the will to power, the flourishing Nietzschean commonwealth cannot restrict itself to pursuing exploitation internally, which is to say, over its existing members. This impetus must also be directed *externally*, toward those deemed foreign:

> It is part of the concept of the living that it must grow – that it must extend its power and consequently take alien forces into itself. [...] At least a people might [...] designate as a right its need to conquer, its lust for power, whether by means of arms or by trade, commerce and colonization – the right to growth, perhaps. A society that definitively and *instinctively* gives up war [*Krieg*] and conquest [*Eroberung*] is in decline [...]. (KSA 13:14 [192], 378)

The type of conquest sanctioned in this text is *not* one necessarily achieved by means of martial force – it can equally be accomplished through the exercise of so-called soft power (i.e., through economic and cultural influence). And certainly, Nietzsche is well aware of the fact that just because we might be able to overwhelm a foreign force by means of military might, this approach is seldom an efficient way of *incorporating* that force (since this method tends to provoke their bitter antagonism).[159]

In the above-cited note, Nietzsche derives his argument for the necessity of incorporative struggle from his description of societies *as will-to-power organizations*. And elsewhere, consistent with his abstract conception of the well-functioning power organization, he theorizes that the ideal social hierarchy is sustained by an underlying moral framework. The soft power of moral education, for instance, plays an essential role in preparing people for slavery: "*Moralities* and religions are the principal means by which one can make whatever one wishes out of man, provided one [...] can assert one's will over long periods of time – in the form of legislation,

[158] On the scholar as "a tool, a piece of slave," see BGE 207.
[159] See KSA 10:16[26], 507f., where Nietzsche attempts to explain the "increasing humanization" of the vital drive for power augmentation: "there is an ever-*subtler* sense of *how hard* it is really to incorporate [*einverleiben*] another: while a crude injury done to him certainly demonstrates our power over him, it at the same time *alienates* his will from us even more – and thus makes him less easy to subjugate."

religions, and customs" (KSA 11:34[176], 478). Christian morality's "glori-
fication [*Veredlung*] of obedience" (BGE 61), for example, can ideologically
condition the lower rungs of society to relish their servility, and to work
as dutiful instruments in the hands of the ruling elite (which happens to
be one of Christianity's most advantageous functions according to
Nietzsche).[160] Those in power can also use moral education to manipulate
the *conscience* of the masses, and thereby codify their behavior. Thus, religion
"binds the ruler together with the ruled, betraying and handing over the
consciences of the latter to the former – which is to say: handing over their
hidden and most interior aspect, and one which would very much like to
escape obedience" (BGE 61).

So far, Nietzsche's stance toward morality may sound like a mere
variation on a theme already salient in Plato's noble lie, or Machiavelli's
infamous prince, who wields religion as a means of ensuring social
stability. Yet Nietzsche's ideal vision of morality is far more complex
than it appears at first glance. In his view, the subjugated masses
relentlessly struggle upward, seeking to usurp their oppressors, and he
affirms the fact that religious practice furnishes the downtrodden with a
means of improving their chances in this endeavor, namely, insofar as it
can endow them with the "spirituality" and capacity for self-overcoming
required to eventually seize power (BGE 61).[161] In statements such as
these, we bear witness to Nietzsche valorizing a mode of social stratification marked by *constant* tension and struggle, a "*continuous* exercise in
obeying and commanding, in keeping away and below" (BGE 257;
emphasis mine).[162] As in Roux's model of the body, the tension generated as the various parts of the community concurrently strive for
dominance is vital to the commonweal. And in this struggle moral
education can be weaponized by *both* sides, albeit in strikingly different
ways.

Our exposition of Nietzsche's abstract account of healthy organization
also revealed how any commanding unit depends upon its subordinates,
whose demands it must, to a certain extent, therefore obey. Otherwise put,
it needs to exercise certain virtues (*Tugenden*) toward its underlings –
accordingly, its struggle to exploit must be *measured* in kind. And in the
later corpus we find political writings that neatly harmonize with this

---

[160] See KSA 12:10[188], 568; KSA 11:35[9], 511; Appel (1999, 134).

[161] In this way, Nietzsche's endorsement of aristocratic subjugation complements his calls for self-
overcoming, *pace* Warren (1991).

[162] See Tongeren (1989, 152–153). See also Nietzsche's discussion of the struggle to engineer "protective
measures" against the rabble in TI Improvers 3.

ontological affirmation of reciprocity. In A 57, for instance, he explains why "in every healthy society" there exist "mutually conditioning" castes:

> Mediocrity is even the *foremost* requirement for there being exceptions: a higher culture is conditioned by it. When the exceptional person treats the mediocre with a more delicate touch *than he treats himself and his equals* [emphasis mine], this is not just courtesy of the heart, – it is simply his *duty* . . .

Though we have to cast our eye back to Nietzsche's middle period, HH 93 gives some well-needed empirical substance to the idea expressed in A 57:

> *Of the rights of the weaker.* – If someone, a besieged town for instance, submits under conditions to a stronger force, the counter-condition is that one is able to destroy oneself, burn the town down, and thus inflict a great loss upon the stronger. For this reason there here arises a kind of *equalization* [*Gleichstellung*] on the basis of which rights can be established. The enemy derives advantage from preserving them. – To this extent there also exist rights as between slaves and masters, that is to say to precisely the extent that the possession of the slave is useful and important to his master. (HH 93)

Reading A 57 together with HH 93, we can plainly see that Nietzsche is not saying that superior individuals *should* grant their subordinates rights in accordance with some objective or transcendent moral law. Nor is he suggesting that subordinates are entitled to *equal* rights. Rather, he is simply stating that exploiters should grant rights to those whom they exploit in direct proportion to their dependence on these exploited subalterns. The ascendant power needs to prevent not just the suicidal rebellion of their vassals, but also their degeneration through neglect or wanton oppression.[163] These texts sufficiently demonstrate that Nietzsche's model of healthy social exploitation is *not* adequately captured by the unidirectional, amoral interpretation of Nietzschean slavery advanced by his radical aristocratic readers. He is more accurately conceived as favoring a paternalistic system of moral reciprocity, one geared toward establishing relations of symbiotic interdependence between hierarchically organized powers. And while there are certainly texts in which Nietzsche endorses amoral political regimes, we can now see that, *pace* the radical aristocrat interpretation, these texts do not cohere particularly well with the notion of command inscribed in his theory of the will to power.

---

[163] In D 112 Nietzsche gives more reasons as to why stronger parties would be well advised to grant rights to those weaker than themselves.

The final reason that Nietzsche advocates aristocratic order concerns its efficacy as an "organization [*Veranstaltung*] with the purpose of *breeding* [*Züchtung*]" (BGE 262). As we have seen, owing to the entrenched nature of our drives, the task of creating higher individuals cannot be accomplished within the span of a single lifetime. Thus, we are faced with the "problem of breeding, because an individual life is too short" (KSA 11:26 [407], 260). But the collective tenacity required to bring a *transgenerational* enterprise of this magnitude to completion can, Nietzsche claims, only be guaranteed by a stringent aristocratic order.[164] This species of political regime represents the necessary corrective to the capricious "multi-willing" (*Vielwollerei*) of democracy's short-term coalition governments. The following note provides us with an indication of what exactly Nietzsche hopes will be enacted by stable aristocratic authority:

> I consider religions and educational systems [*Erziehungs-systeme*] insofar as they gather and bequeath force; no study seems to me to be more essential than that of the *laws of breeding* [*Züchtung*], in order not to lose, again, the greatest amount of force through inexpedient marriages [*unzweckmäßige Verbindungen*] and lifestyles. (KSA 11:34[176], 480)

It is moral, legal and educational order – the preconditions of breeding – that Nietzsche wishes to safeguard. Yet there is extensive scholarly disagreement regarding the precise nature of his proposed breeding program. A large part of the debate hinges on whether his "*laws of breeding*" are biologically oriented toward eugenics or culturally oriented toward education.[165] When discussing "breeding," Nietzsche tends to use the German terms *Zucht* and *Züchtung*, both of which are able, depending on the context, to signify either zoological breeding *or* cultural cultivation.[166] Given that he would have almost certainly been aware of this ambiguity, his equivocation vis-à-vis breeding appears to have been quite intentional. In the above quote, for example, in addition to sanctioning the regulation of breeding partnerships (*Verbindungen*), he also promotes markedly cultural modes of cultivation, such as "education" and the management of people's "lifestyles."[167] As we now know, he declines to draw a clear-cut distinction between biologically and culturally ingrained behavioral impulses; little wonder, then, that we

---

[164] See BGE 262, 188 and 203. In A 58, Nietzsche also affirms durable and intransigent religious-legal orders, such as that of the Roman imperium, as a necessary precondition of flourishing life.

[165] For a more biologically oriented interpretation of Nietzsche's notion of breeding, see Richardson (2004, 190–200). For a cultural interpretation, see Ottmann (1999, 358ff.); Schank (2000).

[166] See entries for "Zucht" and "Züchtung" in DWB; see also Detwiler (1990, 111–113).

[167] On marriage laws as a method of selective breeding, see KSA 12:4[6], 179; see also Richardson (2004, 198). In BGE 61, Nietzsche also underscores the importance of "fortunate marriage customs."

encounter a correspondingly hazy distinction in his breeding project. But be it by cultural or biological means, Nietzsche firmly believes we can, and indeed should, struggle against deeply embedded, harmful drives by blocking their transmission to future generations. This, it should be remarked, constitutes a plainly unmeasured feature of his later sociopolitical philosophy.

Within his ideal vision of healthy social order, Nietzsche endorses a number of further species of unmeasured struggle, many of which are significantly less palatable than the practice of arranged marriage. First, he affirms the need for selective immigration policies – societies must exclude any cultures which they lack the strength to incorporate, and which therefore may cause them harm. It is on these grounds that Nietzsche counsels the Germans to block Jewish immigration from the East: "[. . .] so commands the instinct of a people whose type is still weak and indeterminate enough to blur easily and be easily obliterated by a stronger race" (BGE 251).

In some of his more extreme moods, Nietzsche even calls for the *eradication* of certain members of society. Like Spencer, he disapproves of the Christian endeavor to preserve degenerate segments of the community. Thus, he argues that Christians "have preserved too much of *what should perish [zu Grunde gehn sollte]*" (BGE 62); and setting himself apart from positivistic socialists, he in no way recommends that we eradicate disease or self-destructive vice. For Nietzsche, these conveniently hasten the demise of potentially detrimental members of society: "*Waste, decay, elimination [Ausschuß]* need not be condemned: they are necessary consequences of life, of the growth of life" (KSA 13:14[75], 255). This, it should be added, is not simply a question of passively allowing degenerate members of society to wither away; he often encourages an alarmingly active approach – for example, by preventing certain individuals from reproducing (presumably by means of sterilization).[168] And in other places, his recommendations have an aggressively genocidal tenor. In EH BT 4, for example, he declares the following:

> The new faction in favor of life that takes on the greatest of all tasks, that of breeding humanity to higher levels (which includes the ruthless extermination of everything degenerate and parasitical), will make possible a surplus of life on earth [. . .].[169]

Again, Nietzsche employs a naturalistic argument in order to justify such radical policies:

---

[168] See KSA 13:23[1], 599; TI Skirmishes 39; KSA 13:16[35], 495; Richardson (2004, 198).
[169] See also KSA 13:11[414], 192.

> Life itself recognizes no solidarity, no "equal rights," between the healthy
> and the degenerate parts of an organism: one must excise the latter – or the
> whole will perish [*geht zu Grunde*] – *sympathy* for failures [*Mißrathenen*],
> *equal rights* for the ill-constituted – that would be the profoundest immor-
> ality, that would be *antinature* itself as morality! (KSA 13:23[1], 600)

Those who are of no use whatsoever to the commonwealth have no
legitimate claim to *any* rights from their superiors (unlike those who can
be exploited), not even to the right to life. Accordingly, in such cases
Nietzsche asserts the need for a wholly unrestrained, amoral species of
struggle. We should observe, however, that while he grounds this negative
eugenic project in his conception of the world as will to power, such
policies do not seem to be *entailed* by that ontology. For example, deport-
ation or exile would appear to be equally (if not more) consonant with the
affirmation of excretion that we identified in his organizational model of
the will to power. But no matter how charitably we interpret Nietzsche on
this point, the sheer weight of texts in which he applauds the struggle to
subjugate, exploit, exclude and even destroy large swathes of society gives
the lie to agonistic interpretations of his later political thought. For
Nietzsche, the purposive organization of society is a function of these
very processes.

4.4.2   Initiating Social Synthesis

Though we now have a picture of Nietzsche's healthy body politic, it
remains to be seen how we can *realize* such a community; how he thinks
we can initiate the revitalizing unification of modern society. Reminiscent
of his earlier philosophy, the later Nietzsche seeks to bind Europeans
together by injecting them with a sense of common purpose: "A task
great enough to reunite [*wieder zu binden*] *peoples*" (EH CW 2, KSA
6.360).[170] The task that Nietzsche has in mind here, as we now know, is
that of breeding higher individuals: "My thought: Goals are lacking, and
these must be individuals!" (KSA 12:7[6], 281); "Not 'humanity,' but *overman* is the goal" (KSA 11:26[232], 210). But how can we get this transgenerational enterprise off the ground?

In Nietzsche's view, the first step is to establish a thriving aristocracy,
since, as we saw in the previous section, this represents a precondition of
breeding higher humans.[171] In BGE 251, he refers to the "breeding of a new

---

[170] As Nietzsche laments in Z, "Humanity still has no goal" (Z I Goals, KSA 4.76).
[171] See KSA 12:2[57], 87; KSA 11:37[8], 582.

caste to rule over Europe" as the "European problem"; and it is indeed a problem, for how does Nietzsche think that we can concretely tackle the short-term challenge of cultivating a productive aristocracy? In a *Nachlaß* note entitled "*The strong of the future*," he provides some indication as to how we might set about overcoming this problem – that is, how we might approach the task of propagating a future race of leaders:

> The *means* would be those that history teaches: *Isolation* through interests in preservation that are the reverse of those which are average today; habituation to reverse evaluations; distance as a pathos; a free conscience in those things that today are most undervalued and prohibited. (KSA 12:9[153], 425)

Consonant with UM, Nietzsche again emphasizes the prophylactic need to *isolate* promising individuals. Such isolation creates a sheltered space for *experimentation*, which, as we determined in the previous section, Nietzsche takes to be an essential condition of self-cultivation.[172] He accents the need for "a race with its *own sphere of life* [...]; a hothouse for strange and choice plants" (ibid.). This protected laboratory functions as a crucible within which higher individuals can set about forging not just new moralities of *self-organization*, but also those capable of vibrantly synthesizing the community at large. Elaborating on this idea, in A 57 Nietzsche describes how systems of law honed to ensure aristocratic order, such as that which we find inscribed in the lawbook of Manu, result from the "experimental morality of many centuries."[173] The question is, though: Do we not need an aristocracy – or at least precisely the kind of stable political organization that we currently lack – in order to institutionalize this kind of protected experimental space? In other words, do we not require an aristocracy to be already in place in order to breed an aristocracy? Thus, how does Nietzsche suggest that we bootstrap ourselves out of the crisis of disintegration?

In response to this predicament, Nietzsche presents his own philosophy as the trigger needed to initiate widespread organizational struggle and establish a nascent aristocracy:

> My philosophy brings the triumphant thought of which all other modes of thought will ultimately perish. It is the great *cultivating* thought: the races

---

[172] On the need for isolation, see KSA 12:10[59], 491f. On the need for experimentation, see KSA 12:10[61], 493; or KSA 11:37[8], 582, in which Nietzsche affirms "a *reversal of values* for a certain strong type of human." Conway (1997a, 75–78) claims that this experimentation is private in kind, and that it sets an example of health that provokes emulation in others; in other words, in his view, there is a trickle-down effect.

[173] We should also note Nietzsche's *criticisms* of the laws of Manu. See KSA 13:14[203], 385f.; KSA 13:14[216], 392f.; KSA 13:15[45], 439f.; Brobjer (2004).

that cannot bear it stand condemned; those who feel it as the greatest benefit are chosen to rule. (KSA 11:26[376], 250)

On the one hand, the "great *cultivating* thought" that Nietzsche has in mind here is that of the eternal return – the idea that "[t]his life as you now live it and have lived it you will have to live once again and innumerable times again" (GS 341). This idea represents "existence as it is, without meaning or purpose [*Sinn und Ziel*], yet recurring inevitably without any finale of nothingness" (KSA 12:5[71], 213). There is certainly textual evidence that Nietzsche considered the idea of the eternal return as a trigger for collective organization. This is perhaps most striking in a note from 1883, where he describes this idea as a "*selective* principle, in the service of *force* (and barbarism!!)" (KSA 10:24[7], 646).[174]

The thought of the eternal return has a double effect according to Nietzsche. On the one side, the idea is so unbearably pessimistic that it compels the psychologically infirm to commit suicide. In the hands of the philosopher, it thus represents "a mighty pressure and hammer with which he breaks [*zerbricht*] and clears out of the way degenerate and decaying races to make a path for a new order of life, or to implant into that which is degenerate and wants to die away a longing for the end" (KSA 11:35[82], 547). Christianity grants consolation by artificially imbuing existence with a sense of transcendent purpose (*Zweck*), meaning (*Sinn*) and value (*Werth*) – particularly that of being admitted into heaven subsequent to the final judgment. Yet in accepting the idea of the eternal return, "we deny final purposes [*Schluß-Ziele*]" (KSA 12:5 [71], 211). Nietzsche claims that we are forced into making this denial by dint of our scientific integrity – it is "the *most scientific* of all possible hypotheses"; knowledge "compels this belief" (KSA 12:5[71], 211).[175] Faced with the loss of Christian value, the weak and sick experience the idea of the eternal return as a "curse" (ibid.) and are consequently driven either to destroy themselves (*sich durchzustreichen*) (KSA 11:25[227], 73) or each other.[176] Independent of any aristocratic regime, this thought thereby induces the unmeasured process of elimination (*Ausscheidung*) – "it purifies" (KSA 12:5[71], 217), eliminating the sickest individuals from society.[177]

---

[174] In KSA 11:25[227], 73, Nietzsche again dubs the eternal return "the great *cultivating* thought."

[175] For an argument against the idea that Nietzsche defended the eternal return on scientific grounds, see Clark (1990, 245ff.).

[176] See KSA 12:2[100], 110: "The hammer: a doctrine, which by means of an *unfettering* of the most death-seeking pessimism brings about a *selection* of the healthiest [*Lebensfähigsten*]." On this issue, see Deleuze (1983, 68ff.).

[177] See also KSA 11:27[23], 281, where Nietzsche describes the thought of the eternal return as enacting an elimination (*Ausscheidung*) of "life-hostile elements" from society.

Yet Nietzsche does not think the crisis instigated by the eternal return merely serves to cull the degenerate – it also apportions command to those who prove themselves worthy. In this way it

> brings to light the weaker and less secure among [men] and thus promotes *a rank-order of forces*, from the point of view of health: those who command are recognized as those who command, those who obey as those who obey. Of course, outside every existing social order. (KSA 12:5[71], 217)

According to Nietzsche, then, the idea of the eternal return is able to *sort*, and functionally organize, the European mishmash of modern individuals. Those who are able to affirm the thought are incontrovertibly marked out as higher, and duly thrust into positions of command over their inferiors. In this sense, the thought of the eternal return is meant to ignite and fuel a pervasive struggle for incorporation, and in doing so draw serviceable elements into a social hierarchy. Note that this process is entirely blind to individuals' standing in previous social orders, and can therefore be considered genuinely meritocratic in nature.

Although commentators have highlighted the way in which Nietzsche repeatedly singles out the eternal return as his philosophical "hammer" of choice they often neglect the fact that his theory of the will to power can fulfill much the same organizing function. A case in point is Deleuze (1983, 70), who cites KSA 12:5[71] in order to foreground the destructive force of the thought of the eternal return; however, in this fragment Nietzsche is in fact referring to his theory of the will to power:

> [...] There is nothing to life that has value, except the degree of power – assuming that life itself is the will to power. Morality guarded the *underprivileged* against nihilism by assigning *each* an infinite value, a metaphysical value [...]. *Supposing that the faith in this morality would perish*, then the underprivileged would no longer have their consolation – and would *perish* [*zu Grunde gehen*].
>
> This *perishing* presents itself as a – self-destruction [*Sich-zu-Grunde-richten*], as an instinctive selection of that which *must destroy* [*zerstören*]. *Symptoms* of this self-destruction of the underprivileged: self-vivisection, poisoning, intoxication, romanticism, above all the instinctive need for actions that turn the powerful into *mortal enemies* (as it were, one breeds one's own hangmen) [...]. (KSA 12:5[71], 215–216)

In this fragment, it is the realization that the world is will to power that impels the weak to self-destruction – namely, by divesting them of metaphysical consolation, such as they find in the belief that they possess

God-given worth as human beings. What is also noteworthy about this text is how it frames the idea of the world as will to power as a cultivating thought: in provoking the weak to actively menace the powerful, it indirectly breeds (*züchtet*) these higher individuals to become the hangmen of the weak.

In addition to setting this organizational dynamic into motion, Nietzsche believes that the ideas of the eternal return and the will to power impose collective ends on society. As he says of the eternal return, "it assigns common tasks [*gemeinsame Aufgaben*] to men who have opposite ways of thinking" (KSA 12:5[71], 217). But what common tasks do these two theories foist upon humanity? And how do they *compel* separate members of society to form a coordinated whole? In other words, how do they unify the collective will?

Referring to the eternal return, Nietzsche sketches an answer to these questions in a preparatory note for Z:

> [. . .] Determination of the higher men as the creative ones. Organization of the higher men, cultivation [*Erziehung*] of the future *ruling ones* [. . .]. Your supremacy must itself become joyful in ruling and shaping. "Not only man, *also the overman returns eternally.*" (KSA 11:27[23], 281)

Nietzsche claims that only by creating new goals and values are we able to counteract the despair evoked by the insight that we live in a world devoid of transcendent worth.[178] The idea of the eternal return forces its adherents to take joy in the activity of commanding, inventing new goals and revaluing their values. It becomes exigent that we rediscover the pleasure inherent to overcoming resistances and forming novel, stronger power organizations. Pivotally, in Nietzsche's opinion the creative act that most effectively augments one's power, and which therefore brings the greatest degree of joy, is the creation of the overman – an idea which he further accents in the following *Nachlaß* fragment:

> In order to *bear* the thought of the [eternal] return:
> freedom from morality is necessary, [. . .]
> *greatest enhancement of the force-consciousness of man*, as that of the one who creates the overman. (KSA 11:26[283], 225)

One of the most painful corollaries of the eternal return is that "[h]e returns, the human of whom you are weary, the small human being" (Z III Convalescent 2, KSA 4.274). The only way to combat this abysmal thought,

---

[178] See KSA 11:26[284], 225: "means of bearing it [the thought of the eternal return] / the revaluation of all values [. . .]."

then, is to work toward the overman and thereby grant oneself the uplifting conviction that *"also the overman returns eternally."*[179]

The highest human is, in Nietzsche's analysis, "[h]e who determines values and directs the will of millennia by giving direction to the highest natures" (KSA 11:25[355], 106). Of course, there is no greater or more enduring project than that of breeding a new aristocracy, and with that, the overman. It follows from this that if we wish to maximally discharge our power and thereby endow our life with the utmost pleasure and significance, the most effective creative project that we could possibly engage in is that of fashioning higher individuals, who stand as the fullest "reflection" (*Abbild*) of thriving nature qua will to power (KSA 11:25[140], 51).[180] On purely prudential, egoistic grounds, each of us therefore ought to join the collective struggle to beget overmen, since this constitutes the most empowering, pleasurable and meaning-giving project available to us. And insofar as this requires a social and transgenerational breeding project, the only way that we can work toward the goal of the overman is by acquiescing to it as a shared "common task." According to Nietzsche, this task demands that we cooperate with our equals, obey the directives of our superiors and assume resolute command over our inferiors.

In reconstructing Nietzsche's vision of the overman as the mainstay of social solidarity, we should take care not to overlook just how radically underdetermined he leaves his conception of this ideal figure. As opposed to embodying a fleshed-out exemplar, the overman very minimally symbolizes the *growth*, or *overcoming*, of humanity. As Heidegger (1961, 125) observes, "the essence of the over-man [*Über-menschen*] consists in going 'beyond' [*über*] the hitherto human [*Menschen*]."[181] The affirmation of this thin conception of the overman as a social goal is tantamount to an affirmation of the will to power as a flourishing dynamism free of any essential telos that would predetermine growth.[182] The task of breeding higher humans is therefore a *processual* task, *not* a teleological one – that is to say, it could never be attained in any final manner.[183]

179 See Clark (1990, 261, 271); Ansell-Pearson (1991, 192).
180 See Müller-Lauter (1999, 87ff.); Heidegger (1961, 304). This controverts Philippa Foot (1973, 163), who argues that Nietzsche justifies the pursuit of the overman by appealing to an intuitive aesthetic preference that we have for higher men.
181 See also Heidegger (1997, 26). Bataille (2015, 166) comparably interprets the overman as an unlimited "field of possibilities."
182 Werner Stegmaier (2000, 209–211) has similarly argued that the doctrine of the overman is an anti-doctrine (*Anti-Lehre*) intended to undermine any single concept of "the human" that threatens to become reified.
183 For a contrary interpretation of the overman – that is, as an oft-*attained* and therefore *attainable* ideal – see Conway (1997a, 23). In this context, cf. D 559.

But we do not necessarily have to assent to the abysmal thought of the eternal return in order to view the task of breeding higher humans as a worthwhile enterprise. The logic of the will to power gives us independent prudential reasons to participate in this collective, transgenerational project. This is convenient, since for many of us the idea of the eternal return is not in fact psychologically compelling, and thus turns out to be a rather damp squib. As Ivan Soll (1973, 339–340) has incisively pointed out, if there is no psychological continuity between my repeated selves, there is no real reason why this repetition should present me with any real cause for concern.[184]

When Nietzsche talks of the need for "a doctrine, which *sieves out* [*aussiebt*] humans ... which drives the weak to decisions, and likewise the strong," he could just as well be referring to the teaching of the will to power as to the doctrine of the eternal return (KSA 13:11[149], 71). To be sure, both theories represent radically immanent worldviews that eschew any transcendent realm of meaning, and to that extent they go hand in hand. The world that must be affirmed by he who passes the test of the eternal return is precisely the world *as will to power* (KSA 12:38[12], 610; BGE 56). It is for this reason that we should view the latter as having practical priority within Nietzsche's thought. Affirming the world as will to power entails that we make a decision regarding the future of humanity (since viewing the world in this light casts our present failings into sharp relief). Further, it robs the weak of consolation (insofar as it undermines eschatology); it provides us with a yardstick against which we can revalue our values; and finally, it paints a picture of flourishing life as conflict, creative activity and overcoming, doing so in such a way as to impel us to engage in the struggle to organize ourselves, our fellow humans and our descendants.[185]

One could object that the panpsychic hypothesis built into Nietzsche's theory of the will to power is no more plausible than the doctrine of the eternal return. However, Nietzsche's theory of the will to power does not stand or fall with the supposition of panpsychism. Its practical force

---

[184] Clark (1990, 270) rejects this criticism, arguing that it is based on a misreading of the idea, which she argues should be imagined "in an uncritical or preanalytical manner, suspending all doubts concerning its truth." However, this requires a *charitable* interpretation of the thought, and it completely loses the compulsive force that conditions its organizing effect. After all, why be charitable to a thought that might destroy us?

[185] See KSA 11:34[247], 504, where after giving an account of the world as will to power (against mechanistic theories of existence), he states that "the various philosophical systems are to be considered as *methods of cultivation* of the spirit: they have always *trained* a particular force of the spirit best; with their one-sided demand to see things precisely so and not otherwise." See also KSA 11:40[50], 653.

remains even if we merely accede to it as an abstract theory of organization, one based on the empirical observation that thriving unities are conditioned by functional order, which is in turn generated by an active struggle to incorporate useful elements and to exclude those that are obsolete or injurious. This theory also forcefully denies the existence of essences, as well as the idea of a transcendent realm that could potentially ground objective, universal values. As such, it motivates us to collectively and individually forge our own values and, with this, to shape the direction of our future growth.

Recall that in UM it was insight into two transcendent a priori truths – the nature of our essential self, and the end of natural teleology – that functioned as the lynchpin of Nietzsche's synthetic project. In his later writings, however, a significant transformation has taken place: his remedy to the crisis of disintegration is now grounded in a purely *immanent*, hypothetical and a posteriori view of the world as will to power.[186]

4.5   Conclusion

At the end of the previous chapter, we determined that if the later Nietzsche wanted to remedy the crisis of disintegration, he needed to provide an account of organization purged of the flawed metaphysical presuppositions that compromised his earlier view. We have now exposed how he accomplishes this with his notion of the will to power. The theory conceives nature as entirely composed of actively (even consciously) organizing forces, each of which relentlessly strives to overpower and incorporate that which they deem useful and, correspondingly, to exclude that which they judge to be harmful. The purposive coordination that characterizes any integrated whole is therefore a function of the way in which the superordinate and subordinate component parts of that whole have been contingently shaped in their reciprocal struggle with one another. The part–whole relation is therefore invariably the contingent result of a two-way conflict, and never wholly determined from above – for example, by a substantial essence or Idea.

We then examined how this abstract model translates into an applicable therapeutic. At the psychological level, we saw how his vision of

[186] As Ottmann (1999, 360) has remarked, this starkly contrasts with Plato, for whom cultivation is rooted in gaining insight into "the Idea of the good and the world existing [*seiende*] in itself." Whereas Ottmann figures the eternal return as Nietzsche's immanent cultivating idea, however, I have tried to illuminate how an affirmation of life *as will to power* is equally able to ground his later socially synthetic project.

flourishing will to power, when taken as a normative ideal, impels us to hierarchically order our serviceable values and drives, while, at the same time, demanding that we eradicate those values and drives that turn out to be intractable. Yet we found that Nietzsche discourages any attempt to consciously micromanage this process, or to prematurely determine it according to some preconceived (and inevitably incorrect) notion of our true self. At the very least, he recommends that we affirm the principles of thriving will to power, and seek to radically critique, and thereby remove, any moral constraints that contradict these principles. On the incorporative side, he recommends that we engage in a phase of open-minded experimentation, one rigorously subordinated to the general aim of embodying healthy forms of the will to power – as we experiment, we must, in Nietzsche's view, perpetually assess whether particular phenomena augment or diminish our strength relative to others. From the tumult of our drives, a vibrant economy of functionally organized impulses should naturally emerge – one that leaves us capable of tenaciously pursuing our goals (unlike the depression and caprice that he associates with psychological fragmentation). Yet we should not mistake this for a static telos – any flourishing order must *continually* grow, overcome and reorder itself; nor should we assume that Nietzsche thinks this ideal can be attained in a single individual's life span – its more substantive attainment requires a collective, transgenerational commitment to the project of breeding higher individuals.

At the collective level, his model of healthy organization flows into an affirmation of hierarchical, exploitative order, which is, he claims, exemplified in aristocratic political organization. In opposition to the collective caprice and inefficacy characteristic of modern society, the stability of functional, aristocratic hierarchy enables the community to bear fruit in the form of higher individuals. This said, Nietzsche's conceptions of aristocracy and slavery both admit a remarkably wide spectrum of legitimate interpretations. The reading advanced by the agonistic democrats, however, cannot be located anywhere on this spectrum. Their exegesis of the will to power is excessively soft; and in clear contravention of their interpretation, Nietzsche's endorsement of political exploitation, hierarchy and exclusion *is* cogently grounded in his notion of the will to power. On the other hand, the radical aristocratic interpretation was found to have unique defects of its own. Most importantly, their understanding of Nietzschean exploitation as categorically amoral was seen to clash with the principle of reciprocity that Nietzsche builds into his vision of the world as will to power. Both the agonistic democrats *and* the radical aristocrats therefore misrepresent Nietzsche's politics by failing to remark that healthy organization emerges from a *balance* of measured *and* unmeasured struggle. As we have seen, both of these two schools of interpretation tendentiously magnify one side of this dualism at the expense of the other.

Conclusion

At the beginning of this book, we set out with a single guiding objective: to demonstrate that we ought to read Nietzsche as a proponent of both measured *and* unmeasured conflict. The two separate parts of this book have accomplished this objective by means of two distinct routes: Part I established that he valorizes both *Vernichtungskampf* (unmeasured) and *Wettkampf* (measured) at various points in the corpus; Part II then demonstrated that Nietzsche consistently promotes *organizational conflict*, which consists of both a measured struggle for the incorporation of that which is deemed useful, *and* an unmeasured struggle for the exclusion of that which is not.

Though we turned up myriad discrepancies in his views on conflict, we nonetheless found that the majority of his mature writings on this topic form a systematic whole. We further ascertained how Nietzsche achieves this coherence by eliminating and replacing the flawed metaphysical foundations that compromised his earlier philosophy. In order to clarify the systematicity that structures his later thoughts on conflict, we should briefly recapitulate the interlocking set of philosophical claims that have been established over the course of this book. First, and most fundamentally, everything and everyone struggles for power – primarily by means of striving to incorporate and *organize* that which is serviceable into a functional hierarchy. However, this general impetus was seen to be highly polymorphous and able to express itself through a rich variety of concrete behaviors. Second, the most effective approach to incorporating and exploiting inferior forces involves carefully heeding the demands of those forces. Third, at a social level, one way that relations of exploitation can be established is by means of violently destructive conflict – thus, in war for example, aggressors may seek to eradicate their opponents in order to enslave the individuals, or exploit the resources, commanded by those opponents. Otherwise put, they endeavor to annihilate their adversaries in order to appropriate the so-called spoils of war. This, however, is not the most effective means of establishing relations of exploitation, principally because it tends to provoke an attitude of rebellion that makes it difficult to instrumentalize any conquered individuals. Fourth, though violence may very well represent an indelible *Urfaktum* of life, and even the genetic root of all culture, we are nonetheless able to employ softer means in trying to establish and maintain the relations of exploitation upon which our lives depend – and indeed, it is in our own power-augmenting interests to do exactly this. Fifth, while it may not be necessary for us to engage in *violently* unmeasured conflict, life is nonetheless fundamentally conditioned by unmeasured struggle – that is, insofar as the organization that constitutes any living unity is conditioned by the active exclusion of that which it deems harmful. Finally, seventh, where two powers realize they are too equally matched to establish relations of exploitation, they can, and indeed should, engage in agonally measured contention – this enables both powers to strengthen themselves in their common struggle to exploit third parties.

As this list makes clear, affirming the world as will to power does not entail affirming *either* measured *or* unmeasured conflict, but rather a synthesis of the two. Both forms of conflict are required to achieve the higher goal of organization, which is synonymous with flourishing life. As such, in suppressing one or the other of these two dynamics, both hard and soft readers can, by Nietzsche's very own standards, be likewise charged with fabricating life-denying misinterpretations of his philosophy. With an eye to correcting this imbalance, this book has sought to initiate an aspect change whereby these two sides, instead of being understood as mutually exclusive, can be seen as two ways of looking at a single overarching impetus for organization.

In trying to construct a vision of health, Nietzsche illuminates a constellation of structural analogies that inhere between humans and lower forms of organic of life. Nietzsche does not, however, thereby commit the error of *reducing* human existence to the basic biological processes that define these lower forms of life. He is not claiming that there is no substantive difference between people and single-celled organisms. Rather, he takes these two categories of phenomena to be *mutually* illuminating – in other words, each provides us with an *image-language* (*Bilderrede*) that can be used to shed helpful light on its counterpart.[1] Consistent with this, Nietzsche frequently draws attention to the *differences* that inhere between these two categories. One pertinent example concerns the specifically human phenomenon of higher-order consciousness (*Bewußtsein, Geist*),

---

[1] For more on this charge of biologism (and Heidegger's famous treatment of this charge), see Ioan (2019, 71ff.).

which far from being evidence of our superiority over lower organic forms, Nietzsche takes as proof of "the relative imperfection of the [human] organism, as an experimenting, a groping, a mistaking, as an exertion" (A 14). Whereas lower organic forms enjoy an almost direct relation to themselves and the external world, humans see through a glass darkly, so to speak, thanks to the inefficient mediation of consciousness. Consequently, we are forever condemned to a state of confusion regarding both ourselves and the outside world.

Harmonious with this vision of human fallibility, our study has exposed the way in which we are particularly prone to misconceive the nature of conflict. What is more, the resulting confusions can lure us into adopting unhealthy ethical stances toward the various instances of conflict that arise in our day-to-day lives. However, while we may as human beings be condemned to err on various fronts, the misconceptions that cloud our understanding of conflict seem to be largely preventable. Of course, in order to prevent them, we must first recognize them *as* misconceptions. For this reason, the identification of these conceptual pitfalls is to my mind one of the principal contributions of not just Nietzsche's thoughts on conflict, but also our critical analysis of these thoughts. We should therefore review some of the all-too-human, but nonetheless detrimental errors that we have flagged throughout the course of our inquiry.

First, in Chapter 1 we mapped some of the consequences that follow from conceiving physically destructive conflict in terms of the cathartic discharge of an *essentially* murderous species of energy. The problem was found to be that this supposition denies the very possibility of substantive transformation, and thereby neutralizes the project of modulating struggles of annihilation into culturally productive modes of opposition. While we focused on the way in which this specifically hinders the agonistic program of transforming *Vernichtungskampf* into *Wettkampf*, it likewise undermines the project of modifying violent conflict into nonlethal modes of incorporative or exclusionary struggle. For instance, we can incarcerate or exile, rather than physically eradicate, problematic members or groups of society; and we can even pursue completely nonphysical modes of negation – for example, instead of eliminating troublesome individuals or social groups, we could strive to eradicate the specific drives that render them so problematic (as a truly reformatory correctional system ought to do).[2] But if we assent to the claim that

---

[2] In D 202, Nietzsche endorses precisely this approach to dealing with criminals, though even here he sanctions physical destruction (in the form of encouraged suicide) as a last resort.

murderous energy is at bottom untransformable, then we have to think of such possibilities as merely compressing and displacing our violent dispositions, which we consequently ought to prepare to release in the form of international war. The idea that physically destructive impulses grow unstoppably stronger until they inevitably erupt is therefore a perilous assumption, one that Nietzsche fortunately outgrew.

Chapter 2 then brought into relief how the tendency to confound agonal and destructive conflict likewise undoes the agonal dimension of Nietzsche's transformative project. The issue is that this elision fails to conceptually distinguish between the form of conflict that Nietzsche wants us to *subject* to transformation (i.e., *Vernichtungskampf*) and the form of conflict that he hopes will *result* from such transformation (i.e., agonal contest). Further, in this chapter we also determined that conceiving productive agonal relations as being founded on nothing but the counterbalancing of adversaries led commentators to neglect the foundational importance of cultivating *self*-limitation. Conversely, describing the agon as being entirely grounded in a shift of subjective attitude (i.e., toward respect) blinded interpreters to the need for *educational institutions* designed to instill the ethos of self-moderation that sustains agonal culture.

Chapters 3 and 4 then examined the problematic assumption that in order to effectively struggle for organization we must first identify our metaphysical telos. Contrary to this supposition, we found that the goals toward which humans strive must be forged *by humans themselves*, and, moreover, kept open to continuous revision. Prematurely fixed conceptions of our ideal self or society can, on Nietzsche's account, cause us to inhibit digressions that may very well turn out to be advantageous to our personal and collective evolution.

Chapter 4 then clarified the way in which Nietzsche thinks our picture of the natural world significantly influences our normative orientation toward conflict. Conceiving nature as a purely mechanical system governed by universal natural law is, in his view, not merely scientifically unfounded, but also harmfully serves to vindicate universal moral law. This worldview thus discourages people from fashioning a moral law suited to their own particular organizational needs. Similarly, our mistaken tendency to ascribe a transcendent origin to our values can obfuscate the fact that many of these values are the vestiges of a rearguard ethical policy concocted by the weak for the sake of mere survival (i.e., instead of active flourishing). Moreover, this alleged transcendence makes our values seem out of practical reach, which in turn discourages people from actively reorganizing their normative outlook.

Nietzsche also exposes our predisposition to confuse that which ought to be excluded with that which is merely difficult to incorporate – in other words, we are prone to confound "the useless and the difficult to acquire" (KSA 9:11[134], 492). As such, we often strive to negate that which might, albeit with some effort, prove to be of worth. Contrastingly, our inability to correctly discern that which is serviceable can also lead us to excessively consume that which *cannot* be used, an error exemplified by antiquarian education and the historical sense, both of which Nietzsche thinks are key drivers of subjective anarchy. He thus alerts us to the importance of carefully screening phenomena according to their employability.

Finally, we located two further common errors by reading Nietzsche against his one-sided interpreters. On the one hand, describing exploitation as intrinsically unmeasured led some commentators to overlook the possibility, and indeed the task, of ascertaining softer, more symbiotic forms of exploitation (which, incidentally, Nietzsche himself often specifies). On the other hand, in conceiving measured modes of contest as being divorceable from those of an exclusionary sort, agonistic commentators overlook the multiple ways in which elimination is likely essential to human life. Correspondingly, they neglect the fact that we would do well to focus our energies on engineering forms of elimination that are as soft as humanly possible.

The various fallacies that we are apt to commit when it comes to thinking about conflict are not, it should be added, comparable to the life-preserving errors that Nietzsche elsewhere affirms – such as in BGE 4, where he invites us "to acknowledge untruth as a condition of life." They are rather faulty intellectual dispositions that funnel us into modes of conflict that harm either ourselves or the social wholes to which we belong. Furthermore, they cause us to shirk the beneficial struggle for organization upon which our health depends. If we wish to harness our impulses, and in doing so become more effective individuals, it is therefore imperative that we correct these conceptual errors. This exercise can also teach us the value of behaving virtuously toward our subordinates; and it can prompt us to campaign for the agonal institutions that catalyze cultural flourishing. As such, refining our understanding of the nature and value of conflict can help us cultivate modes of contest that are profoundly beneficial to humans as individuals, communities and even as a species.

These conclusions will no doubt strike many as distortively neat. And to be sure, Nietzsche's views on conflict are admittedly messier than my analysis has generally made out to be the case. Our aim has been to reconstruct the underlying systematicity that reconciles a great many of his apparently contradictory claims about the nature of conflict, struggle and war. Achieving this end has required playing down, and even omitting, a number of significant anomalies and irresolvable tensions. Structured exegesis is an instance of organizational struggle, which as we now know cannot but involve a certain degree of exclusion, simplification and hence *falsification*. But we should nonetheless bear in mind that this systematizing impulse can be pushed too far – that is, to the point where it blinds us to the chaotic nature of the real world, or in this specific case, of Nietzsche's writings; indeed, the later Nietzsche himself declares that "[t]he will to system is a lack of integrity [*Rechtschaffenheit*]" (TI Arrows 26). So, in the interest of scholarly integrity, we should close by taking stock of some of the key remainders generated by our systematic analysis. This should leave us with a more balanced, representative impression of Nietzsche's philosophical project.

In Chapter 1, I argued that Nietzsche abandons his earlier affirmation of violent conflict in favor of agonal transformation. However, we then turned up a number of later texts (particularly GM I 11 and TI Ancients 3, though we might also include GS 362) that did not prima facie hang together with my interpretation. While I have defended the idea that such texts *can* be rendered compatible with my exegesis, there is a case to be made that Nietzsche's mature outlook is irresolvably schizophrenic in nature. Thus, one could argue that he merely vacillates between transformative and essentialist ontologies of violence – between censuring and affirming murderous conflict – and that he does so without ever conclusively committing to one stance or the other. We his readers would then be compelled to choose between these two attitudes, to settle for the benefits of one and forfeit those of the other. Although, as I have demonstrated above, the textual evidence speaks against a schizophrenic reading of this kind, we should acknowledge that the case for such a reading cannot be altogether ruled out of court.

Both parts of this book have also controversially omitted the dark seam of pessimism that runs through Nietzsche's later writings, particularly from 1887 onwards. For the pessimistic Nietzsche, modernity's decadence is simply incurable. We are individually and collectively ensnared in the process of disintegration, and in struggling against this snare we only tighten its grip and accelerate our inevitable decline. As he warns in TI Socrates 11, "[p]hilosophers and moralists are lying to themselves when they think that they are going to extricate themselves from *décadence* by waging war [*Krieg*] on it. Extrication is not in their power" (TI Socrates 11). And in TI Skirmishes 43 he seems to implore his readers to march directly into the jaws of decadence with their eyes firmly open:

we have to go forwards, and I mean step by step further into decadence [. . .].
You can inhibit this development and even dam up the degeneration
through inhibition, gather it together, make it more violent and sudden:
but that is all you can do.[3]

And finally, in GS 356 he laments the fact that "everything is lacking
[. . .]. *We are all no longer material for a society.*"[4] In light of such remarks,
my reading of Nietzsche might strike some as naively sanguine. And
certainly, our study has been consciously centered on the optimistic,
proactive side of Nietzsche's philosophy – for it is cautious hope, as
opposed to cynical fatalism, that in my view shines through his mature
Weltanschauung. But this is not to say that we should simply ignore his
gloomier forecasts. After all, if modern humanity is indeed terminally ill,
then we should take care not to waste our energy in futile pursuit of
a cure; rather, we should refocus our efforts on palliative care, and on
reconciling ourselves with the prospect of inevitable death. But I would
contend that before we can reasonably diagnose our situation as terminal
in kind, we must first exhaust all possible courses of treatment – and for
this, we are best off confining ourselves to the optimistic facet of
Nietzsche's practical philosophy.

In addition to omitting such anomalies and textual tensions from my
analysis, I have also refrained from critically interrogating some of
Nietzsche's more dubious philosophical claims. Thus, in Chapter 2 we
might have asked whether the agonistic appropriation of Nietzsche's
thought, while not strictly representative, is perhaps nonetheless a more
suitable normative philosophy, given the challenges faced by contemporary
society; indeed, is it, as Nietzsche argues (and the agonistic democrats
deny) imprudent to call on people to empower, as opposed to exploit, their
inferiors?

In Chapter 4 we sidelined a number of further objections. We established that Nietzsche's organizational program in no way entails selective
immigration policies, chattel slavery, wars of enslavement, eugenics or
ethnic cleansing. On the contrary, he entreats his readers to contrive softer
means of pursuing both incorporation and exclusion. Yet there appears to
be *so* much flexibility in how we might imagine ourselves realizing these
processes, that their affirmation makes little ethical demand on us. For

[3] It is also worth noting how in this passage he depicts the dynamic of decadence in terms of raw
catharsis.
[4] For an exegesis that foregrounds the pessimistic dimension of Nietzsche's later writings, see Conway
(e.g., 1997b, 90–95).

instance, we saw that Nietzsche considers anyone in gainful employment to be an exploited slave. Thus, on this reading, we already have slavery in abundance. Moreover, in our account of the analogy that Nietzsche posits between political communities and organisms, we have not had space to defend his views against the barrage of criticism to which organic models of society were fatally subjected in the early twentieth century. And regarding his theory of the will to power, there are certainly grounds to doubt whether it is indeed the most empowering, pragmatic hypothesis – certainly, the truth of this claim demands further empirical scrutiny. Lastly, history seems to have demonstrated that Nietzsche's theory of the will to power, much like that of the eternal return, is unable to trigger widespread social regeneration in the manner that he believed it could.

Such objections indicate that we should exercise lively caution when dealing with Nietzsche's views on conflict. To be sure, he would himself encourage such caution, since he openly spurns the uncritical assent of his readers: "I bid you lose me and find yourselves; and only when you have all denied me will I return to you" (Z I Bestowing 3, KSA 4.401). Would-be disciples flout a core requirement of his philosophy: that we create our *own* values, our *own* tables of good and bad – ones tailored to our *own* specific conditions of existence. Paradoxically, then, the more wholeheartedly that we agree with Nietzsche, the more energetically we ought to contradict him. First and foremost, we need to reject those elements in his normative view that we find ourselves unable to assimilate into our particular lived existence. What is more, for Nietzsche, as soon as ideas enjoy unchallenged, absolute rule (*Alleinherrshaft*) – or otherwise put, the moment they lack opposition – they become "boring, forceless, and tasteless" (D 507), or in Mill's words (2015, 35), they are reduced to little more than "dead dogmas." Counterintuitive though it may seem, the most effective way that we can support Nietzsche's philosophy of conflict is therefore by providing it with robust critical resistance.

References

Abdulla, Adnan K. 1985. *Catharsis in Literature*. Indiana: Indiana University Press.

Abel, Günter. 1998. *Nietzsche: die Dynamik der Willen zur Macht und die ewige Wiederkehr*. Berlin: de Gruyter.

Acampora, Christa Davis. 1998. "Nietzsche's Problem of Homer." *Nietzscheforschung: Jahrbuch der Nietzschegesellschaft* 5/6: 553–574.

2003. "Demos Agonistes Redux: Reflections on the *Streit* of Political Agonism." *Nietzsche-Studien* 32(1): 374–390.

2006. "Naturalism and Nietzsche's Moral Psychology." In *A Companion to Nietzsche*, edited by Keith Ansell-Pearson, 314–334. London: Blackwell.

2013. *Contesting Nietzsche*. Chicago: Chicago University Press.

Ansell-Pearson, Keith. 1991. *Nietzsche Contra Rousseau*. Cambridge: Cambridge University Press.

1994. *An Introduction to Nietzsche as Political Thinker*. Cambridge: Cambridge University Press.

Appel, Fredrick. 1999. *Nietzsche Contra Democracy*. Ithaca: Cornell University Press.

Aquinas, Thomas. 1956. *On the Truth of the Catholic Faith*, translated by Vernon J. Bourke. New York: Doubleday.

Arendt, Hannah. 1958. *The Human Condition*. Chicago: Chicago University Press.

Aristotle. 1991a. *Nichomachean Ethics*. In *The Complete Works of Aristotle*, edited by Jonathan Barnes. 2 vols. Princeton, NJ: Princeton University Press.

1991b. *Poetics*. In *The Complete Works of Aristotle*, edited by Jonathan Barnes. 2 vols. Princeton, NJ: Princeton University Press.

1991c. *Politics*. In *The Complete Works of Aristotle*, edited by Jonathan Barnes. 2 vols. Princeton, NJ: Princeton University Press.

1991d. *Rhetoric*. In *The Complete Works of Aristotle*, edited by Jonathan Barnes. 2 vols. Princeton, NJ: Princeton University Press.

Aschheim, Steven E. 1994. *The Nietzsche Legacy in Germany 1890–1990*. Berkeley, CA: University of California Press.

Assoun, Paul-Laurent. 2003. *Freud and Nietzsche*. London: Bloomsbury.

Atwell, John E. 1995. *Schopenhauer on the Character of the World: The Metaphysics of Will*. Berkeley, CA: University of California Press.

Augustine. 2003. *The City of God*, translated by Henry Bettenson. London: Penguin.

Aydin, Ciano. 2007. "Nietzsche on Reality as Will to Power: Toward an 'Organization–Struggle' Model." *Journal of Nietzsche Studies* 33(1): 25–48.

Bailey, Tom. 2013. "Nietzsche the Kantian?" In *The Oxford Handbook of Nietzsche*, edited by Ken Gemes and John Richardson, 134–159. Oxford: Oxford University Press.

Bataille, Georges. 2015. "Nietzsche and National Socialism." In *On Nietzsche*, translated by Stuart Kendall, 165–168. New York: State University of New York Press.

Baumeister, Roy and Brad Bushman. 2003. "Emotions and Aggressiveness." In *International Handbook of Violence Research*, edited by Wilhelm Heitmeyer and John Hagan, 479–494. Dordrecht: Kluwer Academic.

Bäumler, Alfred. 1931. *Nietzsche, der Philosoph und Politiker*. Leipzig: Reclam.

Beetham, David. 1985. *Max Weber and the Theory of Modern Politics*. Oxford: Blackwell.

Bernays, Jacob. 1857. *Grundzüge der verlorenen Abhandlung des Aristoteles über Wirkung der Tragödie*. Breslau: E. Trewendt.

Bismarck, Otto von. 1928. *Bismarck: Die gesammelten Werke (Vol. 10)*, edited by Wilhelm Schüßler. Berlin: Otto Stollberg.

Brandes, George. 1915. "An Essay on Aristocratic Radicalism." In *Friedrich Nietzsche*. 1–56. New York: Macmillan.

Brennecke, Detlef. 1976. "Die Blonde Bestie. Vom Mißverständnis eines Schlagworts." *Nietzsche-Studien* 5: 113–145.

Brobjer, Thomas. 2004. "Nietzsche's Reading about Eastern Philosophy." *Journal of Nietzsche Studies* 28: 3–35.

Brusotti, Marco. 2012. "Reagieren, schwer reagieren, nicht reagieren. Zu Philosophie und Physiologie beim letzten Nietzsche." *Nietzsche-Studien* 41: 104–126.

Burnham, Douglas. 2015. *The Nietzsche Dictionary*. London: Bloomsbury.

Campioni, Giuliano. 2009. *Der französische Nietzsche*. Berlin: de Gruyter.

Caro, Adrian Del. 2004. *Grounding the Nietzsche Rhetoric of Earth*. Berlin: de Gruyter.

Cavell, Stanley. 1990. *Conditions Handsome and Unhandsome: The Constitution of Emersonian Perfectionism*. Chicago: University of Chicago Press.

Church, Jeffrey. 2015. "Nietzsche's Early Perfectionism: A Cultural Reading of 'The Greek State.'" *Journal of Nietzsche Studies* 46(2): 248–260.

Clark, Maudemarie. 1990. *Nietzsche on Truth and Philosophy*. Cambridge: Cambridge University Press.

Clark, Maudemarie and David Dudrick. 2012. *The Soul of Nietzsche's* Beyond Good and Evil. Cambridge: Cambridge University Press.

Conant, James. 2001. "Nietzsche's Perfectionism: A Reading of *Schopenhauer as Educator*." In *Nietzsche's Postmoralism*, edited by Richard Schacht, 181–256. Cambridge: Cambridge University Press.

Connolly, William. 1988. *Political Theory and Modernity*. Oxford: Blackwell.

   1991. *Identity/Difference*. New York: Cornell University Press.

   1993. *Augustinian Imperative*. New York: Rowman & Littlefield.

Conway, Daniel. 1997a. *Nietzsche and the Political*. New York: Routledge.

   1997b. *Nietzsche's Dangerous Game: Philosophy in* Twilight of the Idols. Cambridge: Cambridge University Press.

Cowan, Michael. 2005. "Nietzsche and the Psychology of the Will." *Nietzsche-Studien* 34:48–74.

Crawford, Claudia. 1988. *The Beginnings of Nietzsche's Theory of Language*. Berlin: de Gruyter.

Curtius, Ernst. 1864. "Der Wettkampf." In Ernst Curtius, *Göttinger Festreden*, 1–22. Berlin: Wilhelm Herz.

Darwin, Charles. 2009. *On the Origin of Species*, edited by Gillian Beer. Oxford: Oxford University Press.

Deleuze, Gilles. 1983. *Nietzsche and Philosophy*, translated by Hugh Tomlinson. London: Continuum.

Detwiler, Bruce. 1990. *Nietzsche and the Politics of Aristocratic Radicalism*. Chicago: University of Chicago Press.

Dombowsky, Don. 2004. *Nietzsche's Machiavellian Politics*. Basingstoke: Palgrave Macmillan.

2014. *Nietzsche and Napoleon: The Dionysian Conspiracy*. Cardiff: University of Wales Press.

Drochon, Hugo. 2016. *Nietzsche's Great Politics*. Princeton: Princeton University Press.

Emden, Christian. 2018. "Nietzsches Katharsis. Tragödientheorie und Anthropologie der Macht." *Nietzsche-Studien* 47(1): 1–48.

Emerson, Ralph Waldo. 2000. "The Transcendentalist." In *Transcendentalism: A Reader*, edited by Joel Myerson, 366–380. Oxford: Oxford University Press.

Féré, Charles. 1888. *Dégénérescence et Criminalité*. Paris: Alcan.

Flaig, Egon. 2003. "Kultur und Krieg. Antihumanismus bei Jacob Burckhardt und Friedrich Nietzsche." In *Streit um den Humanismus*, edited by Richard Faber, 137–156. Würzburg: Königshausen und Neumann.

Foot, Philippa. 1973. "Nietzsche: The Revaluation of Values." In *Nietzsche: A Collection of Critical Essays*, edited by Robert C. Solomon, 156–168. Garden City, NY: Doubleday.

Freud, Sigmund. 1955. "Das Unbehagen in der Kultur." In *Gesammelte Werke 14. Werke aus den Jahren 1925–1931*, edited by Anna Freud, 419–506. London: Imago.

1966. "Die kulturelle Sexualmoral und die moderne Nervosität." In *Gesammelte Werke 7. Werke aus den Jahren 1906–1909*, edited by Anna Freud, 143–167. Frankfurt am Main: S. Fischer Verlag.

Gardner, Sebastian. 2009. "Nietzsche, the Self, and the Disunity of Philosophical Reason." In *Nietzsche on Freedom and Autonomy*, edited by Ken Gemes and Simon May, 1–32. Oxford: Oxford University Press.

Gemes, Ken. 2009. "Freud and Nietzsche on Sublimation." *Journal of Nietzsche Studies* 38(1): 38–59.

Gerratana, Federico. 1988. "Der Wahn jenseits des Menschen: Zur frühen E. v. Hartmann-Rezeption Nietzsches (1869–1874)." *Nietzsche-Studien* 17: 391–433.

Goethe, Johann Wolfgang von. 1948–1960. "Zur Morphologie." In *Goethes Werke. Hamburger Ausgabe*. Vol. 13, 53–250. Hamburg: Wegner.

Grote, George. 1851. *History of Greece*. 2nd ed., vol. 6. London: John Murray.

Hamacher, Werner. 1986. "'Disgregation des Willens', Nietzsche über Individuum und Individualität." *Nietzsche-Studien* 15(1): 306–336.

Hatab, Lawrence. 1995. *A Nietzschean Defense of Democracy: An Experiment in Postmodern Politics*. Chicago, IL: Open Court.

2002. "Prospects for a Democratic Agon: Why We Can Still Be Nietzscheans." *Journal of Nietzsche Studies* 24: 132–147.

2005. *Nietzsche's Life Sentence: Coming to Terms with Eternal Recurrence*. New York: Routledge.

2008a. "Breaking the Contract Theory: The Individual and the Law in Nietzsche's *Genealogy*." In *Nietzsche, Power and Politics*, edited by Herman Siemens and Vasti Roodt, 169–90. Berlin: de Gruyter.

2008b. *Nietzsche's* Genealogy of Morality. Cambridge: Cambridge University Press.

Heidegger, Martin. 1961. *Nietzsche*, vol. 2. Pfullingen: Neske.

1997. *Was heisst denken?* Tübingen: Max Niemeyer.

Hesiod. 2006a. *Theogony*. In *Theogony, Works and Days, Testimonia*, edited and translated by Glen Most. Cambridge, MA: Harvard University Press.

2006b. *Works and Days*. In *Theogony, Works and Days, Testimonia*, edited and translated by Glen Most. Cambridge, MA: Harvard University Press.

Hill, Kevin. 2003. *Nietzsche's Critiques: The Kantian Foundations of his Thought*. Oxford: Oxford University Press.

Hobbes, Thomas. 1996. *Leviathan*, edited by Richard Tuck. Cambridge: Cambridge University Press.

Homer. 1975. *The Odyssey of Homer*, translated by Richmond Lattimore. New York: Harper & Row.

2008. *The Iliad*, translated by Robert Fitzgerald. Oxford: Oxford University Press.

Honig, Bonnie. 1993. *Political Theory and the Displacement of Politics*. New York: Cornell University Press.

Huddleston, Andrew. 2014. "'Consecration to Culture': Nietzsche on Slavery and Human Dignity." *Journal of the History of Philosophy* 52(1): 135–160.

2017. "Nietzsche on the Health of the Soul." *Inquiry* 60(2): 135–164.

Hume, David. 1739. *A Treatise of Human Nature*. London: John Noon.

Hurka, Thomas. 2007. "Nietzsche: Perfectionist." In *Nietzsche and Morality*, edited by B. Leiter and N. Sinhababu, 9–31. Oxford: Oxford University Press.

Ioan, Razvan. 2019. *The Body in Spinoza and Nietzsche*. London: Palgrave.

Irwin, Terence. 1988. *Aristotle's First Principles*. Oxford: Clarendon Press.

Janaway, Christopher. 2007. *Beyond Selflessness: Reading Nietzsche's* Genealogy. Oxford: Oxford University Press.

Janz, Curt. 1978–1979. *Friedrich Nietzsche: Biographie*, 3 vols. Munich: Hanser.

Jaspers, Karl. 1981. *Nietzsche: Einführung in das Verständnis seines Philosophierens*. New York: de Gruyter.

Jenkins, Scott. 2011. "What Does Nietzsche Owe Thucydides?" *Journal of Nietzsche Studies* 42(1): 32–50.

Jensen, Anthony K. 2008. "Anti-Politicality and Agon in Nietzsche's Philology." In *Nietzsche, Power and Politics*, edited by Herman Siemens and Vasti Roodt, 319–346. Berlin: de Gruyter.

Johnson, Dirk. 2010. *Nietzsche's Anti-Darwinism*. Cambridge: Cambridge University Press.

Kahn, Charles. 1979. *The Art and Thought of Heraclitus*. Cambridge: Cambridge University Press.

Kalyvas, Andreas. 2009. "The Democratic Narcissus: The Agonism of the Ancients Compared to that of the (Post)Moderns." In *Law and Agonistic Politics*, edited by Andrew Schaap, 15–41. Farnham: Ashgate.

Katsafanas, Paul. 2013. "Nietzsche's Philosophical Psychology." In *The Oxford Handbook of Nietzsche*, edited by Ken Gemes and John Richardson, 727–755. Oxford: Oxford University Press.

  2015. *Agency and the Foundations of Ethics: Nietzschean Constitutivism*. Oxford: Oxford University Press.

  2016. *The Nietzschean Self: Moral Psychology, Agency, and the Unconscious*. Oxford: Oxford University Press.

Kaufmann, Walter. 1974. *Nietzsche: Philosopher, Psychologist, Antichrist*. Princeton: Princeton University Press.

Kirk, G. S., J. E. Raven and M. Schofield, eds. 1983. *The Presocratic Philosophers: A Critical History with a Selection of Texts*. Cambridge: Cambridge University Press.

Kivivuori, J., J. Savolainen and P. Danielsson. 2011. "Theory and Explanation in European Homicide Research." In *Handbook of European Homicide Research*, edited by Marieke Liem and William Alex Pridemore, 95–109. New York: Springer.

Lampert, Laurence. 2004. "Nietzsche and Plato." In *Nietzsche and Antiquity*, edited by Paul Bishop, 205–219. Rochester, NY: Camden House.

LeBlanc, Steven. 2003. *Constant Battles: Why We Fight*. New York: St. Martin's Griffin.

Lemm, Vanessa. 2007. "Is Nietzsche a Perfectionist? Rawls, Cavell, and the Politics of Culture in Nietzsche's 'Schopenhauer as Educator.'" *Journal of Nietzsche Studies* 34(1): 5–27.

  2013. "Nietzsche, *Einverleibung* and the Politics of Immunity." *International Journal of Philosophical Studies* 21(1): 3–19.

Lessing, Gotthold. 1890. *Hamburgische Dramaturgie*. Stuttgart: G. J. Göschen.

Liddell, Henry George and Robert Scott. 1961. *A Greek-English Lexicon*. Oxford: Clarendon Press.

Loeb, Paul. 2015. "Will to Power and Panpsychism." In *Nietzsche on Mind and Nature*, edited by Manuel Dries and P. J. E. Kail, 57–88. Oxford: Oxford University Press.

Lorenz, Konrad. 1998. *Das sogenannten Böse: Zur Naturgeschichte der Aggression*. Munich: Deutschen Taschenbuch Verlag.

Machiavelli, Niccolò. 1998. *The Prince*, translated by Harvey Mansfield. Chicago: University of Chicago Press.

Malthus, Thomas. 1798. *An Essay on the Principle of Population.* London: J. Johnson.
Martin, Nicolas. 2006. "Nietzsche as Hate-Figure in Britain's Great War." In *The First World War as a Clash of Cultures*, edited by Fred Bridgham, 147–166. Woodbridge: Boydell and Brewer.
Mayer, Julius Robert. 1893. "Über Auslösung." In *Die Mechanik der Wärme in gesammelten Schriften*, edited by Jacob Weyrauch. Stuttgart: J. G. Cotta.
Mill, John Stuart. 2015. *On Liberty.* In *On Liberty, Utilitarianism, and Other Essays*, edited by Mark Philp and Frederick Rosen, 5–112. Oxford: Oxford University Press.
Miller, Perry. 1953. "Emersonian Genius and the American Democracy." *The New England Quarterly* 26(1): 27–44.
Miner, Robert. 2011. "Nietzsche's Fourfold Conception of the Self." *Inquiry* 54(4): 337–360.
Mittasch, Alwin. 1952. *Nietzsche als Naturphilosoph.* Stuttgart: Alfred Kröner Verlag.
Moore, Gregory. 2002. *Nietzsche, Biology and Metaphor.* Cambridge: Cambridge University Press.
Mouffe, Chantal. 2000. *The Democratic Paradox.* London: Verso.
Most, Glenn. 2009. "Nietzsche gegen Aristoteles mit Aristoteles." In *Grenzen der Katharsis – Transformationen des aristotelischen Modells seit Bernays, Nietzsche und Freud*, edited by Martin Vöhler and Dirck Linck. Berlin: de Gruyter.
Müller, Enrico. 2005. *Die Griechen im Denken Nietzsches.* Berlin: de Gruyter.
    2020. "Competitive Ethos and Cultural Dynamic: The Principle of Agonism in Jacob Burckhardt and Friedrich Nietzsche." In *Conflict and Contest in Nietzsche's Philosophy*, edited by Herman Siemens and James S. Pearson, 89–104. London: Bloomsbury.
Müller-Lauter, Wolfgang. 1978. "Der Organismus als innerer Kampf: Der Einfluss von Wilhelm Roux auf Friedrich Nietzsche." *Nietzsche-Studien* 7: 189–235.
    1999. *Nietzsche: His Philosophy of Contradictions and the Contradictions of his Philosophy*, translated by David J. Parent. Urbana: University of Illinois Press.
Nehamas, Alexander. 1985. *Nietzsche: Life as Literature.* Cambridge, MA: Harvard University Press.
Niemeyer, Christian, ed. 2009. *Nietzsche-Lexikon.* Darmstadt: Wissenschaftliche Buchgesellschaft.
Nolte, Ernst. 1963. *Der Faschismus in seiner Epoche.* Munich: Piper.
Nozick, Robert. 1974. *Anarchy, State, Utopia.* New York: Basic Books.
Orsucci, Andrea. 1996. *Orient – Okzident: Nietzsches Versuch einer Loslösung vom europäischen Weltbild.* Berlin: de Gruyter.
Ottmann, Henning. 1999. *Philosophie und Politik bei Nietzsche.* Berlin: de Gruyter.
Owen, David. 1994. *Maturity and Modernity: Nietzsche, Weber, Foucault and the Ambivalence of Reason.* London: Routledge.
    1995. *Nietzsche, Politics and Modernity.* London: Sage.
    2002. "Equality, Democracy, and Self-Respect: Reflections on Nietzsche's Agonal Perfectionism." *Journal of Nietzsche Studies* 24: 113–131.

Pape, Wilhelm. 1914. *Handwörterbuch der griechischen Sprache: Griechisch-deutsches Handwörterbuch*. Vol. 1. Braunschweig: Vieweg & Sohn.

Parkes, Graham. 1991. "Ordering the Psyche Polytic: Choices of Inner Regime for Plato and Nietzsche." *Journal of Nietzsche Studies* 2: 53–77.

Paul, Hermann. 1992. *Deutsches Wörterbuch*. Tübingen: Max Niemeyer.

Pearson, James S. 2020. "Unity in Strife: Nietzsche, Heraclitus and Schopenhauer." In *Conflict and Contest in Nietzsche's Philosophy*, edited by Herman Siemens and James S. Pearson, 44–69. London: Bloomsbury.

Plato. 1992. *Republic*, translated by G. M. A. Grube and C. D. C. Reeve. Indianapolis: Hackett.

  2005. *Euthyphro. Apology. Crito. Phaedo. Phaedrus (Loeb Classical Library)*, translated by Harold N. Fowler. Cambridge, MA: Harvard University Press.

Poellner, Peter. 1995. *Nietzsche and Metaphysics*. Oxford: Oxford University Press.

Porter, James. 2009. "Hellenism and Modernity." In *The Oxford Handbook of Hellenic Studies*, edited by G. Boys-Stones, B. Graziosi and P. Vasunia. Oxford: Oxford University Press.

Rawls, John. 1971. *A Theory of Justice*. Cambridge, MA: Harvard University Press.

Ribot, Théodule. 1888. *Les Maladies de la Volonté*. Paris: Alcan.

Richardson, John. 1996. *Nietzsche's System*. Oxford: Oxford University Press.

  2004. *Nietzsche's New Darwinism*. Oxford: Oxford University Press.

Ruehl, Martin. 2003. "Politeia 1871 – Nietzsche *Contra* Wagner." In *Out of Arcadia: Classics and Politics in Germany in the Age of Burckhardt, Nietzsche and Wilamowitz*, edited by Ingo Gildenhard and Martin Ruehl, 61–86. London: Institute of Classical Studies, University of London.

  2004. "'*Politeia*' 1871: Young Nietzsche on the Greek State." In *Nietzsche and Antiquity: His Reaction and Response to the Classical Tradition*, edited by Paul Bishop, 79–97. Rochester, NY: Camden House.

Russell, Bertrand. 2004. *History of Western Philosophy*. London: Routledge.

Salaquarda, Jörg. 1984. "Studien zur zweiten *Unzeitgemässen Betrachtung*." *Nietzsche-Studien* 13: 1–45.

Schacht, Richard. 1983. *Nietzsche*. London: Routledge.

Schank, Gerd. 2000. *"Rasse" und "Züchtung" bei Nietzsche*. Berlin: de Gruyter.

Schiller, Friedrich. 2010. *Über die Ästhetische Erziehung des Menschen*. Stuttgart: Reclam.

Schmitt, Carl. 2002. *Der Begriff des Politischen*. Berlin: Dunkler und Humblot.

Schopenhauer, Arthur. 2009. "On the Freedom of the Will." In *The Two Fundamental Problems of Ethics*, translated by Christopher Janaway, 31–112. Cambridge: Cambridge University Press.

Schrift, Alan D. 2000. "Nietzsche's Contest: Nietzsche and the Culture Wars." In *Why Nietzsche Still?*, edited by A. D. Schrift, 184–201. Berkeley: University of California Press.

Siemens, Herman. 2001a. "Agonal Configurations in the *Unzeitgemäße Betrachtungen*." *Nietzsche-Studien* 30: 80–106.

  2001b. "Nietzsche's Political Philosophy: A Review of Recent Literature." *Nietzsche-Studien* 30: 509–526.

2002. "Agonal Communities of Taste: Law and Community in Nietzsche's Philosophy of Transvaluation." *Journal of Nietzsche Studies* 24(1): 83–112.

2008. "Yes, No, Maybe So... Nietzsche's Equivocations on the Relation between Democracy and 'Grosse Politik.'" In *Nietzsche, Power and Politics*, edited by Herman Siemens and Vasti Roodt, 231–268. Berlin: de Gruyter.

2009. "Nietzsche's Critique of Democracy (1870–1886)." *Journal of Nietzsche Studies* 38: 20–37.

2013. "Reassessing Radical Democratic Theory in Light of Nietzsche's Ontology of Conflict." In *Nietzsche and Political Thought*, edited by Keith Ansell-Pearson, 83–106. New York: Bloomsbury.

2015. "Contesting Nietzsche's Agon. On Christa Davis Acampora's *Contesting Nietzsche.*" *Nietzsche-Studien* 44(1): 446–461.

Soll, Ivan. 1973. "Reflections on Recurrence: A Re-Examination of Nietzsche's Doctrine, *die ewige Wiederkehr des Gleichen.*" In *Nietzsche: A Collection of Critical Essays*, edited by Robert C. Solomon, 322–342. Garden City, NY: Doubleday.

Spencer, Herbert. 1882. *The Data of Ethics*. New York: D. Appleton and Co.

1886. *Principles of Biology*. Vol 2. New York: D. Appleton and Co.

1994. "The Proper Sphere of Government." In *Spencer: Political Writings*, edited by John Offer. Cambridge: Cambridge University Press.

Stegmaier, Werner. 2000. "Anti-Lehren: Szene und Lehre in Nietzsches *Also sprach Zarathustra.*" In *Friedrich Nietzsche: Also Sprach Zarathustra (Klassiker Auslegung Bd. 14)*, edited by Volker Gerhardt, 209–211. Berlin: Akademie Verlag.

Stern, Tom. 2015. "Against Nietzsche's 'Theory' of the Drives." *Journal of the American Philosophical Association* 1: 121–140.

Strong, Tracy. 1988. *Friedrich Nietzsche and the Politics of Transfiguration: (Expanded Edition)*. Berkeley, CA: University of California Press.

Tongeren, Paul van. 1989. *Die Moral von Nietzsches Moralkritik*. Bonn: Bouvier.

2002. "Nietzsche's Greek Measure." *Journal of Nietzsche Studies* 24(1): 5–24.

Tully, James. 2008. *Public Philosophy in a New Key. Volume I: Democracy and Civic Freedom*. Cambridge: Cambridge University Press.

Tuncel, Yunus. 2013. *Agon in Nietzsche*. Milwaukee, WI: Marquette University Press.

Wagner, Richard. 1850a. *Das Kunstwerk der Zukunft*. Leipzig: Otto Wigand.

1850b. *Die Kunst und die Revolution*. Leipzig: Otto Wigand.

1911. "Über Staat und Religion." In *Sämtliche Schriften und Dichtungen*, edited by Hans von Wolzogen and Richard Sternfeld. Vol. 8, 3–29. Leipzig: Breitkopf und Härtel.

Warren, Mark. 1991. *Nietzsche and Political Thought*. Cambridge, MA: MIT Press.

Wölfflin, Eduard, ed. 1900–. *Thesaurus Linguae Latinae*. Lipsiae: B. G. Teubneri.

Wotling, Patrick. 2011. "What Language Do Drives Speak?" In *Nietzsche on Instinct and Language*, edited by João Constâncio and Maria João Mayer Branco, 80–116. Berlin: de Gruyter.

Young, Julian. 1997. *Heidegger, Philosophy, Nazism*. Cambridge: Cambridge University Press.

2005. *Schopenhauer*. London: Routledge.

2010. *Friedrich Nietzsche: A Philosophical Biography*. Cambridge: Cambridge University Press.

Zuckert, Catherine. 1976. "Nature, History and the Self: Friedrich Nietzsche's *Untimely Considerations*." *Nietzsche-Studien* 5(1): 55–82.

Index

aboulia, 189, 244

Acampora, Christa Davis, 8, 19, 40, 41, 76, 77, 84, 119, 131, 146

adventure, 211, 238, 239

aesthetic, *see also* art; music; poetry; tragedy
  agency, 148
  conception of catharsis, 41
  conception of politics, 248
  contest, 95, 102, 103, 124
  judgment, 102
  role of genius, 83
  values, 102, 145

affects, 233, *see also* drives; impulses; inclinations
  aggressive, 88
  channeling of, 127
  competitive, 125
  discharging of, 42
  extirpation of, 224
  relation to drives, 225

agency, 157, 159, 173, 189, *see also* autonomy; command; freedom
  aesthetic, 148
  collective, 70, 197, 199, 250, 253
  creative, 130
  of the drives, 225
  ethical, 148
  guidelines for, 103
  hindered, 194
  of nature, 181
  social, 134

agon, 18, 26–36, 39–41, 52–55, 74–140, 153, 157, 165, 214, 228, 272, *see also* competition
  artistic, 95, 99, 102, 123
  as a means of social unification, 145
  destructive interpretation of, 77–90
  dialogical, 95
  official Greek games, 8, 78, 93, 127
  physical, 11, 80, 95, 99, 102
  political, 101, 105
  psychological, 146

agonistic democrats, 4, 31, 91, 115, 146, 185, 246–247, 267, 268, 275

agonistic readings of Nietzsche, 31, 32, 39–41, 55, 56, 64, 68–69, 71–73, 74–140, 145, 158, 164, 171, 173, 214, 249, 259, 273, 275
  and the will to power, 185, 214, 246

Aidos, 89, 108–116, 137, *see also* reverence; shame

altruism, 13, 16, 191, 194, 235
  as a means to self-organization, 241

ambition, 9, 85, 86, 96, 101, 105, 116, 127, 128, 131

amoralism, 248, 253, 256, 259, 267

anarchy, 199, 221, *see also* chaos; disintegration
  psychological, 189, 225
  social, 128, 197

Anaximander, 6, 11, 16, 82

ancient Greeks, 6–11, 17–19, 29, 41–51, 52–54, 64, 65, 74–140, 154, 157, 250

ancient Romans, 56, 89, 156, 240, 250, 257

anthropomorphism, 22, 114, 132, 175, 181

Aquinas, Thomas, 2–3

aristocracy, 247, 251, 267, *see also* hierarchy; nobility
  and the agon, 91–116
  and agonal values, 99
  and the birth of agonal culture, 79
  biological, 218
  brutal, 60
  and exploitation, 250–260
  hereditary, 93, 96
  how to breed an, 259

Aristotle
  on agency, 189
  on catharsis, 41
  on envy, 125
  on ostracism, 125, 204
  on slavery, 45

art, 9, 10, 16, 27, 49, 52, 86, 88, 95, 102, 115, 130, 167, 174, 193, *see also* aesthetic; music; myth; poetry; tragedy
  as a means of catharsis, 43

flourishing (cont.)
  and morality, 234
  and violence, 39–73
flux, 149, *see also* becoming
  Heraclitean, 6
force, *see also* power; will to power
  argumentative, 10
  destructive, 159
  Empedoclean, 2
  individual, 237
  of love, 2
  martial, 254
  natural, 5, 15, 202, 209
  plastic, 153–160, 205
  psychological, 166
  release of, 67
  unbounded, 90
  of will to power, 64
foreignness, 134, 157, 254
forgetting, 157, 241
Förster-Nietzsche, Elisabeth, 30, 74
fragmentation, 147, 167, 184, *see also*
    disintegration
  psychological, 173
freedom, 135, 198, 213, *see also* agency; autonomy;
    command
  of the blond beasts, 60
  individual, 13
  social, 79
  of the will, 68
Freud, Sigmund, 55, 58
friendship, 91, 114, 123, 134

genealogy, 66, 236
  of the agon, 90
genius, 9, 45, 53, 58, 82, 119, 123, 128, 150, 165,
    167–172, 181, 228
  artistic, 170
  elite, 168, 250
  global, 169
  philosophical, 172
genocide, 46, 258, 275, *see also* eugenics
Germans, 147, 187, 258
Germany, 20, 44, 74, 79, 148
glory, 9, 100, 103, 110, 138, *see also* fame
goals, 169, 181, 193
  agonal, 94, 96, 120
  capricious, 198
  communal, 259
  difficulty of envisaging, 159
  guiding organization, 272
  happiness, 165
  of individual, 238
  long-term, 198
  social, 171

God/gods, 12, 72, 100, 110, 127, 129, 130, *see also*
    Christianity; religion
Goethe, Johann Wolfgang von, 65, 238
Grecophilia, 44
greed, 63, 68, 211, 231
Grote, George, 128
growth, 222, 243, 254
  inorganic, 209
  of organisms, 204, 209
guilt, 179, 193, 230
gymnastics, 11, 53, 88, 89, 99, 127

habits, 172, 173, 225, *see also* drives; impulses;
    inclinations
habituation, 137, 226, 260
happiness, 12, 165, 192, 196
harmony, 9, 25, 41, 148, 150, 163,
    184
  psychological, 224
  within organisms, 204
Hartmann, Eduard von, 49, 150
Hatab, Lawrence, 107, 118, 214, 246
hatred, 2, 63, 86, 100, 159, 163, 194
health, 7, 13, 41, 64, 152, 154, 159, 165, 173,
    188, 194
  cellular, 209
  collective, 187–200
  cultural, 45, 55, 58, 73
  great, 231
  individual, 240
  of organisms, 259
  psychological, 10, 58
  social, 24, 112
Hegel, G. W. F., 3, 150, 220
Heidegger, Martin, 30, 220, 264
Heraclitus, 1, 3, 6–8, 15, 43, 77, 120, 143,
    166
herd, 179, 196, 236, 240, *see also* morality, herd
  and the last man, 65
heroes, 97, 104
heroism, 56, 83, 97
  and the agon, 77, 79, 81, 97
  and happiness, 165
Hesiod, 52, 80, 84, 87, 97
hierarchy, 9, 57, 145, 146, 159, *see also* aristocracy;
    command; exploitation;
    instrumentalization
  as sustained by morality, 235
  of drives, 228
  psychological, 165, 189, 218
  social, 167, 172, 189, 195, 251, 262, 267
  of values, 238
  within organisms, 152
historical sense, 157, 190, 194,
    273

self (cont.)
  self-cultivation, 104, 105, 127, 131, 168, 179,
    223–245
  self-destruction, 262
  self-exploitation, 252
  self-knowledge, 108, 179, 233–234
  self-misunderstanding, 241
  self-organization, 164
  self-preservation, 209
  self-regulation, 204
  self-restraint, 76, 117, 122, 139
  as untransformable, 245
sentience. *see also* consciousness; panpsychism
  inorganic, 215
  nonhuman, 214
shame, 80, 108, 113, 194, *see also Aidos*
sickness, 7, 10, 22, 64, 190, 194, 236, 261
Siemens, Herman, 27, 120, 121, 249
sin, 14, 179, 193, *see also* Christianity; conscience,
  bad; guilt
skepticism, 16, 187, 190
slavery, 45, 64, 93, 105, 248, 251–254, 267, 275, *see
  also* exploitation; instrumentalization;
  morality, slave
social class, 45, 95, 98, 100, 115, 138, 187, 190,
  246
  and the agon, 91–116
  and education, 100
  and leisure, 105
  mixing, 197
  and race, 188
  struggle, 3
socialism, 45, 192
society, 87, 94, 110, 166–172, 245–266, *see also*
  community; politics
  agonal, 74–140
  altruistic, 192
  aristocratic, 195
  exhausted, 56
  of the last man, 196
  productive, 44
  and war, 18, 39–73
Socrates, 8–11, 89, 95
solitude, 108, 109
soul–state analogy, 10, 26, 189, 194, 218
sovereign individual, 135, 230
Spencer, Herbert, 3, 20, 21, 196, 208
Spinoza, Baruch, 12, 208
spiritualization
  of the agon, 89
  of desires, 232
  of enmity, 184, 246
sport, 27, 67, 95, 114
state, 49, 88, 172, 248, *see also* community;
  politics; society

state of nature, 64, 121, 123,
  126
stimuli, 203, 218, 227
struggle. *see also* agon; competition;
  conflict
  of annihilation, 203
  for existence, 21, 22, 103, 201
  for nutrition, 202
  for perfection, 210
  for space and nutrition, 205, 218
  for survival, 210
  as inherent to becoming, 7
  over limited resources, 209
  universality of, 7, 15, 216
subjectivity, 76, 160, 177, 223, 244, *see also*
  consciousness; psyche; self
sublimation, 40, 185, 223–245
  of herd impulses, 241
sublimational readings of Nietzsche, 224,
  243
substance, 12
survival, 20–26, 208, 210
  conscious pursuit of, 212
  of organisms, 203
systematicity
  in nature, 151
  in Nietzsche's philosophy, 30, 75,
  269

talent, 95, 102, 104, 116, 138, 168
taming, 127, 196
taste, 190, 239
teleology, 170–172, 202, 212, *see also* goals;
  purposiveness
  and the overman, 264
  natural, 182
thing in itself, 51, 161, 242
Thucydides, 128
tradition, 155, 156, 173, *see also* customs;
  history
tragedy, 10, 42, 148, *see also* art; myth;
  poetry
truth, 3, 175
  a priori, 12, 266
  desire for, 212
  drive for, 227, 233
  moral, 242
  objective, 207
  of reality, 167
  of the will to power, 217
tyranny, 10, 93, 116, 119, 123, 132, 217, *see also*
  despotism
  of the Christian ideal, 240
  over oneself, 252
  psychological, 224

For EU product safety concerns, contact us at Calle de José Abascal, 56–1°,
28003 Madrid, Spain or eugpsr@cambridge.org.

www.ingramcontent.com/pod-product-compliance
Ingram Content Group UK Ltd.
Pitfield, Milton Keynes, MK11 3LW, UK
UKHW022310060425
457118UK00018B/216